The Politics of 1930s
British Literature

Historicizing Modernism

Series Editors

Matthew Feldman, Professor of Contemporary History, Teesside University,
UK; and Erik Tonning, Professor of British Literature and Culture,
University of Bergen, Norway.

Assistant Editor: David Tucker, Associate Lecturer, Goldsmiths,
University of London, UK

Editorial Board

Professor Chris Ackerley, Department of English, University of Otago, New
Zealand; Professor Ron Bush, St. John's College, University of Oxford, UK;
Dr Finn Fordham, Department of English, Royal Holloway, UK; Professor
Steven Matthews, Department of English, University of Reading, UK;
Dr Mark Nixon, Department of English, University of Reading, UK; Professor
Shane Weller, Reader in Comparative Literature, University of Kent, UK;
and Professor Janet Wilson, University of Northampton, UK.

Historicizing Modernism challenges traditional literary interpretations by
taking an empirical approach to modernist writing: a direct response to new
documentary sources made available over the last decade.

Informed by archival research, and working beyond the usual European/
American avant-garde 1900–45 parameters, this series reassesses established
readings of modernist writers by developing fresh views of intellectual contexts
and working methods.

Series Titles:

Arun Kolatkar and Literary Modernism in India, Laetitia Zecchini

British Literature and Classical Music, David Deutsch

Broadcasting in the Modernist Era, Matthew Feldman,
Henry Mead, and Erik Tonning

Charles Henri Ford, Alexander Howard

The Politics of 1930s British Literature

Education, Class, Gender

Natasha Periyan

BLOOMSBURY ACADEMIC
LONDON • NEW YORK • OXFORD • NEW DELHI • SYDNEY

BLOOMSBURY ACADEMIC
Bloomsbury Publishing Plc
50 Bedford Square, London, WC1B 3DP, UK

BLOOMSBURY, BLOOMSBURY ACADEMIC and the
Diana logo are trademarks of Bloomsbury Publishing Plc

First published in Great Britain 2018

Cover design: Eleanor Rose

A catalogue record for this book is available from the British Library.

Library of Congress Cataloging-in-Publication Data
Names: Periyan, Natasha author.
Title: The politics of 1930s British literature : education, class, gender /
Natasha Periyan.
Description: London ; New York : Bloomsbury Academic, 2018. |
Series: Historicizing modernism | Includes bibliographical references and index.
Identifiers: LCCN 2017060027 | ISBN 9781350019843 (hardback) |
ISBN 9781350019867 (epdf)
Subjects: LCSH: English literature–20th century–History and criticism. |
Great Britain–Intellectual life–20th century. | Politics and literature–Great Britain–
History–20th century. | Education in literature. | Social classes in literature.
Classification: LCC PR478.P64 P47 2018 | DDC 820.9/3581–dc23
LC record available at https://lccn.loc.gov/2017060027

ISBN: HB: 978-1-3500-1984-3
          ePDF: 978-1-3500-1986-7
          eBook: 978-1-3500-1985-0

Series: Historicizing Modernism

Typeset by Integra Software Services Pvt. Ltd.
Printed and bound in Great Britain

To find out more about our authors and books visit www.bloomsbury.com
and sign up for our newsletters.

To Barbara, Robert,
Anoushka, and Laurence – with thanks.

Contents

Acknowledgements

The origins of this book came in my PhD thesis at Royal Holloway. I am grateful to Finn Fordham, who was an encouraging and supportive supervisor, and my advisor, Betty Jay. I am grateful also for the funding that I received from the English Department at Royal Holloway and the Bradley De Glehn Scholarship from the Arts Faculty, both of which enabled this doctoral research. Ian Patterson and Anna Snaith examined the thesis upon which this book is based with wisdom and insight and I am grateful for their comments on the work.

This book was completed while I was a Postdoctoral Teaching Fellow at Goldsmiths and I am grateful to my colleagues there and to Lucia Boldrini, Rita Sakr, Carole Sweeney, Carole Maddern, and Tamar Steinitz, in particular for the practical and moral support that I received. Isobel Hurst and Chris Baldick provided invaluable feedback on chapters of this work and it is with particular gratitude that I acknowledge the generosity of Lara Feigel throughout the process of completing this project, and for reading sections of the book manuscript. Alice Wood provided advice on the publishing process and conversations with Clara Jones on Woolf and the 1930s were thought-provoking. Thanks are due to Matthew Feldman and Eric Tonning, the series editors of Historicizing Modernism, and the staff at Bloomsbury Academic, particularly David Avital, Clara Herberg and Vinita Irudayaraj. Bloomsbury's anonymous reader offered invaluable advice that helped shape this into a fuller study. David Gillott worked scrupulously and attentively in helping to prepare the manuscript for publication and Janet Zimmermann did sterling work in preparing the index. I am grateful to the staff at the British Library, the New York Public Library, the Institute of Education archives, the Hull Archive and History Centre, the Bridlington Local Studies Centre and Ian Johnstone at the Walter Greenwood archive at the University of Salford. Students I have taught at Royal Holloway, Falmouth, and Goldsmiths have encouraged me to think about learning and literature in new ways and, in a book about education, it would be remiss of me not to thank my teachers, past and present, who have informed so much of my thinking. Particular thanks are due to Sos Eltis, Madeleine Carnwath, Mary Curran, and my grandparents, from whom I learnt so much.

I am lucky to have a wide network of lovely friends who have provided much fun along the way. Thanks are especially due to Ellie, Nick, Jo, Beth, Nicola,

Michi, Finn, Sophie, Elinor, Camilla, and Amanda. My parents-in-law, Pete and Madeleine, have lent books and provided encouragement. My family, and particularly my parents, Barbara and Robert, and my sister, Anoushka, have been a loving and supportive presence throughout and have had boundless faith in me. In small ways and big, and with much good humour, patience, and love, my husband, Laurence, has made this book possible – thank you.

I am grateful to the following Literary Estates and Executors for permission to use materials: the archival material from *The Dog beneath the Skin* is quoted with permission from the Estate of W. H. Auden; the extract from W. H. Auden Public school letters. Holograph transcripts. 1v. is quoted with permission from The Henry W. and Albert A. Berg Collection of English and American Literature, The New York Public Library, Astor, Lenox and Tilden Foundations; the unpublished letter by Vera Brittain is included by permission of Mark Bostridge and T. J. Brittain-Catlin, Literary Executors for the Estate of Vera Brittain 1970; the material from the National Union of Women Teachers is used with the permission of the UCL Institute of Education archive; the archival material from the Winifred Holtby Collection at the Hull Archive and History Centre and the Bridlington Local Studies Centre is quoted with permission from the Hull City Council, who administer the literary estate of Winifred Holtby. An earlier version of Chapter 4 appeared as an article in *Textual Practice*: 'Altering the Structure of Society': An Institutional Focus on Virginia Woolf and Working-Class Education in the 1930s', published online 25 January 2017. I am grateful to Taylor & Francis for permission to republish here. Every effort has been made to contact the copyright holders for the unpublished material in this book; I apologize for any inadvertent omissions.

Key to Editorial Symbols

The following symbols have been used when transcribing archival manuscript sources:

<word>	:	indicates that text has been inserted in the main body of the text
∧	:	indicates a marginal textual insertion
~~word~~	:	indicates crossed out text
<u>word</u>	:	indicates underlined text
[indeciph]	:	indicates indecipherable text

Editorial Preface to Historicizing Modernism

This book series is devoted to the analysis of late-nineteenth- to twentieth-century literary modernism within its historical contexts. *Historicizing Modernism* therefore stresses empirical accuracy and the value of primary sources (such as letters, diaries, notes, drafts, marginalia, or other archival materials) in developing monographs and edited collections on modernist literature. This may take a number of forms, such as manuscript study and genetic criticism, documenting interrelated historical contexts and ideas, and exploring biographical information. To date, no book series has fully laid claim to this interdisciplinary, source-based territory for modern literature. While the series addresses itself to a range of key authors, it also highlights the importance of non-canonical writers with a view to establishing broader intellectual genealogies of modernism. Furthermore, while the series is weighted towards the English-speaking world, studies of non-Anglophone modernists whose writings are open to fresh historical exploration are also included.

A key aim of the series is to reach beyond the familiar rhetoric of intellectual and artistic 'autonomy' employed by many modernists and their critical commentators. Such rhetorical moves can and should themselves be historically situated and reintegrated into the complex continuum of individual literary practices. It is our intent that the series' emphasis upon the contested self-definitions of modernist writers, thinkers, and critics may, in turn, prompt various reconsiderations of the boundaries delimiting the concept of 'modernism' itself. Indeed, the concept of 'historicizing' is itself debated across its volumes, and the series by no means discourages more theoretically informed approaches. On the contrary, the editors hope that the historical specificity encouraged by *Historicizing Modernism* may inspire a range of fundamental critiques along the way.

Matthew Feldman
Erik Tonning

Introduction

The 1930s was a decade where writers were also teachers. The range and scope of their pedagogic activity is striking: W.H. Auden taught throughout the 1930s; former teacher Vera Brittain gave speeches at schools, as did her friend Winifred Holtby, who also spoke at teachers' conferences; both Holtby and Antonia White contributed articles to the teachers' weekly *The Schoolmistress*; Stephen Spender taught at Blundell's in 1940; from 1932 to 1933, George Orwell taught at The Hawthorns, a small private school; card-carrying communist Arthur Calder-Marshall taught at a minor public school in the 1930s and Virginia Woolf lectured to the Workers' Educational Association (WEA) in 1940. In her lecture, Woolf commented: 'No other ten years can have produced so much autobiography as the ten years between 1930 and 1940.'[1] The preoccupation with the autobiographical that Woolf registers in her lecture often centred on schooldays: former tutor Graham Greene, whose father was a headmaster, played head boy in the decade, rounding up a collection of his generation's A-grade writers to produce a collection of memoirs on school experiences.

So pervasive was the pedagogic that it permeated more standard literary forms: Cyril Connolly described his autobiography as a 'textbook', and Virginia Woolf's essay 'The Leaning Tower' was originally a lecture. By the end of the decade, Woolf's analysis of the presiding literary tenor of the decade was one infected by the testing tones of the teacher as she identified 'the pedagogic, the didactic' strain in the Auden group's writing (E6, p. 272). In no other decade, it seems, could one of the leading lights of the literary scene have composed a school motto or penned a school song so characteristic of their wider verse, as Auden did; or an autobiography become a stimulus for pacifist educational practice, as Brittain's *Testament of Youth* was. The line between the pedagogic

---

[1] Virginia Woolf, 'The Leaning Tower', in *The Essays of Virginia Woolf Volume VI 1933–1941*, ed. by Stuart N. Clarke (London: Hogarth Press, 2011), pp. 259–83 (p. 273). Further references to this edition will be included in brackets after the citation as E6 and then the page number.

and the political was also blurred: Arthur Calder-Marshall and W.H. Auden produced educational tracts in the decade, and Holtby's feminist politics were informed by her active work for the National Union of Women Teachers. The pedagogic provided a mode that allowed for both campaigning and creativity.

This was a decade with much to be taught, but it was also one with much to be learnt. A decade where the vast majority left school at fourteen; where industrial areas were afflicted by poverty and unemployment; and where, as Walter Greenwood portrayed, what was learned at school took second place to what was earned at the factory. By the late 1930s, when the nation seemed to be slipping, ineluctably, into another war, education became the means through which a bright, gleaming, egalitarian future could emerge from the destruction and carnage of the battlefield. But this was also a future that, for the Eton-educated writer Henry Green, held ambivalence and even fear.

It is a conviction of the pressing nature of the pedagogic in the 1930s that underpins this book's overriding contention that, to those perennial symbols of the decade – the gramophone and the loudspeaker – should be added the textbook and the blackboard. It considers a wide range of 1930s writers to argue that engagement with education elucidates their politics, conceptions of gender and selfhood, cultural critique, and aesthetics. Ross McKibbin argues that 'more or less everyone in the interwar years agreed that England was a democracy. The question was – whose democracy?'.[2] He suggests that 1930s democracy was 'defined by the "modern" middle class [...] individualist, but also socially engaged', while in the 1940s the 'ruling definition was social-democratic [...] its proponents [...] the organized working class'.[3] This book argues that 1930s writers' engagement with education registered this shift in democratic ideals, while also exposing the tensions inherent in McKibbin's association between 'individualist' and 'socially engaged' claims in 1930s democracy. This reveals a crucial narrative of the intelligentsia's struggle to arrive at a democratic form that manages the bourgeois individual's stake in the collective community, representing a frequently uneasy accommodation of the bourgeois 'I' alongside the proletarian 'we', and a mutual refashioning of class and cultural codes. This book departs from Valentine Cunningham's foregrounding of the Spanish Civil War's communist call to submerge bourgeois identity in the collective as a determinant of the period's political reckonings.[4] It argues that

---

[2] Ross McKibbin, *Classes and Cultures: England 1918–1951* (Oxford: Oxford University Press, 1998), p. 533.

[3] Ibid.

[4] Valentine Cunningham, *British Writers of the Thirties* (Oxford: Oxford University Press, 1988), pp. 211–40.

the Spens Report, which considered comprehensive schooling in a government document for the first time, sat alongside the Spanish Civil War as a way in which a socialist future was imagined.

This book renders education central to a reading of the decade's cultural critique, in dialogue with John Coombes, who argues that 'Education and Self-Improvement' is that 'perennial liberal panacea' with 'very little' 'to do with a genuine cultural politics of the Left'.[5] Readings of the influence of pedagogy on 1930s writing as 'didactic' are complicated by contextualizing writers' pedagogy against their creative work to open up an understanding of the open and interrogatory qualities in the decade's literary register and the conflicts inherent in its didactic voice. Leo Mellor, informed by Pierre Bourdieu, argues that George Barker's autodidact status elucidates his culturally transgressive, unstandardized classical knowledge in the 1930s.[6] I explore how writers educated within elite institutions interrogated the forms of culture sanctified by those institutions during a period in which working-class writing was increasingly being encouraged by literary magazines such as *New Writing* and *Left Review*.[7] Expansions in educational access illuminate contemporary tensions between writers' conceptions of a working-class 'new realism', 'democratic' forms of cultural discourse, and right-wing hopes to preserve a working-class language, uninflected by literary influence.

Flogging a dead horse: The historical context of educational reform

By the end of the 1930s, writers were recycling the same metaphors to intone the death of the public school, an institution which held a political and cultural predominance in the period, and which seemed antithetical to democratic social and educational forms. In her lecture to working men and women, Woolf suggested of the public-school-educated Auden group: 'They are flogging a dead or dying horse because a living horse, if flogged, would kick them off its back'

---

[5] John Coombes, *Writing from the Left: Socialism, Liberalism and the Popular Front* (London: Harvester Wheatsheaf, 1989), p. 79.

[6] Leo Mellor, 'George Barker in the 1930s: Narcissus and the Autodidact', *Modernist Cultures*, Vol. 10 No. 2 (Summer 2015), 250–68.

[7] See Christopher Hilliard, *To Exercise Our Talents: The Democratization of Writing in Britain* (London: Harvard University Press, 2006), pp. 98–129.

(E6, p. 271). A few months later, Orwell contended that mocking the public schools 'is flogging a dead horse, or a dying one, for all but three or four schools will be killed financially by the present war'.[8] In his autobiography, written in 1940, Louis MacNeice wearily found:

> The public schools of England have been written down *ad nauseam*. To flog these dying horses is no longer very daring and there have been more than enough autobiographies of rich boys faring ill, of sensitive plants wilting on the playing fields.[9]

Woolf, Orwell, and MacNeice are all responding to an interwar, leftist, political context in which the class and gender values of public-school-education were being critiqued, and education was being held as a mode of social, and even cultural, transformation. However, as MacNeice found in 'The Leaning Tower: Replies', 'some of those old dead horses [...] have a kick in them still'.[10] Despite attempts from the Left throughout the period to establish a democratic educational system with wider access to secondary education, the critical consensus describes a period of failure in developments in educational policy: Gordon, Aldrich, and Dean conclude that 'the overall verdict on this period must be one of stagnation rather than progress', while Ross McKibbin argues that 1918 to 1951 denotes a period of 'failure' in educational reform.[11]

Areas of Britain's education system lay outside the scope of normal levels of state control. Brian Simon notes the 'extraordinary dominance' of the public schools in the interwar period, and, to a large extent, public attitude towards them remained, McKibbin notes, 'benign or neutral'.[12] The tremendous popularity of James Hilton's *Goodbye Mr Chips* (1934), an affectionate depiction of the traditions of the English public school which was adapted for the stage in 1938, and for a film produced by MGM in 1939, with an Oscar-winning turn by Robert Donat, provides a more representative measure of public opinion than the criticisms of Woolf, Orwell, or MacNeice.

---

[8] George Orwell, 'Review of *Barbarians and Philistines: Democracy and the Public Schools* by T.C. Worsley', *Time and Tide*, 14 September 1940, in *The Complete Works of George Orwell Volume 12 A Patriot After All 1940–1941*, ed. by Peter Davison (London: Secker & Warburg, 1998), pp. 261–62 (p. 262).

[9] Louis MacNeice, *The Strings Are False* (London: Faber & Faber, 1996), p. 80.

[10] Louis MacNeice, 'The Leaning Tower Replies: The Tower That Once', *Folios of New Writing* (Spring 1941), pp. 37–41 (p. 38).

[11] Peter Gordon, Richard Aldrich, and Dennis Dean, *Education and Policy in England in the Twentieth Century* (London: Woburn, 1991), p. 59; McKibbin, *Classes and Cultures*, p. 269.

[12] Brian Simon, *The Politics of Educational Reform: 1920–1940* (London: Lawrence & Wishart, 1974), p. 271; McKibbin, *Classes and Cultures*, p. 271.

There was variety of prestige and provision within the non-maintained sector of English education. For some, the term 'public school' included just the 'Clarendon' Nine: Eton, Harrow, Rugby, Westminster, Shrewsbury, Charterhouse, Winchester, St Paul's, and Merchant Taylors', with the latter two predominantly day schools. There were other nineteenth-century institutions of equal reputation, and there also existed a rank of 'minor' public schools for the middle classes. A greater proportion of the more recently founded girls' public schools received state support, and they were generally less beholden to historical tradition. While the public schools were legally charities, there were, in addition, non-state schools run for profit: largely 'private' or 'preparatory' schools, with some secondary schools. Just over half of the public schools received some state assistance and were 'direct grant' schools which, in exchange for some state support, theoretically offered 25 per cent of their places to holders of local authority scholarships, although in practice, the number of schools that complied with this requirement was low.[13]

By 1940, 189 schools with a total of 65,000 students belonged to the Headmasters' Conference, the coordinating body of the independent sector, and there was an increase in the number of pupils enrolled at public schools: from 27,262 between 1927 and 1928, to 36,510 between 1937 and 1938.[14] Nonetheless, state secondary schools were expanding at a greater rate than the public schools, with some of the smaller private and public schools losing pupils to the good grammar schools. The economic effects of the slump, the increase in public-school fees as a result of the Burnham Scale, changes in the socio-economic structure of major towns, and competition from the grammar schools, all contributed to pressures felt by the public schools during this period.[15] The fee-paying progressive sector also offered a potential rival to the traditional public school. Many of these schools declined during the Second World War, although their emphasis on child-centred learning and departure from authoritarian teaching styles was felt widely in pedagogic practice.[16]

Brian Simon argues that the campaign for widening secondary-education provision was the axis on which 'the politics of education in the inter-war years chiefly turned'; however, policy was largely determined by those socially and

---

[13] See McKibbin, *Classes and Cultures*, p. 242.

[14] Simon, p. 272; McKibbin, *Classes and Cultures*, p. 239.

[15] See McKibbin, *Classes and Cultures*, pp. 239–40; Simon, p. 274.

[16] See Robert Skidelsky, *English Progressive Schools* (Harmondsworth: Penguin, 1969) for more on the progressive movement.

culturally alienated from state education provision.[17] The public schools, and particularly the boarding schools, exercised a strong influence on political life in the period: between 1920 and 1940, 68 per cent of Conservative MPs had been educated at public schools, 27.5 per cent of them at Eton.[18] During fourteen and a half years of Conservative rule, including the years of the National Government, all the presidents of the Board of Education had gone to Eton, and all but one had also gone to Oxford.[19]

Robert Morant, permanent secretary for the Board of Education (1902–11), had founded the development of fee-paying secondary schools aided by rates and exchequer grants, but conceived of secondary education as available only for the elite, and for those who would become teachers at the elementary schools. By the post-war period there was a profound shortage in secondary school places: a 1920 Report of the Departmental Committee in Scholarships and Free Places found that less than one in ten of an age group in elementary school could move into the secondary system at age eleven.[20]

In 1918 Virginia Woolf's cousin, H.A.L. Fisher, was president of the Board of Education in David Lloyd George's wartime cabinet. Fisher, Woolf suggested, was 'stamped and moulded by the great patriarchal machine', but he was also, Simon notes, a 'liberal' who was instrumental to the post-war agenda for educational reform.[21] The esteem in which he was held by reforming politicians was clear from the parliamentary reading of the Butler Education Act in 1944, where R.A. Butler claimed that his Act 'gathers up all the dreams of the reformists, and some were in the Fisher Act'.[22] Fisher's April 1917 speech 'Education Estimates', upon which the 1918 Fisher Education Act was based, noted that 'our highway from the public elementary school to the University still needs considerable improvement'.[23] Section 4(4) of the 1918 Fisher Education Act decreed that no child should be debarred 'from receiving the benefits of any form of education by which they are capable of profiting through inability to pay fees'. The *Times*

---

[17] Simon, p. 15.

[18] Simon, p. 272.

[19] Simon, p. 280.

[20] Simon, p. 22.

[21] Virginia Woolf, 'Sketch of the Past', in *Moments of Being: Autobiographical Writings*, ed. by Jeanne Schulkind (London: Pimlico, 2002), pp. 78–160 (p. 155). Further references to this memoir will be included in brackets after the citation as 'Sketch' and then the page number; Simon, p. 281.

[22] The Butler Education Bill Reading, 19 January 1944, <http://hansard.millbanksystems.com/commons/1944/jan/19/education-bill> [accessed 13 November 2017].

[23] H.A.L. Fisher, 'Education Estimates: April 19 1917', in *Educational Reform: Speeches Delivered by the Right Hon H.A.L. Fisher, MP, President of the Board of Education* (Oxford: Clarendon Press, 1918), pp. 1–28 (p. 18).

Educational Supplement found that Fisher had taken a path 'that leads nowhere but to universal secondary education'.[24] In 1918 the school-leaving age was nominally fourteen, but the presence of an 'exemption' clause resulted in nearly half of children leaving school for work at thirteen, with some leaving at twelve. Fisher banished the exemption clause, formalizing fourteen as the official school-leaving age and recommended part-time education for fourteen- to sixteen-year-olds. In 1921 these steps towards reform were frustrated when the Committee on National Expenditure, chaired by Sir Eric Geddes, recommended that education grants should be reduced by a third, jeopardizing educational improvements: consequently, Gordon, Aldrich, and Dean find that the Fisher Act 'did not visibly alter the structure of the system of education'.[25]

Shortly after the cuts, R.H. Tawney published *Secondary Education for All: A Policy for Labour* (1922), and then a popular version, *Education: The Labour Policy* (1924). Tawney linked education with the aims of a democratic society:

> The Labour Party is convinced that the only policy which is at once educationally sound and suited to a democratic community is one under which primary education and secondary education are organised as two stages in a single continuous process.[26]

With the decline of the Liberal Party at the 1924 election, the Labour Party became the main conduit for interwar educational reform. During the tenure of the first Labour government, Charles Trevelyan attempted to reverse the 1922 Geddes Axe, encouraging local authorities to raise the school-leaving age. But Labour's tenure was too brief. During the years of Conservative government (1924–29), Lord Eustace Percy abolished free places in secondary schools, wanting, Denis Lawton notes, 'secondary education to remain highly exclusive'.[27] The 1926 Hadow Report favoured secondary education for all aged eleven to fifteen. However, there was no clear vision of the form this secondary education might take. An expansion of elementary schools was mooted, and a division at age eleven into a selective system of education based on grammar schools, secondary schools, and technical schools: 'All go forward, though along different paths. Selection by differentiation takes the place of selection by elimination.'[28]

[24] *Times Educational Supplement*, 30 October 1919, as cited in Simon, p. 20.
[25] Gordon, Aldrich, and Dean, p. 33.
[26] R.H. Tawney, *Secondary Education for All: A Policy for Labour* (London: Labour Party Advisory Committee and George Allen Unwin, 1922), p. 7.
[27] Denis Lawton, *Education and Labour Party Ideologies, 1900–2001 and Beyond* (London: Routledge, 2005), p. 29.
[28] As cited in Lawton, p. 30.

The Conservatives rejected Hadow's recommendations for raising the school-leaving age to fifteen by 1932, negating the issue of the form secondary education might take, while Labour broadly welcomed the Hadow Report. Throughout the interwar period, Hadow proved influential in shaping a vision for the potential structure of secondary education as strongly marked by division, with different types of school for different children.[29]

The advent of the second Labour government in 1929 gave the fight for secondary education for all renewed vigour. Trevelyan's 1930 Bill sought to raise the school-leaving age to fifteen, but this was blocked by the House of Lords in 1931 through fear of compromising the place of the grammar school, and due to pressure from a voluntary-aided sector concerned about increased state control. Under the National Government, the minimum 50 per cent grant from the Exchequer to local authorities was abolished, and free places in secondary schools were replaced by means-tested places. In 1934, of every 1,000 elementary-school pupils in England, only 119 children moved sideways into the secondary system at age eleven.[30]

The 1936 Education Act has been condemned by educational historians: Brian Simon calls it 'belated and inadequate', while H.C. Dent suggests it was a 'half-baked compromise'.[31] It raised the school-leaving age to fifteen to take effect from 1 September 1939, but the Act's generous exemptions rendered it a compromise on any real reform: in the ten local education authorities (LEAs) where the school-leaving age had already been raised to fifteen and exemptions applied, the exemption rate was typically not less than 79 per cent.[32] Underfunding and the advent of the Second World War frustrated the implementation of the Act. During the war, the Norwood Report (1943) firmly advanced a tripartite system of secondary education on the basis that 'general educational experience' evidenced three 'rough groupings' of pupils: those 'interested in learning for its own sake, who can grasp an argument or follow a piece of connected reasoning' and were suited to the grammar school; those whose abilities lay 'markedly in the field of applied science or applied art' and were suited to the technical school; and those who dealt 'more easily with concrete things than with ideas' would be facilitated by a new institution known as the modern school.[33]

---

[29] Lawton, p. 34.

[30] Simon, p. 256.

[31] Gordon, Aldrich, and Dean, p. 58; Simon, p. 224; H.C. Dent, *1870–1970: Century of Growth in English Education* (London: Longman, 1970), p. 111.

[32] Gordon, Aldrich, and Dean, p. 57.

[33] The Norwood Report as cited in Gary McCulloch, *Failing the Ordinary Child?: The Theory and Practice of Working-Class Secondary Education* (Buckingham: Open University Press, 1998), pp. 55–56.

The 1944 Butler Act claimed to represent 'the first of the Government Measures of social reform' for the post-war world. At the Bill's reading, Butler claimed that it gave 'an opportunity to every child to pass through the primary and secondary stages [...] instead of a rudimentary education, under this Bill we hope to institute the broader training of a citizen for all'.[34] The elementary school was abolished, state-run education was organized into primary and secondary levels, and secondary-school fees were abolished. The compulsory school-leaving age was raised to fifteen in 1947 with the promise (not achieved until 1972) of raising the school-leaving age still higher to the age of sixteen. However, the Act did not define the specific structure of the secondary schools. Following the influence of Hadow, it left the way open for a tripartite system.

Butler also remained evasive on the public schools, which were left to the Fleming Report, much to the chagrin of the Left. In the post-war climate, the Fleming Report recognized that the 'trend of social development is leaving the Public Schools out of alignment with the world in which they exist'; to leave them unchanged would make it impossible to 'close in the world of schools a social breach that ... aggravates, if it does not actually cause, the much more serious divisions in society at large'.[35] However, far from rendering the system obsolete, the Fleming Report sought to replicate the advantages of the public-school system for more pupils through the widening of an expensive and bureaucratic bursary scheme, where schools that entered it would allocate 25 per cent of their places to pupils with local authority bursaries and the suggestion of boarding at some state secondary schools.[36]

From the Hadow Report onwards, the tripartite system of education represented the main vision for secondary education, but there were growing calls from left-leaning teaching unions from 1925 to develop more socially cohesive forms of institutional structures. A form of 'common' school was envisaged, which before the late 1940s, was usually called the 'multilateral' or 'multibias' school, and was later labelled the 'comprehensive' school.[37] The multilateral school was to accommodate all, both the 'modern' and 'grammar' sides. However, the comprehensive school became increasingly associated with weak or no streaming. Despite an openness to the benefits of a multilateral

[34] Butler Education Bill Reading.
[35] The Fleming Report as cited in McKibbin, *Classes and Cultures*, p. 241.
[36] Board of Education, *The Public Schools and the General Educational System* [The Fleming Report] (London: His Majesty's Stationery Office, 1944); McKibbin, *Classes and Cultures*, p. 241.
[37] McKibbin, *Classes and Cultures*, p. 231.

system before the Second World War, support waned for this system in the immediate post-war period, with some alienated by the scale of plans put forward by the London County Council who, in 1944, proposed to adopt 'a system of Comprehensive High Schools', each with over 2,000 pupils.[38]

In the post-war period, problems emerged with the implementation of the tripartite system. While Labour MPs were generally committed to this, there was also a commitment to developing a rewarding and stimulating curriculum in the secondary modern schools, and concern surrounding the perception of these schools as second-rate.[39] The 1944 Education Act gave local authorities power to develop plans for secondary provision in their area, recommending that 70 to 75 per cent of children were provided for by modern schools, and 25 to 30 per cent by technical and grammar schools combined. There was, however, vast regional variation in provision and the expensive technical school failed: in the 1950s less than 4 per cent of pupils attended such schools, rather than the 10 to 15 per cent that had been envisaged.[40] The schools were becoming strongly coded in terms of social class: by 1950, 60 per cent of children of professionals and businessmen could expect to win places at grammar school, compared to 10 per cent of working-class children.[41]

From 1951 the Conservatives maintained the tripartite system while Labour turned against selection. In the 1950s, the Communist Party, and Brian and Joan Simon in particular, played a key role in the campaign for comprehensive secondary education as they discredited the supposedly 'objective' basis of the system of intelligence testing which formed the basis of grammar-school selection.[42] Under Harold Wilson's 1964 Labour government there was a rapid shift in favour of comprehensive schools, while the Conservatives tended to emphasize the success of the grammar schools as they glossed over the failure of the secondary modern school. By the end of the 1960s, 1,300 comprehensive schools were in existence and in 1969, Margaret Thatcher was struck by the 'dominance of socialist thinking' in education policy, even among her own party, as she oversaw the spread of more comprehensive schools under her tenure as education secretary from 1970.[43]

---

[38] See McKibbin, *Classes and Cultures*, p. 234.

[39] See McCulloch, pp. 62–63.

[40] McCulloch, p. 60.

[41] McKibbin, *Classes and Cultures*, p. 262; see also McCulloch, pp. 77–80.

[42] See Matthew Kavanagh, 'British Communism, Periodicals and Comprehensive Education: 1920–56', *Twentieth Century Communism*, Vol. 12 (April 2017), 88–120.

[43] McCulloch, p. 139.

Marxist critics have drawn attention to the profound consequences educational policy held for culture. Brian Simon suggests that the Conservatives' exclusive vision for secondary education rendered it 'dedicated to the aim of separating out a selected few, conceiving of culture itself in terms of exclusiveness, conditioned to consider the nation's school system in terms of a functional preparation for different spheres of a class-divided society'.[44] This is an argument also reflected by Raymond Williams who argues that 'culture is one way in which class [...] shows itself', suggesting that historically education has been a site for a cultural class divide: 'the majority of people [...] were [...] shut out by the nature of the educational system from access to the full range of meanings of their predecessors.'[45] Against this interwar context of continued frustration of educational reform, education proved a significant site of engagement for writers' politics. Education offered a framework within which to critique dominant gender and class ideals, as well as occasioning a kind of proleptic thinking, as writers variously grasped for and resisted a more egalitarian social vision that could offer new institutional structures, associated with new, democratic, cultural forms.

1930s criticism: Leaning towers, gelded towers, and ivory towers

This book's focus on writers' political engagements with education in the 1930s is both indebted to the methods of literary historiography that have informed much 1930s criticism, and resistant to the imperatives that have underpinned traditional conceptions of the 1930s canon. Critical studies of the decade have traditionally focused on male, public-school-educated writers. Samuel Hynes's influential study *The Auden Generation: Literature and Politics in England in the 1930s* (1976) renders Auden, and his surrounding circle of public-school-educated writers, central to the decade's politics and aesthetics. Bernard Bergonzi (1978) follows Hynes in his definition of 1930s writing as largely corresponding to 'the Auden generation'.[46] For Bergonzi, education provided a monologic register that undermined political engagements.[47] Valentine Cunningham's compendious *British Writers of the Thirties* (1988) offers a broader analysis of

[44] Simon, p. 148.
[45] Raymond Williams, 'The Idea of a Common Culture (1967)', in *Raymond Williams On Culture & Society: Essential Writings*, ed. by Jim McGuigan (London: Sage, 2014), pp. 93–100 (p. 94; p. 97).
[46] Bernard Bergonzi, *Reading the Thirties: Texts and Contexts* (London: Macmillan, 1978), p. 1.
[47] Bergonzi, p. 37.

1930s writing, beyond Auden and his immediate circle. He uses the Spanish Civil War as a testing ground of writers' left-wing politics, charting a communist political narrative as he explores bourgeois writers' attempts at self-annulment as they sought to 'go over' to the proletariat. Conversely, educational practice is rendered as a manifestation of an adolescent sensibility.[48] Cunningham suggests that 1930s writers' concern with school is ultimately myopic and negatively inflects education's influence on cultural production in his references to the 'Old Boy racket'.[49] Adrian Caesar's *Dividing Lines: Poetry, Class and Ideology in the 1930s* (1991) debunks the 'literary-historical myth' of the 1930s literary Left as shaped by Auden and other 'young poets of the upper-middle class'.[50] Caesar's study does not fully acknowledge the ways in which writers were aware of how 'both the production and the reception of poetry are inseparably bound to the structures of the society from which it springs' in their consideration of how widening educational access could inform cultural production.[51]

Education has thus been a significant biographical factor in determining a masculinized 'canon' of the 1930s 'generation'. Virginia Woolf who was 'never at school' ('Sketch', p. 79) was excluded from a great number of critical studies of the 1930s. 'The Leaning Tower' identified a 1930s generation defined by their 'expensive education' (E6, p. 265). Woolf's perspicacity as a cultural critic of her contemporary scene makes her exclusion from the masculinized critical tradition of 1930s literature and politics more keenly felt. The relegation of Woolf to the role of outmoded 1920s aesthete has been challenged by Woolf studies, with feminist interventions in the 1970s and 1980s by figures such as Jane Marcus, and most recently in work by Clara Jones, Alice Wood, and Anna Snaith.[52]

Woolf was not the only female writer to be excluded from conceptions of a 1930s canon. The extent to which the educational imperatives which have

---

[48] Cunningham, *British Writers*, p. 127.

[49] *British Writers*, p. 119; p. 134; p. 147.

[50] Adrian Caesar, *Dividing Lines: Poetry, Class and Ideology in the 1930s* (Manchester: Manchester University Press, 1991), p. 22.

[51] Caesar, p. 3.

[52] See *The Bulletin of the New York Public Library: Virginia Woolf Issue*, Vol. 80 No. 2 (Winter 1977); Jane Marcus, *Virginia Woolf and the Languages of Patriarchy* (Bloomington: Indiana University Press, 1987); Clara Jones, *Virginia Woolf: Ambivalent Activist* (Edinburgh: Edinburgh University Press, 2016); Alice Wood, *Virginia Woolf's Late Cultural Criticism* (London: Bloomsbury, 2013); Anna Snaith notes of *The Years* that 'faced with a decade inaugurated and characterized by political and economic crisis, she responded by making that crisis her subject'. Anna Snaith, 'Introduction', in Virginia Woolf, *The Years*, ed. by Anna Snaith (Cambridge: Cambridge University Press, 2012), pp. xxxix–xcix (p. xxxix).

informed the selection of this canon have resulted in a focus on a male, socially exclusive demographic is evident in Maroula Joannou's edited collection *Women Writers of the 1930s: Gender, Politics and History* (1999), which explores the 'many good women novelists' whose reputation suffered as a result of the exclusion of women and working-class writers from the myth of the thirties 'on the grounds of their sex [...] their class [...] and their education (which debars working-class men and many of the liberal-left women who did not go to university)'.[53] Joannou's work is paralleled by other studies, such as those by Alison Light and Janet Montefiore, which brought female voices into the scope of analysis of the decade.[54] Just as the tower has been gelded by feminist critics, Andy Croft has toppled the tower, focusing on the decade's working-class and popular-front writers.[55] The political commitments of communist teachers in the 1930s has been illuminated by Matthew Kavanagh's valuable historical research and Simon Grimble's literary analysis of Edward Upward's 1930s work, but there is scope for more to be done on the decade's communist teachers and how their involvement with the journal entitled *The Ploughshare,* the organ of the Teachers' Anti-War Movement, informed their literary output.[56]

As well as a segmentation of 1930s literature into generations and factions, there is also a well-established conception of the formal and political engagements at stake in the 1930s as distinct from the modernist period. Carol A. Wipf-Miller presents the 'orthodox' position on 1930s literature that 'going over' politically prompted a 'concomitant aesthetic shift' as younger writers '"went over" [...] from modernism to a new realism, from an aesthetic ideal of formal autonomy to one that pursued an active and politicized engagement between life and art'.[57] Keith Williams and Steven Matthews caution against readings that too readily polarize different generations of writers in studies

---

[53] Maroula Joannou, 'The Woman Writer in the 1930s – On Not Being Mrs Giles of Durham City', in *Women Writers of the 1930s: Gender, Politics and History,* ed. by Maroula Joannou (Edinburgh: Edinburgh University Press, 1999), pp. 1–15 (p. 2; p. 9).

[54] Alison Light, *Forever England: Femininity, Literature and Conservatism between the Wars* (London: Routledge, 1991); Janet Montefiore, *Men and Women Writers of the 1930s: The Dangerous Flood of History* (London: Routledge, 1996).

[55] Andy Croft, *Red Letter Days: British Fiction in the 1930s* (London: Lawrence & Wishart, 1990).

[56] See Matthew Kavanagh, '"Against Fascism, War and Economies": The Communist Party of Great Britain's Schoolteachers during the Popular Front, 1935–1939', *History of Education,* Vol. 43 No. 2 (2014), 208–31. Simon Grimble has recently drawn on *The Ploughshare* to consider the tension between 'revolt and constraint' in Edward Upward's writing, occasioned by his depiction of the politically compromised figure of the teacher through whom 'spiritual uplift and moral struggle' is explored. Simon Grimble, '"Only Degradation and Slavery?": The Figure of the Teacher in the Writing of Edward Upward', in *Edward Upward and Left-Wing Literary Culture in Britain,* ed. by Benjamin Kohlmann (Farnham: Ashgate, 2013), pp. 69–82 (p. 70; p. 82).

[57] Carol A. Wipf-Miller, 'Fictions of "Going Over": Henry Green and the New Realism', *Twentieth Century Literature,* Vol. 44 No. 2 (Summer 1998), 135–54 (p. 136).

of the 1930s, positioning Woolf and T.S. Eliot as the 'literary midwives to the younger writers of the thirties'.[58] They 'challenge the [...] aftermyth of the thirties as a homogenous antimodernist decade', instead asserting the complex interrelationship of aesthetics and politics in the period.[59] As Marina MacKay notes, 'Generational change, the old explanation for the end of modernism, won't do.'[60] She complicates the characterization of modernism itself as at an aesthetic remove, noting that the

> characteristic tag used in the 1930s of the 1920s, the 'Ivory Tower' is, most impartially, an attack on literary specialization. But there's a very real sense in which the ivory tower was, to swap metaphors, a straw man. The narrow class and metropolitan base of literary and political culture in interwar England made it impossible for writers not to have social and familial connections with the political establishment.[61]

In the remit of *The Politics of 1930s British Literature*, this 'narrow class' base and strong links to the 'political establishment' is particularly apparent in the case of Woolf, with her connections to the very engine of interwar educational reform via H.A.L. Fisher.

Recent critical accounts have considered the close relationship between literary style and politics in this period. Lara Feigel (2010) recognizes the interrelationship of the formal and political in her analysis of the 'aestheticisation of politics' and the 'politicisation of aesthetics' in socialist, cinematic writing in the 1930s.[62] Benjamin Kohlmann returns to a critical conception that affirms the separation between the 1920s and 1930s in order to offer an understanding of the way in which a younger, politically engaged branch of 1930s writers understood themselves. He considers 'the politics of writing', illustrating the 'variety of politicized writing' in the 1930s by 'focusing on a cultural site where anxieties about art's inadequacy as a political weapon were especially intense.'[63] *The Politics of 1930s British Literature* emerges from these critical discourses which recognize the interrelationship of the political and the aesthetic. It is concerned

---

[58] Keith Williams and Steven Matthews, 'Introduction', in *Rewriting the Thirties: Modernism and After*, ed. by Keith Williams and Steven Matthews (London: Longman, 1997), pp. 1–4 (p. 2).

[59] Williams and Matthews, p. 1.

[60] Marina MacKay, "Doing Business with Totalitaria": British Late Modernism and Politics of Reputation', *ELH*, Vol. 73 No. 3 (Fall 2006), 729–53 (p. 748).

[61] MacKay, 'Doing Business', p. 731.

[62] Lara Feigel, *Literature, Cinema and Politics 1930-1945: Reading between the Frames* (Edinburgh: Edinburgh University Press, 2010), p. 12; p. 155.

[63] Benjamin Kohlmann, *Committed Styles: Modernism, Politics, and Left-Wing Literature in the 1930s* (Oxford: Oxford University Press, 2014), p. 13.

with the 'politics of writing' and the 'politicisation of aesthetics' as education informed debates about a new realism or a democratic art and rendered the class-inflected nature of literary discourse clear.

While this study is implicitly indebted to the 'temporal, spatial, and vertical' expansionist impulse that came with the New Modernist Studies, critical labels such as 'late modernism', 'intermodernism', and 'middlebrow' – categories that, as Kohlmann has noted, rely, ultimately, on the modernist for definition – can obscure the extent to which there was a (sometimes uneasy) mixing and mingling of generations and brows in the period.[64] Indeed, shortly after the publication of *The Orators* in June 1932, Woolf discussed the new generation of strident, young, public-school-educated men at a literary party. Woolf, feeling a parody of the literary ingénue in her white dress, retreated back home:

> Talk about Auden & Naomi Mitchison: her review of Auden read aloud [...] [t]hen they talked about the German youth movement: about bad people [...] I wore my new dress, too white & young perhaps; & so came home across London.[65]

This study groups authors by literary networks and friendships, but writers were also interacting in ways that frustrate these categories: Winifred Holtby wrote the first critical study in English of Virginia Woolf, and the two met and corresponded; Stephen Spender was friends with Woolf; George Orwell fell out with Spender; Henry Green was published by the Hogarth Press; Woolf read Vera Brittain's *Testament of Youth* and Holtby's *South Riding*; Graham Greene reviewed Auden; Holtby reviewed Graham Greene. I contribute to a more amorphous understanding of the ways in which the different factions of the literary scene interacted and influenced one another as education provided a currency for social transformation and a mode of political critique for writers from across the highbrow and middlebrow; the intermodernist and late modernist scenes.

This book joins a critical field that has traditionally been dominated by debates over the way in which education determines the class formations of a literary

---

[64] See Douglas Mao and Rebecca L. Walkowitz, 'The New Modernist Studies', *PMLA*, Vol. 123 No. 3 (May 2008), 737–48 (p. 738); Tyrus Miller, *Late Modernism: Politics, Fiction and the Arts between the World Wars* (London: University of California Press, 1999); Kristin Bluemel, *George Orwell and the Radical Eccentrics: Intermodernism in Literary London* (Basingstoke: Palgrave, 2004). Kohlmann critiques the dependence of intermodernism and late modernism on the category of modernism in *Committed Styles*, pp. 11–12.

[65] Virginia Woolf, *The Diary of Virginia Woolf Volume IV 1931–1935*, ed. by Anne Olivier Bell (London: Hogarth Press, 1982), pp. 105–06. Further references to this edition will be included in brackets after the citation as D4 and then the page number.

'generation', while sidelining consideration of how closely these writers engaged with contemporaneous educational discourse to interrogate their social and cultural position. John Carey's classic study *The Intellectuals and the Masses: Pride and Prejudice amongst the Literary Intelligentsia, 1880–1939* (1992) dominates conceptions of the ways in which writers were responsive to educational expansion. He focuses primarily on modernists, but discusses also writers such as George Orwell, as he argues that writers of the period sought to 'take literacy and culture away from the masses [...] to counteract the progressive intentions of democratic educational reform'.[66] Jonathan Rose largely follows Carey as he polarizes 'middle-class' 'modernist' elites against 'self-educated' autodidacts, offering a negative reading of modernism's depiction of autodidacts.[67] *The Politics of 1930s British Literature* argues that 1930s writers such as Orwell and Woolf were not retrospectively stuck in a rejection of 'late nineteenth-century educational reforms', but instead engaged with contemporary debates surrounding educational expansion.[68] The book's distinctive methodology uses tracts and pamphlets to illuminate a reading of the politics of literary texts, demonstrating writers' engagement with contemporaneous educational discourse through close biographical, archival, and historical research. By bringing pedagogic texts – textbooks, lectures, school songs, anthologies – within the scope of literary analysis, I demonstrate how actively these writers engaged with education, and suggest that the varied registers provided by the pedagogic were co-opted within the scope of the decade's creative work, informing the register of its social critique.

The 1930s has been particularly subject to periodization and re-periodization; its bridge between modernism and late modernism renders it a decade for which critics have demanded some elasticity. In 1980, Hynes critically redressed his earlier study: 'A decade is not a generation. The individuals who matter will not be an age-group, but the sharers of the time.'[69] This was recognized by Spender, who, on reviewing Valentine Cunningham's *British Writers of the Thirties*, commented that 'the 1930s began in 1928'.[70] I focus here on the 1930s as a period loosely conceived, and determined not by rigid chronological

---

[66] John Carey, *The Intellectuals and the Masses: Pride and Prejudice among the Literary Intelligentsia, 1880–1939* (London: Faber & Faber, 1992), p. 18.

[67] Jonathan Rose, *The Intellectual Life of the British Working Classes* (London: Yale University Press, 2001), p. 431.

[68] Carey, 'Preface', unnumbered page.

[69] Samuel Hynes, 'What is a Decade?: Notes on the Thirties', *Sewanee Review*, Vol. 88 (1980), 506–11 (p. 511).

[70] Stephen Spender, '"Where No One Was Well": Review of *British Writers of the Thirties* by Valentine Cunningham', *The Observer*, 7 February 1988, p. 24.

bounds, but by shared critical and imaginative concerns. This originates in political debates founded in the 1920s with the Labour Party's campaign for 'Secondary Education for All' and comes to fruition with the post-war Butler Education Act. The proleptic nature of the thinking of writers such as Virginia Woolf on educational institutions renders some of the ideas considered in this book unexpectedly anticipatory of post-war educational reforms. Through author-based case studies, and analyses of literary networks and friendships, the chapters of this book interrogate its central proposition from different angles.

Chapter 1 argues that W.H. Auden, a writer who has traditionally been positioned as instrumental to critical conceptions of the 1930s, developed his politics and aesthetics through engagement with education. It explores the influence of D.H. Lawrence on Auden's prose register and educational ideals, and departs from depoliticized readings of Auden's involvement in education to argue that education allowed him to evolve his left-leaning politics, while also demonstrating the bourgeois basis of his political convictions. My exploration of the school song Auden composed for Raynes Park School argues that the relationship between Auden's pedagogic and poetic work is dialogic, and through an analysis of *The Orators* and *The Dog Beneath the Skin*, the chapter nuances critical interpretations of Auden's parabolic, didactic tones to consider also the open, interrogatory qualities in his register as he incites the enactment of free, rational choice. Key to my analysis is a consideration of how far the form and genre of Auden's creative work tolerated his pedagogic approach.

Chapter 2 argues that Winifred Holtby's and Vera Brittain's feminist and pacifist politics informed, and were informed by, education, with a particular focus on their mid-1930s works: Holtby's *South Riding* and Brittain's *Honourable Estate* and *Testament of Youth*. It argues that *South Riding* is closely informed by Holtby's feminist activism for the National Union of Women Teachers and the Six Point Group, and her articles for *The Schoolmistress*. The novel is contextualized against cuts to education in the 1930s, and its closure is read as signalling the limitations of education to effect widespread social change. I draw on historical and archival material to argue that Brittain's *Honourable Estate* is in dialogue with late-Victorian and Edwardian educational discourses surrounding women's education, and demonstrate that *Testament of Youth* emerged from pacifist educational debates and inspired pacifist educational practice.

Chapter 3 explores the network of writers who contributed memoirs to Graham Greene's edited collection, *The Old School* (1934), to argue that interest in education resulted in individualistic analyses of schooldays and new literary forms that captured communal modes of experience. Greene's involvement is assessed alongside his autobiographies and novels to suggest the tensions in his leftist politics. A contextualized, genetic reading of *Love on the Dole* demonstrates how Walter Greenwood manipulates narrative and language to depict the social and educational deprivation of the slums. I argue that Stephen Spender's essay in *The Old School* and his autobiographical novel, *The Backward Son*, engage with contemporaneous educational discourses to critique the heroic, while a genetic reading of his poetry demonstrates his manipulation of literary form to evade the heroic narrative. A comparison between the narrative form of Antonia White's essay in the collection and her literary fiction suggests how White was both seduced by, and critical of, her old school, and her feminist and pedagogic politics are illuminated by her previously unconsidered articles for *The Schoolmistress*. A discussion of Arthur Calder-Marshall argues that the pedagogic politics of his anti-public school tract, *Challenge to Schools*, illuminates the Marxist aesthetics in his public-school novel *Dead Centre*.

Chapter 4 focuses on Virginia Woolf, considering *The Pargiters, The Years, Three Guineas*, and 'The Leaning Tower', to depart from the critical focus on Woolf's anti-institutional engagements with working-class education through 'The Common Reader'. I explore instead how Woolf renders institutional working-class education central to the future realization of democratic social and literary forms. The 1880 Education Act is considered in relation to *The Pargiters* and *The Years* and the significance of autodidact, dialect scholar Joseph Wright is suggested for a reading of the children's song and Woolf's characterization of Sam Robson in *The Years*. The marginal role of the working class in *Three Guineas* is assessed through a consideration of the text's marginalia as I nuance critical conceptions of *Three Guineas*'s politics in my argument that the text's endnotes render transparent Woolf's polemical focus on the 'daughters of educated men'. 'The Leaning Tower', Woolf's lecture to the WEA, is assessed as a studied rhetorical performance that draws on contemporaneous educational debates as she anticipates a socially and culturally democratic post-war future.

Chapter 5 focuses on the Eton-educated writers Henry Green, George Orwell, and Cyril Connolly's interrogation of their educational background, literary discourse, and cultural heritage. I argue that Orwell's ventriloquial rhetorical style renders opaque his ironic engagement with the uneducated 'myth of the proletariat' and that he manipulates historical details and literary register in *The Road to Wigan Pier* and *Coming Up for Air* to reflect his anti-heroic politics and his political appeal to the middle class. Connolly objected to criticisms of *Enemies of Promise* which suggested that its literary criticism had 'nothing to do with' its autobiography. This analysis argues that Connolly's memoir self-reflexively suggests that education informs the development of his style and cultural values. The chapter draws on Henry Green's novels, with particular attention to *Living*, to argue that the class and cultural codes arising from education inform Green's elusive self-presentation and his analysis of literary discourse in his public-school autobiography, *Pack My Bag*. The book concludes with consideration of Green's post-war novel *Doting* (1952). Green's rendering of the public school is haunted by a sense of upper-class redundancy in an era of the democratic educational reform so anticipated by many of the writers of the 1930s. This novel offers a compelling coda to this school-minded decade.

1

W.H. Auden: Pedagogy and Freedom of Choice in the 1930s

W.H. Auden had an unconventional classroom practice. His friend, Margaret Gardiner, noted:

> He told me that he believed teachers ought to be clowns; if you stood on your head or played the piano with your feet, the boys would immediately attend, there'd be no difficulty about discipline. You should continuously startle them into interest, he said, keep them alert by letting them catch you out, trip you up.[1]

One of his former pupils, Michael Yates, found that his classes were 'in turn traditional, original, or a plain riot of fun'. Plays replaced essays; astronomy replaced preparation for the Common Entrance.[2]

Louis MacNeice recognized that Auden's 'several years as a schoolmaster, and his general interest in boys' schools has had a huge influence on his poetry'.[3] As he was establishing his literary career, Auden spent the decade teaching in schools: spring 1930 to summer 1932 was spent at Larchfield, a down-at-heel

---

[1] Humphrey Carpenter, *W.H. Auden: A Biography* (London: Allen & Unwin, 1981), p. 112.

[2] Carpenter, p. 143. Michael Yates later confirmed that he had had a relationship with Auden after they first met when Auden taught him at Downs School when Yates was 13. They continued their contact after Yates left the school shortly afterwards. Carpenter is hazy about the precise details of their relationship although Yates is one of his sources. From the mid-1960s Yates and his wife Marny were regular summer visitors to Auden's summer home in Kirchstetten, Austria. Carpenter mentions Yates in p. 143; pp. 201–02; pp. 391–92; pp. 451–52. Yates discusses his influence on Auden's love poetry in 'Tell Me the Truth about Love', dir.by Susanna White, BBC4, 17 May 2009 [first broadcast in 2000]. See also Louise Jury, 'Auden's Schoolboy Inspiration Tells the Truth about Their Love', *Independent*, 18 March 2000, <http://www.independent.co.uk/news/media/audens-schoolboy-inspiration-tells-the-truth-about-their-love-284829.html> [accessed 26 July 2017]. There is some indication that, among Auden's circle, his reputation for an enthusiasm for adolescent boys was well established. As Thekla Clark notes, at a 1966 party, seeing Auden in conversation with a 'young man', his friend, John Clark, turned to a group of friends and remarked '"Wystan is a born pedagogue,"' Chester [Kallman] answered '"Ped-a-*what?*"'. Thekla Clark, *Wystan and Chester: A Personal Memoir* (London: Faber & Faber, 1995), p. 92.

[3] Louis MacNeice, *Modern Poetry: A Personal Essay* (Oxford: Oxford University Press, 1938), p. 85.

school in Helensburgh, Scotland, which mainly took in pupils of preparatory school age; and from autumn 1932 to summer 1935, he taught at the Downs School, a successful preparatory-age Quaker school in Colwall, Herefordshire, with an earnest, puritanical ethos: 'We sing many hymns, and slap our thighs. Those who loiter in the lavatories are not much thought of.'[4] After returning from the Spanish Civil War in 1937, he also returned to Downs for a term's teaching. During the decade, Auden expressed interest in gaining work in a wide variety of schools: he visited the progressive Dartington Hall School in spring 1932, and wrote asking for a job, to which he received a 'friendly but doubtful' reply.[5] In 1935, after some time at the Downs, Auden was lined up for a job at Bryanston, but was ambivalent about teaching in a public school: 'I'm off to Bryanston in September, full of doubts', he wrote to Michael Roberts.[6] The arrangement fell through after Auden urged an ex-pupil of Downs, then at Bryanston, to 'put an onion in the chalice' for the sermon Geoffrey Hoyland, the Downs' headmaster, was due to give at Bryanston.[7] That same year, uncertain whether to go on teaching, Auden wrote to Roberts: 'If I do, I think a secondary day school.'[8]

This is the first critical focus on Auden as educationist, offering a historicized consideration of his involvement with education to nuance interpretations of his politics and aesthetics. Previous critical renderings, by Valentine Cunningham and Edward Mendelson, depoliticize Auden's engagement with education.[9] Cunningham offers a communist standard of left-wing political commitment (negatively) critiquing Auden on the basis of how effectively he submerged the bourgeois 'I' in the proletariat 'we'.[10] Where the political implications of education have been considered, the public school has frequently been figured as a site of generational conflict.[11] Stan Smith's essays on Auden have usefully asserted the influence of the politics of

---

[4]   Richard Davenport-Hines, *Auden* (London: Heinemann, 1995), p. 120.

[5]   Carpenter, p. 137.

[6]   Carpenter, p. 174.

[7]   Ibid.

[8]   Carpenter, p. 175.

[9]   See Cunningham, *British Writers*, p. 447; Edward Mendelson, *Early Auden* (London: Faber & Faber, 1981), p. 294.

[10] *British Writers*, p. 219; p. 224. For other critical readings of Auden's relationship with Marxism, see Justin Replogle, 'Auden's Marxism', *PMLA*, Vol. 80 No. 5 (1965), 584–95; Patrick Deane, 'Auden's England', in *The Cambridge Companion to W.H. Auden*, ed. by Stan Smith (Cambridge: Cambridge University Press, 2004), pp. 25–38.

[11] Frederick Buell, *W.H. Auden as a Social Poet* (London: Cornell University Press, 1973), pp. 72–73; Samuel Hynes, *The Auden Generation: Literature and Politics in England in the 1930s* (London: Bodley Head, 1976), p. 19.

1931 on Auden's work on education, while this chapter more directly suggests how contemporaneous educational movements stimulated Auden's politics.[12] Stephen Parsons's research has found that membership of the Communist Party rose among the professional middle classes in the 1930s, of whom a disproportionate number were teachers.[13] Auden's political foregrounding of the role of the teacher, analyzed in this chapter, is responsive to contemporary social and political concerns, as education informed Auden's self-reflexive socialism, shaped by his class position.

Critics have also suggested that teaching negatively informs Auden's poetic register: Bergonzi notes the 'schoolmasterly' tone of 1930s writing and Caesar comments on 'Auden's hectoring, pedagogical tones'.[14] The parabolic properties of Auden's verse (and thirties writing in general) are also associated with his pedagogic register; Samuel Hynes bases his critical terminology surrounding 1930s 'parable-art' on Auden's own formulation in *The Poet's Tongue* (1935), and Mendelson similarly alludes to Auden's 'didactic historical parables'.[15] In tension with such critical observations of Auden's didactic pedagogic register, Mendelson notes Auden's thesis that 'the purpose of education was to enlarge the freedom in which [...] choices were made'.[16] This chapter's historicized consideration of Auden's engagement with education considers this seeming impasse between critical conceptions of his authoritarian, pedagogic register and his wider advocacy of pedagogy's anti-authoritarian aims. It explores the open and interrogatory *pedagogic* qualities of Auden's register, and his attempts to mitigate against the instructional and didactic *parabolic*. Key to my analysis will be a consideration of how far Auden's creative work tolerated his pedagogic approach. With a particular focus on his pedagogy and prose writings on education, but with consideration also of his creative work in the period, this chapter argues that Auden was concerned with education's role in inciting the development of moral freedom. The chapter unpicks the influence of Auden's ideologues in the 1930s, D.H. Lawrence and Homer Lane, to interrogate the ways in which this principle informed Auden's pedagogy and aesthetics, as well as considering how it informed his conceptualization of political principles.

---

[12] Stan Smith, 'Loyalty and Interest: Auden, Modernism and the Politics of Pedagogy', *Textual Practice*, Vol. 4 No. 1 (1990), 54–72; Stan Smith, 'Remembering Bryden's Bill: Modernism from Eliot to Auden', in *Rewriting the Thirties*, ed. by Williams and Matthews, pp. 53–70.

[13] As cited in Grimble, p. 71.

[14] Bergonzi, p. 32; Caesar, p. 78.

[15] Hynes, *Auden Generation*, pp. 14–15; Mendelson, *Early Auden*, p. 305.

[16] *Early Auden*, p. 305.

'Writing' and Ode V of *The Orators*

Auden's early essay 'Writing', a contribution to Naomi Mitchison's textbook *An Outline for Boys and Girls and Their Parents* (1932), expresses concern for talent to 'make itself understood [...] to bridge the gulf between one person and another' and find a 'united' community of readers beyond the coterie 'circle of clever people'.[17] These comments are striking for the extent to which they seem personally motivated: obscurity is a criticism held against early Auden, and particularly *The Orators*, a text that has an enigmatic dedicatory verse to Stephen Spender that points to – and indeed revels in – this very obscurity: 'Private faces in public places | Are wiser and nicer | Than public faces in private places.'[18]

Early reviewers were perplexed by the poem. F.R. Leavis, for whom Auden went on to contribute reviews on education, found the work 'remarkable' but suggested that 'too often, instead of complexity and subtlety, he gives us a blur'.[19] In August 1932 Auden himself apologized to a befuddled reader calling *The Orators* 'far too obscure and equivocal'.[20] This equivocality is extended to the instability of Auden's political critique, recognized by Graham Greene, who found that 'the subject of the book is political, though it is hard to tell whether the author's sympathies are Communist or Fascist'.[21] In 1966 he wrote: 'My name on the title-page seems a pseudonym for someone else [...] who might well, in a year or two, become a Nazi'; and in 1932, Auden suggested that the poem is 'meant to be a critique of the fascist outlook, but [...] I see that it can [...] be interpreted as a favourable exposition'.[22] The influence of D.H. Lawrence is evident in this early work, and much of the poem's ambiguity stems from the ways in which Auden is both critical of, and seduced by, the nameless Leader figure.[23] Mendelson suggests that the poem is 'about hero-

---

[17] W.H. Auden, 'Writing', in *The Complete Works of W.H. Auden Prose and Travel Books in Prose and Verse Volume I 1926–1938*, ed. by Edward Mendelson (London: Faber & Faber, 1996), pp. 12–24 (p. 24). Further references to this essay will be included in brackets after the citation.

[18] W.H. Auden, *The Orators: An English Study* (London: Faber & Faber, 1932), front matter. Further references to this edition will be included in brackets after the citation.

[19] F.R. Leavis, 'Unsigned Review', *Listener*, 22 June 1932, in *W.H. Auden: The Critical Heritage*, ed. by John Haffenden (London: Routledge & Kegan Paul, 1983), pp. 100–01 (p. 101; pp. 100–01).

[20] Mendelson, *Early Auden*, p. 104.

[21] Graham Greene, 'Three Poets', *Oxford Magazine*, 10 November 1932, in *Auden: Critical Heritage*, ed. by Haffenden, pp. 115–16 (p. 115).

[22] W.H. Auden, *The Orators: An English Study*, 3rd edn (London: Faber & Faber, 1966), p. 7; Mendelson, *Early Auden*, p. 104.

[23] I am grateful to Professor Chris Baldick for this point. Auden described 'The Initiates' section of *The Orators* in an August 1931 letter to Naomi Mitchison as 'my memorial to Lawrence [...] the theme is the failure of the romantic conception of personality'. Mendelson, *Early Auden*, p. 97.

worship' and Auden's 1966 'Preface' isolates this as the poem's 'central theme'.[24] The school setting provides the locale for much of this criticism – to the extent that Michael Roberts read the poem as a critique of the public school classes.[25] My analysis considers the influence of Homer Lane on 'Ode V' of *The Orators*. It recognizes the multiplicity of this enigmatic text, while offering one way of understanding elements of the ambiguity of Auden's verse, as part of his pedagogic attempts to incite a sense of the significance of individual choice, a parabolic message of his verse that, I argue, is reflected in his pedagogic strategies in 'Writing'.

Addressed 'To My Pupils', 'Ode V' of *The Orators* is positioned as speaking to the schoolboys of Larchfield, a school of largely preparatory-age intake, at which Auden was teaching as he wrote the poem. The specific differences between the public and preparatory school were a concern of Auden's 'Public-School Notebook'. This includes a clipping from the June 1921 issue of the *St. Edmund's Chronicle*, the school magazine of Auden's former preparatory school, which comments on the relative autonomy of the public, as opposed to preparatory, schoolboy: 'The boys seemed more purposeful, more businesslike [*sic*]; more as if they were doing things on their own and not under compulsion.'[26] Homer Lane's 'Age of Loyalty' coincides with some of the years of preparatory-school age; Lane called this period the 'stage of transition', noting its crucial implications for heroism: 'From eleven is the most difficult age; it is the self-giving age and the "storm period", it sees the breaking up of self-assertion, of the desire to be hero, and the search for a hero not oneself.'[27] Under Lane's thesis, hero-worship and aspiration to the heroic coincided with some of the years of preparatory schooling, which was typically from eight to thirteen.[28] Indeed, the autobiographical 'Letter to Lord Byron' (1937) suggestively noted of preparatory-school teaching: 'It's pleasant as it's easy to secure | The hero-worship of the immature'.[29]

Auden had encountered Lane's work for the first time in 1928, through John Layard, one of Lane's former patients, and in April 1930, he had celebrated Lane

[24] Mendelson, *Early Auden*, p. 97; Auden, *The Orators*, 3rd edn, p. 7.

[25] Michael Roberts, 'Untitled Review', *Adelphi*, August 1932, in *Auden: Critical Heritage*, ed. by Haffenden, pp. 107–10.

[26] [Public-school letters. Holograph Transcripts of 13 letters] The Henry W. and Albert A. Berg Collection of English and American Literature, The New York Public Library.

[27] Homer Lane, *Talks to Parents and Teachers* (London: Allen & Unwin, 1928), p. 103; p. 105.

[28] Lane, p. 103.

[29] W.H. Auden, 'Letter to Lord Byron', in *The English Auden: Poems, Essays and Dramatic Writings 1927–1939*, ed. by Edward Mendelson (London: Faber & Faber, 1986), pp. 169–99 (p. 196).

as a 'healer[s] in our English land'.[30] Lane's psychoanalytic teachings advocated the morally desirable nature of free, instinctive behaviour, and his advocacy of freedom found a practical application in his work in education: from 1913 to 1918, Lane established and was the 'Superintendent' of the Little Commonwealth, a reformatory school in Dorset.[31] Lane formalized his ideas on education in *Talks to Parents and Teachers,* published posthumously in 1928. In a 1934 book review, Auden demonstrated his familiarity with Lane's teachings, as he wondered if the author 'is acquainted with the work of Homer Lane, but everything she says is a striking confirmation of his teaching'.[32] Lane's Little Commonwealth was shaped by ideals of freedom, which, in turn, had a profound influence on A.S. Neill. After the Little Commonwealth's demise, Neill founded Summerhill in 1921, on the model of Lane's school: 'How can I say I'd have run a Summerhill even if Lane had never lived?'.[33] Neill dedicated *A Dominie in Doubt* (1920) 'to Homer Lane [...] I owe much to him'.[34] Like the Little Commonwealth, Summerhill similarly used self-government as an educational method: 'You cannot have progression unless children feel completely free [...]. When there is a boss, freedom is not there.'[35] In 1955, Neill retrospectively commented on a 1950 meal he had shared with Auden: 'P.S. Hell, I lunched with Auden in New York five years ago, and we didn't know of the Lane link.'[36]

Mendelson notes Auden's 'subversive writing from within' in *The Orators,* comments echoed by Richard R. Bozorth.[37] This liminal position is particularly reflected in 'Ode V', where Auden's stance is illuminated with reference to Lane's liminal positioning of the teacher in group relations. Lane develops a pedagogy that undermines boys' hero-worshipping tendencies:

> The only way to carry on a class is to work through the crowd mind. But, though the teacher *can* in this way become a group leader, yet, if his attitude to the group is one of command, he will only increase its dislike both of himself and of his subject. [...] Until [...] the teacher can become a *member* of the crowd, and

---

[30] W.H. Auden, 'XXXI', in *English Auden,* ed. by Mendelson, pp. 48–49 (p. 49).

[31] Carpenter, p. 86.

[32] W.H. Auden, 'To Unravel Happiness', in *W.H. Auden Volume I 1926–1938,* ed. by Mendelson, pp. 77–79 (p. 78).

[33] A.S. Neill, *All the Best, Neill: Letters from Summerhill,* ed. by Jonathan Croall (London: Deutsch, 1983), p. 96.

[34] A.S. Neill, *A Dominie in Doubt* (London: Jenkins, 1920).

[35] A.S. Neill, *That Dreadful School* (London: Jenkins, 1937), p. 46.

[36] Croall (ed.), p. 97.

[37] Mendelson, *Early Auden,* p. 95; Richard R. Bozorth, *Auden's Games of Knowledge: Poetry and the Meanings of Homosexuality* (Chichester: Columbia University Press, 2001), p. 135.

do away with the emotional attitude of the crowd by himself resigning his own authoritarian position, he will find both disciplinary problems and a dislike of his instructions.[38]

Lane's recommendations for anti-authoritarian educational techniques are formulated in opposition to Freud's analysis of hero-worship. Freud argued that in 'group psychology' the individual 'gives up his ego ideal and substitutes for it the group ideal as embodied in the leader'.[39] In his analysis of 'The Group and the Primal Horde', a similar deferral to group will is described; individual will is surrendered and 'no impulses whatever came into existence except collective ones; there was only a common will, there were no single ones'. Individual reason is abandoned in favour of a kind of collective consciousness.[40] For Auden, the term 'hero-worship' was laden with Freudian associations. 'Psychology and Art Today' (1935) contended that Freud has 'revised hero-worship' away, it is implied, from Victorian Carlylean ideals, while Humphrey Carpenter notes Auden's familiarity with Freud through his father's medical practice, commenting that by 1928 he 'was already well read in Freud's writings'.[41] For Lane, the teacher must be a 'member' of the crowd, a part of its group consciousness, not its hierarchical leader and a projection of its ego-ideal.

Auden republished 'Ode V' as 'Which Side Am I Supposed to Be On?' in the 1940s. The revised title is suggestive: the interrogatory form reflects an ambiguity of allegiance, combined with an element of coercion ('supposed'). Various forces conspire to render the enactment of free will in the poem difficult. The boys act under a repressive cloak of enforced ignorance, calling the 'us' of group ties into doubt: 'They speak of things done on the frontier we were never told' (p. 107). The leaders exploit the boys by keeping them in a state of ignorance: 'Boy, the quarrel was before your time, the aggressor | No one you know' (p. 104). Any attempts at elucidation are met with rebuttal; the 'veteran answers' a recruit's question with an evasion: 'Go to sleep, Sonny!' (p. 104). The closure presents the dissolution of group ties as those who had once '*identified themselves with one another in their ego*' are slipping away.[42] Thus there is a 'leakage' (p. 108) to the enemy side; the boys recognize familiar faces 'we seem

[38] Lane, pp. 112–13.
[39] Sigmund Freud, *Group Psychology and the Analysis of the Ego*, trans. and ed. by James Strachey (London: Hogarth Press, 1959), p. 61.
[40] *Group Psychology*, pp. 54–55.
[41] W.H. Auden, 'Psychology and Art Today', in *W.H. Auden Volume I 1926–1938*, ed. by Mendelson, pp. 93–105 (p. 104); Carpenter, p. 86.
[42] Freud, *Group Psychology*, trans. and ed. by Strachey, p. 48, emphases in original.

to have seen before' (p. 107). The shifting distinguishing referent, them versus us, throughout the poem, undermines any easy sense of alliance and affiliation. This creates an emotional landscape that deliberately invokes ambiguity and uncertainty; obscurity is part of the poem's pedagogic strategies in a reflection of Lane's appositional analysis of the teacher's role in group psychology, as a figure that 'work[s] through the crowd mind' rather than 'command[s]' the crowd.[43] Auden's stance as he addresses 'My Pupils' in 'Ode V' has a pedagogic import. As the bonds of group life dissolve, are Auden's Larchfield pupils capable of taking free and individual action? Obfuscation of allegiance in the poem deliberately heightens a sense of the moral weight inherent in the individual act of volition: with no coherent group consciousness to which the pupils can defer, the prime importance of individual responsibility for decision-making is revealed.

Auden's essay 'Writing' defined the 'epic' in Freudian terms as 'long stories in verse about the exploits of a small group of young warriors under a leader [...] held together by their devotion to their leader' (p. 24). Christopher Isherwood, who later noted the 'cult of the public-school system' as 'The Test' of 'fundamental "Manhood"',[44] a phrase derived from 'Ode V', which presents the recruits who, feeling the pressure of the 'names to live up to' wonder if they are capable of 'passing | The endurance test?' (p. 105), commented that, for early Auden, 'the saga-world is a schoolboy world'.[45] In *The Orators*, the school setting is merged with this world as Auden renders a Freudian application to the Old English heroic verse, 'The Battle of Maldon':

> What have we all been doing to have made from
>   Fear
> That laconic war-bitten captain addressing them
>   now?
> 'Heart and head shall be keener, mood the more
>   As our might lessens':
> To have caused their shout 'we will fight till we lie
>   down beside
>   The Lord we have loved'. (p. 106)

---

[43] Ibid.
[44] Christopher Isherwood, *Lions and Shadows: An Education in the Twenties* (London: Minerva, 1996), p. 47.
[45] Christopher Isherwood, 'Some Notes on Auden's Early Poetry', *New Verse No. 26–27*, November 1937, p. 5.

Resolution must be the tougher, hearts the keener, courage must be the more as our strength grows less [...] I mean to lie at the side of my lord, by the man so dear to me.[46]

S.A.J. Bradley comments that 'Maldon' presents 'an exemplary dynamic of warfare': it therefore offers the perfect vessel for the boys' ego-ideal.[47] Chris Jones notes that Auden uses 'an almost direct translation' of his source 'to expose the ways in which this group willingness to die is manufactured'.[48] Auden also gives a Freudian application of group psychology to this Anglo-Saxon statement of loyalty to one's liege lord. Byrhtwold's words of individual sacrifice are transferred into a statement of group sacrifice in the collective pronoun ('we will fight ... '). Auden splits Byrhtwold's words between the boys and the captain, creating an enactment of the process of group identification where the individual 'gives up his ego ideal and substitutes for it the group ideal as embodied in the leader'.[49] The shared ego-ideal is reflected in the shared lines. The rhetorical question, 'What have we all been doing to have made from Fear | That laconic war-bitten captain addressing them now?', recognizes a degree of complicity in the cultivation of this leader that reflects a central tension of *The Orators*: its degree of complicity in, or critique of, the hero-worship it presents.

Where the pedagogic figures in 'Ode V' frustrated pupils' attempts at elucidation, in 'Writing' there is a clarity and directness of pedagogic intent that suggests the ways in which Auden developed his own pedagogic strategies in tandem with the pedagogic poetics of 'Ode V'. Simple sentences ('This is the first language.' (p. 12)) and subheadings are used throughout, such as 'SPEECH' (p. 12) and 'MEANING' (p. 14). The register is informal and anti-authoritarian. Colloquialisms and the collective plural are used: 'but suppose' (p. 13), 'language as we know it [...] [t]o go back to our sketch' (p. 15). Jokes are used (in the form of humorous names): 'Mr Stinker' (p. 15), and analogies explain verse form in more accessible terms: 'Imagine a circle of people dancing; the circle revolves and comes back to its starting place [...] [w]hen words move in this kind of repeated pattern, we call the effect of the movement in our minds the metre' (p. 19). Expansions and exemplars are used for clarification: 'It is unlikely [...] that language was entirely onomatopoeic, that is, that words were sounds imitating

---

[46] S.A.J. Bradley, trans. and ed., *Anglo-Saxon Poetry* (London: Dent, 1982), p. 527.

[47] Bradley, p. 519.

[48] Chris Jones, *Strange Likeness: The Use of Old English in Twentieth-Century Poetry* (Oxford: Oxford University Press, 2006), p. 111.

[49] Freud, *Group Psychology*, trans. and ed. by Strachey, p. 61.

the sounds of things spoken about […] (e.g. hissing, growling, splashing)' (p. 15). Most importantly, Auden foregrounds the role of choice as part of his open and interrogatory pedagogic strategies: 'Another question. What is the difference between writing as a work of Art, what we call literature, and other kinds of writings. Again, it depends how you choose to look at it.' The reader is guided through the process of making an independent decision: 'suppose I take up […] [i]f on the other hand'. Ambiguity of perception is finally tolerated: 'The most we can say is that' (p. 21).

Reading across Auden's prose and verse elucidates the ways in which they share a pedagogic purpose. The clarity of Auden's prose writing for textbooks reinforces the opaque elements of his early verse, providing a relationship between the two modes that is at once complementary and contradictory.

D.H. Lawrence's disciple: Auden's early reviews on education

In the 1930s Auden supplemented his teaching salary with reviewing, developing a particular niche as a reviewer of books on education. 'Private Pleasure', Auden's September 1932 review for *Scrutiny*, is ostensibly a review on three different educational books, but it moves from a very brief consideration of these to an exploration of the faults of the education system more broadly, finding that until wider social change takes effect 'teaching will continue to be, not a public duty, but a private indulgence'.[50] Written from the perspective of the schoolmaster ('some of us will go on teaching what we can' (p. 27)), the review gains authority from its writer's specialist expertise. The review's polysemous narrative voice occupies different subject positions to articulate – and ultimately ironize – different aspects of the education system, but these different voices are pitched against the commanding register of the review's own naturalized voice that has been described as both Leavisite and Lawrentian.[51] The arresting, prophetic voice as well as the arguments of Lawrence's *Fantasia of the Unconscious* (1922) – a text centrally concerned with education which, Carpenter notes, Auden read while an undergraduate or shortly after – informs Auden's early reviews.[52]

[50] W.H. Auden, 'Private Pleasure', in *W.H. Auden Volume I 1926–1938*, ed. by Mendelson, pp. 25–27 (p. 27). Further references to this essay will be included in brackets after the citation.
[51] Davenport-Hines comments on the Leavisite voice of the review in *Auden*, p. 130; Mendelson comments on the Lawrentian voice of the review in *Early Auden*, p. 129.
[52] Carpenter, p. 87.

Auden, taking on the role of diagnostician, intones the central problem for England, in the interjectory, interrogatory style that also characterizes Lawrence's prose: 'Education, all smoothly say, is the production of useful citizens. But, good God, what on earth is a useful citizen just now?' (pp. 25–26). Auden borrows Lawrence's disdain for the localized concerns of parental interest, expressed in similar terms: 'Teach every little Mary to be more and more a nice little Mary out of her own head' (*Fantasia*); 'Fathers sell grand pianos or give up tobacco, that little Adrian or Derek may go to Marlborough or Stowe' ('Private', p. 25).[53] Lawrence's style of frequent citation of other voices for comment within his own discourse is evident throughout Auden's piece. Progressive education comes under particular scrutiny. Progressives are 'comfortably off, with no right to fear' yet they 'have nightmares' (p. 26). Auden's satire is evident in his parodic, class-based discourse: 'Even if there is anything wrong with the world, if I do try to do anything about it, I shouldn't make any difference: I should only lose my money. It's all so very diffy. Let's go and ask the children' (p. 26). Lawrence's cynicism surrounding education's emphasis on the 'development of the powers of so-called self-expression in a child' (p. 89) informs Auden's critique of progressive education's emphasis on imaginative expression, which produces imitative copies, rather than evidencing personal creativity: 'Girls of eleven paint like Picasso, boys of sixteen write pastiches of Joyce' (p. 26). Auden's disdain for the 'love-smarm' (p. 26) which 'emotionally [...] withers' (p. 26) is also indebted to Lawrence's *Fantasia,* which rails against the

> disease of love [...] the disease of niceness and benevolence [...] it is all a gangrene. We can retreat upon the proud, isolate self, and remain there alone like lepers, till we are cured of this ghastly white disease of self-conscious idealism. (pp. 86–87)

In 'Private Pleasure', and a near contemporary corollary review of Bertrand Russell's *Education and the Social Order* (1932), 'Problems of Education', published in the *New Statesman and Nation* on 15 October 1932, Auden develops a Lawrentian rebuttal to progressive education. This conflict of ideals is compelling, given that Russell and Lawrence themselves fell out over their contrasting social philosophies in 1915.[54] 'Problems of Education' refers to

---

[53] D.H. Lawrence, *Fantasia of the Unconscious and Psychoanalysis and the Unconscious* (London: Penguin, 1975), p. 86. Further references to this edition will be included in brackets after the citation.

[54] Russell and Lawrence shared a period of intense friendship and intended to conduct a lecture tour together. However, their conflicting social philosophies were brought into focus after Lawrence read (and commented disparagingly on) Russell's 'Philosophy of Social Reconstruction'. Lawrence's biographer, Mark Kinkead-Weekes, notes that by June 1915, 'the gap between his [Russell's] secular and humanist reformism and Lawrence's intensity about spiritual revolution deepened [...] into a chasm'. Mark Kinkead-Weekes, *D.H. Lawrence: Triumph to Exile 1912–1922* (Cambridge: Cambridge University Press, 1996), p. 258.

Lawrence's idea of man's 'dual' nature (p. 28), which, Auden suggests, is not accommodated in Russell's educational principles.[55] *Fantasia* maintains the place of the 'proud, isolate self' which, Lawrence argues, is distorted by an education system that pursues academic education for the many, when it is only suitable for the few: 'It is not the *nature* of most men to know and to understand and to reason very far' (p. 84). Both reviews echo this, but avoid Lawrence's fascistic exclusivity, as they oppose 'liberal' or progressive education with man's authoritative qualities: 'to command or obey [...] to live with others in a relation of power' ('Private Pleasure', p. 26); 'to obey and to command, to strut and to swagger' ('Problems of Education', p. 28). 'Problems of Education' contends that the public school is one of the 'old methods' (p. 28) capable of 'satisfying' (p. 28) this aspect of man's nature. While Russell hoped that progressive education would provide an ideal model of citizenship balanced by 'individual judgement and individual initiative', Auden associates progressive education with a form of moral coercion that transforms Russell's idealized product of progressive education – 'educated in fearless freedom' – into a prop to state interests: 'Its most powerful weapon against social revolution' ('Private Pleasure', p. 26).[56] The aversion expressed to the 'spiritual bully' ('Problems of Education', p. 28) and the 'liberal' methods of education which 'can only bully the spirit' ('Private Pleasure', p. 26) is also borrowed from Lawrentian principles. *Fantasia of the Unconscious* notes the profoundly 'dangerous' nature of 'ideal bullying. Bullying people into what is ideally good for them' (p. 52).

Auden suggests that education's focus on educational technique, rather than social change, is futile as a means to effect a real change:

> The failure of modern education lies not in its attention to individual needs, nor to methods, nor even to the moral ideas it preaches, but in the fact that nobody genuinely believes in our society, for which the children are being trained. (p. 28)

The contention that educational reform, in the absence of wider social reform, is futile is reflected also in a January 1933 review: 'Education succeeds social

---

[55] W.H. Auden, 'Problems of Education', in *W.H. Auden Volume I 1926–1938*, ed. by Mendelson, pp. 27–28 (p. 28). Further references to this essay will be included in brackets after the citation.

[56] Bertrand Russell, *Education and the Social Order* (London: Allen & Unwin, 1932), p. 244. Auden's criticism of progressive education's secret tyrannies is paralleled elsewhere. For instance, Russell previously registered an awareness of potential charges of moral coercion: '[A] man who is to educate really well [...] must be filled [...] with the spirit of reverence.' Russell found that 'the man who feels this can wield the authority of an educator without infringing the principle of liberty'. Bertrand Russell, *Principles of Social Reconstruction* (London: Allen & Unwin, 1916), p. 146; p. 148.

revolution, not precedes.'[57] The review adapts Marxist principles to offer a pertinent self-critique of the discourses within which ideologies become naturalized:

> Whoever possesses the instruments of knowledge, the Press, the Wireless, and the Ministry of Education, is the dictator of the country; and, my friends, it becomes increasingly difficult to overthrow a bad one because imitating our voice, he makes us believe that he does not exist. (p. 31)

Mendelson suggests that Auden is expressing here 'his own difficulty in finding a language for social criticism.'[58] While the tone in these early essays may be derivative of Lawrence's prophetic voice, Auden's adoption of elements of Lawrence's register and educational ideals, so polarized from more anodyne journalistic discourses, offers a striking, charismatic tenor from which to critique and diagnose society's problems.

Values by ideals and *The Dog beneath the Skin*

Auden's engagement with Lawrence's ideals continued in his reviews on education in the mid-1930s, a period in which his pedagogic attempt to incite the need for individual volition also met with formal conflict in his co-written play with Isherwood, *The Dog beneath the Skin* (1935).

The original title of 'Honour', Auden's 1934 essay for *The Old School*, 'The Liberal Fascist', reveals a debt to his own 1932 articles on education. The essay considers the 'education of our morals' in the 'Honour System' at Auden's former public school, Gresham's in Holt.[59] Instead of corporal punishment, Gresham's utilized a more 'liberal' system of 'promises': '(1) Not to swear. (2) Not to smoke' and '(3) Not to say or do anything indecent' (p. 59). This system enacts a form of moral tyranny akin to the fascistic methods of the 'secret service' ('Private', p. 26) and the 'intellectual watch committee' ('Problems', p. 28) that he had previously mentioned in his 1932 reviews. The system encouraged pupils to become informants: both on themselves and on others. It was particularly effective because 'the only emotion that is fully developed in a boy of fourteen is the

---

[57] W.H. Auden, 'A Review of *The Evolution of Sex*, Dr Gregorio Marañón and *The Biological Tragedy of Women*, by Anton Nemilov', in *W.H. Auden Volume I 1926–1938*, ed. by Mendelson, pp. 29–31 (p. 30).

[58] *Early Auden*, p. 131.

[59] W.H. Auden, 'The Liberal Fascist [Honour]', in *W.H. Auden Volume I 1926–1938*, ed. by Mendelson, pp. 55–61 (p. 58). Further references to this essay will be included in brackets after the citation.

emotion of loyalty and honour' (p. 59). Auden engages with Freudian discourse in a consideration of the effects of the Honour System which turned schoolboys into 'neurotic innocents [...]. By appealing to it [honour], you can do almost anything you choose; you can suppress the expression of all those emotions, particularly the sexual, which are still undeveloped' (p. 59). The suppression of the expression of 'indecent' (or homosexual) acts at Gresham's transforms the libido into an 'internal enemy' and renders the pupils 'neurotics'.[60] 'Sentries' are created 'against inner and outer' as the pupils 'report' on themselves.[61]

Auden adapts *Fantasia,* which holds that 'morality which is based on ideas, or on an ideal, is an unmitigated evil' (p. 79), to criticize the 'Honour System':

> There is far too much talk about ideals at all schools. Ideals are the conclusions drawn from a man of experience, not the data: they are essentially for the mature. [...] For the young without experience, ideals are as grave a danger in the moral sphere as book learning is in the intellectual, the danger of becoming a purely mental concept, mechanising the soul. ('Honour', p. 60)

> An idea which is merely introduced into the brain [...] is the cause of all our misery today. Instead of living from the spontaneous centres, we live from the head. [...] Our primary affective centres, our centres of spontaneous being, are so utterly ground round and automatized that they squeak in all stages of disharmony and incipient collapse. We are a people – and not we alone – of idiots, imbeciles and epileptics, and we don't even know we are raving.
>
> And all this is due [...] to that hateful germ we call the Ideal. The Ideal is *always* evil, no matter what ideal it be. (*Fantasia,* pp. 82–83)

Auden here acts as an interpreter of Lawrence, translating his obtuse physiological language, and reflecting his principle that education should be drawn from experience, rather than abstract principles. Auden maintains Lawrence's language from the semantic field of industry in 'Honour', but condenses this into the phrase 'mechanising the soul' which captures Lawrence's meaning more directly. By undermining the 'orthodoxy' (p. 60) of ideals as a governing principle of education, Auden recognizes that 'education has to rely almost entirely upon the quality of the teacher' (p. 60). The essay argues that the pedagogue must have 'no moral bees-in-his-bonnet' but should instead 'be an anthropologist', combining the skills of the sociologist and the psychologist

---

[60] Sigmund Freud, 'Introduction to *Psychoanalysis and the War Neuroses*', trans. by Ernest Jones, in *The Complete Psychological Works of Sigmund Freud Volume XVII (1917–1919),* trans. by James Strachey (London: Hogarth Press, 1955), pp. 205–15 (p. 210).

[61] W.H. Auden, 'XIX', in *English Auden,* ed. by Mendelson, p. 33.

(p. 60; p. 61). This teacher-anthropologist is captured in Auden's later, 1937 poem, 'Schoolchildren', in which the poem's speaker observes the children as if witnessing some anthropological specimen: their 'strangeness is difficult to watch [...] But watch them'.[62]

The conviction that ideals play a nefarious role in education is evident also in 'Life's Old Boy' (March 1934), a review of Lord Baden-Powell's biography.[63] The review argues that it is a 'mistake' to educate 'values by ideals', as it encourages 'living at second hand'.[64] The scout promise 'To do his duty to God and the King' is a 'dangerous principle' as 'reform is always disloyalty' (p. 63; p. 64). Instead, a 'state has to train its youth not only to be its good citizens' but also 'to change it, i.e. to destroy its present existence' (p. 66). To encourage this progress in values, 'educationalists must always be revolutionaries', ready to make the 'attack on the psychological front' of middle-class conservatism (p. 66). Baden-Powell, however, is a propagator of old values – in the terms of the review's title, he is life's perennial old boy, incapable of revolutionary action.

There is, however, an unresolved ambiguity in 'Life's Old Boy': Does Auden suggest that the teacher can educate 'values by ideals' as long as he or she advocated revolutionary, rather than conservative, values? This is resolved in revisions made to *The Dog beneath the Skin* as Auden foregrounds the need for individual choice in the play's action. *The Dog beneath the Skin* was originally published by Faber & Faber in 1935 and Mendelson also notes its performance by the Group Theatre in January 1936. The play's revisions are informed by Auden's contemporaneous writing on education while also revealing the problems inherent in the transference of his pedagogic critique into his creative work.

In the original published version, Francis and Alan return from their travels around fascistic Europe to their home town of Pressan Ambo, to discover that fascism has similarly taken hold. The Pressan Ambo Lads' Brigade is depicted, with the 'objects of the brigade' a distinct echo of those of the scouts, only with more explicitly fascistic ends: 'standing outside all political parties and factions, for Church, King and State, against communism, terrorism, pacifism and other forms of international anarchy'.[65] In Faber's 1935 published version, Francis

[62] W.H. Auden, 'Schoolchildren', in *English Auden*, ed. by Mendelson, pp. 216–17 (p. 216).

[63] Lord Baden-Powell's name appears unhyphenated in Auden's review.

[64] W.H. Auden, 'Life's Old Boy', in *W.H. Auden Volume I 1926–1938*, ed. by Mendelson, pp. 62–66 (p. 64). Further references to this essay will be included in brackets after the citation.

[65] W.H. Auden and Christopher Isherwood, *The Dog beneath the Skin or Where Is Francis?* (London: Faber & Faber, 1935), p. 160. Further references to this edition will be included in brackets after the citation.

delivers a speech that prompts the conversion of one member of the Lads' Brigade from the side of conservatism to the side of progress:

> FRANCIS. You are units in an immense army: most of you will die without ever knowing what your leaders are really fighting for or even that you are fighting at all. Well, I am going to be a unit in the army of the other side: but the battlefield is so huge that it's practically certain you will never see me again. We are all of us completely unimportant, so it would be very silly to start quarrelling, wouldn't it? Goodbye.
>
> *[He turns to go]*
>
> ALAN.   Francis! I'm coming with you!
>
> FRANCIS.   I'm glad.
>
> [...]
>
> A BOY FROM THE RANKS OF THE LADS OF PRESSAN. Let me come too, Francis!
> FRANCIS. We're not going on a treasure-hunt, you know, or looking for pirates.
> BOY. I don't care. I want to help.
> FRANCIS. All right. [*The* BOY *crosses the stage.*] Any more?
>   [*Three other villagers silently join the group*]
>
> (pp. 174–76)

Thus Francis leads a recruit from the Lads' Brigade in an 'army of the other side', against the forces of fascism. The moment of the boy's crossing the stage is filled with dramatic tension, as he symbolically 'goes over'; changing political allegiance. Auden expressed his interest in the moral import of theatre in his June 1935 letter to Spender, written in the month the play was published: 'The theatre-going audience is a bourgeois one. [...] The moral I tried to draw is always: "You have the choice. You can make the world or mar it." Free will means you can choose either to fear or to love.'[66]

Before the play's performance in January 1936 by the Group Theatre, a letter from Isherwood to Auden suggested that 'the appeal for volunteers' was 'horribly quisb [*sic*]'.[67] William Ostrem suggests that changes were made as a result of the 'authors' continuing realization of their own tendencies towards the romantic, fascistic pose of hero leadership [...] [the original ending was] too tainted with the methods of fascism itself'.[68] The member of the Lads' Brigade who changes

---

[66] As cited in Mendelson, *Early Auden*, pp. 279–80.
[67] William Ostrem, 'The Dog Beneath the Schoolboy's Skin: Isherwood, Auden and Fascism', in *The Isherwood Century: Essays on the Life and Work of Christopher Isherwood*, ed. by James J. Berg and Chris Freeman (London: University of Wisconsin Press, 2000), pp. 162–71 (p. 170).
[68] Ostrem, p. 170.

sides may be joining the Left, but his act of political transformation can still be conceived of as lacking any expression of true free will. The entire final scene of the play was rewritten: the British Library's Lord Chamberlain's Plays archive contains a typescript of the new final scene. The version used in performance by the Group Theatre in January 1936 used the moment of the scout's 'conversion' to Francis's cause as a juncture in which to investigate this issue of 'free will'. In the revised version, Francis makes a speech that emphasizes the importance of free choice:

> FRANCIS. You are not individually important. You are just units in an immense army; and most of you would probably die without knowing either what your leaders are really fighting for or even what your are fighting for at all. That is why I have come back. That ignorance at least I can do something to remove. I can't dictate to you what to do and I don't want to either. I can only try to show you what you are doing and so force you to choose. For choice is what you are all afraid of. [...] Anything, you *say* [...] give us a dictator, an authority who will take the responsibility of thinking and planning off our shoulders. [...] You are fighting your own nature which is to learn and to choose.[69]

The emphasis on individual choice in the revised version demonstrates Auden's attempt to counter the social conservatism that he detected in educational movements while also avoiding similar charges of moral coercion or the teaching of 'values by ideals' that he levelled at these movements. The play illuminates how Auden distinguishes between pedagogy's methods and its content. His dictum in 'Life's Old Boy', 'educationalists must always be revolutionaries' (p. 66), is elucidated as an attempt to put the onus on individual choice: pedagogy should be revolutionary via a practice that facilitates a form of individualism (via the enactment of individual choice), rather than through the propagandistic dissemination of a revolutionary agenda.

The changes to the play in performance were unpopular with contemporary reviewers. Cyril Connolly found that 'a different and unsatisfactory ending has been substituted', while Derek Verschoyle critiqued the pedagogic import of the play's new ending, objecting to the 'rather embarrassing conclusion' suggesting that its 'sermon' registered a 'naively evangelistic [...] political attitude' that was reminiscent of Auden's earlier play, *The Dance of Death* (1933).[70] Mendelson suggests that Francis in the revised play is 'an Audenesque instructor in history and

---

[69] British Library, Western Manuscripts Collection, L.C.P. 1935/33, 22.10.1936, Auden/Isherwood, *Dog beneath the Skin*. Lic: 14254. Typescript pp. 5–6.

[70] Cyril Connolly, 'Review', *New Statesman and Nation*, February 1936, in *Auden: Critical Heritage*, ed. by Haffenden, pp. 185–88 (p. 187); Derek Verschoyle, 'Review', *Spectator*, February 1936, in *Auden: Critical Heritage*, ed. by Haffenden, pp. 183–85 (p. 183; p. 184; p. 183).

choice'.[71] He similarly asserts the ineffectiveness of the revised ending: 'Francis's crude *didactic* methods do not inspire much confidence in their powers beyond the stage. [...] In this final version, Francis [...] *explaining* everything, never giving the audience much chance to make the decisions that the play demands'.[72] Mendelson's critique registers a disjunction between the methods of pedagogy and the generic properties of drama: the 'didactic' methods of pedagogy are deemed deadening and unsuited to the formal properties of drama. The revised version of *The Dog beneath the Skin* highlights the tension in the duality between Auden's roles as dramatist and pedagogue; this is a tension less inherent in the private properties of poetry (in 'Ode V' of *The Orators*) which elicits, rather than declares, a need for individual volition.

Auden's mid-1930s poetry teaching: Democracy and the demotic

Simultaneous with the process of revisions to *The Dog beneath the Skin*, Auden was developing a pedagogic practice designed to counter the 'didactic' 'explaining' that Mendelson finds in the play. His mid-1930s teaching of poetry continues to foreground the need for individual choice, a choice incited by the pedagogic strategies he deploys, and demonstrated also in the formal manipulations of the school hymn he composed for Raynes Park School, which draws on tropes and features evident in his poetry. Auden's poetry teaching is, in varying degrees, informed by the context in which it occurs – for Raynes Park School and the Workers' Educational Association (WEA) – as it asserts the significance of demotic cultures. I consider the sources that inform Auden's pedagogy to argue that this interest in demotic cultures is suspended between a progressive, Marxist commitment and a patrician, conservative sanctification of oral cultures.

In a review of *English Poetry for Children*, by R.L. Megroz, Auden commented that, with the rise of English studies, 'anthologies and manuals for the prosaic teacher pour from the press'.[73] Auden objected to the teaching of poetry, finding in it an attempt to remove individual volition:

---

[71] *Early Auden*, p. 278.

[72] *Early Auden*, p. 279, emphases added.

[73] W.H. Auden, 'A Review of *English Poetry for Children* by R.L. Mégroz', in *W.H. Auden Volume I 1926–1938*, ed. by Mendelson, pp. 70–71 (p. 71). Further references to this essay will be included in brackets after the citation.

> Poetry cannot really be taught except by practitioners [...] [t]o those who are
> not one can only suggest that they should get away from attempting to teach
> appreciation which means imposing their personal taste on the immature, a
> spiritual bullying. (p. 71)

Auden echoes the Lawrentian idea of 'the spiritual bully' of progressive education.
Like the scouts in 'Life's Old Boy', the teaching of poetry is deemed to educate
'values by ideals' (p. 64) rather than experience. *The Poet's Tongue*, 'an anthology
primarily intended for schools' that Auden co-edited with the headmaster of
Raynes Park School, John Garrett, develops a pedagogic strategy that puts the
onus on individual volition by rebutting the values of 'hero-worship' inherent
in both the pupil–teacher relationship and ideals of canonicity.[74] The verse is
ordered according to alphabetic sequence of a poem's first word (a method
Auden also employed later in his own 1945 *Collected Poetry*). The opening
'Index of First Lines and Authors' lists the poem's number, its first line, author,
date and then its page number. This is followed by an 'Author and Subject Index'.
The determiners of canonicity, via the heroic 'great names' of literary value, are
lost through anonymity: the actual poems are printed in the volume without
their author. Mendelson notes the ways in which the arrangement of verse in
the anthology banishes 'personal authority to the poets he included'.[75] This
arrangement was also deliberately designed to avoid pedagogic dictatorship,
privileging instead the enactment of the reader's free will:

> The propagandist, whether moral or political, complains that the writer should
> use his power over words to persuade people to a particular course of action,
> instead of fiddling while Rome burns. But Poetry is not concerned with telling
> people what to do, but with extending our knowledge of good and evil, perhaps
> making the necessity for action more urgent and its nature more clear, but
> only leading us to the point where it is possible for us to make a rational and
> moral choice. [...] Poetry may illuminate but it will not dictate. [...] As regards
> arrangement we have, after some thought, adopted an alphabetical, anonymous
> order. It seems best to us, if the idea of poetry as something dead and suitable
> for a tourist-ridden museum [...] is to be avoided, that the first approach should
> be with an open mind, free from the bias of great names and literary influences.
> (pp. 108–09)

---

[74] W.H. Auden and John Garrett, 'Introduction to *The Poet's Tongue*', in *W.H. Auden Volume I 1926–
1938*, ed. by Mendelson, pp. 105–09 (p. 108). Further references to this essay will be included in
brackets after the citation.

[75] *Early Auden*, p. 257.

Auden's anti-didactic theory of poetry as a medium for promoting the act of
'rational and moral choice' is encouraged by the pedagogic method advanced
in the volume. 'Life's Old Boy' found that 'half of the educational battle [...] the
attack on the psychological front, has only just begun' (p. 66). The arrangement
of the anthology attempts to tackle this psychological battle, by refusing to 'teach
appreciation' (p. 71).

The volume is characterized not only by its arrangement of verse, but by
the catholicity of its editorial selection of verse. It offers a 'definition[s]' (p.
105) of poetry as 'memorable speech' (p. 105), drawing on Woolf's early short
story 'The Mark on the Wall' to offer an inclusive sense of what 'counts' as
poetry: 'everything that we remember no matter how trivial: the mark on
the wall, the joke at luncheon, word games, these, like the dance of a stoat
or the raven's gamble, are equally the subject of poetry' (p. 106). David Jones
called the anthology 'one of the best anthologies of English stuff I know of'
and indeed the capaciousness of Jones's term reflects the capaciousness of
the volume itself.[76] The original 1935 edition was in two parts, with Part I
in particular offering an eclectic selection of nursery rhymes, doggerel from
broadsheets, folk songs, sea shanties, carols, extracts from folk plays and
ballads, and verse by Andrew Marvell, D.H. Lawrence, W.B. Yeats, Edith
Sitwell, Lewis Carroll, Edward Lear, and Walter de la Mare. The selection
of verse in Part II is less esoteric, and includes the contemporary poets
Stephen Spender, Cecil Day-Lewis, and Rex Warner, as well as Wilfred Owen,
T.S. Eliot, Rochester, Browning, Chaucer, Byron, Donne, Wordsworth, and
Shakespeare. A reader reading consecutively from the beginning of Part I
would encounter, Davenport-Hines suggests, 'marvellous juxtapositions':
first a folk song, then a nursery rhyme, then a verse by Shelley, followed by
an anonymous verse.[77] The listing of verse without author, and 'independent
of period and unconfined in subject' (p. 109), both of which offer instructive
principles for reading verse creates, as the 'Preface' notes, 'the first impression'
that poetry is 'a human activity' (p. 109). It also promotes a Leavisite reading
model with an emphasis on close reading, and an attentiveness to form rather
than context, for all verses included; from a sea shanty to an extract from *The
Faerie Queene*.

---

[76] Cited in Davenport-Hines, *Auden*, p. 139.
[77] Ibid.

The selection of verse is underpinned by a sense of fun, pleasing to the readership of schoolchildren for whom it is primarily intended, but it is also motivated by social and cultural concerns. The 'Preface' associates industrialization with a process of social and cultural segmentation that has not been mitigated by mass education:

> In spite of the spread of education and the accessibility of printed matter, there is a gap between what is commonly called 'highbrow' and 'lowbrow' taste, wider perhaps than it has ever been.
>
> The industrial revolution broke up the agricultural communities, with their local conservative cultures, and divided the growing population into two classes [...]. Literature has tended therefore to divide into two streams [...].
>
> Nor has the situation been much improved by the increased leisure and educational opportunities which the population to-day as a whole possess. [...]
>
> [A] universal art can only be the product of a community united in sympathy, sense of worth, and aspiration; and it is improbable that the artist can do his best except in such a society. (p. 107)

In *The Poet's Tongue,* the individual's selection of verse is uninfected by literary hierarchies and the very catholicity of the editorial selection of verse expands notions of the poetic to include elements of the demotic. By incorporating this material into the volume, alongside more traditionally 'highbrow' verse, the volume itself aims to counter the problem outlined in its 'Preface': there is an attempt to create an audience 'united in sympathy', and to cultivate a poetic taste that allows for a 'universal art'. These comments are striking for the extent to which they echo Auden's earlier comments in 'Writing' where he considers the social conditions conducive to the fermentation of the literary reputations of Homer, Dante, and Shakespeare:

> There is something common to all three: the small size of the society and the unity of interests. Whenever a society is united (and the larger the society the harder it is to unite [...]) it has a great outburst of good writing [...].
>
> But whenever society breaks up into classes [...] literature suffers. There is writing for the gentle and writing for the simple, for the highbrow and the lowbrow; the latter gets cruder and coarser, the former more and more refined. (p. 24)

There is strong echoing between the two passages as Auden's thesis is explored in strikingly similar language, rendering the 'Preface' a later iteration of the ideas expressed in 'Writing'.

Davenport-Hines compellingly reads the selection of verse in *The Poet's Tongue* against the context of Raynes Park School, suggesting that its focus on demotic cultures is an

> unsentimental, hard-headed celebration of the power of the spoken word for semi-literate people and [...] [a] tribute to the local cultures whose extermination was signalled by the existence of Raynes Park County School, built on a by-pass between a fish- and meat-paste factory and a second-hand car emporium.[78]

The consistency of outlook demonstrated between 'Writing' and *The Poet's Tongue* indicates, however, that this is a thesis held by Auden in the 1930s, rather than one stimulated by the immediate context of the school itself. *The Poet's Tongue* sees Auden and Garrett take an active pedagogic role in encouraging the creation of a certain universal taste in readers, conducive to the reception of a poetry that encompasses the high and low and a broad spectrum of human experience – the poetry, perhaps, Auden wants to write, rather than merely diagnosing the problem of socially and culturally divided taste from the perspective of the coterie poet.

Auden's personal relationship with Garrett and the volume's emphasis on 'memorable speech' informed other elements of Auden's pedagogic-poetic activity in the mid-1930s. John Garrett was a dynamic, young headmaster and the first head at Raynes Park School, a secondary boys' grammar school in the southern suburbs of London. The charismatic Garrett attracted various luminaries to teach at his school, including Rex Warner and the painter Claude Rogers.[79] Visitors to the school included T.S. Eliot, John Lehmann, Louis MacNeice, Stephen Spender, Naomi Mitchison, Walter de la Mare, David Cecil, and George Lansbury.[80] This was a school, Davenport-Hines suggests, for 'socially disconnected, educationally aspirant lower-middle-class people', but Garrett nonetheless had a conscious sense of creating a new educational ethos, rather than merely aping the public schools.[81] Auden's composition of the Raynes Park School song, a version of which is still sung by pupils of the school today, should be seen in the context of a dynamic, modern institution. The song was possibly written in summer 1936, and published as 'Raynes Park School Song' in the school magazine, *Spur*, in October 1936, before it was reprinted

---

[78] *Auden*, p. 139.

[79] Davenport-Hines, *Auden*, p. 138.

[80] Ibid.; Raynes Park High School website, 'School History 1935 and onwards', <http://www.rphs.org.uk/75/1935-and-onwards> [accessed 17 July 2017].

[81] *Auden*, p. 138.

in *The Badger*, the Downs School magazine initiated by Auden, in which it was signed 'Very Anon':

Time will make its utter changes,
Circumstance will scatter us,
But the memories of our schooldays
Are a living part of us.
Chorus
So remember then when you are men
With important things to do,
That once you were young and this song have sung
For you were at school here too.

Daily we sit down in form rooms,
Inky hand to puzzled head:
Reason's Light, and Knowledge Power;
Man must study till he's dead.
Chorus
Man has mind but body also
So we learn to tackle low,
Bowl the off-breaks, hit the sixes,
Bend the diver's brilliant bow.
Chorus
Man must learn to like his neighbour
For he cannot live alone;
Friendships, failures and successes,
Here we learn to make our own.
Chorus
Tractors grunt where oceans wandered,
Factories stand where green grass grew;
Voices break and features alter,
We shall soon be different too.
Chorus
Boys and cities, schools and nations,
Though they change like you and me,
Do not simply grow and happen:
They are what they choose to be.
Chorus[82]

[82] Richard Davenport-Hines, 'School Writings', in *W.H. Auden: 'The Language of Learning and the Language of Love', Auden Studies 2*, ed. by Katherine Bucknell and Nicholas Jenkins (Oxford: Clarendon Press, 1994), pp. 1–47 (pp. 32–33).

A former pupil of Raynes Park, Alan Wright, notes the mnemonic qualities of the verse: the 'scansion that makes the words easy to remember and [...] rhymes which come trippingly off the tongue'.[83] Characteristic features of Auden's verse, including pararhyme in the chorus ('young [...] this song have sung'), as well as partial rhymes ('utter' | 'scatter', 'then' | 'when'), along with the regular rhyme scheme (abcb) and verse length, render the verse easy to commit to memory. The song contains familiar elements of the Audenesque: the imperatives 'So remember ... ' and 'Man must ... ', and the classificatory proper nouns used throughout, which not only universalize the song's pedagogic messages, but also elevate lessons for boyhood to the world of manhood, rendering them more palatable.

Various pedagogic messages are contained in the song: the first verse reinforces the significance of school as a formative influence; the second the empowering role of study; the third the public-school emphasis on school sports, here adopted for grammar-school boys; the fourth has an emphasis on the peer group drawn from the Christian teaching of the Sermon on the Mount ('Man must learn to like his neighbour'); the fifth reinforces a sense of the transience of youth and the sixth contains an Audenesque emphasis on individual choice.

Images from the school song are used in Auden's verse, indicating a reciprocal relationship between his pedagogic and poetic modes. The 'diver's brilliant bow' is used in 'No Trenchant Parting This', composed in August 1927, and 'As I Walked Out One Evening', composed in November 1937, around the time of the composition of the school song. Here it is contextualized within the arena of school sports, a context in which the image held particular resonance. While at Gresham's, Auden watched his school friend, Robert Medley, for whom, Carpenter notes, Auden held 'sexual feelings', dive in the school pool.[84] In 1922 Medley came to stay with the Auden family and Dr Auden found a poem describing Medley at a swimming pool in which he thought he detected an erotic element.[85] Dr Auden confronted the boys about the poem but they assured him that their relationship was purely platonic.[86] The *OED* notes that the first usage of 'bent' as both an adjective and a noun to allude to things 'out of order, spoiled. Of persons: eccentric, perverted; *spec.* homosexual' is in 1930.[87] Auden may not

---

[83] Raynes Park High School website, 'The School Song', <http://www.rphs.org.uk/77/the-school-song> [accessed 17 July 2017].

[84] Carpenter, p. 31.

[85] Carpenter, p. 33.

[86] Ibid.

[87] 'bent', adj., 5c, *OED*, <http://www.oed.com> [accessed 26 July 2017].

be consciously engaging with this meaning in 'Bend the diver's brilliant bow', but it is clear that school swimming had homoerotic associations for him, aside from the image of athletic finesse that is also summoned by this line.

In verse five, the Audenesque industrialized setting of the 'Factories' is also a gesture to the quasi-industrial, suburban setting of the school. The alliterative 'green grass grew' adds a lyricism to this evocation of the area's rural past. The change in the physical locale of the school from the rural to the industrialized also offers an analogy for the shift from childhood to adolescence and manhood. This verse with its humorous personification of 'Tractors grunt' and the curious reference to the physicality of the boys ('Voices break') shifts the tone of the verse into something approaching farce as Auden plays with the traditional solemnity of the form of the school song and mitigates the instructive elements of the verse. The chorus's conspiratorial, teasing reference to the grown-up men 'with important things to do' places Auden the lyricist firmly on the side of the boys, poking fun at the self-important adult world. Recordings of the school song, with its jaunty music by composer Thomas Wood, reflect the song's light qualities.

The final verse reinforces the significance of individual choice through the emphatic colon and climactic monosyllables of its final line. This sentiment is consistent with Auden's wider message and is untypical of the more traditional school ethos of *esprit de corps*. The song's emphasis on freedom of choice contained in its final verse rendered its message particularly apt for end-of-term renditions, as Wright comments:

> The end of term versions were the more important because they signified freedom, and the imminence of the holidays led to the assembled students bellowing the words and drowning a piano accompaniment. [...] [T]he din was no doubt appalling, but nevertheless the memory of the song as an expression of release at the end of a term is the most affectionate of my recollections.[88]

There is a certain irony in the final verse's emphasis on the primacy of individual choice, in a song that is sung by the collective. The shift to the demonstrative pronoun 'they' in this final line may be motivated by an attempt to mitigate this tension. The alternative, 'We are what we choose to be', which would be consistent with the closure of the two previous verses, annuls any sense of individual will.

John G. Blair's analysis of Auden's poetry contributes to an understanding of the ways in which Auden's conception of poetry seems particularly apt for the form of a school song. Blair notes Auden's 'basically didactic poetics' but crucially nuances this assessment:

---

[88] Raynes Park High School website, 'The School Song'.

> He is committed to [...] the poem as a performance for the sake of impact
> on that audience. He hopes that his words will stimulate some tangible moral
> change, but he refuses to tell his reader what to think or do. Any reorientation in
> the reader's life [...] must be left to him.[89]

This emphasis on 'performance' and 'impact' lends Auden's poetry to the form
of the school song. The provocation of his verse to a 'tangible moral change'
is reflected in the song, which encourages self-reflection on the part of the
singers. The perspective of former pupil Alan Wright is instructive for offering
a measurable sense of the effect of Auden's pedagogy in the song, while also
recognizing its performative aspects. He notes the song's avoidance of a 'didactic
tone' by its arrangement, whereby school students sing both the 'we' parts of
'the shrewd or contemplative verses', and the part of the '"you", the unconvinced,
perhaps, in the choruses. As a consequence, it is the students themselves who
hand out any moralising advice which is included.'[90] The song's form thus
mitigates the 'didactic' elements of the verse.

'Poetry, Poets, and Taste', Auden's December 1936 contribution to *The
Highway*, the journal of the WEA, written shortly before his departure to Spain,
suggests the conflicted ways in which his interest in the demotic is inflected by
class concerns. Adrian Caesar argues that Auden's contribution to the journal is
'condescending and ingratiating'.[91] In his defence of the worth of poetry against
imaginary 'objections', Auden does appear to be preaching to the converted:
the WEA was an organization already deeply committed to liberal education.[92]
Mendelson's editorial notes suggest that the subheadings to Auden's article in
The Highway are 'arbitrarily placed' (p. 765). This editorial intervention also
mediates – and ameliorates – readers' responses to Auden's contribution. The
subheading, 'In this article the modern poet and writer of plays discusses
some of the typical prejudices against poetry', serves as an editorial disclaimer,
distancing *The Highway* from the stance of the article.[93] Auden's teaching in this
piece is consistent, however, with his wider pedagogy (previous instances of
which were, however, for a more naive audience). The empowering debunking
of canonicity evident in *The Poet's Tongue* is at play: 'as for taste, it ultimately
rests with the individual reader' (p. 164), as is the emphasis on an expansive

---

[89] John G. Blair, *The Poetic Art of W.H. Auden* (London: Princeton University Press, 1965), p. 63.

[90] Raynes Park High School website, 'The School Song'.

[91] Caesar, p. 63.

[92] W.H. Auden, 'Poetry, Poets, and Taste', in *W.H. Auden Volume I 1926–1938*, ed. by Mendelson,
    pp. 162–65 (p. 162). Further references to this essay will be included in brackets after the citation.

[93] W.H. Auden, 'Poetry, Poets, and Taste', *The Highway*, December 1936, p. 43.

notion of poetry and its vital human significance: 'poetry has as varied a subject matter and treatment as human character' (p. 163), rendering it accessible and quotidian. Auden even reuses an idiom deployed in the 'Preface' to *The Poet's Tongue*: 'fiddling while Rome burns' (p. 162).

The closure of the essay is notable for the two ideological positions that Auden cites, the associations of which sit in tension with one another. Following his encouragement of the necessity of standing by one's individual taste, whatever it may be, the end of the article notes: '"To each according to his needs; from each according to his powers", in fact. Personally the kind of poetry I should like to write but can't is "the thoughts of a wise man in the speech of the common people"' (p. 165). The first citation here is an adaptation of the full version of the Marxist phrase that calls upon the community to meet the full needs of the individual in a schema of distributive justice, a message that would chime with the readers of *The Highway*. Auden also supplied a simplified version of this phrase for the Raynes Park School motto: at the official school opening, in November 1935, a statement from Garrett was read out: 'Our opportunity lies in our freedom from tradition, for thus we are able to create our own ... the motto of the school is no latin tag, but rather the words of the contemporary poet, W.H. Auden: "To each his need: from each his power."'[94] In the context in which Auden uses the phrase, it seems to express the need for education to meet the potential of each individual.

It is tempting to suggest that this maxim was close to Auden's mind due to the influence of his communist schoolmaster-friend, Cecil Day-Lewis. In 1935 Day-Lewis, writing as Nicholas Blake, published *A Question of Proof*, a murder mystery set in a preparatory school, featuring a tea-drinking, nail-biting detective with a talent for poetry, based on Auden: Nigel Strangeways. The phrase's usual iteration occurs in the novel, when Michael, the left-wing schoolteacher notes: 'The best slogans I know are the ones in the Sermon on the Mount and "to each according to his need, from each according to his ability".'[95] Auden's adaption of the injunction to 'Love thy neighbour' from the Sermon on the Mount in the Raynes Park School song, composed the following year, and his further use of the Marxist maxim in the school motto and his article for *The Highway*, sees him fulfil the wishes of this fictional schoolteacher, consolidating the play between life and art already evident in *A Question of Proof*. This serves as both an elaborate in-joke and an earnest educational message.

---

[94] Raynes Park High School website, 'The Beginnings', <http://www.rphs.org.uk/76/the-beginnings> [accessed: 17 July 2017].

[95] Nicholas Blake, *A Question of Proof* (London: Penguin, 1935), p. 139.

In his attempt to empower the working class to write in their own language, Auden then cites Yeats's *Dramatis Personae* (1935) as he recalls Lady Gregory's frequent recantation of Aristotle's motto: 'To think like a wise man, but to express oneself like the common people.'[96] Auden's early essay 'Writing' expresses a similar conviction that 'the speech of a peasant is generally better, i.e. more vivid, better able to say what he wants to say, than the speech of the average University graduate' (p. 18). In 'Poetry, Poets, and Taste', the sentiment is infected with a Yeatsian, aristocratic veneration of peasant cultures that sits uncomfortably alongside the Marxist term; the celebration of the demotic is compromised by the conservative associations of Auden's source. There is a reflection here of Auden's earlier refusal to join the Communist Party on Rupert Doone's invitation, after the publication of 'Problems of Education', a rejection which was couched in a sense of the ineluctability of class identity: 'No. I am a bourgeois [...] I shall not join the C.P.'[97]

Auden's late-1930s polemical works on education render clear his rejection of fascistic elements of Lawrence's educational critique while demonstrating his bourgeois background, as his political critique of the education system in the last years of the decade demonstrates a left-leaning politics, formulated in self-reflexive terms.

Politics and the teacher

On 12 January 1937 Auden joined the roll call of left-wing poets and writers who supported the Spanish Civil War effort. He had intended to stay for four or five months but was home by 4 March 1937; his time in Spain was, Davenport-Hines suggests, 'spent [...] drinking, waiting for action that never came.'[98] Back in England, he returned for a term's work at the Downs School, a move motivated by financial necessity that has been read by critics as an abandonment of politics: Valentine Cunningham notes, 'Auden's period as political activist was over, and he'd chosen to mark it by re-entry into schoolmastering'; while Mendelson similarly argues that Auden 'discarded any serious wish to affect the political future' and therefore agreed to return to Downs.[99] Adrian Caesar detects an increasing conservatism in Auden's politics in the decade: 'High Toryism vies

---

[96] A. Norman Jeffares, *W.B. Yeats: A New Biography* (London: Continuum, 2001 [1988]), p. 84.

[97] As cited in Mendelson, *Early Auden*, p. 19.

[98] *Auden*, p. 165.

[99] Cunningham, *British Writers*, p. 447; Mendelson, *Early Auden*, p. 294.

with a more liberal conservatism, and as the decade progressed the latter began increasingly to dominate.'[100] During the late 1930s, Auden's integration of educational theory with left-leaning political theory became more overt, and the line between pedagogue and politician also became increasingly blurred, as he formulated a hopeful response to that 'low dishonest decade' through an exploration of the teacher's role in social change.[101]

In the late 1930s Cecil Day-Lewis and Edward Upward, in *Starting Point* (1937) and *Journey to the Border* (1938) respectively, were also exploring the political allegiances at stake within the role of the left-leaning public schoolmaster and the private tutor in the wealthy upper-class home. Day-Lewis's *Starting Point* holds public-school teaching and left-wing commitment as mutually exclusive. The book follows a group of four friends from Oxford, during the General Strike, to adulthood. Anthony, a member of the group, is forced to contemplate the relative weight of his commitment to teaching and his commitment to communism:

> Anthony would have to choose between the good he could do in this school [...] and on the other hand the good he could do if he joined in the active work of the Party. Where would he be most useful?[102]

He leaves his teaching job after his sympathetic headmaster confronts him about parental complaints of his frequentation of pubs and his dissemination of communist 'propaganda' among his students (p. 301). The decision to leave teaching later seems 'simple and ineluctable' to Anthony; 'a formal acceptance of something which his own life in society had made inevitable' (p. 307). Upward's novel, written while he was on the editorial board of *The Ploughshare,* the organ of the Teachers' Anti-War Movement from 1936 to 1938, sees his protagonist, an unnamed tutor, experience a series of tests and 'experiments in vision' before resolving to join the 'Internationalist Movement for Working-class Power'.[103] The novel's final moments indicate that the tutor will leave his old life behind to join the communist cause: 'His decision to join it [the workers' movement] would not make life easier for him. But at least he would have come down to earth, out of the cloud of his irresponsible fantasies; would have begun to live' (p. 135). The use of the subjunctive reflects, as Benjamin Kohlmann notes, the 'undescribed and undescribable' nature of the communist society the novel

[100] Caesar, p. 64.

[101] W.H. Auden, 'September 1, 1939', in *English Auden,* ed. by Mendelson, pp. 245–47 (p. 245).

[102] Cecil Day-Lewis, *Starting Point* (London: Cape, 1937), p. 294.

[103] Feigel, p. 124; Edward Upward, *Journey to the Border* (London: Enitharmon Press, 1994), p. 116. Further references to this edition will be included in brackets after the citation.

anticipates, and contributes to Rod Mengham's assessment of the mood of the novel: 'The revolutionary message of the novel is out of synch with its chronic morbidity.'[104] It is in this context of the late 1930s, where teaching and politics were becoming increasingly interlinked for Auden and his circle, that Auden's late-1930s writings are situated, as he takes on the role of teacher-cum-polemicist in his tract *Education Today and Tomorrow,* and in his speech at a conference of schoolteachers, 'Democracy's Reply to the Challenge of Dictators'.

Written in autumn 1937, *Education Today and Tomorrow* calls for educational democracy in response to the hierarchical, class-bound nature of educational structures. The tract is a collaboration with schoolteacher and journalist, T.C. Worsley, who later wrote *Barbarians and Philistines* (1940), which pitted the public school against democratic social structures and asked, 'Is oligarchy [...] compatible with democracy?'.[105] Worsley wrote the majority of the first section, 'Fact', but the last two sections, 'Theory' and 'Suggestion', were predominantly Auden's work.[106] The pamphlet was eventually published on 2 March 1939 in the Hogarth Press's *Day to Day Pamphlets* series.

In the intervening period between writing and publication, the Spens Report was published. The report was similarly concerned with developing a more democratic education system, promising 'substantial changes' to education.[107] Driven by an egalitarian ethos, it deliberated over the concept of multilateral schooling in an official government document for the first time: 'Many benefits might accrue if children above the age of 11 were educated together in multilateral schools [...] children differing in background and objective would be working in close association within the same school.'[108] Multilateralism was deemed to be 'too subversive', however, and 'with some reluctance' this idea was dropped.[109] Instead, an equal, but separate, class-based system of state

---

[104] Rod Mengham, 'The Thirties: Politics, Authority, Perspective', in *The Cambridge History of Twentieth-Century English Literature,* ed. by Laura Marcus and Peter Nicholls (Cambridge: Cambridge University Press, 2004), pp. 359–78 (p. 368); Benjamin Kohlmann, 'Writing of the Struggle: An Introduction to Edward Upward's Life & Works', in *Edward Upward and Left-Wing Literary Culture in Britain,* ed. by Kohlmann, pp. 1–17 (p. 6).

[105] Thomas Cuthbert Worsley, *Barbarians and Philistines: Democracy and the Public Schools* (London: Hale, 1940), p. 13.

[106] See *W.H. Auden Volume I 1926–1938,* ed. by Mendelson, pp. 805–06.

[107] Board of Education, *Report of the Consultative Committee on Secondary Education with Special Reference to Grammar Schools and Technical High Schools* [The Spens Report] (London: His Majesty's Stationery Office, 1938), p. ii.

[108] Board of Education [The Spens Report], pp. 375–76.

[109] Board of Education [The Spens Report], p. 291; p. 376.

education was advocated: Spens recommended 'parity of status'[110] between all types of state-maintained secondary education, allowing all to take their place as 'citizen[s] of a democracy'.[111] *Education Today and Tomorrow* acknowledges the report: 'The Spens Report on Secondary Education was published after this pamphlet was written and set up.'[112] It recognizes its positive recommendations for reform, mentioning its promise of 'universal free education' to all age eleven to sixteen, and its 'redressing the lack of provision for any but academic ability by establishing technical high schools parallel with the present secondary schools' (p. 408). However, it notes that the report works within 'the framework of the present system' (p. 408), while Auden and Worsley go further, finding fault with 'the prevailing social philosophy' (p. 407).

Auden's sections of the tract critique a class-based education system, exploring how the 'ladder theory' of liberal education policy renders the public school as a decidedly middle-class institution. This theory was associated with liberal conservative values, offering funded scholarships for the few, rather than open access for all. Denis Lawton notes that it enforced a 'top-down' approach to 'social progress and efficiency' via society's leaders, while social democracy advocated the 'broad highway' of equal opportunity.[113] A 1917 leaflet from the Independent Labour Party expressed disdain for the policy: the working class 'do not want ladders ... and patronage' but 'culture, independence and power'.[114] Auden suggests that the '"ladder" theory' is 'a barely concealed "leadership theory"', the logical end of which is seen in the modern Nazi training colleges' (p. 412), referencing the 'Ausleselager' or 'Selection Camps' founded by the Nazi Party in 1937 to form a 'school elite'.[115] He facetiously assures his reader that 'it has never been brought to anything like its logical conclusions in England' and juxtaposes this with the comment that 'the exclusiveness of the public schools was largely retained' (p. 412), as Auden implies that fascist education policy finds its kin in England's class-based education system. Via this 'liberal theory',

---

[110] This phrase recurs throughout the report. Board of Education [The Spens Report], p. xvii; p. xxxiii; p. xxxv; p. xxxvi; p. 168.

[111] Board of Education [The Spens Report], p. 85. This idea also recurs throughout the report, for example: p. 145; p. 223; pp. xxxvii–xxxviii.

[112] W.H. Auden and T.C. Worsley, *Education Today and Tomorrow*, in *W.H. Auden Volume I 1926–1938*, ed. by Mendelson, pp. 389–424 (p. 408). Further references to this essay will be included in brackets after the citation.

[113] Lawton, p. 12.

[114] As cited in Lawton, p. 26.

[115] Jürgen Schiedeck and Martin Stahlmann, 'Totalizing of Experience: Educational Camps', in *Education and Fascism: Political Identity and Social Education in Nazi Germany*, ed. by Heinz Sünker and Hans-Uwe Otto (London: Falmer Press, 1997), pp. 54–80 (p. 59).

the few working-class boys the public school does admit through scholarships are submitted to 'a thorough de-classing process' (p. 413). Auden identifies that the avowed intent of both 'old schools and new schools' is to 'produce leaders' (p. 415), and notes that 'to be a leader you must be middle class' (p. 413), as the democratization of the public school, the passport to leadership, is a fallacy.

Auden criticizes a system that fails to cultivate free and individual thought in all social groups. He presents an education system that sees a coincidence of D.H. Lawrence's 'higher, responsible, conscious class' and 'the lower classes, varying in their degree of consciousness' (p. 77) in *Fantasia*. Under the heading 'D.H. Lawrence, Anti-Idealism, and Fascism', Auden commends Lawrence's teaching that 'the mind is only a part of the whole man' (p. 415), but suggests that other elements of his doctrine are 'dangerous' (p. 414):

> [Lawrence's theory] is a very attractive doctrine for an authoritarian state, because once you begin by saying that some people are born to think and therefore to rule, while the mass are born not to think but to carry out the way of life which the thinkers decide is best for them, it is a short step to saying that those who are actually ruling are born to think and those who oppose them must not be allowed to think. (pp. 414–15)

Auden's implicit criticism of the anti-democratic elements of Lawrence's fascistic doctrine in 'Problems of Education' and 'Private Pleasure' is tackled more directly. The leader who is 'born to think' is critiqued as unremarkable, as the education system cultivates the 'pleasant-mannered yes-man with executive ability' (p. 415). This 'yes-man' will accept that society is 'final and absolutely just' rather than rebelling against it. Auden adapts Lawrence's thinking as he reflects social democratic arguments which call for equality of educational opportunity: 'The question of whether there are some people who are followers by nature, and others who are leaders, can only be discussed when education up to the age of maturity is open to all' (p. 415).

Auden's recommendations for educational reform initially presuppose 'radical social changes' that will give 'every child [...] the same educational opportunities' (p. 416; p. 415). However, a 'Short Term Programme' suggests a solution 'in the event of a Socialist Government being returned to power without a radical change in the class system and the private ownership of capital' (p. 422). The more moderate social democracy Auden proposes tolerates the public-school system – for now:

> If making State elementary education compulsory for all would [...] raise such a dust that no government could survive, this must be an objective which

is never lost sight of, as it probably has more to do with class feeling on its psychological side in this country than any other factor. We shall never have a [...] democracy till we do, however excellent some of the preparatory schools may be. (p. 423)

Auden advocates the abolition of the preparatory-school system, rather than the establishment of universal elementary-level schooling, which was established in 1880, as he ventriloquizes the voice of the middle-class parent in free indirect discourse ('however excellent... '). The schools' legislative immunity is noted as Auden refuses to give a wholesale recommendation of their abolishment in his use of the conditional tense ('if [...] would'), despite the fact that the demands of democracy and preparatory schools are antithetical.

Auden's approach to the debate surrounding educational democracy is informed by his class position: in Christopher Caudwell's terms, his 'aspirations for bourgeois freedom and bourgeois equality'.[116] This is elucidated with reference to Max Morris's tract *The People's Schools*, also published in 1939, by the left-leaning New People's Library. Morris similarly considers 'the class bias that marks [the British education system] [...] dangerous from the standpoint of a truly democratic community'.[117] Both tracts approach a similar argument for educational democracy from a contrasting perspective: where Morris argues for the advancement of working-class rights to ensure the 'fullest development of the mind and body of every child', Auden hopes to create a democratic educational system by debunking middle-class hegemony, rather than focusing on working-class advancement.[118] In correspondence, Auden explained his failure to advocate for a wholesale rejection of the public school in terms of political expediency:

Ultimately it will be better to have compulsory state elementary education for all, but at present it isn't practical politics in this country for a Labour or any other Government. Class-feeling in this country is so strong, bourgeois parents would go to any lengths to avoid the state school.[119]

---

[116] Christopher Caudwell, *Illusion and Reality: A Study of the Sources of Poetry* (London: Macmillan, 1937), p. 319.

[117] Max Morris, *The People's Schools: The New People's Library Volume XX* (London: Left Book Club; Gollancz, 1939), p. 93.

[118] Morris, p. 94.

[119] W.H. Auden, letter to E.R. Dodds, 13 November 1938, 'Textual Notes: Education', in *W.H. Auden Volume I 1926–1938*, ed. by Mendelson, pp. 805–10 (p. 807).

For Stephen Spender, Auden's political position around this time owes its debt to personal integrity:

> The ultimate criticism of Auden and the poets associated with him is that we haven't deliberately and consciously transferred ourselves to the working class. The subject of his poetry is the struggle [...] seen, as it were, by someone who whilst living in one camp, sympathises with the other; a struggle [...] which while existing externally is also taking place within the mind of the poet himself, who remains a bourgeois.[120]

Spender's comments saliently define the political tension in Auden's work as attributed not to a lack of commitment, but rather to a point of ontology. Auden interprets the proletarian struggle on the basis of his subjective, decidedly middle-class experience. Rather than diagnosing political failure, Spender argues that the group inhabits a far more complex subject position, in which the poem is about the process of 'going over' for a member of the bourgeois. In this reading, the difficulties of submerging the 'I' in the 'we' become the point; part of the 'struggle' is this experience of attempted self-annulment. *Education Today and Tomorrow* responds to the 'struggle' with its interpretation of a dominant ideal in education at the time – the search for democratic education – from a middle-class perspective.

Education Today and Tomorrow overtly aligns the qualities of the heroic with the attributes of the ideal pedagogue. In 1934 Auden drew on William McDougall's *Outline of Abnormal Psychology* to define his conception of the hero: 'The truly strong man lounges about in bars and does nothing at all.'[121] Auden found an exemplar of 'the truly strong man' in T.E. Lawrence, whose 'life is an allegory of the transformation of The Truly Weak Man into the Truly Strong Man' (p. 61). In *Education Today and Tomorrow*, Auden's heroic ideal has evolved beyond such machismo: 'The psychology a teacher needs is that of a sensitive, observant, intelligent man or woman of the world, or else that of a fat, stupid, kindly saint; not potted McDougall' (p. 416). He revisits his previous analysis to suggest that, for teaching, 'the truly wise men must be found' (p. 416).

'Democracy's Reply to the Challenge of Dictators' develops Auden's thesis on the political role of the teacher while continuing to dismiss progressive

---

[120] Stephen Spender, 'Oxford to Communism', *New Verse*, Nos. 26–27, November 1937, pp. 9–10 (p. 10).

[121] W.H. Auden, 'T.E. Lawrence', in *W.H. Auden Volume I 1926–1938*, ed. by Mendelson, pp. 61–62 (p. 61). Further references to this essay will be included in brackets after the citation. Edward Mendelson suggests that the true origin of 'the Truly Strong Man' lies in Eugen Bleuler's case studies. *Early Auden*, pp. 135–36.

education's emphasis on pedagogic technique expressed in his early reviews. Originally a speech delivered at the progressive New Education Fellowship's October 1938 conference on 'The Schools and the State', 'Democracy's Reply to the Challenge of Dictators' was later published in their organ, *The New Era*, in the January 1939 special issue on 'Education and Democracy'. Founded in 1921, the organization was part of the post-war progressive education movement, promoting 'Freedom, and Tolerance and Understanding' in education.[122] Auden was held in high esteem as an educationist by the Fellowship: he delivered the last address at the conference and the speech was published as the leading article in the journal. 'Democracy's Reply' envisages a solution to political crisis through pedagogic activity, a message that, delivered a few weeks after the Munich Agreement, held urgency.

The speech demonstrates that contemporary educational discourse informed Auden's solution to fascistic political crisis. Bertrand Russell's *Education and the Social Order*, the book Auden reviewed in 1932, directly informs the arguments in the speech and when it was published in *The New Era*, *Education and the Social Order* was listed under the section headed 'Some Books recommended by our Contributors'.[123] Russell's chapter on 'Education and Heredity' warns against advocating a link between these factors: 'The only scientifically sound position is to confess our ignorance as to the distribution of native ability and the laws of its inheritance.'[124] Characteristic of Auden's technique in his reviews, in which he felt the critic 'must quote with as little comment as possible' in order to capture interest, 'Problems of Education' (1932) quoted some of this chapter: 'Conservatives and Imperialists lay stress on heredity because they belong to the white race but are rather uneducated. Radicals lay stress on education because it is potentially democratic' (p. 27).[125] This principle proved provocative for Auden, as the debate between education and heredity informs his conceptualization of political systems in 'Democracy's Reply', which notes that fascism 'has attacked' democracy by saying that 'heredity is far more important than environment'.[126]

[122] Beatrice Ensor, 'The Outlook Tower', *The New Era*, January 1920, p. 3. The Fellowship was inspired by Freud: Robert Skidelsky notes that their 'catchword' was 'making the unconscious conscious'. Skidelsky, p. 145.

[123] Unsigned article, 'Some Books Recommended by Our Contributors', *The New Era in Home and School*, January 1939, p. 26.

[124] *Education and the Social Order*, p. 55.

[125] Auden cited in Carpenter, p. 114.

[126] W.H. Auden, 'Democracy's Reply to the Challenge of Dictators', in *W.H. Auden Volume I 1926–1938*, ed. by Mendelson, pp. 463–66 (p. 465). Further references to this essay will be included in brackets after the citation.

Conversely, Auden outlines the 'common' features of liberal and social democracy: 'All democracy [...] rests first and foremost on one simple thing – that you believe environment to be more important than heredity. If you do not believe that [...] you cannot possibly believe in democracy' (p. 463). The climax of the speech reinforces the political role of the teacher:

> As long as society is unequal as it is, the whole idea of democratic education is a sham. Unless all the members of a community are educated to the point where they can make a rational choice, democracy is a sham. [...] The primary demand of all educationists must be for equality of educational opportunity; otherwise, the first law of democracy – that environment should master heredity – is violated. (p. 466)

'Democracy is a sham' – the speech's soundbite is repeated three times and formed the headline of the *Birmingham Post*'s conference report: 'When Democracy is a Sham.'[127] The call for all to be able to make a 'rational choice', evident also in *The Poet's Tongue,* is reflected in Auden's 'Introduction' to *The Oxford Book of Light Verse* (December 1937). This 'Introduction' argues that '[a] democracy in which each citizen is as fully conscious and capable of making a rational choice, as in the past has been possible only for the wealthier few' is the task for all, including the 'modern poet'.[128] In 'Democracy's Reply', Auden tasks the realization of this 'genuine community' (p. 435) to progressive schoolteachers through their potential role in creating 'equality of educational opportunity', urging them to focus on 'social justice' rather than 'educational technique' (p. 466).

The concern expressed so forcefully in 'Democracy's Reply' – that education's role is to equip each individual with the intellectual and spiritual tools to make a 'rational choice' – is an underlying proposition that unites Auden's work in the 1930s: from his early, Lawrentian reviews, to his late-1930s polemical writings, which campaign for educational democracy. It is also a thesis that informs his aesthetics and pedagogy. In January 1939, to the interest of the London literary scene, Auden decamped to America with Christopher Isherwood: Cyril Connolly in *Horizon* called it 'the most important literary event since the outbreak of the Spanish War', suggesting it symbolized the rejection of the involvement of literature in politics in the 1930s.[129] Stephen Spender was dismayed by this

---

[127] Unsigned article, 'When Democracy is a "sham"', *Birmingham Post,* 24 October 1938, p. 13.

[128] W.H. Auden, 'Introduction to *The Oxford Book of Light Verse*', in *W.H. Auden Volume I 1926–1938,* ed. by Mendelson, pp. 430–37 (p. 436; p. 435). Further references to this essay will be included in brackets after the citation.

[129] Carpenter, p. 290.

exodus, but Auden defended it in correspondence, with the shared terms of his self-identification suggesting the shared intent behind his poetry and teaching: 'As a writer and a pedagogue the problem is different, for the intellectual warfare goes on always and everywhere.'[130] From across the Atlantic, Auden continued to criticize the English education system, interpreting it for an American audience. In a 1940 review of *Enemies of Promise* he found that

> The Public School boy comes away with a first-class political training, but one which he can only use in the interests of six percent of the nation, for that is all the nation he knows. Democrats, who rightly condemn the English system for its one-class nature, can learn a good deal from it.[131]

He continued, also, to teach, giving weekly lectures on poetry to the pro-Soviet League of American Writers in autumn 1939, and to the New School for Social Research in spring 1940. Auden's rueful March 1940 letter to Professor Dodds demonstrates his anti-authoritarian pedagogic techniques and his improvisatory, experimental approach to teaching – even if, this time, it was one experiment too far: 'The lectures at the New School are going alright but I have learned not to let them have discussions but talk all the time. Democracy in education *method* doesnt [sic] seem to work, at least not with a large class.'[132]

[130] Letter from W.H. Auden to Stephen Spender, c. 14 March 1941, Nicholas Jenkins, 'Eleven Letters from Auden to Stephen Spender', in *W.H. Auden 'The Map of All My Youth', Auden Studies 1*, ed. by Katherine Bucknell and Nicholas Jenkins (Oxford: Clarendon Press, 1990), pp. 55–93 (p. 76).

[131] W.H. Auden, 'How Not to Be a Genius', in *Prose of W.H. Auden: Prose Volume II 1939–1948*, ed. by Edward Mendelson (London: Faber & Faber, 2002), pp. 18–21 (p. 20).

[132] Kathleen Bell, 'A Change of Heart: Six Letters from Auden to Professor and Mrs E.R. Dodds Written at the Beginning of World War II', in *The Map of All My Youth*, ed. by Bucknell and Jenkins, pp. 95–115 (p. 113).

2

Winifred Holtby, Vera Brittain and the Politics of Pedagogy in *South Riding, Honourable Estate,* and *Testament of Youth*

In 1960 Vera Brittain wrote of her friendship with Winifred Holtby:

> The most creative aspect of a university education arises from the stimulus of ideas exchanged with contemporaries. In our long conversations at Oxford and after […] Winifred helped me to think more clearly, and I hope I did the same for her […] we were feeling our way to conclusions not immediately obvious or easily reached.[1]

The description signals a sense of how formative their period at Somerville was for both of them, suggesting a relationship that is complementary, supportive, and ultimately, pedagogic: the pair teach one another to 'think more clearly' and to think differently, beyond the 'immediately obvious'. This emphasis on the pedagogic was, perhaps, inevitable. University-level education for women arose, in part, out of the need to improve the education of female teachers: Queen's College was founded at the University of London in 1848 to improve educational standards for governesses, while Bedford College was founded in 1849 with a broader aim of educating women who desired further education.[2]

Both Holtby and Brittain were graduates of Somerville College, Oxford. While the college was founded in 1879, it was not until 1920 that its female students were granted the right to matriculate and gain a University of Oxford degree. As Brittain notes, she and Holtby were among the first women at Oxford to receive their degrees: 'the victorious result of a battle half a

---

[1] *The Selected Letters of Winifred Holtby and Vera Brittain (1920–1935)*, ed. by Vera Brittain and Geoffrey Handley-Taylor (London: Brown, 1960), p. vii.

[2] See Joan N. Burstyn, *Victorian Education and the Ideal of Womanhood* (London: Croom Helm, 1980), p. 23.

century old against academic masculine prejudice'.[3] Janet Howarth and Mark Curthoys note that most women who went up to Oxford in the early days envisaged teaching as a career.[4] For Holtby and Brittain, teaching seemed an inevitable next step – and was, perhaps, one to be resisted. In 1921 Brittain wrote to Holtby, reporting a conversation with her former headmistress at St Monica's: 'Miss Heath Jones says there are heaps of good History posts going but she thinks we are very wise to refuse the "safe" jobs [...] until we have first tried the literary work we prefer.'[5] *Testament of Friendship* suggests that teaching was merely a financial expedience to facilitate a more exciting life of letters: 'We both pictured a vague but wholly alluring existence of novel-writing and journalism, financially sustained by the barest minimum of part-time teaching, and varied with occasional excursions into lecturing and political speaking.'[6] Nonetheless, teaching formed a significant part of both women's working lives. In autumn 1921 Brittain was invited to return to her old school to give a weekly lecture on international relations, with Holtby invited the following semester to give a series of history lectures. For a period of two and a half years, both Brittain and Holtby made weekly visits to St Monica's to teach. At one stage, Winifred taught English when the English mistress became ill, while Vera gave lessons in political history.[7] In the early stages of her career, Holtby, Brittain says, suffered an '*embarras de richesses*' of teaching jobs; as well as history teaching at Brittain's former school, St Monica's, where she was later offered a headship, she gave lectures at schools in Forest Gate, Notting Hill, and, in autumn 1923, worked for the Oxford University Extension Delegacy.[8]

While Brittain reported in 1921 that 'the thought of lectures rather bores me at present' and noted that she had 'no love or gift for teaching as such', for Holtby, teaching offered sustenance: 'I am really looking forward to having something

---

[3] Vera Brittain, *Testament of Friendship: The Story of Winifred Holtby* (London: Virago, 2012), p. 120.
[4] Janet Howarth and Mark Curthoys, 'The Political Economy of Women's Higher Education in Late Nineteenth and Early Twentieth-Century Britain', *Historical Research*, Vol. 60 No. 142 (June 1987), 208–31. For more on the place of women at Oxford in the nineteenth and twentieth centuries, see Janet Howarth, '"In Oxford but ... not of Oxford": The Women's Colleges', in *The History of the University of Oxford Volume VII Nineteenth Century Oxford, Part Two*, ed. by M.G. Brock and M.C. Curthoys (Oxford: Clarendon Press, 2000), pp. 237–307; Janet Howarth, 'Women', in *The History of the University of Oxford Volume VIII The Twentieth Century*, ed. by Brian Harrison (Oxford: Clarendon Press, 1994), pp. 345–75.
[5] *Selected Letters*, ed. by Brittain and Handley-Taylor, p. 9.
[6] *Testament of Friendship*, p. 125.
[7] Paul Berry and Mark Bostridge, *Vera Brittain: A Life* (London: Chatto & Windus, 1995), p. 170.
[8] *Testament of Friendship*, p. 144. For further details on Holtby's teaching in this period, please see pp. 143–47.

else to do which will be to some extent communicative and reciprocal. [...] It will be quite a relief either to teach or be taught for a bit.'[9] Despite her indifference, Brittain did receive praise for her 'splendid lecture' on international relations, while Holtby's references for teaching posts from her university lecturers reveal a particular aptitude for teaching; one reference describes her as an 'unusually successful lecturer', while another notes 'Miss Holtby's enthusiasm for her subject & her sense of humour should make her an interesting & exhilerating [*sic*] teacher'.[10]

The pay and conditions of the work of women teachers also formed a significant stimulus for both women's feminist activism in the interwar period. Both campaigned against the marriage bar and for equal pay for teachers through their involvement with the Six Point Group, a political pressure group, founded in 1921. Holtby and Brittain joined this group in March 1922, with Holtby sitting on the Executive Committee during this period.[11] The group consisted of 'Equality First' 'old' feminists, who campaigned for six specific objectives founded on social justice for women: pensions for widows, equal rights of guardianship for married parents, reform of the laws dealing with child assault and the position of the unmarried mother, equal pay for teachers, and equal pay for women in the Civil Service.[12] Both Holtby and Brittain were actively involved in campaigning against the imposition of the marriage bar by the London County Council (LCC) when, in March 1923, it decided to include women teachers within the terms of its 1906 Standing Order which required that women resign their jobs upon marriage. In May 1925 the Six Point Group resolved to organize deputations 'containing representatives of the leading Women's Societies' to 'lay the case for the employment of married women before 1) The Municipal Reform women members of the L.C.C. 2) The Labour women members of the L.C.C. 3) The Education Committee of the L.C.C.'.[13] Correspondence from the archive of the National Union of Women Teachers (NUWT) demonstrates that 'Miss Vera Brittain [...] is organising the deputations on behalf of the Six Point Group' while Holtby was 'Acting Secretary to the Deputation'.[14] NUWT records reveal that Holtby

[9]   *Selected Letters*, ed. by Brittain and Handley-Taylor, p. 16; Berry and Bostridge, p. 171; *Selected Letters*, ed. by Brittain and Handley-Taylor, p. 17.
[10] Berry and Bostridge, p. 170. Winifred Holtby Collection, Hull Archive and History Centre: LWH/5/5.12/01a-01i.
[11] Berry and Bostridge, p. 176.
[12] Ibid.
[13] 'Six Point Group – Deputation to LCC on Married Women Teachers', UWT/D/11/28 ©UCL Institute of Education Archives.
[14] Ibid.

corresponded with key NUWT members, including Emily Phipps, to organize a representative from the NUWT for the Six Point Group deputation to the LCC Education Committee in November and December 1925.[15] An amendment to Holtby's letter from 8 December reveals that the deputation, originally organized for 11 December, was postponed: 'phoned to say Mrs W. Phipps ill & could not receive deputation.'[16] The deputation was eventually held on 15 January 1926, in the absence of Holtby, who was sailing to South Africa.[17] Mrs Wilton Phipps – chairman of the Education Committee received the deputation. Notes from the meeting suggest a degree of sympathetic ambivalence to the cause: 'One could not say that she had been converted, but she listened attentively and seemed impressed that there certainly was another point of view to be considered.'[18]

Both were also actively involved with the NUWT: Holtby spoke at their conferences and events in 1929, 1931, and 1935, while Brittain spoke at their final 'Victory Luncheon' in 1961. The NUWT, a campaigning feminist organization and trade union, was founded in 1920 after the findings of the 1919 Burnham Committee, which investigated teacher pay and established that female teachers would start on 90 per cent of a schoolmaster's salary, a ratio which would drop to 80 per cent after a couple of years due to differential increments and allowances. Women's voices were largely occluded on the Burnham Committee, with only thirty-nine men and five women holding posts. The government and the National Union of Teachers (NUT) committed to a renegotiation of the Burnham Scale only once every five years; this, combined with the sidelining of the results of a 1919 referendum by the NUT executive, whereby 19,965 members came out in favour of equal pay, acted as a stimulus for the formation of the NUWT. Emily Phipps, an influential early figure in the NUWT, found that 'the only conclusion to be arrived at was that it was impracticable to work through the N.U.T. for any reforms which did not meet the approval of the men members.'[19] The warm relationship Holtby and the NUWT shared, in particular, is evidenced by the

---

[15] Ibid.

[16] Ibid.

[17] Holtby writes from on-board the ship on 14 January 1926. *Selected Letters*, ed. by Brittain and Handley-Taylor, p. 76.

[18] UWT/D/11/28 ©UCL Institute of Education Archives.

[19] Emily Phipps, *History of the National Union of Women Teachers* (London: National Union of Women Teachers, 1928), p. 9. For more on the history of the NUWT, please see Patricia Owen, '"Who Would Be Free, Herself Must Strike the Blow" The National Union of Women Teachers, Equal Pay, and Women Within the Teaching Profession', *Journal of the History of Education Society*, Vol. 17 No. 1 (1988), 83–99; Helen Corr, 'Sexual Politics in the National Union of Teachers 1870–1920', *Women, Education and the Professions: History of Education Society Occasional Publication*, Vol. 8 (1987), 53–65.

correspondence surrounding her involvement with the Equal Pay Luncheon she spoke at in May 1931. Holtby accepted the invitation to speak on 15 March 1931, noting 'I admire the N.U.W.T. so much that I shall be very proud to accept their invitation'.[20] The letter of thanks dated 12 May 1931 from the acting general secretary of the NUWT notes Holtby's 'delightful and provocative speech. [...] The Luncheon was quite one of the most successful features of the Week-End Conference, and this was mainly due to the most enjoyable speeches given by you and Mrs. Le Sueur'.[21]

Previous studies have suggested the ways in which Brittain's and Holtby's educational experiences at Somerville College informed their literary output and their feminist critique.[22] This chapter considers the influence of education on these writers' works through a focus on their literary representations of the pedagogic figure in their mid-1930s texts: Holtby's *South Riding* (1936), and Brittain's *Testament of Youth* (1933) and *Honourable Estate* (1936). It reads across their letters, draft manuscripts, research notes, and journalism, to suggest how their depictions of teachers were informed by contemporaneous educational debates, their own pedagogic activity, and their political activism in feminist groups and teachers' unions, while also suggesting the ways in which their work had a demonstrable impact on pedagogic practice.

South Riding and the marriage bar

Winifred Holtby's novel, *South Riding,* posthumously published in March 1936, has a headmistress, Sarah Burton, as a central character, whose professional and personal fortunes are portrayed against 'the drama of English local government'.[23]

---

[20] 'Educational Week-end Conference and Equal Pay Luncheon', UWT/B/5/35 ©UCL Institute of Education Archives.

[21] Ibid.

[22] Susan J. Leonardi considers them in her study of the 'Somerville College Novelists', suggesting how the figure of the educated woman generated 'variations on novelistic assumptions', particularly surrounding the traditional, romance marriage plot. Isobel Hurst has considered the ways in which Brittain's classical education at Somerville College informed her feminist appropriation of classical texts associated with a typically masculine, public-school-education in *Testament of Youth*; while Ann K. McClellan has considered how Brittain's representation of the competing demands of academe and war work critiques competing definitions of women's duty in wartime. Susan J. Leonardi, *Dangerous by Degrees: Women at Oxford and the Somerville College Novelists* (London: Rutgers University Press, 1989), pp. 175–226; Isobel Hurst, *Victorian Women Writers and the Classics: The Feminine of Homer* (Oxford: Oxford University Press, 1996), pp. 211–19; Ann K. McClellan, '"I was my war; my war was I": Vera Brittain, Autobiography and University Fiction during the Great War', *Paedagogica Historica*, Vol. 52 (2016), 121–36.

[23] Winifred Holtby, *South Riding* (London: Collins, 1949), p. v.

The novel was of clear interest to teachers; teachers' papers reviewed the book, with *Teacher's World* recognizing its 'extraordinary blend of the individual story and the community novel'.[24] *The Schoolmaster*, the organ of the NUT, skirted around Holtby's feminist involvement with the NUWT by noting in their review that 'readers of this paper will remember Miss Holtby's visit to the last Union Conference and will recall her deep interest in social problems, and her sustained work for the establishment of Peace through Education'.[25] The documentary sources on which the novel drew, including minutes of council meetings and Labour Party pamphlets, helped render the novel a recognizable portrayal of the experience of schoolteaching: 'It will make a particular appeal to teachers who are not unfamiliar with some of the well depicted characters and the community in which they are placed.' The reviewer found that 'it is a book with a purpose'.[26] The social engagement of *South Riding* arises from the recognizable mould of the Victorian social problem novel, and the political intent behind this novel was symptomatic of Holtby's wider feelings about her work; in a letter to Lady Rhondda in December 1933, Holtby wrote: 'I shall never quite make up my mind whether to be a reformer-sort-of-person or a writer-sort-of-person', and earlier that same year she described herself in a letter to Phyllis Bentley as '50% a politician'.[27]

In *South Riding*, the tension between these categories of writer and artist is felt in Holtby's negotiation of Sarah's relationship with Robert Carne, a gentleman-farmer and father of a pupil at Sarah's school, which is informed by debates surrounding the marriage bar. Kristin Ewins argues that 'Holtby's primary achievement as a political novelist is her ability to bridge the gap between the novel's contrasting political and romantic interests [...] the romance is intensified by the political context'.[28] In the case of the marriage bar, however, the romantic becomes political. The imposition of the statutory marriage bar in 1922 as part of the economy measures instituted by cuts in public spending had the effect of reducing the proportion of married women teachers from 16 per cent in 1921 to 9 per cent in the 1930s.[29] The LCC removed the marriage bar on 16 July 1935, while it was eventually revoked on a national level in 1944. Holtby continued to work on her book after the marriage bar in London had been revoked: writing to

[24] Winifred Holtby Collection, Hull Archive and History Centre, *South Riding* materials, L WH/8/8.22.
[25] Ibid.
[26] Ibid.
[27] See Marion Shaw, *The Clear Stream: A Life of Winifred Holtby* (London: Virago, 1999), pp. 233–34.
[28] Kristin Ewins, '"Revolutionizing a Mode of Life": Leftist Middlebrow Fiction by Women in the 1930s', *ELH*, Vol. 82 No. 1 (Spring 2015), 251–79 (p. 262).
[29] Penny Summerfield, 'Women and the Professional Labour Market 1900–1950: The Case of the Secondary Schoolmistress', *Women, Education and the Professions: History of Education Society Occasional Publication*, Vol. 8 (1987), 37–52 (p. 47).

Brittain from Malvern on 29 July 1935 she noted, 'I'm working hard here on the last draft of my book.'[30] The novel itself, however, is set between June 1932 and 6 May 1935 (the date of George V's Silver Jubilee celebrations).

Holtby wrote against the marriage bar repeatedly in her political journalism and tracts. In *Women* (1934), Holtby laments that 'still, in 1934 [...] public authorities dismiss married women employees upon marriage.'[31] In a 1930 article, Holtby considered the results of a ballot by the Civil Service Clerical Association, whereby 4,795 to 138 female members of the Civil Service voted in favour of the marriage bar if it involved the forfeit of the gratuity awarded to civil service employees upon marriage. The article creates a link between popular culture's cultivation of models of femininity tied to marriage, and the political consequences of the ballot:

> Now, say the wiseacres, you see what happens. The feminists have been making a desperate fuss, protesting against the enforced resignation of women teachers and civil servants upon marriage. [...] Who are the girls who have voted for the marriage bar? Nine out of ten swing daily to their offices in suburban trains and trams and buses, carrying in their suitcases a powder-puff and a love-story or *Home Chat.* They are the public which creates the demand for light fiction in libraries [...]. The love stories so wisely stop on the sound of wedding-bells and the scent of orange-blossoms.[32]

Home Chat (1895–1958), a penny weekly for mothers and housewives, signals middlebrow, or even lowbrow, concerns.[33] The magazine's subject matter was relentlessly domestic. In *The Land of Green Ginger* (1927), Holtby alludes to the magazine to signify the comforts (and constraints) of Joanna's domestic life: Agnes, Joanna's friend, ironically suggests that she may enjoy a copy of '*Home Chat* to read and a fire in your room every night' if she comes to visit her in China, while on hearing of her husband Teddy's tuberculosis she takes a numb, escapist, comfort in the 'fashions' in a copy of *Home Chat.*[34] Holtby's article critiques the tradition in 'light fiction' whereby romance-plot conventions position marriage

---

[30] *Selected Letters*, ed. by Brittain and Handley-Taylor, p. 349.

[31] Winifred Holtby, *Women* (London: John Lane The Bodley Head, 1941), p. 82.

[32] Winifred Holtby, 'The Wearer and the Shoe', in Vera Brittain and Winifred Holtby, *Testament of a Generation: The Journalism of Vera Brittain and Winifred Holtby*, ed. by Paul Berry and Mark Bostridge (London: Virago Press, 1985), pp. 64–67 (pp. 64–65). Further references to this article will be included in brackets after the citation.

[33] Margaret Beetham and others, *Women's Worlds: Ideology, Femininity and the Woman's Magazine* (Basingstoke: Palgrave, 1991), p. 103.

[34] Winifred Holtby, *The Land of Green Ginger* (London: Virago, 2011), p. 106; p. 35. Further references to this edition will be included in brackets after the citation.

as the climax of a woman's life; 'wisely' avoiding the exposure of the realities of married life. Her own fiction repeatedly frustrates this romantic ideal: Susan J. Leonardi observes the ways in which Holtby's novels engage with, but ultimately evade, the marriage plot, suggesting that while this is 'a limited and limiting strategy, it is nonetheless effective for telling the story of the educated woman' without 'eschew[ing] the romance plot altogether or endlessly repeating the inevitability of that plot'.[35] Indeed, Holtby's fiction repeatedly looks beyond the marriage plot to consider new, less conventional, forms for women's life: *The Land of Green Ginger*, for instance, describes the unhappy reality of Joanna's marriage to Teddy, while the novel's closure sees Joanna leave Yorkshire to reunite with her two school friends in South Africa, one of whom, Rachel, is a university lecturer in the Transvaal, and has asked Joanna to help her run a boarding house in Johannesburg 'for young women earning their own living' (p. 267). Here girls' schools facilitate the formation of an all-female social network that allows for the development of female communities based on work and enterprise.[36] Holtby's 1930 article on the marriage bar envisages a future whereby marriage need not preclude a professional life: she suggests that the 138 women who voted against the marriage bar 'saw the prospect of marriage before them, but not marriage demanding that cruel alternative – a home or a career' (p. 66).

It is this 'cruel alternative' that Sarah Burton is anxious to avoid. While Charlotte Brontë's *Jane Eyre* (1847), a text that informs Sarah's self-conceptualization in the novel, is a significant intertextual source for *South Riding*, so too is *Villette* (1853), with its denial of marriage for the educated woman and suggestion that work may be a more fulfilling path.[37] We learn, early on in the novel, that Sarah has been engaged three times: her first fiancé died in the Somme, the politics of her second became increasingly disagreeable to her, while

> the third, an English Socialist member of Parliament, withdrew in alarm when he found her feminism to be not merely academic but insistent. That affair had shaken her badly, for she loved him. When he demanded that she should abandon, in his political interests, her profession gained at such considerable *public* cost and *private* effort, she offered to be his mistress instead of his wife and found that he was even more shocked by this suggestion than by her previous

---

[35] Leonardi, p. 201.

[36] For more on the role of education in the formation of all-female communities please see, Nina Auerbach, *Communities of Women: An Idea in Fiction* (Cambridge: Harvard University Press, 1978) and Martha Vicinus, *Independent Women: Work and Community for Single Women 1850–1920* (London: Virago, 1985), pp. 121–210.

[37] I am grateful to Dr Isobel Hurst for this suggestion.

one that she should continue her teaching after marriage. [...] She knew herself to be desirable and desired, *withheld only from marriage by the bars of death or of principle*. (pp. 48–49, emphases added)

The allusion to the 'public' and 'private' signals the impact the public realm has on the individual's private life.[38] The terms of the marriage bar legislation are ironically inscribed into the final line of this quotation: 'withheld only from *marriage* by the *bars* of death or of principle.' However, in the case of her third fiancé, it is the necessity to make a choice between work and marriage due to the marriage bar, rather than principle per se, that bars Sarah from marriage. The end of the novel alludes directly to the marriage bar in Sarah's speech to her schoolgirls: 'question [...] the rule that makes women have to renounce their jobs on marriage' (p. 488).

Sarah's personal history renders it clear that the marriage bar itself did not necessarily preclude her from pursuing romantic interests. Indeed, on encountering Carne in a Manchester hotel, Sarah agrees to be his 'little tart' for 'one night' (p. 351). She has full cognizance of the possible implications of this decision: 'I am Sarah Burton; I have Kiplington High School; he is a governor. [...] Even if I do not have his child, this may destroy me' (pp. 350–51). Sarah's feelings for Carne are expressed in conflicted terms:

She could find no comfort, for she had thrown away the one chance she had ever had of being his friend. [...] If I could see him, tell him just what I feel for him – that I am his friend, that I don't care what he thinks of me [...] so long as he knows that I stand by him, that I am here, always, loving him, trusting him, caring for him.

Christ, that my love were in my arms! (p. 398)

The insistent repetition of 'friend' gives way to the anguished cry for her 'love' as Sarah grapples with the nature of her feelings for Carne in the context of her own increased dedication to her profession: 'The school, the school, the school filled her deliberate mind. "You're becoming a monomaniac," Pattie had told her' (p. 392). While Muriel is given the choice against marriage in the closure of *The Crowded Street* (1924), when she rejects Godfrey's proposal to pursue professional interests, acting as secretary to the feminist activist Delia, who lives in London, *South Riding* deprives Sarah Burton of her choice against marriage

---

[38] Jean Kennard has commented more broadly on the frequent interplay of the terms 'public' and 'private' in *South Riding*, suggesting that 'Holtby shows the public world to be the private worlds of other people. She stresses our membership in one another's lives'. Jean Kennard, *Vera Brittain & Winifred Holtby: A Working Partnership* (London: University Press of New England, 1989), p. 166.

in her relationship with Carne; their relationship is forestalled and eventually frustrated by Carne's heart attack at her hotel bedroom door, and his eventual death. Carol Dyhouse is puzzled by this plot twist, commenting: 'it is difficult to know exactly what Holtby wants us to understand by this for the moment never comes. [...] Sarah is not made to face the consequences of her impulse – and neither, more significantly, is Winifred Holtby.'[39]

Carne's death represents the strategic denial of a choice for Sarah that both preserves the significance and integrity of her passion for Carne while allowing Holtby to maintain and validate the status and femininity of the single, professional woman. In a grief-stricken state after his death Sarah notes 'for this, there is no remedy. [...] I cannot bear it. There will be no end for ever to this pain' (p. 426). Susan J. Leonardi suggests that, with Sarah Burton, Holtby 'presents unambiguously the possibility that the educated, unattached woman lives a more fulfilling and exciting life than her married sister'.[40] Such an analysis overrides, however, the emotional complexity established in Sarah's conflicted relationship to her work, and her romance with Carne. The review of *South Riding* by the Labour MP Ellen Wilkinson, a figure with whom Sarah Burton is notably associated in the novel, also recognized the departure Holtby's fiction provided from accepted romance-plot conventions in favour of her heroine's intellectual and professional life.[41] Unlike Leonardi, however, Wilkinson's analysis accounts for the complexity of Sarah Burton's emotional life:

> The triumph of this book is its gospel of the saving power of worth-while work. The heroine of the twentieth century cannot fall luxuriously into a decline if her love-story is broken. [...] When the telephone is ringing for a committee, [...] girls demanding to be taught, the modern woman takes a stiff dose of something, and somehow carries on. Life may be several tones greyer. The sparkle and the ecstasy are gone. But no one guesses the inward smash as the cool, efficient woman takes the platform or pulls on the operating gloves. There are some grim but heartening stories to be written on the trail that Winifred Holtby has blazed.[42]

Wilkinson suggests that Holtby's emphasis on the redemptive power of work is genre busting. Refusing to 'stop on the sound of wedding-bells and the scent

---

[39] Carol Dyhouse, *Girls Growing Up in Late Victorian and Edwardian England* (London: Routledge and Kegan Paul, 1981), p. 38.

[40] Leonardi, p. 201.

[41] Joe Astell asks Sarah if Ellen Wilkinson is a 'relation' due to their shared physical feature of red hair: 'No, I'm not. I wish I were. I think she's a grand girl' (p. 103), Sarah replies.

[42] Ellen Wilkinson, 'Winifred Holtby's Last Novel', *Time and Tide,* 7 March 1936, p. 324, in Winifred Holtby Collection, Hull Archive and History Centre, *South Riding* materials, L WH/8/8.22.

of orange-blossoms' (p. 66), *South Riding* establishes new, intellectual, and emotional pathways for the independent woman, torn by, but not defined by, personal loss and grief. One may point to the closure of *Anderby Wold* (1923) for an earlier instance of the same pattern. In this novel's ending, Mary Robson takes spiritual and intellectual consolation from her work after the death of both her husband and lover: 'Those fine things were there just the same – courage, service, progress. [...] she must be practical and get to work.'[43] In the case of *South Riding*, Carne's death allows Holtby to maintain both the text's politicized protest against the marriage bar and her protagonist's professional identity, while preserving middlebrow romance codes.

South Riding, the NUWT, and the equal pay debate

The validation of the role of women's work in *South Riding* during a period in which marriage and teaching represented competing claims signals Holtby's maintenance of the position of the single woman. Holtby's depiction of Sarah Burton's professional identity is informed by her feminist activism with the NUWT as she campaigned for equal pay for women teachers, and reflected also in her articles for the teachers' magazine *The Schoolmistress*, and her early 1930s satirical travelogue, *The Astonishing Island* (1933). Here, I read across these sources to suggest that Holtby depicted the female teacher as an emancipated, empowered professional.

Dale Spender perceives an increased radicalization in Holtby's politics in the 1930s as a response to the social and political sidelining of the concerns of women spinsters.[44] This was of particular pertinence in the field of education where 90 per cent of women teachers were unmarried.[45] With the marriage bar in place, women were perceived not to have the need to earn a wage sufficient to support a family. An October 1929 issue of *The Woman Teacher*, the NUWT organ, demonstrates that at the 1929 NUWT conference at Westminster Hall at which Winifred Holtby spoke, Mr E.F. Wise MP, an invited speaker who delivered his address just before Holtby, exposed this reasoning against equal pay as a fallacy, putting forward a key argument in favour of equal pay to the assembled delegates:

---

[43] Winifred Holtby, *Anderby Wold* (London: Virago, 2011), p. 277.

[44] Dale Spender as cited in Diana Wallace, *Sisters and Rivals in British Women's Fiction 1914–1939* (Basingstoke: Macmillan, 2000), p. 149.

[45] Alison Oram, *Women Teachers and Feminist Politics 1900–1939* (Manchester: Manchester University Press, 1996), p. 185.

'In the community as a whole the number of women with dependants is nearly as large as the number of men with dependants, so this argument against equal pay is statistically unsound.'[46] In *South Riding*, Holtby considers the economic imperative behind teaching through her depiction of Miss Sigglesthwaite and her dependant mother. Jean Kennard notes that 'through Sarah Burton Holtby creates respect for her scholarship and understanding for her need to teach to support her elderly mother'.[47] Sarah's sympathy for Miss Sigglesthwaite's situation, despite her cynicism surrounding her ability to teach effectively, is rendered clear: 'Poor devil, thought Miss Sarah. This is desperate for her. There's an invalid mother, isn't there?' (p. 116). The reference to 'Miss Sarah' here, where elsewhere the narrative refers to 'Sarah', seems to align her with 'Miss Sigglesthwaite', underpinning the sense of kinship Sarah feels for her colleague, while preserving a distinction between the more formal way in which Sarah is referenced when the narrative is focalized through Agnes Sigglesthwaite's perspective (as 'Miss Burton').

Sarah Burton's situation provides Holtby with a more radical argument against equal pay, however. With dead parents, Sarah has no living dependants. She teaches out of professional pride and personal ambition, as well as a wider sense of public service: 'I shall enjoy this. I shall build up a great school here. No one yet knows it except myself. I know it. I'll make the South Riding famous' (p. 49). Such motivations are significant in the context of Holtby's own assessment of the arguments in favour of equal pay for teachers. At the 1929 NUWT conference, Holtby defended equal pay based on gender parity, rather than economic need:

> The speaker wondered why folks were always so ready to call on the public spirit of others – especially of women. [...] She asked whether the mass of women benefited by this unselfishness on the part of some. Would not the countries be healthier if we recognised that justice for all is a fundamental principle of good statesmanship? We must recognise the value of human beings as such, and learn to pay workers for their work alone – all other considerations were irrelevant.[48]

This argument of equality for equality's sake is one put forward in Holtby's journalism: 'Josephine Butler, whose main concern was not with economics but with the sanity and kindliness of the relationships between the sexes, [...] replied once to a questioner: [...] "the most important thing is the principle of equality,

[46] 'Equal Pay Meeting 18 October 1929', IOE Archive UWT/D/1/42 ©UCL Institute of Education Archives.
[47] Kennard, p. 169.
[48] IOE Archive UWT/D/1/42 ©UCL Institute of Education Archives.

equality and equality'".[49] Penny Summerfield argues that, through Sarah Burton, *South Riding* 'can be read as a defiant reply to the secondary schoolmistress's detractors, celebrating the qualities of feminine intellectual and economic independence and authority'.[50] While women in the teaching profession suffered unequal pay in relation to their male colleagues, they had 'relatively good pay and high status' in relation to other female-dominated professions, such as nursing.[51] Sarah's economic empowerment is made much of in the novel. She travels, socializes, and can afford a car: 'I'll have to buy a car' (p. 45). The detail is significant both biographically and in relation to the historical tensions surrounding equal pay for women teachers. In April 1933 Holtby wrote to Jean McWilliam, celebrating the freedom car-ownership provided for her former teacher: 'I was glad to see that my old history mistress at Queen Margaret's has got a car [...] I made her come out to dinner and then take me for a moonlight ride. [...] I haven't got a car yet.'[52] The ability of women teachers to buy their own cars seems to have proved a particular point of provocation for male teachers who resented women's calls for equal pay. The Association of Assistant Masters' (AAM) report to the Royal Commission on Equal Pay in 1945 found that in the 1930s, male teachers complained that 'women teachers can have cars and holidays abroad more frequently than their male colleagues', who the AAM noted, had families to support.[53]

Holtby's 1929 speech at the NUWT conference offered a defence of the place of leisure in the schoolmistress's life as a support to her professional commitments: 'Women teachers worked at great pressure, and therefore needed change and refreshment out of school time. External stimuli had to be paid for, and when a teacher had to lose cultural opportunities the school suffered.'[54] Her observations of the delegates of the 1935 NUT Scarborough conference, at which she delivered a lecture on 'Woman in the Modern World' which was met with 'bursts of delighted laughter' (*Testament of Friendship*, p. 449) and was 'described as being the most brilliant ever heard at the Women's Annual Meeting', emphasized the schoolmistresses' position as economically liberated professionals, with a full and active life:[55]

---

[49] Winifred Holtby, 'Fear and the Woman Who Earns', in *Testament of a Generation*, ed. by Berry and Bostridge, pp. 81–83 (p. 83).

[50] Summerfield, p. 37.

[51] Summerfield, p. 42.

[52] Winifred Holtby, *Letters to a Friend*, ed. by Alice Holtby and Jean McWilliam (London: Collins, 1937), p. 457.

[53] Parliamentary Paper, Cmd 6397 Royal Commission on Equal Pay, Minutes of Evidence. London, HMSO, 1945, 23 March 1945, statement submitted by Association of Assistant Mistresses.

[54] UWT/D/1/42 ©UCL Institute of Education Archives.

[55] Editorial matter in Winifred Holtby, 'The Scarborough Conference', *The Schoolmistress*, 2 May 1935, p. 121. Winifred Holtby Collection, Hull Archive and History Centre, WH/2/2.21/04/05a.

They were active, efficient, self-respecting people. They wore pleasant, attractive garments; they discussed pleasant and invigorating holidays which they had taken in Switzerland, in France, or on North Sea cruises. Hundreds drove themselves to the Conference in their cars, and used the brief intervals between the many sessions for expeditions up to the inland moors.

The time has passed when teaching was the Cinderella of the professions.[56]

While Agnes Sigglesthwaite provides Holtby with the more stereotypical instance of the schoolteacher as the 'Cinderella of the professions', who teaches out of financial necessity to support her aged mother, Sarah Burton accords with the image of the modern, cultured, emancipated professional summoned in the implied reader of her articles for *The Schoolmistress,* to which Holtby contributed between 1931 and 1935. There was a perceived link between the members of the NUWT and the readers of this weekly teachers' paper. After Holtby spoke at the 1931 NUWT Equal Pay Luncheon, the acting general secretary wrote to her noting, 'your name is known to so many members that they were glad to have this opportunity of meeting you and of hearing you make some of the witty criticisms which they have learned to expect in your articles!'.[57] Holtby's articles for *The Schoolmistress* discuss 'in intimate fashion the various interests that go to make the intellectual and social life of a cultured woman of to-day'.[58] Their diverse subject matter, including pieces on middlebrow culture ('Arnold Bennett's Library') and high culture ('Nijinsky', 'The Voice of Youth', which considers poets, including the Auden Group), indicates Holtby's perception of the wide-ranging, culturally esoteric, concerns of her schoolmistress readership.[59] The articles express affection for the work of teaching and recognition of the varied talents of teachers. 'What a Revue Should Be' (1933) discusses a stage version of *1066 and All That,* written, as the article points out, by 'two young schoolmasters' and comments 'for myself, I almost longed to be back at teaching'.[60] The political role of the teacher is privileged and sanctified: an article published after the 1931 election found

[56] Holtby, 'The Scarborough Conference', p. 122. Winifred Holtby Collection, Hull Archive and History Centre, WH/2/2.21/04/05a.

[57] UWT/B/5/35 ©UCL Institute of Education Archives.

[58] Winifred Holtby, 'My Weekly Journal', *The Schoolmistress,* 18 June 1931, p. 329. Winifred Holtby Collection, Hull Archive and History Centre, WH/2/2.21/01/01a.

[59] Winifred Holtby, 'Arnold Bennett's Library', *The Schoolmistress,* 19 November 1931, front page WH/2/2.21/01/06a; Winifred Holtby, 'Nijinsky', *The Schoolmistress,* 16 November 1933, p. 189 and p. 196. Winifred Holtby, 'The Voice of Youth', *The Schoolmistress,* 16 May 1935, p. 185.

[60] Winifred Holtby, 'What a Revue Should Be', *The Schoolmistress,* 27 June 1935, front page. Winifred Holtby Collection, Hull Archive and History Centre, WH/2/2.21/04/06b.

that 'our salvation may lie with the teaching profession'.[61] While some articles are concerned with the political situation more widely, others offer specific comment on NUT conferences and events.[62] Evelyne White, the editor of the journal, observed the 'scholarly way' Holtby approached her subject matter, as well as the pedagogic quality of her contributions: 'Her very real conception of teaching as well as her skill as a teacher were shown over and over again in the articles she contributed to the Press.'[63] Indeed, Holtby's article on 'Miss Helen Waddell' offers an informative and accessible analysis of Holtby's former Oxford tutor's translation of medieval Latin lyrics, while expressing admiration and respect for her scholarship: 'Had I known that the unexpected auditor of my undergraduate efforts was to be the translator of *Mediaeval Latin Lyrics,* the author of the exquisite *Wandering Scholars,* my bashfulness would have struck me dumb.'[64]

The articles suggest a readership with a rich social and intellectual life, far removed from the 'three overlapping negative images of the single woman teacher: as an unfulfilled celibate, [...] the predatory lesbian teacher, and as the militant man-hating spinster', noted by Alison Oram.[65] While a fellow Six Point Group member, Clemence Dane, had rehearsed 'reactionary lesbophobic and anti-spinster discourse' in *Regiment of Women* (1917), Holtby offers a more varied depiction of the spinster teacher.[66] While Agnes Sigglesthwaite is the archetypal woman teacher, seen through Sarah's eyes as 'tall, faded, nervous, with a nose perpetually polished by dyspepsia, and dust-coloured hair that dripped from a dreary bun' who 'justified all too well the libels spread by their detractors about school teachers' (p. 116), Sarah Burton is a woman who relishes her single status: 'I was born to be a spinster, and by God, I'm going to spin' (p. 49), yet remains committed to the coexistence of values of professionalism and femininity. In the company of Alderman Beddows and his conservative friends, Sarah offers a spirited defence of the role of lipstick in teaching: 'thinking of Miss Sigglesthwaite, but also by this time feeling irritably perverse', she comments that

---

[61] Winifred Holtby, 'After the Election', *The Schoolmistress,* 29 October 1931, front page. Winifred Holtby Collection, Hull Archive and History Centre, WH/2/2.21/01/05c.

[62] Winifred Holtby, 'On the NUT Conference', *The Schoolmistress,* 27 April 1933, front page. Winifred Holtby Collection, Hull Archive and History Centre, WH/2/2.21/02/04c.

[63] Evelyne White, *Winifred Holtby as I Knew Her* (London: Collins, 1938), p. 123; p. 147.

[64] Winifred Holtby, 'My Weekly Journal', *The Schoolmistress,* 25 June 1931, front page. Winifred Holtby Collection, Hull Archive and History Centre, WH/2/2.21/01/01b.

[65] Oram, p. 189.

[66] Heather Julien, 'School Novels, Women's Work and Maternal Vocationalism', *NWSA Journal,* Vol. 19 No. 2 (Summer 2007), 118–37 (p. 125).

'I regard lipstick as a symbol of self-respect, of interest in one's appearance, of a hopeful and self-assured attitude towards life.' She maintains that in the case of two candidates with 'equal qualifications' she would pick the candidate who 'looked as though she could hold down the post of head mannequin at Molyneux's, but had chosen to teach instead' (p. 184). Such terms echo the description of Robinson Lippingtree Mackintosh, a castaway from Tristan da Cunha, who arrives washed up on British shores in Holtby's 1933 text, *The Astonishing Island*. As Regan notes, 'His perspective is used to defamiliarize various aspects of, and trends within, British culture.'[67] Thus, where Mackintosh is told that spinster women are 'warped and embittered' and is faced with headlines that deride single women as redundant ('SPINSTERS: FRUSTRATED LIVES [...] CENSUS REVEALS 1,000,000 SUPERFLUOUS WOMEN'), his own experience belies this.[68] Mackintosh notices a 'most beautiful lady, dressed like a princess, in furs and silk [...] with a ravishing figure [...] step out of a sumptuous-looking motor car and cross the pavement into a Hairdresser's Establishment [...] I well believed that such beauty and elegance might wreck many Homes' (p. 89), before being surprised to learn of her professional status:

> 'That's Miss Fairweather, Head Mistress of the Girls' High School [...] Says there's nothing like a hair-wave to make you able to face your own Sixth Form [...]'
> 'Is she a Spinster?' I asked.
> 'I should say so. They don't let teachers marry here.'
> 'Don't let?' I cried. 'Are not teachers, then, True Women? Can you trust your children to be taught by frustrated, bitter, soul-warped, festering spinsters?'
> 'Soul-warped, festering my uncle!' said the young man. 'Fairweather's a daisy. She's Lady Golf Champion for the district, too.' (p. 90)

As in *South Riding*, femininity is figured as a support to effective pedagogy. In the conversation, the term 'spinster' is redefined as having positive associations, as the aptly named Miss Fairweather is described as sexually alluring ('a daisy') and a good sportswoman to boot. Like Miss Fairweather, much is made of Sarah

---

[67] Lisa Regan, *Winifred Holtby's Social Vision: 'Members One of Another'* (London: Pickering and Chatto, 2012), p. 141.

[68] Winifred Holtby, *The Astonishing Island* (London: Lovat Dickson, 1933), p. 82. Further references to this edition will be included in brackets after the citation. The 1921 census had revealed a post-war imbalance between male and female populations and Lord Norwood provoked a national controversy in his reference to the problem of what to do with 'superfluous' women. For more on this and a discussion of the prevalence of the spinster in 1920s fiction, see Chris Baldick, *Literature of the 1920s: Writers among the Ruins: The Edinburgh History of Twentieth-Century Literature in Britain: Volume 3* (Edinburgh: Edinburgh University Press, 2012), pp. 22–24.

Burton's physical appearance in *South Riding*: while not beautiful, she remains attractive to men. This is evident when she is perceived through the lingering eyes of Councillor Huggins, who is ogling an unrecognized swim-suited woman in the middle distance, who is, in fact, Sarah Burton:

> He propped his plump stomach against the sun-warmed paling, and remained there, enjoying the pose of her slim muscular body, her lifted arms, her hair like a flaming cresset. From that distance he could not see her physical defects, her hands and head too big, her nose too aggressive, her eyes too light, her mouth too obstinate. Nor did he dream that here was the headmistress whose appointment he, as a member of the Higher Education Sub-Committee, had recently sanctioned.
>
> [...] Aware of approving eyes upon her, she increased unconsciously and almost imperceptibly, the slight swagger of her walk. (p. 51)

Ashlie Sponenberg considers *South Riding*'s 'cinematic tropes, socialist intent, and erotic subtexts', noting here that 'Sarah [...] emerges from the passage as having shifted the balance of power away from Huggins['s] [...] because her imperfections remain hidden; her sexuality is kept within her control and that of the text'.[69] The shared 'cinematic' narrative perspective also contributes to the book's overriding message: 'we are members one of another', a message repeated in the book and used also in a 1935 book review Holtby wrote for *Good Housekeeping*.[70] While, as Marion Shaw notes, Sarah Burton provides a 'vantage point from which the social landscape can be viewed', the text's switch between different narrative perspectives offers a broader analysis of the individuals within the *South Riding* community, as well as creating a sense of the ways in which individual subjectivity is formed communally, whether that be through an impression of Sarah formed through Mr Huggins, or Sarah's objectification of members of the community in class or gender terms, as Sponenberg discusses.[71] This sense of communality is sometimes achieved through the cultivation of discordant perspectives. The impression of inter-social relationships formed through this narrative device nonetheless remains significant, and ultimately contributes to a sense of the ways in which individual identity is formed in relation to a collective identity, however fractured that communal identity may be depicted.

---

[69] Ashlie Sponenberg, "The Long Arm of Discipline: *South Riding*, Documentary Writing, and the Cinematic Gaze', *The Space Between*, Vol. III No. 1 (2007), 65–78 (p. 77).

[70] Sponenberg, p. 89. Winifred Holtby, 'The Best of Life', in *Testament of a Generation*, ed. by Berry and Bostridge, pp. 87–89 (p. 89).

[71] Shaw, p. 242.

The communal and the individual in *South Riding*: The limitations of education's power for social reform

The tension between the communal and the individual on the level of narrative perspective in *South Riding* also animates the novel on the level of both plot and in the text's critique of the possibilities the education system allows for social reform. Attention to Holtby's research during the composition period of *South Riding* suggests how both of these are informed by contemporaneous left-wing educational debates surrounding cuts to school-building grants and the inclusiveness of the educational system. The novel's closure, I suggest, indicates the limitations of Sarah Burton's educational vision for offering broader social reform.

The novel's communal vision is reflected in its resolution of a key subplot: Sarah's quest for her new school buildings. The decrepit state of the buildings of Kiplington High School for Girls is referenced throughout the novel. At her interview Mrs Beddows acknowledges: 'The buildings are not up to much, and I don't see, with the country in the way it is, that they'll soon be put right' (p. 25). Sarah is determined to build up a 'great school' in the South Riding, and takes on her unpromising raw material with determination and relish: 'Four wretched houses. A sticky board of governors. A moribund local authority. A dead end of nowhere. That's my material. I shall do it' (p. 49). Sarah wants to take her cause to the council's Higher Education Committee: 'I'd like to do a bit of lobbying. Have you seen my buildings? How would you like to run a school with a basement full of blackbeetles?' (p. 105). Finding it difficult to secure public funds for her school, the indefatigable Sarah takes remedial measures:

> The grant for her boarding-house was hideously inadequate. The place looked desolate, and she had no money to spend on decorations. She pillaged her cottage for vases, books and woodcuts. She designed cupboards, bullied local carpenters, hung pictures and curtains, pestered governors. Far into the night she sat writing letters, drafting memoranda. She dragged any member of the Higher Education Committee whom she could lure into her buildings from cellar to garret, exposing their enormities. Her energy was unremitting. If the South Riding was not prepared to build a new school for her, she would make this old one a perpetual torment. And always as she planned and wrote and argued, she saw Councillor Carne in her mind's eye as the apostle and ringleader of reaction, the author of false economies, the culprit really responsible for leaking taps in the science room and blackbeetles in the basement [...] she never forgot to remember him with resentment. (pp. 175–76)

Carne, as a conservative force in the local council, becomes the embodiment of the barrier to the fulfilment of Sarah's ambitions to replenish her crumbling school. Holtby was aware of the ways in which cuts to education grants had impacted upon the fabric of school buildings. In researching her novel, she took notes of local county council meetings and recorded dates of key public events that occurred in January and February 1932, just before the opening of the novel in June 1932. One event recorded is 'Jan 4th Cut in education building programme', and later in her notes Holtby lists local economy measures: 'Economy 1. Kingston Secondary Schools others to be cut down. save £84, 650.'[72]

The appeal against such cuts to educational buildings formed a source of Labour Party activism in the period. In her research for *South Riding*, Holtby consulted Labour's policy report on *Labour and Education*, dated July 1934. The report condemns the National Government's education policy, suggesting that it had 'arrested educational progress and degraded educational standards.'[73] The National Government abolished the special building grant established by the Labour government, and, as a result 'schools long condemned have been retained in existence, and requests by local education authorities for permission to reconstruct them have been summarily rejected. Reorganisation, which till September, 1931, was proceeding rapidly, has been almost arrested.'[74] The policy document notes that

> the next Labour Government must reverse that policy decisively and at once. In addition to restoring the cuts in teachers' salaries, it must [...] [r]eintroduce the special building grant abolished by the 'National' Government, and [...] ensure that local education authorities proceed as rapidly as possible with the building of new schools.[75]

Holtby's depiction of Sarah's struggle to secure funds for new buildings for her school is staged against this context of educational cuts and left-wing political pressure.

Just as Carne provides a symbol to Sarah of the resistance against which she must battle to secure her new school, the novel's closure holds its two plots in tension: the private resolution of her relationship with Carne in the novel's final chapter, and the public resolution of her quest for new school buildings in the

[72] Winifred Holtby Collection, Bridlington Local Studies Centre, Series of sixteen manuscript notebooks.
[73] *Labour and Education* (London: The Labour Party, 1934), p. 1. Winifred Holtby Collection, Hull Archive and History Centre, WH/8/8.2/03a.
[74] *Labour and Education*, pp. 4–5.
[75] *Labour and Education*, p. 1.

epilogue. The final chapter ends with the reconciliation of Sarah's feelings for Carne, as she returns to Maythorpe:

> She knelt on his threshold, her arms round the crumbling pillar, her cheek on the cold stone. [...] All my life I can do nothing but destroy where you have builded and build where you destroyed. Forgive me. Forgive me. [...]
>
> Something had happened. Quite simply she knew that she was not entirely alone, not arrayed against him; for he was within her. She had become part of him and he of her, because she loved him. He had entered into her as part of the composition of her nature, so that they no longer stood in hostile camps. She could no longer hate herself, for that would be hating him too. [...] She entered at last into part of his experience, and understanding him, felt isolated no longer. [...]
>
> She rose slowly, and began to move forward, groping silently round the dark eyeless house, bidding farewell to it, not for herself, but for him. (pp. 476–77)

Maythorpe – Carne's decrepit country pile – becomes the site of a metaphysical ('composition') synthesis of their souls, reminiscent of a marriage service ('she had become part of him and he of her') as Carne's conservative impulses become absorbed into Sarah's soul, creating an 'understanding' between them. The tradition of old country houses being transformed into schools is an old one, but Holtby deliberately avoids this resolution. Instead, in the novel, Maythorpe is destined to become a home for the mentally ill, a symbolic gesture, perhaps, to the outmoded status of the aristocracy. (One might turn also to Nancy Mitford's satirical portrayal of the country pile, Peersmount, as lunatic asylum-cum-House of Lords in *Wigs on the Green* (1935).) Indeed, far from becoming the new inhabitant of Maythorpe, Sarah 'would help to destroy it, as she had helped to destroy all that Maythorpe stood for' (p. 477). Significantly, however, Victor Saville's 1938 adaptation of Holtby's novel resolves the school-building plot in a conservative manner: Maythorpe becomes the site of Sarah's new school. In the final moments of the film (in which Carne is saved from suicide by Sarah), she watches passively from the public gallery as Carne makes an 'offer' to the South Riding Council; the Maythorpe estate is to provide the land for a housing scheme while Maythorpe Hall and gardens are to be 'reserved and restored as the new premises for the Kiplington High School'.[76] As Regan notes, this closure 'presents a different vision of community where the rural feudalism represented by Carne is left intact and the public remains a male dominated space of tradition'.[77] Such

---

[76] *South Riding*, dir. by Victor Saville (London Film Studios, Victor Saville Productions, 1938) [on DVD].

[77] Regan, p. 137.

a narrative manoeuvre neutralizes the novel's progressive, feminist-socialist impulse.

By contrast, in the novel's epilogue, set on King George V's Silver Jubilee, the novel's balance between individual and collective claims shifts to an emphasis on the latter. The school-building plotline is resolved through the endowment of public money occasioned by the King's Jubilee, as Joe Astell acknowledges in his letter to Sarah: 'Maybe that's why I can't get too indignant even about your Jubilee. I can only feel glad that you'll get your buildings out of it' (p. 483). Sarah's new school, a 'palace of glass and chromium' (p. 483), is an emblem of modernity, in contradistinction to the image of archaic decrepitude in the 'cellar[s]' and 'garret[s]' of the old school buildings and the ruins of Maythorpe. The aesthetics of school buildings is one that concerned Brittain also, informing her amendments to the typescript of *Testament of Friendship*. Her description of Holtby's old school, Saint Margaret's, in *Testament of Friendship* notes that the founders of pre-war church schools 'regarded neither beauty nor comfort', observing the school's 'huge draughty windows and tiny antiquated grates', and adding a manuscript insertion to the typescript that reinforces this image of almost monastic asceticism, in the description of the bedrooms as 'small ugly <unlovely> cubicles'.[78] This was by way of contrast to Brittain's own old school, St Monica's. Holtby's 1927 letter to Jean McWilliam, headmistress of Pretoria High School for Girls, observed her plush surroundings, noting the 'family resemblance all the really nicely furnished girls' schools have. I am staying at St. Monica's for the week-end, and writing this in a charming bedroom which [...] might be yours before your own things were in it.'[79] In *South Riding*, Astell is alert to the legacy to the future that the new school buildings provide – 'I believe in bricks and mortar' (p. 483) – just as Holtby recognized the symbolic significance of school buildings in the prize-giving speech she gave at Pretoria High School for Girls, on 19 March 1926:

> The feature of South African life which has impressed me more than others with a promise for its future development lies in the dignity of its educational buildings. In this century we are acquiring a truer knowledge of the value of education in the life of a state. [...] [I]n this day of young restless nations [...] we may estimate their standard of culture by the value which they place upon their education. By their schools may we judge them. [...] [T]he foundations

---

[78] Winifred Holtby Collection, Bridlington Local Studies Centre, 'Annotated Typescript of Vera Brittain's 'Testament of Friendship', p. 43.

[79] *Letters to a Friend*, ed. by Holtby and McWilliam, p. 445.

here have been well and truly laid, and each successive generation which values loveliness in school buildings will complete the work begun in the Transvaal schools.[80]

The emphasis here is on the pledge to the future an investment in education provides. Sarah's grief for Carne initially compromises her pride in the fulfilment of her professional ambitions: 'What did they matter now, the grand new buildings for which she had struggled, the foundation of her great girls' public school? Her work, her ambition and her reputation?' (p. 485). However, this changes when she narrowly avoids death in a plane crash: 'shaken out of sorrow [...] she faced the future' (p. 487). It is this emphasis on the future which dominates the final pages of *South Riding*, with the new school buildings explicitly linked to symbolic values of renewal and hope: 'That afternoon Sir Ronald Tarkington was to lay the foundation of the new High School buildings as part of the ceremonial of a Jubilee dedicated, by instruction of the Prince of Wales, to youth' (p. 490). The building blocks of the new school are symbolically the building blocks of a new civilization.

Holtby's 1935 *Time and Tide* article on the Jubilee celebrations further elucidates the spirit in which she set the closure of her novel in the seemingly deeply patriotic terms of the Silver Jubilee. Holtby notes that she refused to sign a petition from a left-wing organization protesting at the Jubilee celebrations. Her reasons for doing so were 'not that I am a royalist' but instead because she 'looked back on the past twenty-five years and decided that these were, on the whole, the most propitious that women in this country have ever known'.[81] The article celebrates 'rural community councils' and finds that 'as a countrywoman I cannot protest against Jubilee celebrations' (p. 93). The strong alliance drawn between nationhood and womanhood renders it significant that the keynote to the Jubilee celebrations in *South Riding* is effectively given to Sarah Burton, with her address to the schoolgirls. Indeed, the United Service broadcast from St Paul's is only partially recorded, filtered through Sarah's consciousness as she reflects 'not of the King and Queen' but 'on the people near her' (p. 489). Sarah, a former 'History and Civics' teacher at the South London United Secondary School for Girls, gives a rousing speech to her pupils:

---

[80] *Letters to a Friend*, ed. by Holtby and McWilliam, pp. 407–10.

[81] Winifred Holtby, 'King George V Jubilee Celebrations', in *Testament of a Generation*, ed. by Berry and Bostridge, pp. 89–93 (p. 89; pp. 89–90). Further references to this essay will be included in brackets after the citation.

Question everything – even what I'm saying now. Especially, perhaps, what I say. Question every one in authority, and see that you get sensible answers to your questions. Then, if the answers are sensible, obey the orders without protest. Question your government's policy, question the arms race, question the Kingsport slums, and the economics over feeding school children, and the rule that makes women have to renounce their jobs on marriage, and why the derelict areas still are derelict. This is a great country, and we are proud of it, and it means much that is most lovable. But questioning does not mean the end of loving, and loving does not mean the abnegation of intelligence. Vow as much love to your country as you like; serve to the death if that is necessary [...] But, I implore you, do not forget to question. Lead on, girls. (p. 488)

Sarah's speech strikes a balance between establishing a tone of collective patriotism and individualism. The rhetorical features of the speech – the repetition, direct address, and parallel structures – are clearly modelled on the traditional oratory of public-school prize-givings, parodied in Auden's *The Orators* (1932) with the injunctions of the Old Boy who closes his speech by persuading pupils to partake in a demonic initiation rite: 'Unless my memory fails me there's a stoke hole under the floor of this hall the Black Hole [...] [n]ew boys were always put in it. [...] Well look to it' (p. 17). While the speech's form is traditional, its content is progressive. In May 1934 Holtby wrote to Brittain, after being sent *The Modern Schools Handbook*, introduced by Amabel Williams-Ellis and published by Victor Gollancz, which she was reviewing for *Good Housekeeping*.[82] The book is to be 'read by parents' and provides a series of accounts by the headmasters and mistresses of 'modern schools', which broadly includes not just progressive schools, but schools which have been 'affected by the new spirit' in education.[83]

The emphasis in Sarah's speech on questioning 'every one in authority' chimes with the concerns of progressive education, and a number of the head teachers in the volume discuss the relationship their school has with a key principle of progressive education: self-government. The headmistress of Croham Hurst considers the school's relationship to self-government, noting the school is modelled on 'not so much self-government as government in which staff and girls' representatives closely cooperate'.[84] At Badminton, the headmistress, Beatrice Baker, notes that the school is 'making no great educational experiments, but we are trying to train our girls to be forward-looking citizens of a new world'.[85]

[82] *Selected Letters*, ed. by Brittain and Handley-Taylor, p. 286.
[83] *The Modern Schools Handbook*, ed. by Trevor Blewitt (London: Gollancz, 1934), p. 11; p. 22; p. 22.
[84] *Handbook*, ed. by Blewitt, p. 232.
[85] *Handbook*, ed. by Blewitt, p. 222.

This more moderate approach to the radical principles of progressive education elucidates the tenor of Sarah's speech. Sarah's final injunction 'Lead on, girls' symbolically sees her facilitating the habits of freethinking in her pupils while balancing this with a collective sense in the plural reference to 'girls'. Beatrice Baker's chapter quotes part of a speech she made in July 1931, on the occasion of the school's first speech day after becoming a public school. It contains an outline of the qualities which the school aimed to develop in its girls: '(1) Thoroughness; hard work, accuracy, and perseverance [...] (2) Breadth and depth of interest [...] (3) A spirit of service – national and international'.[86] Such principles elucidate the content of Sarah's speech, orientated around the creation of politicized individuals – 'citizens of the future' (p. 488) – with a strong communal sense and a concern for women's rights.

Amabel Williams-Ellis advises parents on a key way in which to determine the quality of a school, citing a father, who on school visits, 'ask[s] them how they deal with their failures. If they say they never have any, I know it's a bad school.'[87] Later in her introduction Williams-Ellis repeats this principle, reinforcing its significance: 'Having by observation and direct question – such as "What do you do about your failures?" – decided what we believe to be the school's weak points'.[88] This elucidates one of the professional lessons Sarah Burton receives from Mrs Beddows in the book's final chapter:

> You were good with the bright ones, Lydia Holly and Biddy Peckover, and the scholarship girls. [...] But what about the stupid and dull and ineffective? The rather dreamy sort of defeated women? You hadn't much use for the defeated, had you? Not much patience with failure. (p. 472)

Mrs Beddows identifies Sarah's critical neglect of her failing pupils, a deficiency of the education system more widely that Holtby considered in her research for *South Riding* and grappled with in her articles. In 1937 secondary schools catered for approximately 11 per cent of the population aged eleven to seventeen years old and the competition for scholarships was fierce.[89] As part of her research for *South Riding*, Holtby consulted the minutes of the meetings of the East Riding Education Committee, on which her mother sat.[90] They demonstrate that 697 candidates

---

[86] *Handbook*, ed. by Blewitt, p. 223.
[87] *Handbook*, ed. by Blewitt, p. 18.
[88] *Handbook*, ed. by Blewitt, p. 20.
[89] Summerfield, p. 39.
[90] Such research renders unconvincing Holtby's claim in her 'Prefatory Letter' to her mother, Alderman Mrs Holtby, that 'the incidents of the schools, housing estates and committees are not described from your experience. I have drawn my material from sources unknown to you' (p. v).

entered for the Minor Scholarships exam in May 1934, with sixty candidates being found eligible for the offer of scholarships, twenty-eight of whom were girls.[91]

In her manuscript notes for an undated article, entitled 'The Points of Free Education Free Secondary Education' Holtby launched a passionate defence of the role of free, secondary education for all children, not just the exceptional scholarship boy or girl:

> Every child capable of profiting by free education should have it. To those who believe in this principle, the ~~2~~15% of children who in England are today receiving such education seems totally inadequate. Of the ~~7~~85% who leave school at fourteen ~~to [indeciph] all education~~ at least ~~fif~~ 50% we reckon must be capable of profiting by the curricula used by high schools or at least by the technical & commercial schools of this country. Some would place the percentage as high as 70%: others would even declare that ~~except for the subnormal child~~ even the subnormal & mentally defective child requires the attention of educationalists after the age of fourteen: that the years of adolescence & those immediately following them are even more important educationally for the backward child than for his brighter brethren. It is ~~probable~~ a truism therefore, that to those who are interested either in education itself, or in the future of the ~~country~~ nation generally, the extension of secondary education is strongly desired. The obstacle ~~we decl~~ it appears, is economic.[92]

The manuscript reveals the extent to which Holtby revised her vision of secondary education to be all-encompassing and of benefit to 'even the subnormal and mentally defective child', adapting her argument to suggest a higher degree of certainty of the positive effects of post-fourteen education for all children: 'It is ~~probable~~ a truism.' The article makes the support of universal, secondary education an article of faith:

> If ~~we~~ <the Bel.[ievers] Of education> could squeeze from the Treasury sufficient sums to build more high schools, if the parents of prospective wage earners could refrain from putting their children into the Labour market until they have received the mature age of sixteen or seventeen. or matriculation standard [...] Then we might have the millennium of HG. Wells.[93]

The amendment here ('If ~~we~~ <the Bel.[ievers] Of education>') suggests that Holtby aligns a belief in education with a religious commitment.

[91] Winifred Holtby Collection, Hull Archive and History Centre, 'Minutes of the Proceedings of the Education Committee', pp. 67–69. WH/8/8.3/01b.
[92] Winifred Holtby Collection, Bridlington Local Studies Centre, Series of sixteen manuscript notebooks.
[93] Ibid.

In *South Riding*, Sarah Burton fails to persuade Mrs Beddows to support her in asking the County Council to offer a 'boarding scholarship' (p. 187) to Lydia Holly who, after her mother's death, has to 'give up her scholarship and go home and look after the children' (p. 186). Mrs Beddows defends the traditional role of women in the home, while exposing the curtailment of professional opportunities for women: 'What if she does give up her scholarship and doesn't go to college? There'll be one school teacher less, and perhaps one fine woman and wife the more. Is that such a tragedy?' (p. 188). Mrs Beddows's resistance also exposes the problems inherent in Sarah's special pleading in the case of Lydia Holly, which has been defined by Regan as 'selective and meritocratic': 'If it wasn't once in fifty you couldn't do it. [...] [Y]ou can't make exceptions' (p. 187).[94] The irony, of course, is that the highly selective scholarship system and the absence of a system of universal secondary education already makes exceptions to those who can benefit from an education at Kiplington High School. Lydia Holly is kept at school not through the intervention of the state, but through the private solution offered to the Holly problem, in a fortuitous plot twist whereby Mrs Burnham agrees to take on the Holly children as a surrogate mother. *The Labour Woman* found this plot twist to be 'artistically indefensible [...] characteristic of an excessive optimism which is the artistic defect of Miss Holtby's novel'.[95] The resolution to the problem of Lydia Holly signals the limitations of Sarah's emphasis on the transformational potential of education. The final vision of the novel is one that reinforces the significance of maternal nurturing as Sarah's personal relationship with Mrs Beddows becomes emblematic of the broader *South Riding* community:

> In Mrs Beddows' smile was encouragement. [...] Sarah, smiling back, felt all her new-found understanding of and love for the South Riding gathered up in her feeling for that small sturdy figure. She knew at last that she had found what she had been seeking. (p. 492)[96]

The novel's closure is further elucidated by Holtby's dedication to her mother in the 'Prefatory Letter' which at once acknowledges the documentary basis of the 'story' and the narrative's emotional core: 'I dedicate this story, such as it is, to you' (p. vi).

---

[94] Regan, p. 152.

[95] Winifred Holtby Collection, Hull Archive and History Centre, *South Riding* materials, L WH/8/8.22.

[96] Other critics consider the novel's privileging of the maternal bond. Lisa Regan notes, 'Sarah's vision of progress through individual independence and education thus yields to a sense of community founded on maternal nurturing and co-operative effort' while Jean Kennard reads *South Riding* as a narrative of 'reconciliation' with the mother figure. Regan, p. 152; Kennard, p. 161.

Such an emphasis on the maternal occurs in the context of the implicit signalling of the limits of education as a democratic pathway to social progress at the end of the novel, when it is noted that Lydia has 'passed her matriculation' taken in the fifth form, and was 'going to college' (p. 488). The narrative projects us into her future: 'She was sure of a major county scholarship; she would probably win the Snaith Bursary for distinction in mathematics' (p. 488). In 1930 the Board of Education increased the number of state scholarships to university awarded by local education authorities from 200 to 300, but, at the same time, the percentage of scholarships available to girls was reduced from 50 per cent, so that 188 scholarships were allocated to boys and 112 to girls.[97] Mrs Beddows's speech emphasizes the exceptional nature of Lydia Holly and thus reinforces the anomalous trajectory away from the slums that her narrative provides. The education system's inability to cope with its 'failures' in an era when secondary education, let alone university education, was available to the minority, lessens its impact as a vehicle of social progress and reform. Sarah's aim to transform Kiplington High School for Girls into a 'great girls' public school' (p. 485), referenced at the end of the novel, also signals education's limitations as a force for social change. This implicit commentary on the limitations of a highly selective education system is held in tension with Sarah's rousing rhetoric which displays the power of education in building the nation's future citizens. Indeed, this is undercut both by Sarah's ironic observation, after her speech, of the 'subdued [...] schoolgirls in their brown tunics, Lydia, Nancy, Jennifer, Gwynneth, the citizens of the future, she thought, with a grimace for all inadequacy, hers as well as theirs' (p. 488), and the statistical facts of access to secondary education in the interwar period. Only some, it seems, will be empowered 'citizens of the new world' (p. 488), however lacklustre they may seem in receiving this injunction.

Vera Brittain's feminist-pacifist pedagogy in *Testament of Youth* and *Honourable Estate*

Winifred Holtby died in September 1935, before *South Riding* had gone to press. She appointed Brittain as her literary executor, charging her with overseeing the publication of the novel and correcting the novel's typescript.[98] As Jean Kennard notes, *Honourable Estate*, Brittain's historical saga that examines

---

[97] Carol Dyhouse, *No Distinction of Sex?: Women in British Universities, 1870–1939* (London: University College London Press, 1995), p. 31.

[98] Shaw, p. 9; p. 44.

the experiences of work, education, and motherhood of three generations of women, spanning from 1894 to 1930, is 'deeply influenced' by *South Riding*.[99] The simultaneity of Brittain's working processes across the two works contribute to this line of influence: from October 1935 to January 1936, Brittain worked on both the uncorrected typescript of *South Riding*, and the proofs of *South Riding* and *Honourable Estate*. As she corrected proofs of *South Riding*, she 'kept getting ideas for "Hon. Estate" instead', observing 'what a strange experience of communion with her spirit this proof-correcting is!'.[100] Like *South Riding*, *Honourable Estate* also contains a portrait of a forward-thinking schoolmistress, in the guise of Miss Hilton, headmistress of Playden Manor, a 'fashionable private school'.[101]

Where Holtby's portrayal of Sarah Burton and Kiplington High School for Girls is strongly influenced by contemporaneous debates, Brittain's portrayal is grounded firmly in late-Victorian and Edwardian educational thinking. Critics have commented on Brittain's highly autobiographical mode of novel-writing, and, indeed, her portrait of Playden Manor is reminiscent of St Monica's, her old school. The description of Miss Hilton, the headmistress of Playden Manor, who had a 'respect for intellectual integrity and a passionate zeal for social righteousness' (p. 272), resembles Miss Heath Jones, who shared the headship of St Monica's with Brittain's aunt, and whom Brittain later 'suspect[s] to have been secretly in sympathy with the militant suffrage raids and demonstrations [...] an ardent though always discreet feminist'.[102] The covert nature of this 'sympathy' is striking and is reflective of the broader, conservative, paradigms behind education for girls.[103] The socially anachronistic nature of many small, private, day schools for girls, combined

---

[99] Kennard, p. 176.

[100] Vera Brittain, *Chronicle of Friendship: Vera Brittain's Diary of the Thirties*, ed. by Alan Bishop (London: Gollancz, 1986), p. 240; p. 239.

[101] Vera Brittain, *Honourable Estate* (London: Virago, 2000), p. 272. Further references to this edition will be included in brackets after the citation.

[102] Vera Brittain, *Testament of Youth* (London: Virago, 2009), p. 23. Further references to this edition will be included in brackets after the citation.

[103] Sara Delamont argues that reforms in women's education in the late-Victorian period were not necessarily the work of committed feminists, while Carol Dyhouse suggests that, on the whole 'reformers [...] emphasised the desirability of educating women to be cultivated wives and mothers', noting that schools for girls were 'in many ways conservative institutions' that nonetheless 'played a crucial role in the history of the feminist movement'. Dyhouse notes the prominent role men played on the board of organizations such as the Girls' Public Day School Company, rendering it unlikely that the schools could pose any substantial challenge to family life, or conventions of femininity. Sara Delamont, 'The Domestic Ideology and Women's Education', in *The Nineteenth Century Woman: Her Cultural and Physical World*, ed. by Sara Delamont and Lorna Duffin (London: Croom Helm, 1978), pp. 164–87; Dyhouse, *Girls Growing Up*, p. 59; p. 60; p. 57.

with her recent work researching Bethnal Green schools for the MP Percy Harris, contributed to the vehemence of Holtby's rejection of the offer of the headship of St Monica's in 1925:

> She [Brittain's aunt] besought me again with tears in her eyes to consider the possibility of taking on the school. My dear, how could I explain to her that it is one of my intentions to remove such schools, however admirable, from England altogether? I could only say 'Impossible', and be very sorry.[104]

Holtby's frustration with traditional gender models disseminated in girls' education is clear in a March 1932 letter to Lady Margaret Rhondda where she notes that she was

> in the throes of [...] [t]rying to compose a School Song ... I am so terrified of the mawkish stuff about purity and what-not that some of the more ladylike laureates might write, that I boldly said I would ... I am praying to the souls of Kipling, Shaw and Dame Ethel Smyth to help me. I must have something rousing and muscular that goes to a good marching tune and tramples down all nasty little giggling feminine inferiority complexes. [...] I want something grandiloquent [...] I'll look at the red, white and blue flowers and try to get that Kipling Feeling[105]

Holtby's plans to compose a school song that subverts clichéd feminine qualities and adopts instead a more stereotypical masculine form ('marching tune') and tone ('rousing', 'muscular'), reminiscent of Dame Ethel Smyth's 'The March of the Women' (1911), the anthem for the Women's Social and Political Union, which had lyrics penned by Cicely Hamilton. Holtby's reference to that 'Kipling Feeling' is partially in jest, but in the allusion to the 'red, white and blue flowers' Holtby indicates a determination to link patriotism and feminism, an association evident also in the closure to *South Riding*. Holtby's and Brittain's perceptions of the influences at play on Edwardian education for girls, in particular the concern with 'purity', are evident in correspondence from April 1935. Brittain wrote to Holtby:

> I wonder if among your or your mother's possessions at Cottingham you happen to have anything of the nature of pious talks to girls (period 1908–12)? I want my headmistress at Playden School [...] to preach a sermon to the girls on 'Purity' and would like an authentic model if possible. I thought I had a copy of Miss

---

[104] *Selected Letters*, ed. by Brittain and Handley-Taylor, p. 46. See Berry and Bostridge, *Vera Brittain: A Life* for speculation on the reasons behind Holtby's refusal, pp. 171–72.

[105] Lady Margaret Rhondda, 'Some Letters from Winifred Holtby', *Time and Tide*, 11 April 1936, p. 519.

Soulsby's 'Stray Thoughts For Girls', which would be just right, but can find no trace of it.[106]

In her reply a few days later Holtby noted:

> I'm afraid Purity doesn't seem to have been a very fruitful subject in our household. [...] But dear Miss Soulsby seems suggestive [...] Dean Farrar's talks may give the peculiarly 'Christian' atmosphere – and I suggest a quotation or two from 'Sesame & Lilies'.
>
> I looked through old *Quivers*, but the fact seems to be that Purity in girls was so much taken for granted that it was not discussed much. I never remember hearing one single school sermon (and we had two a week!) on such a questionable subject.[107]

The pedagogic models provided by Dean Farrar, Miss Soulsby, and John Ruskin closely inform the tone of the headmistress's address in *Honourable Estate*, given on the occasion of girls leaving Playden Manor and 'going out into that wider world' (p. 272). Ruskin's *Sesame and Lilies* had an avowedly pedagogic purpose: his 'Preface' notes that 'I take on me the function of the teacher'.[108] Carol Dyhouse has observed that the pattern, established in the late-Victorian period, which saw middle-class girls educated at home by a governess until the age of around ten, before being sent to a local day school, and then a select boarding school from the age of twelve or thirteen until seventeen, continued until the First World War.[109] The persistence of this tradition is reflected in Miss Hilton's address, whereby Ruskin's Victorian values are held as valuable for the schoolgirls of 1910 despite the current 'period of transition [...] with its strong movements for women's independence, for democratic freedom and for social reform' (p. 272). Miss Hilton alludes to 'the principles laid down in 1864 by Ruskin in his Preface to *Sesame and Lilies*', suggesting that they 'apply just as much to you to-day as they did to the girls of that time'.[110] Miss Hilton cites precepts by Ruskin that emphasize qualities of industry, godliness, and benevolence:

> Whatever else you may be, you must not be useless, and you must not be cruel.
> [...] God dislikes idle and cruel people more than any others – that His first

---

[106] *Selected Letters*, ed. by Brittain and Handley-Taylor, pp. 343–44.

[107] *Selected Letters*, ed. by Brittain and Handley-Taylor, p. 344.

[108] John Ruskin, *The Works of John Ruskin Volume 1 Sesame and Lilies* (Orpington: Allen, 1887 [1864]), p. xxvii.

[109] Dyhouse, *Girls Growing Up*, p. 41.

[110] There is some factual inaccuracy here: Ruskin's 'Preface', was, in fact, published in 1871, slightly later than the publication of the first edition of *Sesame and Lilies* in 1864.

order is, 'Work while you have light'; and His second, 'Be merciful while you have mercy.' (p. 273)

The second lecture of *Sesame and Lilies*, 'Lilies of Queens' Gardens', more fully addresses issues surrounding female education touched upon in the 'Preface'. Dinah Birch characterizes the critical perception of Ruskin's writings on women's education as being reflective of his 'crudely oppressive lapse from good sense and judgement'.[111] In the text, Ruskin maintains the 'separate characters' of men and women and, while he dismisses the idea of the 'superiority' of one sex over the other, he values the inculcation of qualities of subordination in the female sex. Women's education is to focus on the development of their sensibility and critical abilities in order to support men:

> Knowledge should be given her as may enable her to understand, and even to aid, the work of men: and yet it should be given, not as knowledge, – not as if it were, or could be, for her an object to know; but only to feel, and to judge.[112]

The wife is strongly associated with the home, but the home itself is envisaged as a spiritual condition, rather than a physical site: 'Wherever a true wife comes, this home is always round her.'[113]

Ruskin's emphasis on the guiding principle of the home was reflected in the philosophy of other educationists in the late-Victorian era, particularly Miss Lucy Helen Muriel Soulsby, the writer of *Stray Thoughts for Girls* (1893), one of the texts recommended by Holtby. In 1885 Miss Soulsby was appointed by Dorothea Beale to the staff of Cheltenham Ladies' College, before she took up the position of headmistress at Oxford High School for Girls in 1887. In 1897 she left to become headmistress of a small, private school for girls aged between fifteen and eighteen at Manor House, Brondesbury which rendered reverence to the home central to its educative principles and 'stood for a belief in the old-fashioned idea that a child's sympathies, memories, aspirations should be coloured and dominated by her mother'.[114] Schools along this model were in evidence elsewhere in the period; Dyhouse describes the intimate 'family-like'

[111] Dinah Birch, "'What Teachers Do You Give Your Girls?'": Ruskin and Women's Education', in *Ruskin and Gender*, ed. by Dinah Birch and Francis O'Gorman (Basingstoke: Palgrave Macmillan, 2002), pp. 121–36 (p. 134). Birch discusses Ruskin's antipathy to educating well-to-do girls at home and focuses on the lecture's censure of the role of the governess, noting his practical support of institutional education for girls at both school and university levels.

[112] Ruskin, p. 91; p. 90; p. 96.

[113] Ruskin, p. 92.

[114] *Impressions of L. H. M. S.*, ed. by E.A. and B.H.S. (London: Miss Austin, 1927), p. 80.

environments of middle-class girls' schools with headmistresses who exercised a 'maternal' influence.[115] Soulsby resisted academic, university-level education for girls, and was convinced that men and women should have different types of education: in 1895 she was the only Girls' Public Day School Company headmistress to oppose the opening of the Oxford degree to women. *Stray Thoughts for Girls* reflected these principles. In the text's first chapter, entitled 'The Virtuous Woman' which was a 'A FAREWELL BIBLE LESSON TO GIRLS ON LEAVING SCHOOL', Soulsby cautions girls about the threat 'Higher education' at university level offered to family life[116]:

> Now, what mental result, what benefit to the world, will result from an ordinary woman's reading, which can [...] be comparable to the value of a woman who diffuses a home atmosphere [...] if it gave your mother pleasure for you to be at the stupidest garden-party, I should think you were wasting your time terribly if you spent it over a book instead.[117]

Soulsby repeats Ruskin's dictum that 'wherever a true wife comes this home is always round her' and encourages an absolute commitment to uxorial and maternal values:

> Girls are often blamed for thinking too much about marriage: I think they do not do it enough [...] you are not fit to be wives now, and you should aim at becoming so, and to do that, you must be fit to manage your house and to teach your children.[118]

Such values are reflected in Miss Hilton's address, where the idealizing language sanctifies the role of the wife and mother as the 'angel in the house':

> Remember, girls, that whether you are going in for careers, or whether, as in the case of most of you here, you intend to adopt that noblest of all vocations, marriage and motherhood, it is part of your high responsibility to set an example to the men with whom you associate – your husbands, your brothers, your sons, your colleagues [...] The happiness and nobility of a Christian home are invariably the creation of the woman at its centre, so do not fail to set always before you the ideal of shining in this dark world like pure lamps of inspiration. (p. 276)

---

[115] Dyhouse, *Girls Growing Up*, p. 68.
[116] L.H.M. Soulsby, *Stray Thoughts for Girls* (London: Longmans, Green, 1910 [1893]), p. 3; p. 3; p. 9.
[117] Soulsby, p. 9.
[118] Soulsby, p. 15.

The tenor of such speeches was satirized in Holtby's 1928 sketch 'Speech Day at St Cyprian's, 2028', a reading of which elucidates both the gender subversion at the heart of Holtby's sketch and the stereotypical nature of Brittain's rendering of Miss Hilton's speech.[119] The framing narration of the story situates the speech day in the future:

> There seems to be no reason why the present custom of Headmasters from Boy's [*sic*] Schools giving good advice to the Staff and pupils of Girl's [*sic*] Schools should be the monopoly of one sex. We have indeed direct evidence that this will not always be the case.[120]

This evidence is gained through a cryptic form of prolepsis: an 'exclusive reading of the Third Inner Corridor of the Lesser Pyramid' has allowed *Time and Tide* to 'calculate the complete wording of an account in the Hants Gazette and Southern Courier for July 6th, 2028', the date and month the piece was published.[121] Both Holtby and Brittain gave speeches at boys' schools; revisions Brittain made to the typescript of *Testament of Friendship* magnify Holtby's role to emphasize how rare such an occurrence was in the interwar period: 'Mr Thornton […] listened in trepidation in 1934 when Winifred was the first woman <ever> invited to give <the address and present> away the prizes at the School Speech Day'.[122] In her sketch for *Time and Tide*, Holtby reverses the gender-specific ideals propagated by educationists such as Miss Soulsby which rendered the domestic the exclusive sphere of women: 'Remember that for the average man, his future still is that he will be a husband […] remember that no career is more sacred and honourable, nay, necessary to society than that of husband and father'; 'you all can achieve Character and Charm, and it is Character and Charm that make the Home.'[123] Such reversal of gender values seemed to cause some confusion in the writing process; material in the Holtby archive demonstrates that she went back and amended the published version of the sketch ('Headmaster <mistress> of Rugby').[124] Terms used by Soulsby ('a noble woman') are reflected in *Honourable Estate* ('lead noble lives' (p. 273)), and deployed also in Holtby's sketch ('Be good, sweet boys […] [d]o noble deeds'), reinforcing a sense of both Holtby's

[119] Winifred Holtby, 'Speech Day at St. Cyprian's, 2028', *Time and Tide*, 6 July 1928, pp. 655–56. Winifred Holtby Collection, Hull Archive and History Centre, LWH/1/1.12/01g.

[120] 'St. Cyprian's', p. 655. LWH/1/1.12/01g.

[121] Ibid.

[122] Winifred Holtby Collection, Bridlington Local Studies Centre, 'Annotated Typescript of Vera Brittain's "Testament of Friendship"'.

[123] 'St. Cyprian's', p. 656. LWH/1/1.12/01g.

[124] Ibid.

subversion of clichéd values associated with femininity and the stereotyped nature of Miss Hilton's address.[125]

Holtby's suggestion of Dean Farrar's lectures as a possible source for Brittain is significant in the context of Farrar's own children's school stories, including *Eric; or, Little by Little* (1858), an edifying tale of school life which 'was written with but one single object – the vivid inculcation of inward purity and moral purpose.'[126] Farrar's emphasis on spiritual purity is felt in Miss Hilton's speech, which reflects upon the 'purity of heart through which [...] we may learn to see God' (p. 273). Such reflections are ironically interrupted in the narrative by Jessie's 'straying' mind (p. 273) as she recalls how she heard about the fate of one of her brother Jack's public-school friends who was suspended for 'immorality'. On hearing her brother's explanation of what this 'immorality' comprised, she flees to the garden, sobbing as the cultivation of ideals of 'purity' is found to be damaging.

The documentary-like fidelity with which Brittain 'manufacture[s]' the headmistress's speech establishes the typicality of Miss Hilton.[127] The narrative voice in *Honourable Estate* casts Miss Hilton's speech into a wider historical framework, rendering the values she espouses symptomatic of Edwardian pedagogy for girls, with its mixture of conservatism and progressivism:

> Jessie did not notice the curious confusion, in Miss Hilton's address, of modern values with ancient standards. Nor did she realise how characteristic was this confusion of the teachers belonging to Miss Hilton's era – the era that was so soon to plunge its bewildered societies into the catastrophe by which their old conventions and continuities would be broken for ever. (pp. 276–77)

The form of the historical saga enables the temporally privileged perspective of the narrator. This is a device Brittain also deploys in *Testament of Youth*, where Jean Kennard has analyzed the 'double perspective' Brittain creates in her description of Uppingham Speech Day in July 1914 to argue that the scene offers a 'forceful introduction to the arguments against war' that 'dominate' the second part of *Testament*.[128] This is evident in Brittain's ironic description of the 'prophetic precept' provided by the headmaster's speech in the Uppingham School Chapel:

---

[125] Soulsby, p. 15; 'St Cyprian's', p. 656. LWH/1/1.12/01g.

[126] Frederic W. Farrar, 'Author's Preface' [1889], in *Eric; or, Little by Little* (Edinburgh: Black, 1890), p. vii.

[127] *Selected Letters*, ed. by Brittain and Handley-Taylor, p. 344.

[128] Kennard, p. 133; p. 142.

I do not recall much of the speech, which ended with a list of the precepts laid down for boys by a famous Japanese general [...] whose qualities were evidently considered entirely suitable for emulation by young English gentlemen. I shall always, however, remember the final prophetic precept, and the breathless silence which followed the Headmaster's slow, religious emphasis upon the words:

'If a man cannot be useful to his country, he is better dead.' (p. 70)

In *South Riding*, Sarah Burton's injunction to 'serve to the death if necessary' is demilitarized, rendered applicable to public – rather than military – service: 'She was thinking of Joe Astell, killing himself by overwork in the Clydeside, dying for his country more surely than thousands of those who to-day waved flags and cheered for royalty' (p. 488). Where Sarah's schoolgirls seem immune to the effect of her oratory, Brittain suggests that the Uppingham school pupils are awed into 'breathless silence' (p. 70) by the headmaster's words.

Brittain's critique of public-school militarism was informed by L.B. Pekin's anti-public school tract, *Public Schools: Their Failure and Reform.*[129] In March 1932, as she was writing *Testament*, she wrote to Holtby: 'Do you know if anyone on "T. & T." is reviewing the L.P. Pekin *[sic]* book on Public Schools? If not, do get them to; it *ought* to be noticed; it is honest, courageous, sincere, yet most devastating in its indictment.'[130] Indeed, *Time and Tide* did review the book, echoing Brittain's terms in describing it as a 'formidable indictment' of the public schools.[131] Central to this indictment is Pekin's pacifist condemnation of the militarized brand of citizenship encouraged by the public-school Officer Training Corps (OTC).[132] The OTC was established in public schools and universities in 1908, following the recommendations of a committee chaired by Lord Haldane, Secretary of State for War, which was asked to consider a solution to the shortage of officers in the armed forces. Pekin describes the OTC as a 'particularly dangerous feature' of public-school-education that is

---

[129] Isobel Hurst has previously considered the ways in which the ideals of military heroism critiqued by Brittain are informed by classical texts she encountered while at Oxford. She interprets the text as a 'feminist reading' of the *Iliad*, noting that this 'was a familiar text for classically educated soldiers; its aristocratic code of male friendship and individual glory resembled the public school culture from which Brittain initially felt excluded by her gender'. Hurst, p. 219; p. 216.

[130] *Selected Letters*, ed. by Brittain and Handley-Taylor, p. 206.

[131] Stephen King-Hall, 'Public Schools and Public Boys', *Time and Tide Second Spring Book Supplement*, p. 467.

[132] Pekin's anti-militarism is informed by a pacifist position. Where Peter Parker mirrors Pekin's emphasis on the role of the OTC in preparing schoolboys for war, Gordon Corrigan's military history demonstrates that, in 1914, Britain was the least militarized nation in Europe and was alone in having no compulsory military service. Peter Parker, *The Old Lie: The Great War and the Public School Ethos* (London: Constable, 1987); Gordon Corrigan, *Mud, Blood and Poppycock: Britain and the First World War* (London: Cassell Military, 2004).

'perverted from a strictly educational instrument' with 'no less than 60,000 boys between the ages of fourteen and eighteen being carefully trained for war'.[133] While technically voluntary, Pekin claims that the 'moral coercion' on behalf of schools and parents to join the OTC 'amounts to absolute compulsion'.[134] Pekin compares the figures spent by the country on the League of Nations (£120,000 a year) and the OTC (£200,000 a year) and impassionedly asks:

> Might it not [...] be time to consider how far we are furthering the peace of the world by teaching our schoolboys to regard war as a natural thing, and training them during their most impressionable years in the business of wholesale killing?[135]

The significant role of the OTC in Uppingham life is evident in Brittain's description of her visit: Roland, like her brother Edward, was in the OTC, and appeared on the morning of the speech day dressed in his 'colour-sergeant's uniform at the corps review' (p. 68). Following the end of term, Brittain notes that Roland, Edward, and Victor were due to spend two weeks in an OTC camp in Aldershot, the annual summer camp which offered different school OTC groups the opportunity to meet one another.[136] Roland with his 'military ancestors [...] took the O.T.C. very seriously' (p. 68) and Brittain suggests that his commitment to military service imbues him with a sense of gravitas that renders him remote: 'I did not feel inclined to tease him any more' (p. 68). In retrospect, the militaristic overtones of the day feel 'prescient' and Brittain acknowledges that while the masters may have sensed this

> I do not believe that any of the gaily clad visitors who watched the corps carrying out its manoeuvres and afterwards marching so impressively into the Chapel for the Speech Day service, in the least realised how close at hand was the fate for which it had prepared itself, or how many of those deep and strangely thrilling boys' voices were to be silent in death before another Speech Day. (pp. 68–69)

Once again, Brittain employs her 'double perspective' which concatenates past and present experience, creating a sense of tragic inevitability to the fate of the schoolboys. Where Brittain positions the schoolboys as depersonalized victims of a militaristic educational ideology ('it had prepared itself'), Pekin's analysis of them is more incriminating; they are 'persuaded into thinking it natural and ordinary

---

[133] L.B. Pekin, *Public Schools: Their Failure and Their Reform* (London: Hogarth Press, 1932), p. 109; p. 109; pp. 109–10.
[134] *Public Schools*, p. 112.
[135] Figures are cited by Pekin, *Public Schools*, on p. 110; p. 123.
[136] Pekin, *Public Schools*, p. 120.

to hunt down and shoot other people who were our "enemies".[137] This double perspective is evident in another book that Brittain records reading at the time of writing *Testament*: Robert Graves's *Good-bye to All That*. In her March 1932 correspondence with Holtby she implicitly compares Graves's memoir with her own: 'He seems to have spent about a year in answering correspondents, writing to newspapers, repudiating libel actions, quarrelling with his family, etc. I suppose if my book *ever* is finished and published I shall have a similar fate.'[138] Like Brittain's, Graves's narrative juxtaposes school experience with First World War experience, inscribing within the memoir a sense of cause and effect. For instance, in describing the results of a school debate on 'this House is in favour of compulsory military service', a motion that Graves suggests was met with only six noes, he notes 'of the six noes, Nevill Barbour and I are, I believe, the only ones who survived the war'.[139]

In May 1934 Brittain was invited to speak at Leighton Park, a boys' Quaker school, that advocated an 'alternative' ideal of citizenship to that propagated by the school OTC.[140] Such pacifistic models of education were praised by Pekin, who notes the 'relief work of [...] the Society of Friends' that offers a 'better training in courage and endurance than school military training does'.[141] Brittain's speech had a strongly pacifist message:

> I talked to the boys about the task of their generation being to make the collective system work [...] and that they must trust my impaired generation to do our best to keep the peace machinery in being for them for ten years.[142]

The tenor of Brittain's speech seems to redeem the militaristic values advanced in the headmaster's speech at Uppingham Speech Day; and, indeed, the speech day at Leighton Park was ineluctably linked in Brittain's mind with this earlier event: 'It was all rather moving, and I couldn't help thinking of Sunday evening chapel at Uppingham Speech Day in 1914 – which I had mentioned to the boys – and wondering what fate was awaiting their particular generation of youth.'[143] The lingering, pastoral description of Brittain's visit to Leighton Park ('outside it was still light; there were lilacs and copper beeches [...] and the wind was blowing long furrows across the bright green long grass') contains echoes of the

---

[137] *Public Schools*, pp. 112–13.
[138] *Selected Letters*, ed. by Brittain and Handley-Taylor, p. 210, emphasis in original.
[139] Robert Graves, *Goodbye to All That* (London: Penguin, 2000), p. 53. Further references to this edition will be included in brackets after the citation.
[140] Pekin, *Public Schools*, p. 123.
[141] Ibid.
[142] *Selected Letters*, ed. by Brittain and Handley-Taylor, pp. 277–78.
[143] *Selected Letters*, ed. by Brittain and Handley-Taylor, p. 278.

description of the 'three radiant days' (p. 69) at Uppingham in 1914.[144] In the retrospective mode that informs *Testament*, Brittain feels that 'an atmosphere of brooding expectation [...]must surely have hung about the sunlit flower gardens and the shining green fields' (p. 69).

Brittain's own pedagogic activity was not only personally redemptive; her pacifist message was disseminated more broadly in educational circles. In 1934 Holtby wrote to Brittain:

> You *must* read 'The Modern Schools Handbook'. The Leighton Park chapter is largely a sermon on the text of that passage from the 'Testament': 'I do not believe that a League of Nations or a Kellogg Pact, or any Disarmament Conference ... ' and he calls it 'that noblest of all war books.'[145]

As Holtby notes, E.B. Castle, the headmaster of Leighton Park, whom Brittain identified as 'young, speculative, and [having] all our own views', cites Brittain's discussion of the need to give peace the same 'element of sanctified loveliness which [...] glorifies war' in the context of his discussion of the OTC, where he suggests that

> one of the problems we have set ourselves consciously to face is that of providing a moral and physical equivalen[t] for the O.T.C. [...] I am convinced that the ultimate influences behind it do not make for a constructive view of citizenship.[146]

Brittain's description of the Uppingham Speech Day thus offers the foundations of her critique of militaristic ideology, providing an analysis of its role in the life of 'middle-class England – its interests, its morals, its social ideals, its politics' (p. xxv). *Testament of Youth* was both informed by anti-militarist educational tracts and contributed to the development of an internationalist and pacifist pedagogy, as educationists such as Leighton applied the text to educational practice and disseminated ideals inspired by Brittain in educational pamphlets.

Coda: Winifred Holtby, Vera Brittain, and the NUWT

For both Brittain and Holtby, the line between their creative work and their work to influence pedagogic practice and educational reform was blurred. Both self-consciously produced critiques of the politics of pedagogy based on

[144] Ibid.
[145] *Selected Letters*, ed. by Brittain and Handley-Taylor, p. 288.
[146] *Selected Letters*, ed. by Brittain and Handley-Taylor, p. 277. *Handbook*, ed. by Blewitt, pp. 206–07; p. 206.

documentary sources and educational debates. While their engagement with organizations such as the NUWT and the Six Point Group, as well as their work in schools, reinforced the urgency of their critique, for Woolf this documentary method also signalled creative limitations: after reading *South Riding* she noted of Holtby: 'She has a photographic mind. [...] She's a ventriloquist, not a creator' (L6, p. 382). The impact the two had on educational reform was acknowledged on 5 April 1961, when the NUWT hosted a Victory Luncheon at the Café Royal, Regent Street. The meeting represented both the culmination of the work of the NUWT and its grand finale. Coinciding with the date of the establishment of equal pay for men and women teachers, it was decided that the union should be disbanded: the feeling was that further work to advance equality of status between men and women teachers would be better achieved by 'other means than a union for women teachers only'.[147] Brittain enthusiastically agreed to speak at the event, and there was a degree of timeliness to the invitation:

> I am just back from a series of commemorations in Yorkshire of the 25th anniversary of Winifred Holtby's death. You will recall the many articles that she wrote in favour of equal pay for teachers in 'Time and Tide' and elsewhere, and I know how she would rejoice with me that your objective is achieved.[148]

Holtby's memory suffused the event, with the NUWT organizer noting in correspondence with Brittain: 'I wish that Miss Holtby and Miss Froud could have been present next year'.[149] On the day a 'tribute' was paid to Brittain and Holtby, when Brittain was introduced as one of the event's three speakers who were 'representing not only themselves but a partner'.[150] The pair were

> journalists and novelists [...] who gave their time and their talents to helping [...] women to gain justice – equal franchise and equal pay. We thank you Vera Brittain and Winifred Holtby for this and for the colour they brought to the movement.[151]

In correspondence, NUWT organizers both emphasized the significance of the two women's involvement in the movement and demonstrated the same commitment to the politics of pedagogy inherent in both writers' fictional depictions of teachers, and their feminist-pedagogic activism: 'I cannot express how much we owe to you both and how greatly we enjoyed that work'.[152]

---

[147] 'Victory Luncheon', UWT/B/10/1 ©UCL Institute of Education Archives.
[148] Ibid.
[149] Ibid.
[150] Ibid.
[151] Ibid.
[152] Ibid.

3

Writers of *The Old School*: Graham Greene, Walter Greenwood, Stephen Spender, Antonia White, and Arthur Calder-Marshall

In July 1933 Graham Greene wrote in his diary: 'I want to propose a symposium to a publisher. "The Old School", studies of the horror of the public school by about ten prominent young authors with the schools mentioned by name.'[1] The volume, edited by Greene, eventually also included essays on girls' schools, one essay on a grammar school, and one essay by Walter Greenwood on a council-run state school. It was published in July 1934 – its essayists symbolically bursting out of the school gates with their rebellious insurrection on the cusp of the summer holidays. Greene clearly intended to attract the brightest and best to contribute: in correspondence he noted that he had 'various distinguished authors telling candidly the horrors of their schools. Among others I have Harold Nicolson, Richard Hughes, Arnot Robertson, Elizabeth Bowen, Theodora Benson, William Plomer.'[2] Richard Hughes was not included in the final volume, but Greene added W.H. Auden, Antonia White, Walter Greenwood, L.P. Hartley, Seán O'Failáin, Anthony Powell, Arthur Calder-Marshall, J.N. Richards, Stephen Spender, Derek Verschoyle, and E.L. Grant Watson to his list. The fact that Greene frames the political critique of his generation through the lens of school experience is peculiarly 1930s; yet, as I shall discuss, in many of the volume's essays there is a real resistance to making an overt political statement.

My reading of *The Old School* acknowledges the diversity of the voices presented through an analysis of the collection itself and Greene's editorial contribution, as well as the essays of Walter Greenwood, Stephen Spender, Arthur Calder-Marshall, and Antonia White. These contributors were all, more broadly, school-minded in the period, producing, as I shall explore, novels,

---

[1] Norman Sherry, *The Life of Graham Greene: Volume I 1904–1939* (London: Cape, 1989), p. 492.
[2] Sherry, pp. 492–93.

autobiographies, poetry, contributions to teachers' papers, and educational tracts, and they were all interested in the social, ontological, and cultural implications of education. Max Saunders recognizes the form of latent social critique evident in 1930s autobiography, emphasizing the 'documentary' element in life-writing of the period that provided 'testimony not of the self alone but of society'.[3] This analysis considers these writers, from an array of educational backgrounds, to suggest how, alongside their individual analyses of educational experience, they attempted to arrive at more communal forms of literary expression to both critique current social realities and represent alternative political structures.

Graham Greene, social class, and old school loyalty

In August 1934 Greene wrote to his brother: '*The Old School* went into a second impression this week-end, 1500 copies sold. Not bad for a joke of that kind.'[4] The volume was produced during the brief, six-month window of Greene's membership of the Independent Labour Party from August 1933, and his later comments register an embarrassment at the collection that could be attributed to the political positions it embodies. This section considers the range of attitudes expressed in the collection as a whole, and the editorial decisions that seem to underpin *The Old School*. Through reference to Greene's other autobiographical works which reflect upon his schooldays, *The Lawless Roads* (1939) and *A Sort of Life* (1971), I also add to the diverse range of critical perspectives on Greene's politics, which variously position him as politically ambivalent, vaguely left-wing, and right-wing, to consider how his editorial contributions to *The Old School* in the volume's 'Preface' and conclusion ('The Last Word') reveal both the nature of, and the tensions in, his politics at his most 'Leftist' moment.[5]

3   Max Saunders, *Self-Impression: Life-Writing, Autobiografiction, and the Forms of Modern Literature* (Oxford: Oxford University Press, 2010), p. 510.
4   Graham Greene to Hugh Greene, 18 August 1934, in *Graham Greene: A Life in Letters*, ed. by Richard Greene (London: Little, Brown, 2007), p. 65.
5   Valentine Cunningham explores Greene's involvement with the politically neutral publication, *Night & Day*, which ran from 1 July 1937 to 23 December 1937, suggesting that he was the magazine's 'reddish literary editor'. Brian Diemert notes that Greene was 'politically ambivalent, sympathetic to ideals of social change but reluctant to tie himself to any single political platform', while Bernard Bergonzi suggests he was 'apolitical or right wing'. Maria Couto, however, reclaims Greene from the implicit conservatism of his faith: 'Catholicism did not mean for Greene [...] a conversion to conservatism.' Valentine Cunningham, 'Neutral?: 1930s Writers and Taking Sides', in *Class, Culture and Social Change: A New View of the 1930s*, ed. by Frank Gloversmith (Brighton: Harvester Press, 1980), pp. 45–69 (p. 54); Brian Diemert, *Graham Greene's Thrillers and the 1930s* (London: McGill-Queen's University Press, 1996), p. 23; Bergonzi, p. 3; Maria Couto, *Graham Greene: On the Frontier: Politics and Religion in the Novels* (Basingstoke: Macmillan, 1988), p. 4.

Greene's decision to produce the volume was, in some ways, a natural consequence of his background. He was from a family of educationists: his father was headmaster of Berkhamsted, the public school that Greene not just attended, but also grew up in; his uncle was a civil servant at the Board of Education; and one of his aunts was a 'progressive' who ran a school in South Africa and was friends with Olive Schreiner.[6] Greene himself 'had a horror of becoming involved in teaching. It was a profession into which you could so easily slip [...] by accident' (p. 112). After graduating, he did briefly take an undemanding job in a Derbyshire village, working for a widow who was concerned about her son being 'overworked' (p. 113), with lodgings provided in a hotel. The curriculum blended the typical and the esoteric: in addition to teaching his pupil games, mathematics, and Latin (both of which Greene had 'forgotten'), and with no expertise in the area himself, Greene decided to teach carpentry, and together they embarked on building a toy theatre. This was a challenge too far, so a rabbit hutch for a non-existent rabbit was settled on instead.

Greene's reading in this period also more immediately stimulated the production of *The Old School*. In June 1933 he wrote a review of Hugh Talbot's *Gentlemen – the Regiment*, the story of Alastair Chappell's life in the army during the period of the Crimean War. Greene suggested that it was 'an embarrassing book [...] a school-boy's daydream of Honour, Love, Back to the Wall, The Regiment'.[7] Greene went on to criticize school honour in his conclusion to *The Old School* as 'silly' and a 'hypocritical tradition'.[8] The same July 1933 diary entry in which Greene conceived of this project also alludes to his reading of Robert Graves's autobiography, *Good-bye to All That* (1929). Greene found that the volume was 'full of the right kind of anecdote, ones which set the creative instinct going'.[9] Graves felt, on leaving Charterhouse, that the public-school spirit was 'fundamental evil' (p. 36), but after discussing the 'very worst' (p. 37) of Charterhouse with his friend, they recognized that 'in another twenty years' time we'll forget [...] and we'll send our sons to Charterhouse for sentiment's sake' (p. 37). The titular phrase of *The Old School* is used by Graves as he notes: 'This must not be construed as an attack on my old school' (p. 37). Greene's frustration with the persistence of the public-school spirit, and a contention

---

[6] Graham Greene, *Fragments of Autobiography: A Sort of Life and Ways of Escape* (London: Penguin, 1991), p. 26. Further references to this edition will be included in brackets after the citation.

[7] Graham Greene, 'Fiction', *The Spectator*, 30 June 1933, p. 956.

[8] Graham Greene, *The Old School: Essays by Divers Hands*, ed. by Graham Greene (London: Cape, 1934), p. 253. Further references to this edition will be included in brackets after the citation.

[9] Sherry, p. 492.

of the system's urgent need for reform against a backdrop of complacency, is a driving force behind his collection, as his editorial interventions demonstrate. The same diary entry also records an idea for a 'slightly Kafka novel' about an insurrectionary pupil who, at night, causes disarray to school classrooms.[10] The idea for a school novel is one to which Greene returned. In *A Sort of Life*, published in 1971, he records revisiting Berkhamsted 'some twelve years ago, because I had started a novel about school, I revisited the scene and found no change. I abandoned the novel – I couldn't bear mentally living again for several years in these surroundings' (p. 54).

Indeed, as he records in *A Sort of Life*, Greene's time at school was one of psychological strain as he was agonized by conflicting loyalties to his peers and his father. As 'relief' (p. 59) from these tensions, Greene's parents agreed to let him spend Sunday afternoons at home, and his brother, who was undergoing medical training, suggested 'psycho-analysis as a possible solution, and my father – an astonishing thing in 1920 – agreed' (p. 68). Greene underwent psychoanalysis with Kenneth Richmond, who was publishing psychoanalytically informed works on education in this period. Greene records finding his book 'on educational theory' 'rather dull reading' (p. 72) when he was young. By this time, Richmond had published several books in this field: *The Permanent Values in Education* (1917), *Education for Liberty* (1918), and *The Curriculum* (1919). It is difficult to know precisely which of Richmond's books Greene had read, but the underlying tenor of Richmond's educational doctrine; his concern to clear new ground for a curriculum better attuned to psychoanalytic understanding, and his privileging of the freedom of the child, alongside his underlying conviction of the significance of school experience in development, implicitly informs Greene's volume.

Janet Montefiore recognizes the Freudian underpinnings of 1930s autobiography, arguing that they are 'case-book' memoirs that describe the writer's 'social construction'.[11] She suggests of *The Old School* that 'the story of these writers' educations is [...] one of youthful subjection to false values from which the maturing man painfully struggles free'.[12] It is difficult to ascribe a consistent trajectory to the memoirs included, however. The diffuse nature of the collection was recognized in E.M. Forster's review in *The Spectator*: 'The editor, Mr Graham Greene (Berkhamsted), shovels everything together as well

---

[10] Ibid.

[11] Montefiore, p. 45.

[12] Montefiore, p. 49.

as he can, but the book could, I think, have cohered better' and indeed in his 'Preface' Greene suggests the diversity of perspectives awaiting the reader, who will find 'a little that is good and a little that is astonishingly bad and a great deal that is almost too funny to be true' (p. 8).[13] The rather no-nonsense conclusion to Theodora Benson's essay dismisses the significance of schooldays for wider development – a dismissal that imperils the very urgency of *The Old School* itself:

> Many modern writers make out that schools, and unhappiness at schools, have dire effects on the characters and futures of the pupils. It just isn't so. [...] [I]f I ever try to blame anything concerning me off on to the old school I shall be a liar. (p. 44)

Even those who had a wretched time at school seem reluctant to ascribe absolute blame to the school itself. E. Arnot Robertson writes of Sherborne:

> I would like to make clear at the beginning that I know I am being unjust to the school because I was unhappy there; presumably there must have been something good about it, for everyone was not as unhappy as I was. (p. 173)

Writers in the collection show an awareness of the latent, negative, editorial assumptions underpinning the collection. Elizabeth Bowen writes in her happy account of life at Downe House: 'I say with deference to the susceptibilities of possible other essayists in this book that I consider my old school an exceedingly good one' (pp. 57–58).

Whether by coincidence or editorial design, certain themes recur across the collection. In a gesture to the volume's title, most writers in the collection make specific use of the phrase the 'old school' in their essay, creating a loose sense of editorial unification. Greene's correspondence indicates that this title was loaded: the collection would be 'called ironically The Old School'.[14] The precise implications of the title are criticized by one contributor to the collection, the novelist L.P. Hartley: on a sleepless night in a sleeper car, Hartley reviews his time at Harrow 'urging my memories to assume the ironical character suggested by the title of this book' (p. 85), but finds that the nervous complaints with which he is afflicted cannot be attributed to his schooling: 'when I was at Harrow, I remembered, these things afflicted me much less' (p. 86). Like Benson and Bowen, who both offer broadly favourable accounts of their schooling, Hartley 'realized that the objections to the Public School system which I have often voiced [...] were not founded on my own experience at Harrow' (p. 87).

---

[13] E.M. Forster, 'Review of *The Old School*', *The Spectator*, 27 July 1934, p. 136.
[14] Sherry, p. 492.

A number of the essays consider the standardized product of the public school. The tone of this criticism varies. For L.P. Hartley, the accusation of standardization was simply inaccurate: 'The familiar charge that public schools turn out all boys according to a pattern, did not hold good of my contemporaries at Harrow' (pp. 87–88). J.N. Richards takes a benevolent view on the public schools' tendency to standardization: 'It seems to me that in a world where standardization is the rule of life [...] it is the plain duty of our schools to fall into line with this tendency' as outliers to this process are 'misfits and the idle poor of the modern world' (p. 168). W.H. Auden's matter-of-fact comments suggest that the public school's '*raison d'être*' is the 'mass production of gentlemen' (p. 11), while the writer and politician Harold Nicolson, of an older generation than most of those included in the collection, argues that the type of product created by the public school is an anachronism. He notes the pre-war public school's purpose to 'provide a large number of standardized young men fitted for the conquest, administration and retention of a vast Oriental Empire' (p. 105) that was no longer in existence.

Derek Verschoyle offers the most politicized critique of the public schools' products, suggesting that public school 'character' equates to 'a composite of certain standardized qualities [...] in whose perpetuation the system has a vested interest' (p. 209). Verschoyle's scathing criticism deploys imagery drawn from mechanization to reinforce his point: the public schoolboy is a 'product' (p. 213) and 'a smoothly turning cog in the machine' (p. 214). This 'standardized commodity' (p. 202) has all traces of individual personality removed and is 'a model of impersonal orthodoxy, from which personal determination has been eliminated. It is the manufacturer's mark that counts' (p. 202). Most damningly, his loyalty is 'absurd' leading to 'class-consciousness and smug confidence in his own superiority' (p. 214). Such loyalty reflects upon the wider political situation and leads to conservative stagnation: 'It was the Public Schools which pulled the country through in the General Strike' (p. 214). While Verschoyle renders the schoolboy complicit in a conservative social system, Greene, in 'The Last Word', more sympathetically positions the schoolboy as a victim of the educational system:

> To me there emerges from these essays more than anything else the great importance of individuals to the schoolboy's happiness, while the system, by which I mean the rules, routine and tradition of the school, seems generally designed only for the convenience of the authorities and often works for the boy's unhappiness. (p. 250)

The essays in the collection generally focus on individual recollection, rather than educational theories. The only writer to refer specifically to an educational theorist is Harold Nicolson, who considers the French philosopher Alain's *Propos sur l'Education*, published in 1932, which 'proclaims his opposition to the psychological treatment of the young' (p. 103). The writer and biologist E.L. Grant Watson, an early pupil at the pioneering progressive school, Bedales, which became co-educational in 1898, indicates a deliberate aversion to considering educational theories. His comments suggest that such a consideration is outside the remit of the volume: 'It is not within the scope of this essay to discuss the merits or de-merits of co-education; that is far too large and controversial a subject, I only wish to recall memories' (p. 226). A notable exception to this emphasis on personal recollection is Verschoyle's essay which, while nominally about his experience at Malvern, focuses in much more general terms on the conditions and politics of the public school, candidly considering homosexuality in schools, and often confining personal experience to footnotes.

Where Auden reinforces the current relevance of his school experience with his short-sighted declaration that 'at school I lived in a Fascist state' (p. 17), other essayists neutralize their criticism through the suggestion that their experiences are no longer relevant; William Plomer notes of Rugby: 'I refer to the school as it seemed to me then; I believe it no longer exists' (p. 134). This is an attitude directly criticized by Greene in 'The Last Word' which objects in particular to Nicolson's comments:

> The final sentence of Mr. Harold Nicolson's essay will probably be echoed by many of our unfavourable critics. 'All this was true once; but to-day it is out of date: "things" have changed.' When people speak of 'things' changing, they refer [...] not to what is praised but to what is condemned. What Mr. Auden finds to admire in Holt, Mr. Powell in Eton, Mr. Hartley in Harrow, Mr. Spender in University College School is taken as permanent; the public schools, these critics believe, are slowly but surely progressing towards perfection, particularly now that education is in the hands of younger men.
>
> But the young head master is not necessarily more open to modern ideas than the middle-aged. [...]
>
> I am thinking of my own school. I do not believe that it is family pride which makes me admire the headmaster's achievement (he is my father). He was an admirably progressive head master, never more so than in his later years at the school. [...]
>
> But my father retired, a young man was appointed, and it was the young man who preferred to follow the older tradition. (pp. 247–48)

Greene's criticism is evocative of Graves's ironic citation of the conviction of the 'Old Carthusian' that 'The moral tone of the school has improved out of all recognition since those days' (p. 37). This quotation also embodies other characteristics of Greene's editorial interventions in the collection: his allusion to other essays in the work as he pulls its diffuse strands together; his drawing on the qualities of his own school experience at Berkhamsted as an opportunity to deduce wider conclusions on the educational system; and his offering of a more overtly politicized, and negative, assessment of the public school than that which characterizes some of the essays.

The polemical tone of Greene's 'Preface' serves as a contrast to the heterogeneous tone of the essays which follow. The 'Preface' notes the volume's intention of defining the experiences of a generation that missed the war: 'Most of the writers were at school in the years of the war or the years immediately after the war' (p. 8), while also seeking to defer judgement to the current generation of schoolboys, exemplifying the volume's latent masculinized focus, despite the essays on girls' schools by Elizabeth Bowen, Antonia White, Theodora Benson, and E. Arnot Robertson: 'The ideal critics of this book would be found among the boys now at school' (p. 8). Greene notes 'how class-conscious these schools remain' and maintains that the public school is 'doomed' (p. 7), suggesting that 'whatever the political changes in this country during the next few years one thing surely is almost certain: the class distinctions will not remain unaltered and the public school, as it exists to-day, will disappear' (pp. 7–8). Such an assessment in fact offers a rather biased summation of the actual strength of feeling supporting the public schools' continuation: *The Observer*'s reviewer noted that 'he is [...] underrating the toughness of the middle class [...] he has reckoned without the younger schoolmasters, quite a number of whom are determined to build better on the old foundations'; while an August 1934 article in the *New Statesman and Nation* reproached the Labour Party for its refusal to properly address the public-school issue in its 1934 report on education, hoping that 'some of the gaps to which we have drawn attention will be filled in by a further and fuller statement'.[15] On reviewing the collection on its reissue in 1984, Anthony Burgess found that Greene's anticipation of the impact and reach of socialist politics was typically thirties:

> [*The Old School* is] odorous of the time when fascism was a flash in the pan and the future lay with the socialist levellers. What Mr Greene did not foresee was

---

[15] Ivor Brown, 'Looking Backward. Public Schools and Others', *The Observer*, 12 August 1934, p. 5; Unsigned article, 'Towards a Classless Education', *New Statesman and Nation*, 4 August 1934, p. 146.

[...] the general dissatisfaction with State schools, the recovery of the conviction that education has, to be good, to be elitist.[16]

Greene's association between the public-school system and the capitalist structure was being made elsewhere in the period, by figures such as Arthur Calder-Marshall, as I shall discuss, and Winston Churchill's nephews, Giles and Esmond Romilly, who produced the anti-public-school magazine *Out of Bounds*. The brothers noted that 'in criticising the public schools, it is essential to bear in mind the part they play in relation to capitalist society'.[17] Greene makes this association explicit in 'The Last Word' where, in his discussion of the progressive nature of his father's own tenure as headmaster, the school is positioned as a paradigm for society: '[At Berkhamsted] an enthusiast was even allowed to start a system of self-government. It failed (you cannot be a socialist in a capitalist state), but he was given time and sympathy for his experiment' (p. 248). Greene argues for the untenability of socialism within the current social and economic structure. The formulaic, parenthetic comment is also, perhaps, suggestive of a political philosophy based on logic and argument, rather than personal conviction. 'The Last Word' further associates the public school's deficiencies with the impoverished working class in a myopic comparison:

> It is a curious system, but one common to all public schools, which prevents a normal sexual relationship and punishes harshly any temporary substitute. It is the method of the State which offers no other means than theft to an unemployed man to feed his family adequately and then punishes him when he steals. (p. 254)

The rhetorical hyperbole here does not tolerate the many (obvious) differences between the public schoolboy and the working-class unemployed as *The Old School* mounts a class-based critique of an institution, while paradoxically undermining any sense of empathy with the working-class condition.

Greene's original conception of the project reveals that a breach of old school loyalty was an integral part of the volume's intent: he wanted to produce a collection of 'studies of the horror of the public school [...] with the schools mentioned by name'.[18] The exposure and revelatory value of the proper name destroys the cloak of anonymity and advances a new standard of old school *dis*loyalty. Ross McKibbin comments that 'the [public] schools' goals were detached from wider social goals' and Greene criticizes the loyalties prompted

---

[16] Anthony Burgess, 'Class of '34', *The Observer*, 19 August 1984, p. 19.
[17] Julian Symons, *The Thirties: A Dream Revolved* (London: Cresset Press, 1960), p. 29.
[18] Sherry, p. 492.

by the single-class, single-sex nature of the public-school system, suggesting instead that more socially diverse, communal loyalties should be fostered:[19]

> It is at least better that he should learn loyalty to a town which includes all classes and both sexes than to an institution consisting only of his own sex and his own class.
>
> Why, in any case, he should feel more loyal to a school which is paid to teach him than to a butcher who is paid to feed him I cannot understand. I am afraid my want of understanding is responsible for this book. (p. 256)

Winifred Holtby's review of the collection in *The Schoolmistress* 'answers its compiler's [...] challenge from her own [...] experience', finding that a 'modern county secondary school' she had recently visited in Lincolnshire did not display the same alienation between town and school life that Greene detects in the public schools.[20] This school

> has become a centre of activity and culture in the little town [...]. It sets a standard of curiosity, energy and community life. [...] [T]he changes wrought in the towns where they are built by schools of this type answer Mr. Graham Greene's statement [...]. The enthusiasm, idealism and gaiety of such institutions provide a cause for loyalty.[21]

In his later review, Burgess felt Greene's comments here were disingenuous: 'Mr Greene could and can understand. [...] If cookery is an art, how much more is teaching.'[22]

Greene examined the psychological conditions behind old school loyalty in *England Made Me*, which he began planning in August 1933 and started writing in November 1933, as he was compiling *The Old School*.[23] Sherry suggests that the 'ironic title, refers to the forming of a certain type of character not so much by England, as by the English public school', noting that Anthony and Minty 'owe their twisted characters to their schooldays. Neither can rid himself of the indelible stamp of his public school.'[24] While Maria Couto suggests that the novel 'illustrates a last, long, lingering look at the virtues that went into the making of the old nation-states and the values and education of Greene's own social class',

---

[19] *Classes and Cultures*, p. 246.

[20] Winifred Holtby, 'The Old School', *The Schoolmistress*, 9 August 1934, p. 493 and p. 500 (p. 493; p. 500).

[21] 'The Old School', p. 500.

[22] Burgess, p. 19.

[23] Norman Sherry notes that the manuscript is dated from November 1933, and his letters demonstrate that he was planning the novel on 18 August 1933. Sherry, p. 491.

[24] Sherry, p. 491.

Greene cynically presents the manipulations Anthony is able to effect under the premise of old school loyalties as he claims false allegiance to Harrow in order to play the English class system to promote the cause of his various scams:[25]

> 'What is that tie?' she [Kate] asked. 'Surely it's not ... '
>
> 'No, no,' he said, flashing the truth at her so unexpectedly that she was caught a victim to the charm she hated. 'I've promoted myself. It's Harrow.'[26]

Just as Captain Grimes in Evelyn Waugh's *Decline and Fall* (1928) associates his public-school background with an immunity from social ills ('That's the public school system all over. [...] [T]hey never let you down'),[27] while in conversation with Minty, an actual old Harrovian, Anthony plays on the loyalty of old school ties: 'Harrovians ought to stick together anyway. You don't get your pickings unless you stick together' (p. 59).

The attitude that is manifested in *The Old School* is also inconsistent with Greene's analysis of school life elsewhere, as he draws on personal reminiscences which are tainted by the kind of 'memorable' investigation of childhood trauma that Cunningham praises.[28] Greene's position at Berkhamsted was compromised by his status as son of the school's headmaster. *A Sort of Life* recalls that one school bully recognized – and exploited – his 'conflict of loyalties, loyalties to my age group, loyalty to my father and brother' (p. 60), both of whom were figures of authority in the school: 'Was my father not the headmaster? I was like the son of a quisling in a country under occupation. My elder brother Raymond was a school prefect and head of the house – in other words one of Quisling's collaborators' (pp. 54–55). His metaphorical status as a traitor-collaborator with the enemy led to his social exclusion: 'I was not a member of the resistance – I was Quisling's son. I had often to go begging that my name might be included in groups who had no desire for my company' (p. 59).

This image of self-division, the 'struggle of conflicting loyalties' (p. 59), is one that dominates the atmospheric early pages of *The Lawless Roads* (1939). The text opens with a reminiscence of a young Greene, hiding 'in secret – on the dark croquet lawn' where he could 'hear the rabbit moving behind me' and the strains of the school orchestra's Saturday evening concert:[29]

[25] Couto, p. 92.

[26] Graham Greene, *England Made Me* (London: Vintage, 2006), p. 15. Further reference to this edition will be included in brackets after the citation.

[27] Evelyn Waugh, *Decline and Fall* (London: Penguin, 2001), p. 28.

[28] *British Writers*, p. 129.

[29] Graham Greene, *The Lawless Roads* (London: Penguin, 1992), p. 13. Further references to this edition will be included in brackets after the citation.

Two countries just here lay side by side. From the croquet lawn [...] you could always see – dominatingly – the great square Victorian buildings of garish brick: they looked down like skyscrapers on a small green countryside [...] You had to step carefully: the border was close beside your gravel path. From my mother's bedroom window [...] you looked straight down into the quad, where the hall and the chapel and the classrooms stood. If you pushed open a green baize door in a passage by my father's study, you entered another passage deceptively similar, but none the less you were on alien ground. There would be a slight smell of iodine from the matron's room, of damp towels from the changing rooms, of ink everywhere. [...]

I was an inhabitant of both countries: on Saturday and Sunday afternoons of one side of the baize door, the rest of the week of the other. How can life on a border be other than restless? You are pulled by different ties of hate and love. [...] In the land of the skyscrapers, of stone stairs and cracked bells ringing early, one was aware of fear and hate, a kind of lawlessness – appalling cruelties could be practised without a second thought [...] Hell lay about them in their infancy.

[...] I escaped surreptitiously for an hour at a time: unknown to frontier guards, I stood on the wrong side of the border looking back – I should have been listening to Mendelssohn, but instead I heard the rabbit restlessly cropping near the croquet hoops. (pp. 13–14)

The switch between the first person and second person throughout this passage embodies the sense of conflict the young Greene experienced as the son of the school headmaster with the 'green baize door' (referenced again in *A Sort of Life*, and a detail Spender borrows in *The Backward Son*) signalling the uneasy division between home and school life. The rhetorical question ('How can life on a border be other than restless?') impresses upon the reader Greene's personal conflict. The imagery used throughout – of frontiers, borders, and alien ground – evokes Greene's sense, as the headmaster's son, of being an interloper in enemy territory. This evocation of divided loyalties and petrified consciousness echoes 'Ode V' of Auden's *The Orators*, a text Greene had reviewed, as discussed in Chapter 1. It was in these moments on the croquet lawn, Greene suggests, that 'faith came to me [...] I began to believe in heaven because I believed in hell' (p. 14). This was the hell of the school ('Hell lay about them in their infancy') expressed in a corrupting distortion of Wordsworth's adulatory exclamation in 'Ode: Intimations of Mortality': 'Heaven lay about us in our infancy!'.

The 'lawlessness' of school with its cracked bells, skyscrapers, and stone steps (all elements which could themselves evoke the Mexican scene that this 'Prologue' introduces) becomes curiously expressive of the adult world that the text goes on to consider. The end of the 'Prologue' displaces Greene's adult experience at the Mexico–America 'border' (p. 23) onto this childhood scene:

> The rabbit moved among the croquet hoops and a clock struck: God was there and might intervene before the music ended. The great brick buildings rose at the end of the lawn against the sky – like the hotels in the United States, which you can watch from Mexico leaning among the stars, across the International bridge. (p. 21)

The border setting prompts Greene's association between Berkhamsted and Mexico in a curious merging here of the scholastic and the exotic. The 'Prologue' to *The Lawless Roads* finds within the 'lawlessness' of school and the arrival of his faith, the seeds of Greene's journey into the lawless roads of Calles-era Mexico.

The mixed loyalties evoked in *A Sort of Life* and *The Lawless Roads* are evidenced in the opening of the 'Preface' to *The Old School*. Rather than exemplifying the rest of the 'Preface's' more polemical tone, these opening lines are more characteristically Greeneian:

> I regard this book rather as a premature memorial, like a family photograph album, a gathering of the staid and unloved hovering, in the most absurd headgear, unconsciously 'upon the brink' and occasionally among them, in a deerstalker cap or a hobble skirt, somebody who has betrayed one's natural distrust of human nature, somebody one has loved and will miss. Like the family album, this book will, I hope, be superficially more funny than tragic, for so odd a system of education does not demand a pompous memorial. (p. 7)

A 'premature memorial' is inherently political, as Greene simultaneously eulogizes and consigns the public-school tradition to death. The sentiment evoked here is deeply ambivalent: poised between loyalty and disloyalty; affection and ridicule. Greene's simile likens the book to a 'family photograph album' capturing the deeply personal context of his conflicted relationship to his own school experience. The farcical image of the outmoded Edwardian fashions of Greene's youth is interrupted by the more elegiac comment: 'somebody who has betrayed one's natural distrust of human nature, somebody one has loved and will miss.' This comment gains increased resonance from attention to Greene's own family circumstances: Norman Sherry notes that while Greene edited *The Old School*, his father's health was deteriorating.[30] A sense of the precariousness of Greene's emotional investment in the public school is summoned in his linguistic inventiveness that evokes a sense of the murky

---

[30] Sherry, pp. 498–99.

territories of emotional ambiguity. The term 'betrayed' is divorced from its typically negative associations into a more positive context, and the repetition of 'somebody' in this opening paragraph allows the impersonal term to accumulate emotional weight, paradoxically creating a sense of intimate distance.

England Made Me, A Sort of Life, and *The Lawless Roads* examine the psychological impulse behind old school loyalties that Greene treats with incredulity in *The Old School.* It is, perhaps, in Greene's failure to acknowledge the actual emotional bonds of school life in his rabble-rousing rhetoric that razes the nation's public schools to the ground, that there is an indication of his eventual disassociation from the collection which he would later describe as a 'joke'.

Walter Greenwood: Education in the Salford slums

Despite Greene's original intent that *The Old School* would be about 'the horror of the public school', the collection also contains a contribution on state education: Walter Greenwood's essay on 'Langy Road Council School' – an elementary school in the Salford slums.[31] This analysis considers Greenwood's essay in *The Old School* alongside *Love on the Dole* (1933) and his journalism to argue that he associates working-class education with political empowerment, while considering the ways in which he registers his characters' political and educational (dis)empowerment through narrative structure and linguistic coding.

Greene had reviewed Greenwood's novel, *Love on the Dole,* for *The Spectator* the month before his June 1933 diary entry in which he first conceptualized *The Old School,* finding it to be a 'devastating picture of unemployment'.[32] Bernard Bergonzi argues for the 'token' nature of the inclusion of Greenwood's account of a council-run state school in the collection, but Greene's solution to the public-school problem in *The Old School*'s editorial seems to emulate a cultivation of working-class attitudes to education which, for Greenwood, are notable for their denial of public-school codes of loyalty: Greenwood had 'disgust for them [the teachers], and for the School. There was nothing at all of the Harrow-and-Eton Alma Mater affection' (p. 77).[33] Greenwood's school was in the depths of the

[31] Sherry, p. 492.
[32] 'Fiction', p. 956.
[33] Bergonzi, p. 28.

Salford slums: he notes the 'sooty school, smoky streets, the trudge homewards to the cold house and empty grate' (p. 83). The school itself bore the mark of its industrial surroundings when, during the war, it merged with another council school and 'factory idiom was introduced to the time-table. There were to be two "shifts"' (p. 82) for scholars from each school. The essay is as concerned with the economics of home life, detailing as much about his part-time job at a pawn shop and his mother's salary for her work as a waitress, as about his education. His family struggled to make ends meet after his father's death and school was 'a sort of inconvenient necessity [...] an interruption in the earning of a livelihood' (p. 83). It was his mother's infectious enthusiasm for opera, an 'aspect of education quite neglected by the School' (p. 81), as well as his lived experience of poverty that informed Greenwood's true intellectual development: 'Subconsciously I was being educated, at least, preparing to be educated. It was not until years later that the study of Marxian economics satisfactorily explained the causes of my predicament' when he 'accidentally' (p. 83) discovered political pamphlets which had belonged to his grandfather. Greenwood depicts jubilation at leaving school:

> Seventeen years ago, a few days after my thirteenth birthday, the headmaster gave me a testimonial and shook hands with me. I ran out into the schoolyard yelling with triumph. My schooldays were over and I was free to find a full-time job.
> I was envied. (p. 84)

The essay closes here on the brink of the young Greenwood's future; a future that – it is clear – had the odds stacked against it. Another contributor to *The Old School* who was of working-class origins registers a similar sense of freedom from the confines of school – the novelist H.E. Bates, who attended his local elementary school before going on to Kettering Grammar School: 'I was free – I had escaped' (p. 33). The paradox of finding freedom in full-time work is repeated in Greenwood's essay ('I wanted the freedom of a full-time job' (p. 84)) suggesting the irony Greenwood later finds in this naivety, as escape from school signifies a different kind of imprisonment. Greenwood's 1936 article for *The Spectator*, 'Poverty and Freedom', also considered the association between freedom and work, arguing that the working class's inculcation in capitalist ideals prompts them to see freedom from work as 'despicable; we had taught ourselves that if we consumed without producing we were thieves'.[34]

---

[34] Walter Greenwood, 'Poverty and Freedom', *The Spectator*, 22 November 1935, p. 861.

Harry Hardcastle in *Love on the Dole* registers the same disenchantment with education that Greenwood records in his essay. At the start of the novel, Harry is alive to the possibility of working life: 'He'd done with schooling, had finished with it on Friday last! He now was free! His wondering spirits revived. Free!'[35] For Harry, promise at school had left him 'damned in a fair handwriting' to interminably write out 'millions of pawn-tickets' (p. 17) in a part-time job that he hated at Price and Jones's pawnshop, with 'tedious lessons on top of it all' (p. 16), a detail borrowed from Greenwood's own life: 'As I hated school so I hated the shop' (p. 83). Now, Harry can apply for work at Marlowe's, the local factory. On gaining work here, his short trousers encode him with the naivety of youth; instead, manly overalls are what are needed: 'An see y'come in a pair overalls. This ain't a bloody school' (p. 26). He feels 'shame of his schoolboy clothes' (p. 44) until he can afford the appropriate, manly garb. The narrative presents Harry's association of manual work with masculinity through free indirect discourse, while indicating authorial attitude through a simile that ironizes the associations made by Harry between factory work and masculinity: '"tat-tat-tat-tat-tat". Such a row. As though a million boys were running stakes along iron railings, simultaneously. Every man stone deaf after a six months' spell of work here. Phew! But they *were* men' (p. 50). The emphasis ('they *were* men') mimics Harry's voice. In tension with this perspective, the simile suggests the repetitive nature of factory work while associating the machine operatives with boys.

The relationship between masculinity and manual work is undercut further in Greenwood's journalism. A July 1936 article, 'On the Dole', discusses the effects of the Means Test and notes the betrayal of the apprentice system: 'Young men who've "served their time" to this or that trade; seven years' apprenticeship at boy's pay, discharged [...] because they are then entitled to man's pay.'[36] Their 'apprenticeship' is in fact to 'able-bodied pauperdom at twenty-one years of age'.[37] The article plays between the terms 'men' and 'boy' to highlight the injustices of the system of indentured labour which infantalizes working-class men through curtailing their economic means, a critique also evident in *Love on the Dole*: 'They now were fully qualified engineers. They also were qualified to draw the dole' (p. 154), as the two parallel sentences indicate a contiguous relationship between eligibility for full pay and unemployment.

[35] Walter Greenwood, *Love on the Dole* (London: Vintage, 2004), p. 16. Further references to this edition will be included in brackets after the citation.
[36] Walter Greenwood, 'On the Dole', *The Spectator*, 17 July 1936, pp. 93–94.
[37] 'On the Dole', p. 94.

Greenwood renders his critique of factory work through Larry Meath in *Love on the Dole*. Ben Harker notes that Meath occupies the 'working-class literary tradition of the socialist autodidactic as authorial mouthpiece' and Larry not only mirrors Greenwood's self-education in Marxist teachings described in *The Old School*, but he also reflects attitudes in Greenwood's journalism, as he denounces Harry's job as a 'swindle' and part of the 'apprentice racket' (p. 47) that inhibits Harry's education, as increased mechanization reduces the skill set necessary to fulfil the role: 'Nobody'll teach you anything simply because there's so little to be learnt [...] they're only machine minders' (p. 47).[38] As Harry nears the end of his apprenticeship, he echoes Larry's earlier prophesies regarding the relationship of education to capitalist production, as well as reflecting Greenwood's association between 'manhood and the dole':

> [The machines] made of inexperienced boys highly skilled men. [...] Every year new generations of schoolboys were appearing, each generation pushing him and his a little nearer to that incredible abyss of manhood and the dole.
>
> Why, the supply of boys was inexhaustible; there were millions of them at school; Marlowe's could keep going for ever. What was to become of him and his when their time was served? Where would openings occur if every firm was playing Marlowe's game? (p. 92)

The repetition of 'he and his' reinforces the way in which Harry's social concern extends beyond his own personal situation as he reflects upon how mass education to elementary level produces an endless supply of low-skilled workers and cheap labour. The figure of Billy Higgs, first introduced when he magnanimously gives Harry half-a-crown after winning a wager, recurs throughout the narrative as a member of an earlier 'generation' whom Harry idolizes, but who is effectively pushed out by Harry's 'schoolboy' generation. The cruel realization of the reality of the figure behind his hero-worship is significant for Harry's own self-perception, as he registers a need for political action (unacted upon): 'They weren't men at all, never had been. [...] Yet they were doing men's work. It was outrageous. Something ought to be done about it' (p. 74). At the close of the narrative, Higgs is referenced again, as the cycle of underpaid labour and consequent unemployment is set to recur: 'The newer and younger end of the neighbourhood's unemployed drifted to where he was standing. Blimey, was he to them as Billy Higgs had been to him?' (p. 233).

---

[38] Ben Harker, 'Adapting to the Conjuncture: Walter Greenwood, History and *Love on the Dole*', *Keywords*, Issue 7 (2009), 55–72 (p. 57).

Indeed, *Love on the Dole*'s emphasis on cyclical inevitability is rendered on the level of both plot and narrative structure. On the day that Harry's daughter is born, Sally Hardcastle symbolically dies, her sense of grief and degradation prompting a personal recklessness and a relinquishing of conventional standards of morality: 'Larry? Ha! Dead, and so was Sally Hardcastle. Aaach! Who cared what happened now. [...] The worst was over; life could hurt her never more' (p. 242). The birth of a new Hardcastle girl implies, however, that there is another family member to be subjected to a similar cycle of poverty. Roger Webster has noted that the novel's closure, depicting the beginning of the working day in Hanky Park, closely mirrors the opening of Chapter 2, 'Getting Up', the first chapter that introduces the reader to the Hardcastle family after an opening that, as Nicola Wilson notes, borrows from the conventions of the social observers of late-nineteenth-century slum narratives.[39] There are, however, elements of this narrative echoing that indicate not just a perpetuation of conditions in Hanky Park, but a further diminution of those conditions, suggesting an intensification of Greenwood's pessimistic vision. There are strong parallels between the description of the doorknocker at the beginning and end of the narrative; but while the opening of the narrative specifies the name of the doorknocker (Joe), the closure depersonalizes him: 'A man wearing clogs and carrying a long pole' (p. 256). The anonymous nature of this figure, coupled also with the loss of prosaic dialogue presented at the beginning of the novel, heightens its sinister undertones, rendering more overt the previously latent echoes of the 'summons' (p. 256) of the grim reaper. There are changes between the opening and the closure that also indicate the aggravation of unemployment within Hanky Park. The opening notes that on Joe's alarm call, 'Lights began to appear in the lower windows of the houses' (p. 14); while the closure adds details that suggest a community divided between the employed and the unemployed: 'He shouldered his pole and clattered out of the street. Those who were unemployed slumbered on. [...] Lights began to appear in some of the lower windows of the houses' (p. 256). Such changes signal the closure's emphasis on social conditions, rather than social community.

Carole Snee suggests that Greenwood 'never challenges the form of the bourgeois novel, nor its underlying ideology'.[40] Roger Webster perceives, however, a relationship between capitalist society and literary form as he

---

[39] Roger Webster, '*Love on the Dole* and the Aesthetic of Contradiction', in *The British Working-Class Novel in the Twentieth Century*, ed. by Jeremy Hawthorn (London: Arnold, 1984), pp. 49–61 (p. 59); Nicola Wilson, *Home in British Working-Class Fiction* (London: Ashgate, 2017), p. 96.

[40] Carole Snee, 'Working-Class Literature or Proletarian Writing?', in *Culture and Crisis in Britain in the Thirties*, ed. by Jon Clark and others (London: Lawrence and Wishart, 1979), pp. 165–91 (p. 171).

argues that *Love on the Dole* departs from the structure of the 'classic realist novel' with its 'affirmation of conventional values by asserting unquestioningly individualized experience'.[41] The circular structure of the novel, its emphasis on cyclical inevitability rather than individual self-determination, creates, as Nicola Wilson notes, a sense of the 'inevitability of the capitalist cycle and the limitations of individuals to change it'.[42] *The TLS* suggested that while the literary value of the novel was high, 'it is in its qualities as a "social document" that its great value lies'.[43] *Love on the Dole* demonstrates the ways in which state policy damages personal lives as social conditions determine novelistic structure.

Graham Greene recognized the political import of the novel in his review, when he commented that *Love on the Dole* depicts

> families tied together by the Means Test [...] The irresponsible workings of State economy [...]: those who hate each other are tied together, and the unemployed man is barred from any relationship which in its tenderness or permanence can make existing a little more like living.[44]

The Means Test was introduced as part of the 1931 austerity measures. Initially, benefits received by those no longer covered by insurance (built up by contributions paid while in work) were means-tested, limiting eligibility. Under the 1934 Unemployment Act, the level of individual income was replaced by a test which rendered the level of benefits contingent upon household circumstances inclusive of pensions, savings, the incomes of children, and even the value of furniture.[45] Juliet Gardiner offers accounts of the divisive effects of this policy, noting that bitterness and even family break-up was the result.[46] The reprehensible effects of the Means Test were detailed in an article Greenwood wrote for *The Spectator* in 1935, which contains a calculation of the effect of the Act on a family in Glasgow, outlining how the changes would leave working children supporting their unemployed parents. Greenwood suggests that the effect of the Means Test is to disempower the young, treating them as 'a "case" or as a child' and curtailing their ability to lead happy personal lives: 'Not all working men and women can afford to be subsidising their adult children

---

[41] Webster, p. 51.

[42] Wilson, p. 97.

[43] Leonora Eyles, '*Love on the Dole*', *The Times Literary Supplement*, 29 June 1933, p. 444.

[44] 'Fiction', p. 956.

[45] McKibbin, *Classes and Cultures*, p. 116.

[46] Juliet Gardiner, *The Thirties: An Intimate History* (London: Harper Collins, 2010), pp. 47–49.

indefinitely even if the children can stand the indignity. Some of them *do* want to get married' [emphasis in original].[47]

While *Love on the Dole* was written in response to the 1931 Means Test, the novel holds love and economic reality in similar tension. Larry's 'condemnation of marriage' stems from a desire to retain 'the things that make life worth while' (p. 142), including cultural and leisure pursuits ('Books, music, brief holidays by seas' (p. 150)), a feat impossible in working-class 'married life with all its scratchings and scrapings' (p. 142). As Pamela Fox and Webster note, Larry Meath occurs in the recognizable mould of the politically conscious autodidact, with both citing his similarity to the figure of Frank Owen in Robert Tressell's *The Ragged Trousered Philanthropists*, who oscillates between, Webster suggests, a form of individualism and a collective social conscience.[48] Larry is repeatedly depicted as attempting to awaken his community to the potentially damaging effects of the Means Test by politicizing Hanky Park through educating its inhabitants in the economic and philosophical arguments behind their social position. Larry's message is repeatedly depicted as failing to resonate, however; when Larry explains Marx's theory of labour, his argument is met with an unthinking maintenance of capitalist thinking: 'Y'can't do without capik ... ' (p. 184). Similarly, his attempts to warn 'everybody' about the Means Test and the potential effects of the National Government fails to contribute to a sense of political urgency in Harry: 'Aw, what the hell does it all matter, anyway. His dull brain refused, listlessly, to care what happened next' (p. 178). Harry's 'dull' inertia is reflected upon in Greenwood's journalism, where he perceived a relationship between poverty and political atrophy as 'one of the tragedies of the Means Test. It kills even the spirit of protest in its victims.'[49]

The novel aligns political activism and education through Larry Meath. This education is signalled in his language. As critics have recognized, Larry's speech is in Standard English, while other inhabitants of Hanky Park speak in non-standard, dialect forms. Chris Hopkins argues that Greenwood's text creates 'a hierarchy of discourse in which Standard English is seen as a more intelligent and articulate discourse than the dialect form.'[50] The text avoids a conflation

---

[47] 'On the Dole', p. 93.

[48] Pamela Fox, *Class Fictions: Shame and Resistance in the British Working-Class Novel, 1890–1945* (London: Duke University Press, 1994), p. 73; Webster, p. 51.

[49] 'On the Dole', p. 93. Ross McKibbin questions 'conventional' readings of the political apathy of the unemployed in the 1930s, but questions also whether the politics of the working class 'was appropriate to their circumstances', noting that the unemployed were 'actively hostile not so much to the general policies of the state [...] as to its agents.' Ross McKibbin, *The Ideologies of Class: Social Relations in Britain, 1880–1950* (Oxford: Clarendon Press, 1990), p. 246; p. 250.

[50] Chris Hopkins, *English Fiction in the 1930s: Language, Genre, History* (London: Continuum, 2006), pp. 46–47.

between non-dialectal forms and intelligence, however: Harry's scholarly flair as a schoolboy quickly positions him as an 'intelligent' character, yet he speaks in dialect forms. In the text, therefore, Standard English denotes an educated pattern of speech. Critics have variously suggested that Larry's educated language is a symbol of his detachment and division from his community (Matthew Gaughan), and one aspect of Greenwood's 'ideological ambivalence' (Stephen Ross).[51] Jack Windle critiques such arguments as offering a limited understanding of the variegated nature of working-class identity, an observation reflected in Pamela Fox's suggestion that 'the "bourgeois" strains of these narratives are not a denial of or regression from working-class experience but another legitimate part of it'.[52] Jonathan Rose details the ways in which the working-class autodidact was a fractional part of working-class identity, not just 'a middle-class interloper in a working-class world' (as Ross renders Larry).[53] Sally wrestles with the extent to which Larry's home, amidst the lodgings of Hanky Park, is a continuation of, or departure from, the working-class identities represented elsewhere in the street: 'Suppose they saw Larry's home? His was no different from her own; it was in the same street, anyway' (p. 97). On seeing it, however, she recognizes the divergent place it accords him within his working-class community:

> Exactly the same kind of room as at No. 17, yet how different. [...] Books arranged on shelves [...] so extraordinary a furnishing of a North Street front room. Their presence enhanced, lent an intangible part of themselves to the meagre rickety furniture provided by the landlady. (p. 190)

This divergent class positioning is signalled in some of Larry's speeches:

> *That* is the price we will continue to pay until you people awaken to the fact that Society has the means, the skill, and the knowledge to afford us the opportunity to become Men and Women in the fullest sense of those terms. (p. 86, emphasis in original)

There is a switch between the unifying collective ('we will have to pay') and the accusatory ('you people awaken') as Larry advocates education ('skill' and 'knowledge') as a means to overcome economic oppression. Larry's educated speech prompts feelings of self-consciousness in Sally that are registered on a lexical level:

[51] Matthew Gaughan, 'Palatable Socialism or "The Real Thing"?': Walter Greenwood's *Love on the Dole*, *Literature & History*, Vol. 17 No. 2 (2008), 47–61 (p. 58); Stephen Ross, 'Authenticity Betrayed: The "Idiotic Folk" of *Love on the Dole*', *Cultural Critique*, No. 56 (Winter 2004), 189–209 (p. 202).

[52] Jack Windle, '"What Life Means to Those at the Bottom": *Love on the Dole* and its Reception since the 1930s', *Literature & History*, Vol. 20 No. 2 (2008), 35–50 (p. 40); Fox, p. 61.

[53] See Rose, *The Intellectual Life of the British Working Classes*; Ross, p. 203.

'I was listening. But I don't know nowt – er – anything about politics.' She raised her eyes to his. [...] She blushed; thought she perceived an appreciative attentiveness in his gaze. [...] He had not yet answered; they still were looking at each other. She was embarrassed but could not avert her gaze.

'I was listening. But I don't know anything about politics,' she had said. He suddenly roused himself. (p. 87)

Larry does not notice the way in which Sally 'corrects' her dialect speech into Standard English – swooning in the lamplight, transported by love, the meaning, rather than the delivery, of her speech is what Larry receives. Critics have commented upon the ways in which Greenwood deploys and critiques discourses traditionally associated with romance fiction; here this discourse fills the rupture of the cultural differences between these two characters, providing an idiom that overwhelms their linguistic divisions.[54] Chris Hopkins finds that the novel has 'some consciousness of this speech difference as a problem for (and feature of) Larry, but it does not always follow up the implications of the interesting problems it raises.'[55] However, one outcome of this 'language difficulty' seems to be a failure of the educated to connect with the very audience that would be most empowered by that education, as Mrs Bull identifies:'Eddicated an' well-read fellers like Larry Meath talkin' till they're blue in face [...] Wot Larry Meath said long ago's all comin' true. Everybody's comin' out o' work' (pp. 164–65).[56] Greenwood's journalism asserted the power of working-class education as a sign of the indefatigable qualities of the human spirit in the face of the intractability of an oppressive social system:

There was [...] the consolation of the public library and of the evening study classes provided by political organisations. Here one could seek historical explanation of one's predicament and find a secret thrill in viewing humanity as engaged in an epic struggle for its own emancipation, or [...] view oneself as a not altogether negligible factor in the ultimate establishment of the millennium. Then the voice within sometimes would rise mocking and derisive to shatter, humiliate and embarrass the two quid a week clerk who thought a world full of rogues could be persuaded by reason and argument to the path of equalitarian rectitude.

---

[54] Webster suggests that Greenwood's 'divided language is not a form of collusion but [...] a reflection and revelation of the divisions in literary and social processes', while Fox suggests that 'despite its criticism' the novel 'finally validates the pursuit of romance'. Webster, p. 54; Fox, p. 185.

[55] Hopkins, p. 48.

[56] Ibid.

> Yet one was not too humiliated, or embarrassed as to want to relinquish the
> idea of a better system of life. One dared not.[57]

Greenwood recognizes the tensions between the means of effecting social
change (autodidact education) and the failure of the medium through which this
means might be conveyed ('reason and argument'). Such an analysis suggests
that he was conscious of the social dimensions of the linguistic problems his
text raises, and that they are part of his analysis of the perpetuation (and indeed
exacerbation) of the conditions in Hanky Park.

A genetic reading of the linguistic and narrative codes in the proof and
manuscript versions of *Love on the Dole* offers evidence to temper perspectives
by Stephen Ross and Pamela Fox, who see elements of contempt in the depiction
of the uneducated working-class characters' language, with Ross noting that the
novel reveals 'a one-sided linguistic privileging of bourgeois discourse that more
or less savagely pokes fun at working-class characters' language'.[58] Greenwood's
deliberate rendering of the dialect of the inhabitants of Hanky Park is indicated
by comparison between the complete manuscript version of the novel and
the novel's proof copy, which demonstrates that he repeatedly reinstates the
dialectal and grammatical forms used in his original manuscript copy of the
novel, following (what appear to be) publisher changes in the printed proof copy,
either deliberate or inadvertent.[59] Such reinstatements suggest that Greenwood
rendered the dialect of the community of Hanky Park with a precision that
supports a reading that privileges a self-consciousness to his engagement with
the problem of language difference. Some changes also reveal Greenwood's
distinction between dialectal forms of English, and inaccurate punctuation.
In conversation between the women of Hanky Park, Greenwood includes
a marginal note, indicating the insertion of an apostrophe to reinstate the
grammatically correct apostrophe, which indicates a contracted form: 'All this
here unemployment^ s doin' *some*body some good.'[60] Later on, in Harry's speech
to his father, he notes in the proof version: 'Ah'll have t'marry 'elen', as Greenwood
marks up the dialectal form of 'Helen' and includes a marginal annotation ('cap')
to indicate that her name should begin with a capital 'e', as in the manuscript

---

[57] 'Poverty and Freedom', p. 860.

[58] Ross, p. 191; Fox, pp. 81–82.

[59] Walter Greenwood Collection, University of Salford. Author's Proof Copy of *Love on the Dole* WGC/1/2/2; Manuscript of *Love on the Dole* WGC/1/2/1.

[60] WGC/1/2/2, p. 214.

version ('Elen).[61] Such amendments suggest that while dialectal variants are used which depart from Standard English grammatical forms and create the audible effect of the Lancashire dialect, this is tempered by punctuation on the page that is recognizably grammatically 'correct'.

When Sally confronts Ned Narkey about Kate's pregnancy, Narkey challenges Sally about her relationship with Larry. The original manuscript copy notes: 'What about that bloody swine as y' let arse about wi' you? How many times has he had wot' e wants?'.[62] The proof version of Narkey's speech sees this editorially amended, with Greenwood's marginal notes: 'What about that bloody swine as y' let arse about wi' you? How many times has he had ^y'skirts up?'.[63] Greenwood includes a marginal annotation that indicates an insertion and amendment back to 'wot 'e wants'.[64] The shift back to the euphemistic, and less graphic, 'wot e' wants' is notable. The final version moderates this speech still further: 'What about that bloody swine as y' let muck about wi' you? How many times has 'e had wot 'e wants?' (p. 167). The term 'muck' is less crude than 'arse' and repeats the term Sally earlier uses in her discussion with Kate about her relationship with Ned ('Fancy bein' such a mug to let a thing like that muck about wi' you' (p. 165)). The overall effect preserves a sense of Narkey's unscrupulous relations with women, while retaining a degree of civility in the language he uses with women in conversation. The fact that, even in the case of Narkey, the villain of the piece, Greenwood preserves a certain reserve surrounding Narkey's discussion of his sexual relations with women suggests a desire to maintain a degree of chivalrous discretion in Narkey's characterization, however exploitative his sexual behaviour. These moderations are in tension with Ross's findings, which see Greenwood as serving bourgeois interests through savage depictions of the working-class community in the novel.

A key area of critical debate on *Love on the Dole* focuses on Greenwood's use of parenthetical translations of working-class dialogue. Ross suggests that the glosses have a 'defamiliarization effect […] carefully preserving his preferred audience's sense of its own discursive normalcy' rendering them 'deeply conservative ideological maneuvers that naturalize the separation between classes by situating bourgeois cultural discourse as a norm into which

---

[61] WGC/1/2/2, p. 297.
[62] WGC/1/2/1, p. 141.
[63] WGC/1/2/2, p. 221.
[64] Ibid.

working-class linguistic deviation must be translated'.[65] Jack Windle suggests, however, that rather than objectifying the novel's working-class community, the glosses point up the ignorance of the middle-class reader: 'Greenwood carefully writes for a dual intended audience and performs a subtle and sophisticated "othering" of the middle-class imagined reader.'[66] Both readings rely on a sense of linguistic alienation occasioned by working-class discourse that necessitates the narrator's intervention and translation. However, there are occasions in the text where the parenthetical glosses are seemingly unnecessary. For instance, in conversation between the women of Hanky Park, Mrs Dorbell notes: 'Ah' votes for none on 'em [...] Me ma an' her ma was blue (Conservative) or they wus red (Liberal), just depended on which o' t' two gev most coal an' blankets' (p. 164). The context alone gives clue to the meaning of 'red' and 'blue' here. The *OED* notes that 'blue' has been used as a metonymic description of the Tory, and then Conservative party, since 1781, listing numerous literary and journalistic usages of the term; it seems likely, therefore, that readers of Greenwood's text would be familiar with the metonymic meaning of the term without the need for a translation.[67]

Elsewhere, there is inconsistency surrounding Greenwood's glossing. The term 'tick', a key means by which the local economy around the streets of Hanky Park is sustained, is repeatedly mentioned in the text: 'women who would come [...] to buy foodstuffs on tick' (p. 14); 'the women were come to redeem the moneys with the family raiment so that they might pay off their tick account for food which stood against their names' (p. 32). These instances, where the term appears unglossed, occur before a later use of the term, this time in Mrs Bull's speech: 'while Ah can get tick (credit) somewhere' (p. 109). The first two instances, arguably, give some indication of the meaning of the term through its context, thus negating the need for a translation. However, even if, in the third instance, the meaning is not clear from the context, it seems curious that the gloss could be deemed necessary, given that the term has already occurred unglossed in the text previously. The overzealous translations make the narrator's role as mediator of these two communities keenly felt, rather than 'naturaliz[e][ing]' linguistic difference. In both instances, the seemingly extraneous translations come within the discourse of the working-class characters; points in the text whereby the middle-class reader may be assumed to feel their sense of class

---

[65] Ross, p. 199.
[66] Windle, p. 38.
[67] 'blue', adj., 9, *OED*, <http://www.oed.com> [date accessed 11 May 2016].

otherness most acutely. In these terms, the emphasis is not on a cruel jibe at the working class by pointing up the deficiencies of working-class language (Ross), or an attempt to 'other' middle-class experience (Windle), but rather a pointing up within the text of the process of translation and negotiation of the linguistic terms of class division.

The hostile reception of Greenwood's work by critics such as Snee and Ross to some degree signals the problems of the working-class writer who has inherited a literary idiom that can never neutrally convey his message; the text's foregrounding of problems of discourse and communication suggests a consciousness of the class-based implications of language from which both its characters and author cannot escape. Greenwood's depiction of working-class life is indeed vulnerable to the very censure it has attracted, as the text reveals a frustration of the ability of a politically conscious autodidact culture to translate to a wider, working-class community, which, as Greenwood repeatedly renders in *Love on the Dole* and *The Old School*, is alienated from institutional educational structures. This is a problem played out by *Love on the Dole*'s depiction of the inefficacity of Larry Meath's teaching, and its cyclical structure.

Stephen Spender: Heroism and education

While Greenwood exemplifies the problems facing the working-class writer in a bourgeois literary environment, John Coombes comments that the left-wing, middle-class writer Stephen Spender had an 'awareness of literary production as a form of political practice in itself'.[68] I consider Spender's essay in *The Old School*, 'Day Boy' alongside his tract, *The New Realism* (1939), his novel *The Backward Son* (1940), and different versions of his poem, 'An Elementary School Class Room in a Slum', to analyze the ways in which he saw education as informing literary discourse. Where Valentine Cunningham argues that after the Spanish Civil War 'the period's taste for heroizing was soured well nigh irrevocably', focusing his analysis on Spender, this section suggests the ways in which Spender critiqued the heroic in *The Backward Son* through the depiction of a protagonist born of the institutionalization of the anti-heroic present in contemporary educational discourse.[69] In dialogue with readings of Spender's verse by Adrian Caesar, I suggest that 'An Elementary School Class Room in a Slum' considers

---

[68] John Coombes, 'British Intellectuals and the Popular Front', in *Class, Culture and Social Change*, ed. by Gloversmith, pp. 70–100 (p. 79).
[69] *British Writers*, p. 459.

the role of education in social change, as, through textual revisions, Spender, like Greenwood, finds a form that evades more individualized narratives as he depicts the impersonal force of history in the regeneration of cultural forms and political structures.

Spender's essay in *The Old School* considers University College School as the 'gentlest of schools' (p. 189), an assessment that renders it a sharp 'contrast' (p. 185) to Spender's 'sadistic' (p. 189) preparatory school, which he considers in more detail in *The Backward Son*. George Orwell detected that the novel was 'autobiographical' while T.C. Worsley called it 'a fascinating document of our time'.[70] Worsley echoes Storm Jameson's analysis of bourgeois involvement in 'socialist literature' through the documentary novel in the July 1937 issue of *Fact*, an issue to which Spender also contributed his theories surrounding the role of poetry in political change. Jameson had suggested that bourgeois writers could locate 'change [...] decay [...] growth' within the self while avoiding cringing cross-class encounters: 'a novel about Lord Invernairn, written from full insight into what this man is actually doing, a novel which exposed him, laid him open [...] would still be socialist literature'.[71] *The Backward Son* presents Geoffrey Brand's trials as he encounters traditional models of upper-class masculinity at his preparatory school. Elizabeth Bowen suggests that the novel is 'not [...] strictly a school novel – primarily it is a study of temperament', and indeed the novel depicts Geoffrey Brand wrestling with ideals of selfhood sanctified by the public-school system.[72] *The New Realism*, written as Spender was making notes for *The Backward Son*, attributes 1930s writers' 'divided position' to their 'bourgeois environment' during their formative years spent at public and preparatory schools: 'the most sensitive years of an artist's experience are his childhood and adolescence, when he is not able to alter his environment by exercising his political conscience'.[73] Spender's later work also alludes to this sense of entrapment; his introduction to a radio broadcast of *The Backward Son* in 1993 noted that his school had 'conditions like a prison', an association also

---

[70] George Orwell, 'Review', in *The Complete Works of George Orwell Volume 12*, ed. by Peter Davison, pp. 163–65 (p. 163); T.C. Worsley, 'Father to the Man: *The Backward Son* by Stephen Spender', *New Statesman and Nation*, 4 May 1940, p. 594.

[71] Storm Jameson, 'Writing in Revolt 1. Theory – Documents', *Fact*, July 1937, pp. 9–18 (p. 10).

[72] Elizabeth Bowen, 'Introduction', in Antonia White, *Frost in May* (London: Virago, 1981), pp. v–x (p. vi). Further references to this edition will be included in brackets after the citation.

[73] Stephen Spender, *The New Realism: A Discussion* (London: Hogarth Press, 1939), p. 21; p. 19; pp. 19–20. Further references to this edition will be included in brackets after the citation.

made in *World within World*, in which Spender noted 'my prison of school'.[74] The novel presents the pressures on the formation of Geoffrey's selfhood in relation to different educational discourses and ideals.

In its depiction of Geoffrey's 'temperament' the novel draws on debates emerging in the late 1930s surrounding the education of backward children. Indeed, Spender's biographer, John Sutherland, comments that he was 'preoccupied' by the education of 'backward' children, and was toying with becoming a schoolmaster about this time, spending winter of 1940 teaching at Blundell's.[75] Sir Cyril Burt, the originator of IQ testing, published his book on *The Backward Child* in 1937, finding that 'the problem of the backward child has never been attacked by systematic research until quite recently'.[76] In the same year, the first report on the education of backward children was published by the Board of Education, and, following this, educational psychologists released reports on dealing with 'backward' children in the classroom. Traditional teaching methods were found to be unsuccessful in educating these children; instead, 'progressive' methods were favoured.[77] The academy deemed 'backward' children morally suspect. In the 'Foreword' to the *1936 Year Book of Education,* which was dedicated to an exploration of the relationship between backwardness and juvenile delinquency, Sir Percy Nunn, director of the Institute of Education, commented: 'Professor Cyril Burt and others have made clear that the path from scholastic backwardness to delinquency is often sadly easy [...] the two states must be regarded as to some extent correlative'.[78] Educationists wrestled with the terms associated with 'backwardness'. Burt himself 'distinguished so clearly between "dullness," which is innate intellectual defect, and "backwardness," which is educational inferiority'.[79] Other terms also creep in, all ideologically weighted, rather than medically diagnostic: 'a child may be dull *or* backward; or he may be both dull *and* backward. A backward child is not necessarily dull, nor is a retarded child necessarily backward'.[80]

[74] Stephen Spender, *The Backward Son,* dir. by Richard Wortley, adapted by Pauline Spender. *Saturday Playhouse,* BBC Radio 4 (20 March 1993); Stephen Spender, *World within World* (London: Hamish Hamilton, 1951), p. 332.
[75] John Sutherland, *Stephen Spender: The Authorized Biography* (London: Penguin, 2004), p. 263; pp. 274–75.
[76] Cyril Burt, 'Preface', in *The Backward Child* (London: University of London Press, 1937), p. v.
[77] M.E. Hill, *The Education of Backward Children* (London: Harrap, 1939), p. 5.
[78] *The Education of Backward Children and Juvenile Delinquency in England and Wales,* ed. by Sir Percy Nunn (London: Evans Brothers, 1937), p. 4.
[79] H.R. Hamley, 'Introductory Survey', in *The Education of Backward Children,* ed. by Nunn, pp. 5–19 (p. 5).
[80] Hamley, p. 6, emphases in original.

The term seems to describe any child who was not hardy enough to adjust themselves to the intellectual, social, or emotional rigours of school life. Burt finds that among the 'type' of backward children exist '*sensitive and repressed*' children who are 'solitary, shy, unsociable beings, quickly scared and easily depressed', they may 'want[s] to be "an author"'.[81] Backwardness also registered itself on a physiological level: Cyril Burt's book found that 'spinal curvature' is 'the most conspicuous characteristic' of backwardness: 'His shoulder tips droop. His arms drag down. His shoulder-blades project backwards like lumpy little wings.'[82] Spender engages with this eugenicist, degeneracy discourse in the presentation of his protagonist, as Geoffrey's brother diagnoses his backwardness in terms that echo Burt's findings: 'the unresisting curved fixture of your spinal column (causing your notorious round-shoulderedness), not to speak of the slowness of your reflexes, and your lack of conscious intelligence'.[83] The novel's drama is founded in the psychic struggle staged between the type advocated by the public school and Geoffrey's failure to accord to this type: his 'backwardness'.

This discourse informs the development between Spender's essay in *The Old School* and his later novel. Both 'Day Boy' and *The Backward Son* detail the same incident at Spender/Geoffrey's preparatory school, precipitated by school bullies who infiltrate the relationship between Spender/Geoffrey and his brother, teasing them about their German heritage. Both recount the nefarious effect this has on the siblings' relationship: 'turning our love into a feeling of frightened and hysterical rivalry' (*The Old School*, p. 187). Both narratives describe the climax of this torment, as they detail how Spender/Geoffrey uncharacteristically confronts the school bullies and pushes one boy through a glass window. Unlike 'Day Boy', however, *The Backward Son* draws on the context of contemporaneous debates surrounding backwardness in the expression of Geoffrey's attempt to overcome the boys' bullying: 'now when he decided to fight he knew that he was being disloyal to his father, the headmaster, the other boys, disloyal above all to their idea of him as a backward boy' (pp. 229–30). In both narratives, there follows a confrontation with the school authorities, as the headmaster suggests that the incident reveals a fundamental – and it is implied hideous – aspect of Spender/Geoffrey's characters. The words that he delivers are very similar in both cases: 'You are a boy who has always puzzled us. Now at last I think I understand you'

---

[81] Burt, p. 546; p. 546; p. 547; p. 550, emphases in original.

[82] Burt, p. 184; p. 184; p. 183.

[83] Stephen Spender, *The Backward Son* (London: Hogarth Press, 1940), pp. 118–19. Further references to this edition will be included in brackets after the citation.

(*The Backward Son*, p. 237); 'You are a boy, who for a long time has puzzled me. I think now I understand you' (*The Old School*, p. 188).

While 'Day Boy' notes that UCS took 25 per cent of its intake from London County Council schools, and attributes the presence of working-class boys to the school's 'gentleness' (p. 191), *The Backward Son* depicts the snobbish atmosphere of Geoffrey's preparatory school, where his social background (his father is a Liberal MP) renders him particularly promising material for Tisselthorp House's preferred brand of masculinity:

> Some of our boys [...] come from a type of home which is not far removed from that where the children are sent to rough, ill-mannered elementary schools. As *your* father is indisputably a gentleman, we are relying on you to have a good influence here. (pp. 29–30, emphasis in original)

In the school chapel, the headmaster suggests that 'the greatest ambition of every boy was [...] to win a scholarship to a public school' (p. 70). This education provides 'the mark of a gentlemen' (p. 71) distinguishing the public- and preparatory-school pupil from 'the common herd' (p. 72). Geoffrey feels 'cramped and forced into a mould' (p. 45) as he struggles to assume 'the rigid mask of a character which Tisselthorp House imposed on him' (p. 57). These masculine ideals are advanced in literary models of selfhood:

> On Sunday evenings, half an hour before supper, it [the new staff room] became the School Library, when the boys were allowed to go and choose a tattered copy of *Tom Brown's Schooldays, St Winifred's*, or *The Bending of a Twig*. In order to give him a 'taste of responsibility', Geoffrey was made school librarian, and he had a note-book in which he was supposed to enter the books which had been taken out. (p. 190)

Jenny Holt notes that the public-school story was 'a popular vehicle for the transmission of civic values, but a very problematic one' and here the school library is a vessel for indoctrination as the books listed, all influential Victorian school stories, advance the spiritually pure and hearty public-school ideal.[84] The 'tattered' well-read appearance of these books suggests the influence of these models on the schoolboys at Tisselthorp House. Isabel Quigly suggests that Dean Farrar's work (which includes *St Winifred's*) is 'shrill and overwrought' with a 'fervent biblical atmosphere', with Graham Greene alluding to 'its sentimentality, its complacency, its uneasy attitude to sex' (*The Old School*, p. 249).[85] Thomas

---

[84] Jenny Holt, *Public School Literature, Civic Education and the Politics of Male Adolescence* (Farnham: Ashgate, 2008), p. 2.

[85] Isabel Quigly, *The Heirs of Tom Brown: The English School Story* (London: Chatto & Windus, 1982), p. 71; p. 72.

Hughes's *Tom Brown's Schooldays* (1857) provided an influential civic ideal for all social groups: in 1910 and 1911, the Board of Education recommended the inclusion of the novel in every elementary school library.[86] Holt asserts the 'death of an [i]deal' of public-school masculinity after the First World War, when 'widening democracy brought demand for changes in the way adolescents were educated as citizens and the formal teaching of civics'.[87] Holt argues that in the 'modernist climate, an "everyboy" such as Tom Brown is not worth reading about; the literary adolescent must be something problematic, marginal and, essentially, pathological'.[88] The allusion to the childhood school story signals that Geoffrey is ironically made a guardian of a literary culture that advocates the heroic models of public-school boyhood which so torture him. He is symbolically the protector of an ideal that he is haunted by, prompting a typically modernist division of the self that highlights how late modernism's rejection of the public-school ideal creates a battleground over which to reject Victorian values and to test modernist notions of selfhood.

The narrative switches to the intimacy of Geoffrey's first-person voice as he fantasizes about coming into his own selfhood through the act of writing: 'I will get up at six o'clock each morning, two hours before breakfast, and start printing *My Life, by Geoffrey Brand. Collected Works. Kiyudkoo, or Who Am I? A Play in Three Acts*' (p. 114). In the 'clear, hard, cold print' (p. 114) of his autobiography, 'they will have to recognize me' as his words will stand in for a strong and undeniable self-presence that Geoffrey cannot manifest in person. He fantasizes about future inclusion in '*The Boys' Book of Wonder Boy Heroes, published in the Year Two Thousand and Twenty-One, A.D*' (p. 114), reflecting Spender's wider preoccupation with ideals of 'greatness' in poems such as 'I think continually of those who are truly great'.[89] Indeed, Geoffrey reflects: 'Unless I am Great, what else am I? It is the only thing to be' (p. 115). His imagined apotheosis to greatness finds its summation in the attainment of a scholarship to a public school: 'What happens to those who are never able to pass examinations, get into any public school, any university, any profession?' (p. 115). Spender denies the place of the hero, while simultaneously asserting the influence of the ideal on Geoffrey's psychic formation: 'Things like that do not happen today. There are no saints nor heroes. All I have is ambition surrounded by an emptiness' (p. 115). Spender's

[86] Holt, p. 3.
[87] Holt, p. 209; p. 213.
[88] Holt, p. 210.
[89] Stephen Spender, *New Collected Poems* (London: Faber & Faber, 2004), p. 16.

introduction to his 1939 collection of poetry, *The Still Centre*, explains 'why I
do not strike a more heroic note', suggesting that 'poetry does not state truth, it
states the conditions within which something felt is true'.[90] *The Backward Son*
critiques an education that advocates an aspiration to old cultural models of the
heroic found in public-school literature, while simultaneously institutionalizing
a version of the anti-heroic, or the backward, leaving Geoffrey condemned to a
neurotic engagement with the heroic ideal.

Spender's poem, 'An Elementary School Class Room in a Slum', a version
of which is published in *The Still Centre*, sees him depart from the 'utilitarian
heroics' to which Geoffrey Brand is prey, in order to explore an alternative
to conventional heroic structures.[91] John Coombes notes the poem's 'liberal
romanticism', finding in it 'an escape from politics rather than an enactment of
it', while Caesar has suggested that the poem reveals a 'negative romanticism
of the working class' in its opening.[92] Commenting on the poems 'I think
continually' and 'Beethoven's death mask', Caesar argues that Spender is
committed to

> an idea of history predicated not upon the economic relations of classes to
> the means of production, but on crude notions of the biography of great men.
> [...] Spender never reveals himself to be at all interested in a Marxist view of
> history. Nowhere is this clearer than in his attitudes towards language. Rather
> than perceiving language to be part of the 'superstructure' predicated upon the
> economic base, and thus subject to change, he espouses Eliot's conservative view
> that language is the repository of somehow 'pure' meanings which have to be
> preserved by poetry against corruption.[93]

Where Caesar measures Spender's cultural politics against his 1933 essay,
'Poetry and Revolution', Spender's 1939 pamphlet, *The New Realism*, which, as
Sutherland notes, 'redefined his [Spender's] aesthetic [...] post-Spain and post-
Communism', identifies the ways in which literary discourse is socially coded.[94]
Spender echoes Woolf's arguments in 'The Niece of an Earl' as he argues that
literature exists only in a bourgeois form:

> This [middle-class] tradition is so strong that even if a writer springs from the
> working class, he writes in that medium and about that kind of life. The best

[90] Stephen Spender, *The Still Centre* (London: Faber & Faber, 1939), p. 10.
[91] Ibid.
[92] Coombes, *Writing from the Left*, p. 5; p. 4; Caesar, p. 87.
[93] Caesar, pp. 85–86.
[94] Sutherland, p. 243.

working-class writers [...] have completely changed their environment, in order to write for a middle-class audience. And since there is no working-class tradition of art that is not very rudimentary, they are justified in doing so.

It follows that when any good work of art about working-class life is created, it is within the bourgeois tradition. (p. 15)

Both Woolf's 'truly democratic age' and Spender's 'classless society' (p. 15) provide the impetus for the production of a 'new realism'.[95] Spender's interest in the potential of the working class to produce 'a culture of its own' (p. 15) stimulates revisions to later versions of 'An Elementary School Class Room in a Slum', the first version of which was composed in April 1935 after a visit to Clemence Pain school in the East End of London, and published in the *London Mercury* in May 1935 as 'An Elementary School Classroom'. Revisions to the poem's closure complicate previous readings of Spender's politics as, in the 1939 version, he positions education as part of the impersonal forces of history (rather than great men) that stimulate social change. The original version of the poem – and particularly its closure – was 'entirely rewritten' for inclusion in *The Still Centre*, and then later adapted for Spender's *Collected Poems* (1955):[96]

> Unless, dowager, governor, these pictures, in a room
> Columned above childishness, like our day's future drift
> Of smoke concealing war, are voices shouting
> O that beauty has words and works which break
> Through coloured walls and towers. The children stand
> As in a climbing mountain train. This lesson illustrates
> The world green in their many valleys beneath:
> The total summer heavy with their flowers.[97]
>   *The London Mercury*, 1935

> Unless, governor, teacher, inspector, visitor,
> This map becomes their window and these windows
> That open on their lives like crouching tombs
> Break, O break open, till they break the town

---

[95] Virginia Woolf, 'The Niece of an Earl', in *The Essays of Virginia Woolf Volume 5: 1929–1932*, ed. by Stuart N. Clarke (London: Hogarth Press, 2009), pp. 529–34 (p. 533). Further reference to this essay will be included in brackets after the citation as E5 and then the page number.

[96] *Still Centre*, p. 9.

[97] Stephen Spender, 'An Elementary School Classroom', *The London Mercury*, Vol. 32 No. 187 (May 1935), 8.

And show the children to the fields and all their world
Azure on their sands, to let their tongues
Run naked into books, the white and green leaves open
The history theirs whose language is the sun.[98]
> *The Still Centre*, 1939

Unless, governor, teacher, inspector, visitor,
This map becomes their window and these windows
That shut upon their lives like catacombs,
Break O break open till they break the town
And show the children to green fields, and make their world
Run azure on gold sands, and let their tongues
Run naked into books, the white and green leaves open
History theirs whose language is the sun.[99]
> *Collected Poems*, 1955

The 1935 version is romantic as 'these pictures' facilitate the children's redemptive, imaginative escape into a pastoral idyll. The revised 1939 stanza is more politicized in tone, attributing power to the working classes through their possession of 'history'. Julian Symons recognizes the potent notion of the ownership of 'history' in the 1930s:

> *History is on our side.* I must have read the words in a dozen poems. They express the conviction which led many writers to view the future with complete assurance. [...] The belief that history is on one side or another is a heady one.[100]

For Spender, 'history' itself connoted a dominion of the future rather than the past: in *Forward from Liberalism* he paradoxically argues that 'the greatest asset of the lowest social classes is the history of the future' (p. 191); his inversion of the usual formulation (history is 'theirs', not notably, 'ours') prefigures Symons's observation of the public schools that 'history was not on their side'.[101]

A. Kingsley Weatherhead suggests that emendations for Spender's *Collected Poems* were made which 'enriched the imagery' of the poem, but a comparison between the 1939 and 1955 versions also highlights Spender's political vision in the 1930s as he explores the issue of social class and agency in shaping the

---

[98] Stephen Spender, 'An Elementary Class Room in a Slum', in *Still Centre*, pp. 28–29 (p. 29).
[99] Stephen Spender, *Collected Poems 1928–1953* (London: Faber & Faber, 1955), p. 81.
[100] Symons, p. 20, emphasis in original.
[101] Symons, p. 26.

forces of history.[102] The 1955 version dispenses with the paradox evident in the 1939 version, which alludes to an impoverished education system that inscribes limitations, rather than creates possibilities, in the shift between the windows that 'open on their lives like crouching tombs' (1939) versus the more direct windows that 'shut upon their lives like catacombs' (1955): the 'crouching tombs' evokes a death more imminent than the subterranean 'catacombs'.

Spender found that education was part of the middle-class 'great reformist tradition' (*Forward from Liberalism*, p. 121) and the 1939 emendments reflect this conviction, replacing references in the 1935 version of the poem to the aristocratic 'dowager' with the middle-class 'teacher' and school 'inspector': revisions that are carried over into the 1955 version. Caesar suggests that these figures are called upon in 'a spirit of Victorian philanthropy', but the revisions seem designed to avoid such readings of patrician philanthropy.[103] Instead, Spender invokes the enabling force of the middle-class reformer in order to explore the contested place of education as both the site of middle-class benefaction and working-class empowerment. Indeed, the competing forces of the middle-class, liberal reformer, and the working-class children animate this stanza. While the middle-class reformers are invoked in the poem's peroration, it is the trappings of education (the map, the broken school windows), not the educators themselves, which directly facilitate the children's revolutionary awakening. Such factors are referenced earlier in the poem, and rendered active agents; the 'maps' which allow the children to conceive of another social reality refer back to the generous potentiality of the map on the classroom wall, which is parodied by the windows which reveal the slum setting: 'Open-handed map | Awarding the world its world. And yet, for these | Children, these windows, not this world, are world'.

Forward from Liberalism posits that 'one may choose between [...] two worlds: the compromise of the bourgeoisie, and a classless society' (p. 137), suggesting that a classless society alone allows the achievement of true educational equality: 'by political freedom in a liberal democracy I mean [...] the right to a good education [...] these freedoms all point to the freedom of an equal and classless society' (p. 136). The 1955 version of the poem is more direct in ascribing the facilitation of 'political freedom' (p. 136) to the agency of education in the series of imperatives: 'show [...] make [...] let'. In comparison, the working-class

[102] A. Kingsley Weatherhead, *Stephen Spender and the Thirties* (London: Associated University Presses, 1975), p. 191.

[103] Caesar, p. 87.

children seem to drive historical agency in the 1939 version, in the absence
of the verb 'to make'. The earlier version is also more insistent in ascribing
language, land, and culture to the working-class subjects and agents through
the repetition of the possessive pronoun; 'their world [...] their sands [...] their
tongues'; whereas the latter version repeats this pronoun only twice: 'their world
[...] their tongues'. In the 1939 version, there is a greater sense of the children
taking over the lines as middle-class facilitation of education, and thus social
change, is downplayed.

The poem reveals Spender's exploration of how far education, and, in turn,
impersonal historical process, can offer an alternative to the narrative of middle-
class, liberal reform without directly ascribing heroic agency to the working
classes. Such a reading complicates Caesar's analysis of Spender's commitment to
a 'great men' version of history and his suggestion that he 'never reveals himself
to be [...] interested in a Marxist view of history'.[104] 'An Elementary School Class
Room in a Slum' reveals Spender attempting to conceive – and depict – history as
an impersonal force, eschewing models of the heroic. Nonetheless, the agency in
the final lines of this poem remains – to a large extent – ambiguous. Can history
truly be driven by impersonal process, facilitating the avoidance of the heroic
pioneer? Or will the middle-class reformer, or the working-class revolutionary,
drive historical change and cultural regeneration? Spender's attempt to negotiate
between the poles of middle-class liberalism and working-class communism
is inscribed in this poem's closure. The poem reveals the transitional tensions
in this shift in political forms through the ambiguous agency inscribed in the
poem's final lines. The uneasy and incomplete resolution of these concerns is
paralleled by the 'muddled' nature of Spender's own political thinking in this
period.[105] *Forward from Liberalism* rather cryptically suggested that 'I am a
communist because I am a liberal' (p. 202) and that 'communism [...] is the final
goal of liberalism' (p. 203). Spender's introduction to 1955's *Collected Poems*
claimed that he had 'avoided [...] any attempt to remove inconsistencies of idea
or feeling, or to bring the beliefs expressed in the early poems into line with my
later ideas'.[106] Analysis of the revisions to 'An Elementary School Class Room
in a Slum' challenge these claims, as Spender neutralizes much of the tension
expressed in the 1939 version of the poem.

---

[104] Caesar, p. 85.
[105] Randall Swingler used this adjective to describe Spender's politics in his review of *Forward from Liberalism*. Randall Swingler, 'Spender's Approach to Communism', *Left Review*, March 1937, p. 110.
[106] *Collected Poems*, p. 15.

The 'Foreword' to *The Still Centre* ties literary production to the concept of the hero: 'One day a poet will write truthfully about [...] heroism [...] but such a poetry will be very different from the utilitarian heroics of the moment.'[107] Consideration of education complicates Cunningham's denial of the heroic after the Spanish Civil War, suggesting instead that heroism remained a significant conceptual framework for Spender, as he explored the possibility of a 'still centre' or self, untroubled by heroic ambition.

Antonia White: Feminist and pedagogic politics

Stephen Spender's *The Backward Son* is closely informed by aspects of Antonia White's novel, *Frost in May* (1933): both texts depict climactic moments of confrontation with school authorities that claim a chillingly privileged insight into their pupils' characters. White's analysis of her school life is concerned with the ways in which religious discipline and authority is imposed from above to infiltrate the very essence of the self. She depicts a conflation of academic, familial, and religious authority where what is at stake is not merely temporary opprobrium at the hands of the school authorities, but eternal damnation. The influence of White's novel extends beyond her immediate contemporaries. *Frost in May* was the first book to be included in Virago's Classics list, the cool detachment of the novel's narrator and the muddled obfuscation of the child's perspective combine to provide a searing critique of the convent school. This section explores the narrative perspectives in White's essay in *The Old School*, her short fiction, and *Frost in May*, to argue that the essay demonstrates how White was both critical of, and seduced by, her old school. White's contributions to *The Schoolmistress* are also considered as a compelling commentary on the feminist and pedagogic politics of her 1933 novel.

As critics have noted, *Frost in May* is 'ostensibly a novel but really a fictionalized memoir'.[108] The novel closely coheres with White's 1934 essay for *The Old School*, 'Child of the Five Wounds'. Both detail her life at Lippington (actually Roehampton) a strict, socially exclusive convent school led by the Order of the Sacred Heart, which is fictionalized as the Order of the Five Wounds. The climax of both narratives pivots around the same incident: the discovery of the opening

---

[107] *Still Centre*, p. 10.
[108] Chris Baldick, *The Oxford English Literary History Volume 10: 1910–1940 The Modern Movement* (Oxford: Oxford University Press, 2004), p. 362.

chapters of a racy novel by Nanda/Antonia which represented the sordid lives of her protagonists, without the final chapters (as yet unwritten) which would have presented the characters' miraculous 'conversion' to the path of righteousness. As a consequence of the discovery of the manuscript, White was effectively expelled from Lippington and attended St Paul's Girls' School, the sister school to the boys' school St Paul's, where her father, the eminent classicist, Cecil G. Botting, taught. This narrative of rejection through aesthetic creation has informed the critical reception of the novel. Regenia Gagnier argues that 'Nanda's opposition to religious and class domination expresses a failure to conform to an external identity as well as the internalized creation of an adversarial "self" henceforth to be associated with aesthetics.'[109] Elizabeth Bowen notes the analogies between *Frost in May* and *Portrait of the Artist as a Young Man*, analogies that Elizabeth Podnieks considers in relation to both Joyce and White.[110] Indeed, the narrative trajectories of both *Portrait* and *Frost in May* are striking in their opposition: where the closure of *Portrait* sees Stephen assert the power of his own creativity, Nanda's act of writing is subject to surveillance and repression. In *The Old School*, White suggests that the very act of writing is both indebted to, and in resistance against, the education she received at Lippington:

> In the matter of writing I owe a great deal to that education and I may as well admit it. I have not used my pen for purposes of which the Lippington authorities would approve but, were it not for them, I should probably never have used it at all. (p. 242)

Where Podnieks notes that the novel's 'underlying theme is the daughter trying to please the father and the devastating consequences that befall her when she fails', White's essay in *The Old School* focuses on the imposition of school authority, in line with the collection's editorial intent.[111] The essay remains devastatingly reticent surrounding the father's words that broke Nanda's 'last thread of self-control' in *Frost in May* – 'if a young girl's mind is such a sink of filth and impurity, I wish to God that I had never had a daughter' (p. 216) – instead noting 'the interview with my father was one which, after twenty years, I don't care to remember' (p. 244). By contrast, in both *Frost in May* and 'Child of the Five Wounds', the nun's words which are expressive of the central philosophy

[109] Regenia Gagnier, *Subjectivities: A History of Self-Representation in Britain, 1832–1920* (Oxford: Oxford University Press, 1991), p. 230.
[110] Bowen, p. vii; Elizabeth Podnieks, *Daily Modernism: The Literary Diaries of Virginia Woolf, Antonia White, Elizabeth Smart, and Anaïs Nin* (London: McGill-Queen's University Press, 2000), pp. 206–17.
[111] Podnieks, p. 189.

of White's education are closely paralleled. Mother Radcliffe in *Frost in May* exhorts: 'No character is any good in this world unless that will has been broken completely [...] [b]roken and re-set in God's own way.' (p. 145). The novel's denouement recalls these words, as Mother Radcliffe notes the fulfilment of her spiritual and pedagogic intent: 'Every will must be broken completely and re-set before it can be at one with God's will. [...] I had to break your will before your whole nature was deformed' (p. 219). The same phrase is used in 'Child of the Five Wounds': 'Your will had to be broken and re-set in God's own way' (p. 245). In the novel's closure, Nanda's father expresses the wish that she may go to 'some Protestant school where she was completely unknown' in order to keep 'the scandal [...] from becoming public' (p. 217), but details of this subsequent life are undisclosed as the narrative parameters remain within the bounds of the hermetically sealed world of the convent school. Instead, the narrative ends with the devastating, ominous realization that 'Nanda knew that whatever might happen in the future, nothing for her would ever be the same again' (p. 221).

Frost in May demonstrates an immersion in the child's perspective without the rationalizing perspective of maturity.[112] Like the third-person narrative voice in Henry James's *What Maisie Knew* (1897), which plays with the bounds of the eponymous heroine's knowledge of events, the consciousness of Nanda (named after another heroine of Henry James, Nanda/Fernanda in *The Awkward Age* (1899)) remains at an enigmatic remove from the reader, partly through the way in which *Frost in May* controls and manipulates time. In Chapter V, when an outbreak of 'feverish colds' occurs at the school, Nanda spends three days in 'snuffling misery' (p. 96) before presenting herself at the infirmary. In order to give Nanda a bed in the infirmary, the sisters decide to let another girl, Theresa Leighton, go back to her lessons. The chapter plays out the saga of Nanda's illness: the 'irrational[ly]' improvement in her condition on admittance to the infirmary; her concerns that it was a 'sin against charity' (p. 100) not to let the 'very delicate' (p. 97) Theresa have her bed. The end of the chapter sees Nanda usurped from her sanatorium bed because 'Theresa Leighton is very ill indeed' (p. 106). At the start of the next chapter, time has elapsed and there is a shocking revelation

---

[112] This characteristic of White's fiction has been analyzed by critics. Anna Jackson comments that 'Nanda's response is [...] emotional rather than analytical. The narrative, written in the past tense, looks back with immediate feeling, belonging always to the present tense of the story itself.' Hermione Lee notes the 'characteristic' 'pull' in White's fiction 'between the controlling writer, digging up her past as though she were her own analyst, and the unredeemed, "untreated" self in the fiction, unable to make coherent shape of, or distance herself from her state of mind'. Anna Jackson, *Diary Poetics: Form and Style in Writers' Diaries, 1915–1962* (London: Routledge, 2010), p. 22. Hermione Lee, 'Introduction', in Antonia White, *Strangers* (London: Virago, 1981), pp. i–vii (p. v).

regarding Theresa's fate: 'Nearly two years after Theresa Leighton's death came the happiest summer Nanda had ever known' (p. 106). The narrative gap means the immediate effect on Nanda of Theresa's death is undisclosed – but there is an indication that the intervening summers after Theresa's death and before this period of happiness have been less than happy. White's more forthright essay in *The Old School* closes down ambiguities of authorial attitude evident in the novel when similar details of Lippington life are recounted. In *The Old School,* White suggests that she was largely ignorant of the strong will that provokes the nuns' censure: 'Deep inside me[,] a tough little core of rebelliousness was growing. I was hardly aware of it myself, but the nuns, with their infallible eyes, knew all about it and watched me with suspicion' (p. 243); in *Frost in May,* however, a greater degree of uncertainty is maintained over the extent to which Nanda is in active rebellion against the school's authority: 'A small core of rebelliousness which had been growing secretly for four years seemed to have hardened inside her' (p. 156). The adjective 'secretly' is ambiguous here: To what extent is the rebelliousness a secret to Nanda herself, or to what extent is it her secret from the school authorities?

White's essay in *The Old School* temporally moves beyond the parameters of school life, to offer a reflection on her far more mundane education at St Paul's Girls' School where 'the gentle social pressure of "good form" and "loyalty" meant absolutely nothing to me' (p. 245). White's 1928 short story 'The Saint' also moves beyond the frame of childhood experience, as the first-person narrator reflects upon the child's experience to offer comment and explanation of the story's action, in this case on the miraculous powers of one of the convent's teachers:

> It must be thirty or forty years since it all happened. [...] I might even have forgotten all about it if I had not read in my *Universe* yesterday that the Canonization of the Blessed Keziah MacDowell had just been ratified by the Holy See.[113]

The essay in *The Old School* similarly moves out into a broader perspective, as White offers an analysis of the effect of her expulsion from an adult's perspective. White 'felt *déclassé* and an exile' (p. 246): 'It was a relief when the heavy door shut behind me and I was back again in the suburban lane, in the world to which I, an outsider from first to last, really belonged' (p. 246). Such a closure foregrounds themes latent in *Frost in May* surrounding the effect of the school's spiritual and

---

[113] Antonia White, *Strangers* (London: Harvill Press, 1954), p. 78.

social exclusivity on Nanda while also cohering with Greene's final analysis of the class-based significance of the current education system. The essay's closure also suggests how Gagnier's consideration of White's depiction of a version of the '"self" antagonistically[,] in spiritual rebellion against parents, school, and/ or Church', does not fully acknowledge the ways in which Nanda is as much seduced as oppressed by the nuns' strictures; as intoxicated by convent life as she is imprisoned by it.[114] It is notable that while part of the intent of *The Old School* was, Greene suggested, that the schools were 'mentioned by name', thus symbolically breaking ties of old school loyalty, White's essay in the collection instead uses the same false name for the school and its religious order that were used in *Frost in May*: Order of the Five Wounds instead of the Order of the Sacred Heart, and the school is known as 'Lippington', with the inverted commas signalling the false name for Roehampton.[115]

The role of spiritual and academic freedom in education interested White in her later diaries and journalistic contributions. Coupled with her essay in *The Old School*, they elucidate the complexity surrounding her attitude to the education she received at Roehampton. In August 1935 White stayed at A.S. Neill's progressive school, Summerhill, as the location for the Group Theatre's summer school. Although she noted that Bertrand Russell – with whom she had enjoyed a flirtation after meeting him in 1926 – had told her a 'great deal' about Telegraph House (the first location of the progressive Beacon Hill school Russell had founded with his wife, Dora), White notes that this was 'my first experience of an "experimental" school in action'.[116] She remained hesitant about the efficacy of the school's ethos, finding it was 'difficult to judge the experiment till these children have gone out into a society which still imposes certain rules of behaviour' while the school's founder, A.S. Neill, also provoked ambivalence: 'Neill I feel uncertain about. There is so much of the exhibitionist about him, something callow and shallow too [...] He strikes me as being radically vain.'[117]

In 1938 White wrote in her diary of her conflicted relationship with teaching: she 'hated *the idea* of being a schoolmistress, having a picture of a schoolmistress as a grotesque, unloved spinster. In practice, have always enjoyed teaching [...] Those who *can't,* teach. Haunted by that.'[118] After leaving school, White spent six

---

[114] Gagnier, p. 249.

[115] Sherry, p. 492.

[116] Antonia White, *Diaries 1926–1957 Volume I*, ed. by Susan Chitty (London: Constable, 1991), p. 52.

[117] *Diaries*, p. 52; p. 53.

[118] *Diaries*, p. 145, emphases in original.

months as a governess with a wealthy Catholic family and two terms teaching Latin, French, and Greek at a prep school where she had taken the place of a master who had gone to the Front. In 1933 she conducted a series of interviews with various eminent figures for *The Schoolmistress*, the teachers' magazine to which Holtby also contributed. Featured on the front page, a subheading introduced White as 'the brilliant author of "Frost in May"', noting that the interviews intended to 'discover[ing] what various distinguished people have found in their own school lives to have been most helpful and inspiring'.[119] They suggest the interest with which *Frost in May* was received in educational circles, and White's knowledge of current educational debates; she asks her interviewees about the role of the classics, co-education, and universities. The interviews are almost novelistic in tone. White starts each one by setting the scene, introducing her interviewee and capturing a sense of the quality and tenor of each interaction by noting the effect her interviewee had on herself. Of David Garnett she notes: 'The literary editor of the *New Statesman and Nation* is a shy interviewee. And shyness is infectious. In fact, my hand trembled so much that my notes are even more indecipherable than usual.'[120] She notes, conversely, of Sir William Crawford:

> SIR WILLIAM CRAWFORD, like Wordsworth, has two voices. One is the voice of command [...] The other is gentle, persuasive, [...] diffident and is reinforced by a remarkably charming smile. People are impressed and intimidated by the first, but they are completely vanquished by the second. And it was in the second that he talked to me about education.[121]

Her own persona in the interviews is inquisitive: 'I COULD not help asking him about his methods of work.'[122] At times, she charms her interviewees: '"But you're an admirable speaker, Sir William," I said. He smiled.'[123] By placing herself so strongly in her interviews as a foil for her interviewees' ideas, the interactions appear conversational, polite yet informal.

A central concern of the interviews is the role of authority in education. The progressive nature of her interviewees' thinking is clear: David Garnett discloses that he sends his son to Bertrand Russell's school where 'he seems not only

---

[119] Antonia White, 'Mr Gordon Selfridge', *The Schoolmistress*, 14 September 1933, p. 601 and p. 604 (p. 601).

[120] Antonia White, 'David Garnett', *The Schoolmistress*, 23 November 1933, p. 217 and p. 234 (p. 217).

[121] Antonia White, 'Sir William Crawford', *The Schoolmistress*, 28 September 1933, p. 658 and p. 674 (p. 658).

[122] 'David Garnett', p. 217.

[123] 'Sir William Crawford', p. 658.

happy and well-adjusted but actually in process of being very well educated'.[124] White asks the actress Flora Robson, with whom she was at drama school: 'If you had a daughter, would you like her to have more freedom than you had yourself at school?'.[125] Robson interprets this question as an issue of academic, rather than spiritual freedom: 'I'd have a certain number of compulsory subjects and the rest on free study lines rather in the way of the Dalton Plan'.[126] The Dalton Plan was inspired by progressive education. Devised by Helen Parkhurst and influenced by John Dewey and Maria Montessori, it encouraged freedom as 'part and parcel of the child's school life'.[127] This allowed the child to direct their own learning; instead of classrooms, subject rooms allow the child 'freedom of movement [...] freedom of choice of subject to be worked, and freedom as to the time of working the subject'.[128] The plan put an emphasis on 'Individual Work' where the 'ultimate aim [...] should be the expression of individuality', tempered by the belief that 'individuality finds its highest expression in the Social group'.[129] In the first interview of the series, White (rather leadingly) asks the retailer and businessman Gordon Selfridge 'if he was in favour of the Dalton plan which encourages children to develop their own powers of initiative and research as opposed to the old method of cramming them with the teacher's pre-digested notes'.[130]

A concern for the efficacy of exams is one that recurs throughout the interviews: White asks the scientist Dr Jordan Lloyd if 'you're against too much cramming for examinations?', where the negative inflection of the question discloses White's own attitude, and she is 'struck' by an 'extremely good' point made by Sir Alfred Hopkinson, the chancellor of Manchester University, that exams give 'the modest ones a chance'.[131] *The Old School* reflects interestingly upon Lippington's academic education, favourably comparing it to St Paul's. White notes that although the curriculum was 'narrow [...] the teaching was admirable' (p. 242), its cultivated curriculum a consequence of its social exclusivity: 'it was hoped that none of us would ever fall into such dire necessity as to be forced to earn

[124] 'David Garnett', p. 217.

[125] Antonia White, 'Flora Robson', *The Schoolmistress*, 12 October 1933, p. 33 and p. 36 (p. 33).

[126] 'Flora Robson', pp. 33–36.

[127] A.J. Lynch, *The Rise and Progress of the Dalton Plan* (London: Philip, 1926), p. 4.

[128] Ibid.

[129] Lynch, p. 5; p. 7; p. 8.

[130] 'Gordon Selfridge', p. 604.

[131] Antonia White, 'Dr. Jordan Lloyd', *The Schoolmistress*, 26 October 1933, p. 93 and p. 96 (p. 93); Antonia White, 'Sir Alfred Hopkinson', *The Schoolmistress*, 9 November 1933, p. 157 and p. 160 (p. 157).

our own living, so we competed for no public examinations' (p. 242). St Paul's Girls' School, however, was exam focused at the expense of the cultivation of true knowledge:

> The excellent digests of other people's books which were later crammed into me at St Paul's [...] have left no impression whatever [...] but I have never forgotten anything I learnt at Lippington. Languages, music, and the history of painting were taught with far more intelligence and efficiency at the Five Wounds than at any ordinary secular school. (p. 242)

Figures in White's interviews repeatedly meditate upon the need for the child to be an active participant in the educational process, rather than a passive recipient of knowledge and morality. Gordon Selfridge notes: 'If only schoolmasters and schoolmistresses would [...] study their pupils and bring out what is in *them* rather than just stamp their own personalities and views on the children they teach, then we'd have *real* education.'[132] In a similar vein, Dr Jordan Lloyd notes: 'What a child's mind needs [...] is not merely a pouring in of stuff from outside, but a chance to get going on its own. And a young mind needs plenty of time to itself to develop.'[133]

By focusing her interviews on interaction, the character and ideas of the interviewee are foregrounded, and her own political stance is obliquely presented. This is a contrast to another, more forthright article White wrote for *The Schoolmistress* under the headline 'The Position of Women in the World To-day', which reflects Holtby's defence of the married female teacher and the feminist politics of *The Schoolmistress*. The article 'stressed the case of the married woman'.[134] Its writer emerges as forceful ('I feel very strongly that the wind is blowing against women's right in general, and that, if we are not careful, we shall be blown back into a state of nonentity'), internationalist in perspective ('in Italy and Germany she is being driven "back to the home"'), and well-informed: White refers to a public meeting protesting 'against the increasing restrictions laid on married women's right to earn' and notes the rates of pay decreed by the Burnham Scale and statistics relating to the low rate of women's pay.[135] Cogent, summative analysis is offered: 'the battleground has shifted from

---

[132] 'Gordon Selfridge', p. 604, emphases in original.

[133] 'Dr. Jordan Lloyd', p. 93.

[134] Antonia White, 'The Position of Women in the World To-day', *The Schoolmistress*, 28 December 1933, p. 345.

[135] Ibid.

woman's political to her economic rights', and experts are alluded to: White closes the article by citing the feminist activist Mrs Pethick Lawrence.[136]

The lucidity of the article forms a contrast to the obfuscation of the child's perspective established in *Frost in May.* White's support to the campaign for married women teachers stands in interesting relation to her own educational background by celibate nuns. Her articles for *The Schoolmistress,* with their focus on anti-authoritarian education and feminist politics, suggest her profound aversion to the psychic crippling and recasting that formed the basis of Lippington's school discipline, however seductive White found the school's curriculum in her essay in *The Old School.*

Arthur Calder-Marshall: The community and the individual in Marxist aesthetics and public-school pedagogy

The communist writer Arthur Calder-Marshall taught at Denstone College, a minor public school, between 1931 and 1933. He offers a comedic, semi-fictionalized account of his entry into teaching in his 1951 autobiography, *The Magic of My Youth,* where he describes presenting himself at the scholastic agency Gabbitas & Thring and announcing: 'I want to declass myself. I should like a job in the worst school you have on your books.'[137] He is invited to provide cover for the Classics master at the comically titled 'Bogglesham Grammar School' which had recently been 'elevated' from the status of 'modest grammar school to the dignity of being represented at the Headmasters' Conference' (p. 208). Calder-Marshall describes visiting the school, where he was presented with a classroom that resembled a 'corrugated-iron shed' in which he found 'a mound of ordure that could have been produced by no dog smaller than a St Bernard or the Hound of the Baskervilles' (p. 210). Here, he finds 'exactly what I've been looking for' (p. 211).

This irreverent tone is evident in Calder-Marshall's essay about his alma mater St Paul's in *The Old School,* where his contribution focuses on spiritual life in school. His essay triangulates with his other works on education around this time: his public-school novel *Dead Centre* (1935) and his political and pedagogic tract *Challenge to Schools* (1935), published by the Hogarth Press. Elinor Taylor

[136] Ibid.

[137] Arthur Calder-Marshall, *The Magic of My Youth* (London: Hart-Davis, 1951), p. 207. Further references to this edition will be included in brackets after the citation.

argues that Calder-Marshall is the 'archetypal fellow traveller', and the nature of his pedagogic focus in the 1930s – a left-wing critique of the public-school system – exemplifies the middle-class origins of his political convictions.[138] I argue that Calder-Marshall's work on education illuminates his Marxist aesthetics as, like Stephen Spender, his creative writing on education manipulated literary form to accommodate a less individualized, and more communal, social vision.

Calder-Marshall's account in *The Old School* is characterized by the humour that also dominates Seán O'Failáin's essay in the collection, as he recounts the collusion between the monks and the boys in the face of school inspectors. However, where O'Failáin and White focus on relations between teacher and pupils, Calder-Marshall's view of school spiritual life is one informed by the peer group. In parentheses at the end of his essay, Calder-Marshall offers a corrective to any impression that his essay is a 'condemnation' (p. 72) of St Paul's. He draws on professional expertise – 'I have been a schoolmaster and know about schools' (p. 72) – to validate the quality of education his former school provides: 'I think that St. Paul's is a very fine school and I can advise parents who wish their sons to have a good academic education, to send them there' (p. 72). The essay focuses on Calder-Marshall's spiritual – rather than academic – experiences at school. The fact that religious experiences are depicted as largely motivated by peer interaction, with little spiritual guidance from authority figures is not, however, intended as a criticism: a footnote in Calder-Marshall's *Challenge to Schools* indicates that a schoolmaster friend who reviewed the pamphlet 'criticizes the fact that I have ignored the question of religion in schools […] I have not dealt with religion because I do not think it should enter into teaching'.[139] The title of Calder-Marshall's essay, 'More Frank than Buchman', alludes to the founder of the Protestant spiritual revivalist movements, the Oxford Group and the Moral Re-armament Movement. Buchman's teachings put an emphasis on the Holy Spirit, listening to God in silence and intercessory prayer, in order to promote 'life change' and spiritual awakening.[140] Buchman described the Oxford Group as an 'organism rather than an organisation', and it was characterized by the socially exclusive nature of its demographic; the group had no formal connection with Oxford, but Buchman was 'particularly successful', Juliet Gardiner notes,

---

[138] Elinor Taylor, 'Popular Front Politics and the British Novel, 1934–1940' (unpublished doctoral thesis, University of Salford [2014]), p. 2.

[139] Arthur Calder-Marshall, *Challenge to Schools: A Pamphlet on Public-School-Education* (London: Hogarth Press, 1935), p. 31. Further references to this edition will be included in brackets after the citation.

[140] Richard Overy, *The Morbid Age: Britain between the Wars* (London: Penguin, 2009), p. 69.

in recruiting Oxford undergraduates to the movement.[141] The group's spiritual practice was characterized by 'house parties', mass gatherings that involved public confession of sins, and 'quiet time' whereby, as Philip Boobbyer notes, 'God could give people wisdom or guidance as to what to do.'[142]

Calder-Marshall's account in *The Old School* mentions his involvement in both quiet time and house parties. He first takes an interest in the Oxford Group after attending a talk at the school whereby Christ is fatuously associated with the public-school's athletic ideal as the parallel statements comically deflate the preacher's logic: 'He said he thought Christ would have played hard for His school, if He was at school to-day. [...] He said, Christ might have rowed for the Varsity if there'd been any Varsity to row for' (p. 64). For the large part, however, the religious practices described are founded in peer activity, rather than formalized school services. In the essay, the intimacy of quiet time and spiritual reflection becomes a proxy for homoerotic intimacies. Spiritual practices are mistaken for sexual fumblings by boys who are not involved in the movement, a misapprehension that the young Calder-Marshall plays with: '"What's all this about? What do you do to one another when you lace up those tent tapes?" "You wouldn't be interested," I said. "It's not your line"' (p. 66). The movement was also used as an opportunity to guard against homosexual practices as one house party used the gathering as a means of warning boys of the evils of masturbation. After a talk the 'bigger boys' explained to the 'smaller boys' what masturbation was, so, Calder-Marshall sardonically notes 'they shouldn't do it' (p. 67). Ironically 'there was great competition for who should walk with whom' (p. 67), as boys wished to share intimate time with the better looking of the boys. Calder-Marshall's account of 'how I lost God' (p. 68) details a comic play between the sexual and the spiritual. It is based around an occasion of 'Quiet Time' when 'Philips and I went up to have Q.T. together' (p. 68). The solemnity of the spiritual occasion and the innuendo of a heaving mattress sparks an eruption of laughter, in recognition of the farcical nature of it all: 'We caught eyes across the bed. And suddenly the air was filled with laughing [...] down, like a precariously balanced pyramid in a shop window, all Pi-squash religion crashed, smashed and lay in fragments on the floor' (p. 68). Even after this, however, 'I couldn't tell them I didn't believe in what I had believed' so 'I kept it all dark about not being religious' (p. 69).

---

[141] Gardiner, p. 504.

[142] Philip Boobbyer, *The Spiritual Vision of Frank Buchman* (Philadelphia: Pennsylvania State University Press, 2013), p. 5.

Calder-Marshall's other significant publications concerned with education during the 1930s, his novel *Dead Centre* and his tract *Challenge to Schools*, show a strong correlation in a number of areas, with the former often presenting in dramatic form the polemical arguments evident in the latter. The novel, a collection of first-person narratives from sixty-three characters, exemplifies what Calder-Marshall later defined in the 1937 'Writing in Revolt' issue of *Fact* as the 'composite method', exemplified by the work of John Dos Passos.[143] While bourgeois literature emphasized the individual, Calder-Marshall believed the progressive writer should depict society as a whole. In a 1937 *Left Review* article, he noted:

> I face the fact that this life of ours is very difficult to group around any central character; that, indeed, it obstinately refuses to be so grouped; and that it refuses to be so much more than used to be the case.[144]

The *Guardian* review of *Dead Centre* noted that 'no school story hitherto written has succeeded so well in analysing the complex variety of personalities that go to make up such a community'.[145] The novel's wide cast of characters, all of whom are associated with Richbury, a minor public school, include a cross-spectrum of the social scale; the majority are pupils, some are teachers, while the school matron, a teacher's wife, servants, the school porter, and gardener are also included.

The multivocal nature of the novel renders its title formally applicable; while some characters are given more than one chapter, it formally has no central voice or perspective. The terms of the novel's title also thematically recur across the text in various contexts which are expressive of the ontological, cultural, pedagogical, and politically defunct nature of the public-school system. One chapter presents the perspective of Mr Biddles, Richbury's OTC officer, who trained up schoolboy officers who enlisted in the army and were killed on the Front. He 'half-believed' the 'lies' told about war, 'while the other part of myself repeated over and over again that awful phrase, "Cannon Fodder" for guns whose appetites seemed insatiable'.[146] The death of the model of public-school masculinity, Cook – 'Captain of my house and Captain of School, I regarded him as my superior' (p. 31) – devastated Biddles: 'Cook's death was the worst shock

---

[143] Arthur Calder-Marshall, 'Fiction', *Fact*, July 1937, pp. 38–44 (p. 42).

[144] *Left Review*, January 1937, as cited in Croft, p. 261.

[145] S.W., 'The Truth about School', *The Manchester Guardian*, 17 September 1935, p. 5.

[146] Arthur Calder-Marshall, *Dead Centre* (London: Cape, 1935), pp. 30–31; p. 30; p. 31. Further references to this edition will be included in brackets after the citation.

of all' (p. 31). Biddles heroizes Cook in his personal rituals of memorialization: 'I put him rightly in the centre of my Old Boys' photographs' (p. 31). The terms of the novel's title become representative of the chasm left behind by a generation of lost adolescents, little more than schoolboys, as Calder-Marshall echoes Vera Brittain's critique of public-school militarism, discussed in more detail in Chapter 2.

In another chapter, the Classics teacher, Mr Small, rails against the classical curriculum of the public school for its extinction of a literary appreciation of the classics in a focus instead on grammar and philology: 'Why in God's name, I say, should philology hold the position of supreme importance, the word becoming more important than the man who wrote it or the occasion on which he wrote?' (p. 60). The boys are left alienated from classical culture as a result of the dry syllabus: 'To the boys, they are dead; dead languages and dead people' (p. 58). *Challenge to Schools* similarly regrets a classical curriculum which 'since the Renaissance has degenerated from the study of what was then the sum total of secular knowledge to a dry, antiquarian and philological exercise' due to the 'demands of examiners for fact' (p. 36).

Calder-Marshall's examination of the tension between cultural and philological concerns in the teaching of the classics is also discussed by Christopher Stray, who analyzes 'the shift from culture to discipline' in the perception of the classics (and particularly Latin) from the Victorian era to 1960, a shift which he suggests 'belonged to a process of marginalization which led [...] to disestablishment'.[147] As Stray notes, by the mid-1880s, there was a perception that the 'regimented corpus of language denied the creative variety of literature', a perception that persisted, until by the 1970s a well-established image of Latin had emerged as 'an arid disciplinary grind'.[148] Stray suggests that St Paul's, the school Calder-Marshall attended, was a 'strong source' for Latin prose composition by North and Hillard, and Greek unseens by Hillard and Botting, the latter, in fact, Antonia White's father who taught at St. Paul's.[149] Where Mr Small in *Dead Centre* regrets the pedagogic tools available to him, 'North and Hillard' (p. 58), the standard Latin prose textbook of the period, *Challenge to Schools* discusses in greater detail objections to the North and Hillard syllabus: 'A textbook such as North and Hillard states rules at the head of each section, rules which, if got by heart [...] will achieve the results necessary for examination success' (p. 36). Such a

---

[147] Christopher Stray, *Classics Transformed: Schools, Universities and Society in England, 1830–1960* (Oxford: Clarendon Press, 1998), p. 297.

[148] Stray, p. 195; p. 296.

[149] Stray, p. 190.

regimented method occludes the fact that 'these rules are [...] not rules, but part of a logical system of thought' (p. 36). While North and Hillard promote the teaching of grammar 'by rote' rather than 'by intelligence' (p. 36), Calder-Marshall suggests that knowledge should be approached by 'intellect[,] instead of memory' (p. 37). The 1934 Latin course *Balbus* embodies some of the tensions Calder-Marshall considers here, exemplifying, Stray suggests, the 'tension between classics as culture and as discipline'.[150] Designed to make the early stages of Latin learning more engaging, the book included illustrations and cultural notes on aspects of Roman life. The book's preface notes an intent to demonstrate the 'lighter [...] more humane aspect' of the classics, while elsewhere noting that 'some pain' was involved in learning, and asserting the need for 'firmness and determination' in order to 'master' the grammar of Latin.[151]

Challenge to Schools further elucidates the critique underlying *Dead Centre* as founded in an ontological principle of the egotism of adolescence from which pedagogic principles should derive:

> To a boy, the centre of the world is himself. From that core radiate the school, the home, the country, the world of present to the outer circumference, the history of that world. [...] If he can be shown that what he is learning is relevant to himself and the world in which he lives, he will welcome it. The struggles of Clodius and Milo are dead [...] But if he can see in them a similar situation to the conflict of Fascists and Communists, they take on new significance. [...] A constant reference from what is being taught to what is being lived; the rescue of the living truth from the debris of history, is the true salvage work of teaching. (p. 38)

The aridity of the curriculum described in *Dead Centre* is reflected here in the description of the 'dead' struggles of classical figures. Archaeological metaphors are used to describe pedagogic principles which impress upon pupils a sense of the applicability of the past to the present, a pedagogic method which echoes Mr Small's desire to show the boys 'time's measuring rod by which they may judge the present. [...] What I could teach and want to is the humanity of "the humanities"' (p. 59). Calder-Marshall advocates the abandonment of the arid, philological approach to the teaching of Latin in order to focus instead on the cultural and political relevance of classical civilizations for contemporary politics. Elinor Taylor includes Calder-Marshall's literary works in her assessment of the popular front's 'sustained attempt to mobilise cultural resources for anti-fascist

---

[150] Stray, p. 280.

[151] *Balbus*, pp. 9–10, as cited in Stray, p. 281.

ends'.[152] In *Challenge to Schools*, Calder-Marshall's pedagogy itself becomes part of this effort as he suggests that political change can stimulate a renewal of the social system in a vision charged with a concern for vitality and novelty:

> A new type of individual is necessary, a type more capable of adjusting himself to new conditions, more alive in every way. Uncritical acceptance of society [...] makes [...] for chaos, by trying to apply a formula that is out of date. The old type cannot persist as before. It must develop in one of two ways, towards Fascism or towards Communism. (p. 29)

The 'new' 'alive' individual is a contrast to the dead centre critiqued in his novel. The openness of 'towards Fascism or towards Communism' reflects Calder-Marshall's pedagogic practice as a schoolteacher, whereby, although holding communist sympathies, he believed in pedagogic 'impartiality': 'When I was a schoolmaster I considered it an essential part of my job to argue and present capitalist and socialist positions also' (p. 29). For him, it was the schoolmasters' duty 'to present not one, but every side of a question' (p. 32).

Challenge to Schools criticizes the public school's ability to cultivate the kind of political and ontological liberation Calder-Marshall advocates. It concludes by arguing that the public schools exist to 'maintain the present system' (p. 40), thus their curriculum and ethos are purposively moribund: 'A deliberate policy, based on the need to perpetuate a capitalist state at all costs' (p. 40). It is in the schools' own interests to cling to their dead centres of authority; any reform threatens their existence: 'The sterile curriculum must be preserved, because live knowledge is dynamic, and dynamitic. [...] They are, from their point of view, wise to suppress, to thwart and deaden as long and fully as they can' as reform 'would release a power that would destroy the economic basis on which they rest.' (p. 41).

The types of selfhood cultivated by public-school-education are also designed to support the current social model. In the public school, 'the good of society (that is, society as constituted at present) and not the good of the individual is desiderated' (p. 12). An experienced teacher, Calder-Marshall notes that 'I have never heard a schoolmaster ask whether the school was good for a certain boy. The statement that a boy is not good for the school is heard constantly' (p. 12). This position is dramatized in *Dead Centre,* where the school headmaster, always with one eye to balancing the books and one eye to PR opportunities, asserts that 'we cannot allow personal considerations to outweigh the good of

---

[152] Taylor, p. 5.

the community' (p. 190). The novel repeatedly enacts this principle, as signs of individuality are suppressed, from the caning of Fothergill, who grows his hair long, to the story of how one of the school's teachers, Cartwright, enacted a 'transcending of personal considerations by public duty' (p. 234) in his request for his rebellious son to be expelled from the school. The novel's final chapter presents 'The Porter' reminiscing about his interactions with various old boys who return to the school. His narration of their conversation indicates how seemingly standardized the product of Richbury is in social interaction: "'I'm runnin' a garage," he says, or such like' (p. 285); "'Well, Sandy," he says, "there's no denying it's a warm day" (or a cold day, depending on the time of year)' (p. 286).

The *Guardian* praised *Dead Centre* for the 'psychological insight' of the first-person portraits, which avoid clichéd portrayals: 'in each we get the human being and no stereotyped figure' and indeed the first-person narratives of the novel frequently express the tension between the fulfilment of the social perception of the public-school product, as advanced by the Porter, and individual identity.[153] *Challenge to Schools* directly criticizes the type of individual cultivated by the public school as 'muted individuals, whose mean is mediocrity' (p. 12). Their personalities cramped by the demands of school life, Calder-Marshall draws an analogy between public-school men and Japanese bonsai trees, cultivated and interfered with 'till they become for ever dwarfed, not too big for their pots' (p. 13). A natural consequence of this is war, which allows 'the stunted individual to give rein to anti-social ideals under guise of heroism' (p. 14). *Challenge to Schools* maintains that 'the ideal public school man never exists' (p. 12), and instead argues that the 'social ideal' of the public school 'cramps, distorts and stunts, for a social ideal which it is incapable of realizing' (p. 14). In *Dead Centre*, the only two pupils or ex-pupils who fulfil the model of school life are literally non-existent; both are dead: Cook, the war hero who died at the front, and Jeffers, killed in a sporting accident who is also recognized as attaining the qualities of the public-school ideal, when the headmaster celebrates him as a 'future captain of the school' (p. 242) with 'the makings of "a perfect Christian gentleman"' (p. 243). This suggests that a seeming consequence of the fulfilment of the public-school ideal is death, or that death allows the projection of the public-school ideal onto individuals. In Woolf's *The Waves*, Percival, the novel's public-school 'hero', is introduced in the novel's school scenes. His voice is not presented directly to the reader and, similarly, the direct perspectives of both Jeffers and Cook are not

[153] S.W., 'Truth about School', p. 5.

presented; instead, impressions of them are formed through the narratives of others.

Dead Centre plays with the tension between individual and communal identity: chapter headings reflect the institutionalized nature of public-school identity as they allude to different boys by their surnames, while the first-person narratives frequently express the complexities and tensions in reconciling individual identity to the demands of the public-school community. The narrative of Ridgway, the Head of the School, poignantly ends with his relief at his imminent liberation from the alienating pressures of his position: 'I shall be free from responsibility for the conduct of other people [...] I can be a person once again, with his own likes and dislikes' (p. 280). Andy Croft notes Calder-Marshall's 'growing preoccupation' in the 1930s with 'the relationship between individual character and the wider society'.[154] Where Calder-Marshall advocated aesthetic principles founded in a concern for a communal vision, his pedagogic principles strongly derive from a focus on the individual, as he critiques the public school's personally compromising emphasis on communality. In the 'composite' form of *Dead Centre*, with its array of first-person narratives expressive of the pressures of according to communal life, Calder-Marshall found a form that could both express the urgency behind his pedagogic principles and accommodate his Marxist aesthetic vision.

Conclusion: *The Old School* and its cultural moment

The writers included in *The Old School* were engaged by education. Essays in the collection, as demonstrated here, offered, in Stephen Spender's case, a stimulus to other creative works that focused on school and schooling; in Antonia White's case, a creative reimagining of existing works from a different temporal perspective; and, in the cases of Greenwood and Calder-Marshall, a corollary to other writing that considered education in the period. The significance of the volume lies less in the interest of the individual essays, however, but in the very fact of the volume itself, which embodies that peculiarly 1930s moment whereby the political and social urgency behind education was keenly felt.

There was a perception on the part of reviewers, however, that authors were not in the best position to be offering opinions on education: David Garnett's review of *The Old School* in the *New Statesman and Nation* cites the opinion of a

[154] Croft, p. 262.

schoolmaster who found it 'a cloak for a number of literary fledgelings to make muling complaints about their education'.[155] Garnett notes that 'he thought also that the book would have been more valuable had it included stockbrokers and clerks and "ordinary people" among the contributors'.[156] E.M. Forster's review presents a dialogue between two of his characters from his own public-school novel, *The Longest Journey* (1907), to dismiss the volume and its contributors: 'Oh, there's nothing to take any notice of [...] [t]hey turn out to be only authors – not people who matter – they are just writing to one another about how they didn't get on at their schools.'[157] This accusation of self-involvement obscures the political earnestness behind the collection itself, and the sense of prescience behind school experience that motivated Greene's editorial involvement.

The literary focus of the collection is indicative of the ways in which education played a role in the formation of cultural ideals in this period. Reading across these writers' novels, poetry, autobiographical works, and educational engagements demonstrates the extent to which their pedagogic and creative works are contiguous: the former feeding into the latter. Where both White's *Frost in May* and Spender's *The Backward Son* offer studies of a consciousness formed under the pressures of school life that are illuminated by reference to these writers' broader engagements with educational discourses, elsewhere the individualistic focus of these narratives is contrasted with experiments in literary form and narrative structure that gesture to attempts to capture a more collective, communal experience: from the circular structure of *Love on the Dole*, Greenwood's examination of the uneducated, depoliticized Salford slums; to Calder-Marshall's 'composite' novel examining the public-school community; to Spender's depiction of ways in which working-class education could precipitate cultural change through the workings of historical process. For these writers of *The Old School*, socialist politics are figured not only in their political and educational ideals, but also in their experiments in literary form, as they found new ways to envisage and represent alternative political and social realities.

[155] David Garnett, 'Current Literature: Books in General', *New Statesman and Nation*, 25 August 1934, p. 239.
[156] Ibid.
[157] 'Review of *The Old School*', p. 136.

4

'Altering the Structure of Society': Virginia Woolf's Class-Critique of Educational Institutions in the 1930s

Virginia Woolf attended the 1935 Labour Party Conference as she was revising *The Years*. The experience provoked prevarication: 'Altering the structure of society: yes, but when its [*sic*] altered? [...] Ought we all to be engaged in altering the structure of society?' (D4, pp. 345–46). Woolf's interrogation of 'the structure of society' reflects Labour's concerns with precisely such a wholesale overhaul. It called for 'a bold policy of Socialist Reconstruction', in which the expansion of education beyond the official school-leaving age of fourteen was to play a key role: 'The Labour Party stands for a big move forward in education, including the raising of the school-leaving age.'[1] Woolf's diary comments recall her 1928 essay on Thomas Hardy, in which she regretted Hardy's 'pessimism' about structural overhaul through the continued exclusion of Jude from Christminster, a version of Oxford.[2] On 26 July 1933, in the early stages of writing *The Years* (*The Pargiters*, the essay-novel from which *The Years* emerged, was finished in December 1932), Jude sprang to mind once again: 'couldnt [*sic*] settle on any [book] save T. Hardy's life just now [...] he felt bitter about the treatment of working men at Oxford; hence Jude' (D4, p. 169). Shortly before the Labour Party Conference, on 13 September 1935, Woolf was similarly exploring how accessible Oxford was to the working classes: '[A] man could live on £200 at Oxford if he lived at home' (D4, p. 341).

Woolf's interest in social class and the institutional structures of education has largely been overlooked in the trend of critical discussion on Woolf and pedagogy,

---

[1] 'Labour Party General Election Manifesto 1935: The Labour Party's Call to Power', in *Labour Party General Election Manifestos, 1900–1997*, ed. by Iain Dale (London: Routledge, 1999), pp. 45–47 (p. 47).

[2] Virginia Woolf, 'The Novels of Thomas Hardy', in *The Essays of Virginia Woolf Volume 5: 1929–1932*, ed. by Clarke, pp. 561–72 (p. 569).

which has focused on two main areas. Critics who have taken an institutional focus have centred on Woolf and gender, with Anna Snaith, Carol T. Christ, and Ann K. McClellan exploring Woolf's critique of women's exclusion from elite male institutions.[3] Concomitant to this, exploration of Woolf's engagement with working-class education has generally taken an anti-institution approach. Melba Cuddy-Keane, Hermione Lee, and Beth Rigel Daugherty have all asserted the significance of Woolf's model of the Common Reader, who uses the public library or the essay, to support a pedagogical strategy that enacts a classless model of autodidacticism.[4] Institutional applications of social class and pedagogy have been marginalized in these debates: Cuddy-Keane argues that Woolf was concerned with democracy as 'social discourse rather than social structures.'[5]

Alison Light and Sean Latham have explored Woolf's class-consciousness, with Light suggesting that this served as a fault line in her socialist political commitment: 'Servants, as ever, were Virginia's window on the world, the chinks of light glimpsed through the thick hedges of class feeling which boxed her in.'[6] Frank Gloversmith aligns Woolf with the cultural theories of Clive Bell, but, I suggest, Woolf was also informed by R.H. Tawney's work.[7] Woolf read Tawney (who was president of the Workers' Educational Association (WEA) from 1928 to 1944) immediately after war was announced, and shortly before her 1940 lecture to the WEA.[8] Jim McGuigan has drawn an opposition between Tawney's conception of 'common culture', which connoted a dissemination of high culture to the masses via education and cultural policy, and Raymond Williams's suggestion that, with

[3] Anna Snaith, 'Introduction', in Virginia Woolf, *The Years*, ed. by Anna Snaith (Cambridge: Cambridge University Press, 2012), pp. xxxix–xcix; 'Chapter 4: Negotiating Genre: Revisioning History in *The Pargiters*', in Anna Snaith, *Virginia Woolf: Public and Private Negotiations* (Basingstoke: Macmillan, 2000); Carol T. Christ, 'Woolf and Education', in *Woolf in the Real World: Selected Papers from the Thirteenth International Conference on Virginia Woolf, Smith College, Northampton, Massachusetts 5–8 June 2003*, ed. by Karen V. Kukil (Clemson: Clemson University Digital Press, 2005), pp. 2–9; Ann K. McClellan, 'Adeline's (bankrupt) Education Fund: Woolf, Women and Education in the Short Fiction', *Journal of the Short Story in English*, Vol. 50 (2008), 2–12.
[4] Hermione Lee, *Virginia Woolf* (London: Chatto & Windus, 1996), p. 414; Beth Rigel Daugherty, 'Virginia Woolf Teaching/Virginia Woolf Learning: Morley College and the Common Reader', in *New Essays on Virginia Woolf*, ed. by Helen Wussow (Dallas: Contemporary Research Press, 1995), pp. 61–77 (p. 74); Melba Cuddy-Keane, *Virginia Woolf, The Intellectual and the Public Sphere* (Cambridge: Cambridge University Press, 2003), p. 109.
[5] *Virginia Woolf*, p. 40.
[6] Alison Light, *Mrs Woolf and the Servants* (London: Penguin, 2007), p. 235.
[7] Frank Gloversmith, 'Defining Culture: J.C. Powys, Clive Bell, R.H. Tawney and T.S. Eliot', in *Class, Culture and Social Change*, ed. by Gloversmith, pp. 15–44 (p. 25).
[8] Virginia Woolf, *The Diary of Virginia Woolf Volume V 1936–1941*, ed. by Anne Olivier Bell (London: Hogarth Press, 1984), p. 233. Further references to this edition will be included in brackets after the citation, as D5 and then the page number.

increased access to education, the very form of a common culture would be transformed.[9] Williams himself was a WEA tutor from 1946 to 1961, and located the origins of cultural studies in the post–Second World War adult education movement 'with notable precedents [...] in the thirties'.[10] Attention to Woolf's engagement with contemporaneous educational discourses – relating to both emergent ideals surrounding comprehensive education and the adult education movement – reveals how her work was informed by early manifestations of debates surrounding the role of education in the cultivation of social and cultural democracy.

Such a focus on Woolf's political engagements in the 1930s supplements work done by David Bradshaw, who has documented Woolf's involvement with the anti-fascist organizations: the IAWDC (International Association of Writers for the Defence of Culture) and FIL (For Intellectual Liberty). Both organizations had similar aims: the defence of 'peace, liberty and culture' in response to the growing menace of continental fascism.[11] Despite Woolf's resignation from the IAWDC in June 1936, her role as a supportive writer-artist panellist in FIL meant that, in the mid to late 1930s, she 'still moved very much within that milieu [of anti-fascist activity]' yet operated as an 'Outsider, working against fascism in her own way and on her own terms'.[12] During this period, Woolf's ideas on cultural democracy were simultaneously being forged through her reading of key thinkers in educational reform. Where the IAWDC and FIL's efforts were pan-European, Woolf's engagement with 1930s educational discourses emerged from a more distinctively British perspective. These discourses provided Woolf with a framework through which to interrogate the limitations of existing 'democratic' values. This chapter joins recent interest on Woolf's cultural critique in the 1930s to consider *The Pargiters* (1932), *The Years* (1937), *Three Guineas* (1938), and her 1940 essay 'The Leaning Tower' (originally delivered as a lecture to the Sussex branch of the WEA on 27 April 1940), alongside her diaries and letters, to argue that she positioned education's institutional structures as playing a significant role in the development of cultural and political democracy in the 1930s.[13] In

[9] Raymond Williams, "The Idea of a Common Culture (1967)', in Raymond Williams, *On Culture & Society: Essential Writings*, ed. by Jim McGuigan (London: Sage, 2014), pp. 93–100 (p. 93).

[10] Raymond Williams, 'The Future of Cultural Studies', in *Politics of Modernism* (London: Verso, 1989), pp. 151–62 (p. 154).

[11] FIL's 'Resolution', as cited in David Bradshaw, 'British Writers and Anti-Fascism in the 1930s, Part I: The Bray and Drone of Tortured Voices', *Woolf Studies Annual*, Vol. 3 (1997), 3–27 (p. 24).

[12] David Bradshaw, 'British Writers and Anti-Fascism in the 1930s, Part II: Under the Hawk's Wings', *Woolf Studies Annual*, Vol. 4 (1998), 41–66 (p. 48).

[13] See Wood, *Virginia Woolf's Late Cultural Criticism*.

working across published and unpublished materials, written in different genres and for different purposes, this chapter also recognizes that the variable contexts of Woolf's political involvement inform the tenor of her negotiation of these debates.

The Pargiters and Woolf's ironic acts of naming

Woolf's early conceptualization of *The Years* came in *The Pargiters,* which, in addition to its feminist critique of education,[14] contains a significant critique of the role of the institution in working-class education. Indeed, while the first women's colleges were established in the second half of the nineteenth century, this period was also significant for the expansion of working-class, university-level education: Ruskin College was founded as a 'Labour' college at Oxford in 1899.[15] Although advances were made in facilitating access to university for women and working men, in reality, Oxbridge remained an upper-class male world: R.D. Anderson describes it as a 'finishing school for young gentlemen'.[16] Between 1878 and 1879, only 4 per cent of men matriculating at Oxford had fathers who were 'Tradesmen, Clerks, Working Class'; this figure rose marginally to 5 per cent from 1897 to 1898.[17] Lawrence Goldman suggests that Oxford and Cambridge's University Extension lecturing system in fact 'saved them from further reform', preserving the space inside the college walls for the public-school elites.[18] This is reflected in *The Pargiters* where both middle-class women and the working classes are described as 'ignorant' (p. 78) of the public-school tradition. Andrew Thacker argues that Woolf's novels 'constantly play across the spatial borders of inner and outer'.[19] In *The Pargiters,* the space outside the elite

---

[14] See Mitchell A. Leaska, 'Introduction', in Virginia Woolf, *The Pargiters: The Novel-Essay Portion of The Years,* ed. by Mitchell A. Leaska (London: Hogarth Press, 1978), pp. vii–xxiv (p. viii). Further references to this edition will be included in brackets after the citation; Snaith, 'Chapter 4', in *Public and Private.*

[15] In terms of the women's colleges, Queen's College was established at the University of London in 1848, Girton at Cambridge in 1869, and Lady Margaret Hall at Oxford in 1878.

[16] R.D. Anderson, *Universities and Elites in Britain since 1800* (Cambridge: Cambridge University Press, 1995), p. 43.

[17] M.C. Curthoys and Janet Howarth, 'Origins and Destinations: The Social Mobility of Oxford Men and Women', in *The History of the University of Oxford VII,* ed. by Brock and Curthoys, pp. 571–95 (p. 578).

[18] Lawrence Goldman, *Dons and Workers: Oxford and Adult Education since 1850* (Oxford: Clarendon Press, 1995), p. 35.

[19] Andrew Thacker, *Moving through Modernity: Space and Geography in Modernism* (Manchester: Manchester University Press, 2003), p. 152.

institution's walls is symbolically inscribed into the institution itself, as Edward reminisces about his public school while at Oxford:

> There had seemed to be none of that feeling of fellowship that had made the last [*year*] terms of his life at Morley so [*tremendously*] important, so exciting [...] the Headmaster [...] said one night what Edward [ha] felt to be the summing up of the whole spirit of Morley – how they belonged to a great & famous fellowship [...] even the most thoughtless, could not leave Morley without feeling that our character as members of a society or fellowship is something different from our individual character. (p. 60)

Oxford is aligned with the public-school tradition in Edward's repeated reference to his ambition to be awarded a 'Fellowship' (p. 59; p. 60) at his college. This title for an academic appointment is echoed here by the term Woolf uses to represent the spirit of kinship engendered by the public school. The public-school system is also, however, presented as excluding the working classes through the ironic implications of the name 'Morley'. Woolf taught English Composition and held a 'Reading Circle' at Morley College in Lambeth from 1905 to 1907.[20] Her adoption of this name for Edward's public school is an ironic statement of social protest at the public school's exclusivity. In the essay section, Morley becomes Rexby. 'The Leaning Tower' later rallied its audience to remain valiant in the struggle for education and political power: 'Nor let us shy away from the kings because we are commoners' (E6, p. 277). The naming strategy in *The Pargiters*, the transference of the working man (Morley) to the King (in the Latin origin of the name 'Rexby'), prefigures this later, more overt political statement.

The ironic intent of Woolf's naming is made explicit in the description of Mr Gabbit/Sam Hughes. As Anna Snaith has noted, aspects of the characterization of this figure are based on the real-life Joseph Wright, the Oxford academic of working-class origins, who created the first *English Dialect Dictionary*

---

[20] Hermione Lee notes that Woolf's attitude to her students while teaching at Morley was a 'blend of conscience and condescension'. Beth Rigel Daugherty's analysis of Woolf's teaching at Morley College contributes to a reading of her essays as transgressing hierarchical models of authority and social class. She notes that Woolf's 'essays become classrooms, spaces permeated with the "understanding of a teacher"', in which she creates a space where 'learning, not hierarchy, is paramount, and where class boundaries can be crossed'. Beth Rigel Daugherty's analysis of the implications of Woolf's teaching for her class politics is a reading that Clara Jones 'complicate[s]' in her analysis of the influence of Morley College on Woolf's political and social thought and her early fiction. Lee, *Virginia Woolf*, p. 224; Daugherty, 'Virginia Woolf Teaching/Virginia Woolf Learning', p. 74; Clara Jones, *Ambivalent Activist*, p. 22.

(1898–1905).[21] In July 1932 Woolf was reading Wright's biography, written by his wife, Elizabeth. Her diary notes that Joseph 'had his old working mother to Oxford. She thought All Souls would make a good Co-op' (D4, p. 116). These reading notes make their way into *The Pargiters*:

> He [Mr Gabbit] would tell them how his mother [...] had taught herself to read when she was over forty; and how she had a better brain than any professor in the place; and how when she came to Oxford, she had remarked of All Souls that it would make an admirable Co-operative hall. (p. 127)

Woolf's inclusion of Mrs Wright's comment speaks to the irony of an Oxford college that names itself 'All Souls' but, unlike the Co-op Hall, does not accommodate all social groups. J.S.G. Simmons notes the 'persistence' of the exclusive 'social stamp' of All Souls and its 'uniquely high' 'social profile': in 1880 it counted five honourables, knights, or baronets among its fellows, and seventeen of its thirty-two fellows went to Eton, Rugby, or another school listed in the Clarendon Commission.[22] Woolf's source for Mrs Wright's comment is less politicized, however; Elizabeth Wright positions her mother-in-law's words as a gripe against the wasteful nature of a college as a seat of research for fellows, rather than education of students: 'Contemplating All Souls, he [Joseph Wright] remarked that there were no undergraduates there. Whereupon Mrs Wright, always a practical woman, unwilling to see anything wasted, exclaimed with fervour: "Eh, but it wod [*sic*] mak [*sic*] a grand Co-op!"'[23] Woolf's adaptation of her source allows her to intensify her critique of socially exclusive educational structures and reinforces her polemic.

Woolf's ironic acts of naming disrupt the territorial and psychological hegemony connoted by the public school and university, making the absence of the working classes from these structures present to readers. Through nomenclature, she implicitly colonizes these spaces for the working class, while working within a social model that dichotomizes the working class and the established middle class.

---

[21] Anna Snaith first asserted the significance of Joseph Wright as a source for Sam Robson in her exploration of the generic transformation of *The Pargiters* into *The Years*. In her editorial notes to *The Years*, Snaith further alludes to William Alexander Robson as a source for this character. An academic at the London School of Economics, Robson was also joint editor with Leonard Woolf on *Political Quarterly*, a journal Robson co-founded in 1930 with Kingsley Martin. Both Leonard and Virginia Woolf saw Robson 'frequently' in the 1930s, and Virginia Woolf later became 'close' to his daughter, Elaine. Snaith's explanatory notes to the Cambridge edition of *The Years* nonetheless emphasize Woolf's 'interest in Joseph Wright and his prominent place' in the novel. *Public and Private*, pp. 108–09; *The Years*, p. 428; p. 394.

[22] J.S.G. Simmons, 'All Souls', in *The History of the University of Oxford VII*, ed. by Brock and Curthoys, pp. 209–20 (p. 216; p. 209; p. 217).

[23] Elizabeth Wright, *The Life of Joseph Wright: Volume I* (London: Oxford University Press; Humphrey Milford, 1932), pp. 4–5.

The Years: 1880 and working-class education[24]

Hermione Lee asserts that the historicity of *The Years* is incidental to ahistorical philosophical problems confronting the individual.[25] The novel poses, however, a degeneracy narrative with a political *and* psychological context. Each chapter – '1880', '1891', etc. – corresponds to a specific historical event that gradually erodes the hegemonic power of the imperialistic, paternalistic, Pargiter family. The start date of *The Years*, '1880', is key. It denotes the establishment of universal, compulsory, elementary schooling for all children, in a significant expansion of the 1870 Education Act that theoretically advocated elementary education for all, but allowed for the discretion of local school boards in enforcing school attendance.[26] An explicit reference to the establishment of working-class education was introduced as *The Pargiters* was transformed into *The Years*, suggesting the significance of advancements in working-class education to the reformulated project. The former refers to 1880 as a time when 'Mr Gladstone was in power; Mr Bradlaugh had declined to take the oath; and at the head of the Irish party was a new leader, Charles Stewart Parnell' (p. 159), while *The Years* also considers the role of working-class education in social change:

> 'Yes, just what I was saying to Bigge this morning', she said, laying down the paper. [...] That man almost always said the very thing that she was thinking, which comforted her, and gave her a sense of security in a world which seemed to her to be changing for the worse.
> '"Before the rigid and now universal enforcement of school attendance ... ?"' Kitty read out.
> [...]

---

[24] This focus on Woolf and working-class education in *The Years* supplements previous readings which focus on the novel's feminist and anti-fascist politics. Anna Snaith in the Cambridge edition of *The Years* notes the developments in women's education during the period covered by the novel, before noting the development of fascism contemporary to Woolf's writing of the text. David Bradshaw has found that Woolf symbolically inscribes within *The Years* an allegiance to the Jews through the use of the colours of the Star of David. Joanna Lipking's reading of the class politics of the novel considers the master/servant relationship between Martin and Crosby. Anna Snaith, 'Introduction', in *The Years*, pp. xxxix–xcix. David Bradshaw, 'Hyam's Place: *The Years*, the Jews and the British Union of Fascists', in *Women Writers of the 1930s*, ed. by Joannou, pp. 179–91; Joanna Lipking, 'Looking at the Monuments: Woolf's Satiric Eye', *Bulletin of the New York Public Library: Virginia Woolf Issue*, Vol. 80 No. 2 (Winter 1977), 141–45.

[25] Hermione Lee, *The Novels of Virginia Woolf* (London: Methuen, 1997), p. 182.

[26] Joanna Bourke, *Working-Class Cultures in Britain 1890–1960: Gender, Class and Ethnicity* (London: Routledge, 1994), p. 116.

"' ... the children saw a good deal of cooking which, poor as it was, yet gave them some taste and inkling of knowledge. They now see nothing and they do nothing but read, write, sum, sew or knit,'" Kitty read out.[27]

The passage includes direct reference to an editorial in *The Times* from 16 April 1880, which objects to the imminent introduction of universal, elementary-level education, regretting that such education has withdrawn 'poor children' from 'their old healthy and instructive share in household duties'.[28] Mrs Malone cites sections of this article, approving of the columnist's conservative stance, as she laments the introduction of compulsory elementary education for its threat to the maintenance of the extant servant class.

Kitty is 'thinking of the Robsons' while Mrs Malone reads the paper aloud (p. 56). Woolf's diary demonstrates that, when writing *The Years*, she was formally concerned with two main aims, compaction and contrast: 'My idea is to <space> contrast the scenes'; 'the thing is to contract: each scene to be a scene, much dramatised; contrasted [...] compacting the vast mass' (D4, p. 266; p. 261). Woolf's juxtaposition of this scene with the immediately preceding scene of Kitty's visit to the self-educated, working-class Robson home ironizes Mrs Malone's conservatism while avoiding the overt 'the burden of something that I wont call propaganda. [...] I have a horror of the Aldous [Huxley] novel' (D4, p. 281). Mrs Robson has already made the journey from servant to scholar that Mrs Malone so disapproves, exposing her concerns as myopic:

'Your mother's family?' said Mr Robson.
'Rigby,' she said, and blushed slightly.
'Rigby?' said Mrs Robson, looking up.
'I wur-r-rked for a Miss Rigby before I married.'
  [...] 'My wife was a cook, Miss Malone, before we married,' he said. Again, he increased his accent as if he were proud of it. (p. 51)

Robson's dialect speech suggests how Joseph Wright informed aspects of Woolf's characterization of this figure. Wright was a dialect scholar from Yorkshire who retained his regional accent and speech after arriving at Oxford. Elizabeth Wright notes that her husband deliberately 'allowed his dialect to be perceptible'.[29] The scene is filtered through the consciousness of Kitty Malone, who registers the alien force of Mr Robson's 'Yorkshire' (p. 51) accent. Such a narrative manoeuvre

---

[27] Virginia Woolf, *The Years*, ed. by Jeri Johnson (London: Penguin, 2002), pp. 56–57. Further references to this edition will be included in brackets after the citation.
[28] Unsigned editorial, *The Times*, 16 April 1880, p. 9.
[29] Elizabeth Wright, *Life of Joseph Wright: Vol. I*, p. 89.

allows Woolf to register the effects of historical verisimilitude on individual consciousness, while maintaining an oblique authorial perspective through the use of scenic juxtaposition.

Sam Robson and Joseph Wright

Margaret Comstock suggests that *The Years* is anti-fascist in intent through its refusal to focus on one 'leader' or 'central figure'.[30] Although there is no central character, Sam Robson emerges as the novel's heroic figure. Woolf's January 1931 speech to the London/National Society for Women's Service found that heroism underpinned subversion: 'If I were to overcome the conventions I should need the courage of a hero' (p. xxxix). Woolf's approving 1932 diary entry reveals how she found, in Wright, an alternative to the conventional public-school leader. Wright offered a new ideal, born of autodidactic education:

> Old Joseph Wright & Lizzie Wright are people I respect. [...] He was a maker of dialect dixeries: he was a workhouse boy – his mother went charing. [...] Their attitude to life much our own. [...] His notion of learning. I sometimes would like to be learned myself. (D4, pp. 115–16)

Wright was born in 1855, fifteen years before the 1870 Education Act, the first parliamentary legislation to address working-class education in any depth. Here he is celebrated for his autodidacticism in a period before the introduction of working-class education. Wright's 'notion of learning' refers to his deep commitment to reading and his cultivation of private libraries; *The Life of Joseph Wright* notes that Wright transported books from Hamburg to Hull in order to form his own personal library.[31] He did, in fact, have some formal education: his biography reveals that he attended Saltaire Mill School, evening classes at the Mechanics' Institute in Bradford, and spent some time at university in Germany as an adult. Such institutional education was, nonetheless, piecemeal: 'It is a fact that never in his life did he have a full day's schooling'.[32] *The Life* refers repeatedly to his 'self-education'.[33] Like Wright, Woolf had little formal

---

[30] Margaret Comstock, 'The Loudspeaker and the Human Voice: Politics and the Form of *The Years*', *The Bulletin of the New York Public Library: Virginia Woolf Issue*, Vol. 80 No. 2 (Winter 1977), 252–75 (p. 254).

[31] Elizabeth Wright, *Life of Joseph Wright: Vol. I*, p. 78.

[32] Elizabeth Wright, *Life of Joseph Wright: Vol. I*, pp. 30–31.

[33] Elizabeth Wright, *Life of Joseph Wright: Vol. I*, p. 39; p. 58.

education – she noted in her memoir, 'Sketch of the Past', that 'I was never at school' (p. 79). Anna Snaith and Christine Kenyon-Jones have demonstrated, however, that the young Virginia Stephen was registered on courses at King's Ladies' Department between 1897 and 1901.[34] Woolf's self-characterization as autodidact-scholar overlooks this fact. Arguably, her avowed exclusion from the establishment structures of education relates to her 'outsider' status, mobilizing the political objectivity that she favoured.[35] Reference to Wright's biography also suggests the pride associated with autodidactic scholarship and reveals that the label 'autodidact' did tolerate some degree of institutional education.

Histories of Oxford reveal the extent to which Wright was an anomaly among Oxford academics: both D.J. Palmer and Janet Howarth position him as 'remarkable' for his working-class, autodidactic background.[36] In *The Years*, Robson is given Wright's autodidactic educational training, and his exceptional status is registered: 'A Professor, who had done it all off his own bat, "a most creditable performance," to quote Dr Malone' (p. 48). Woolf had used similar terms to describe her own independent intellectual work. In September 1925, before the publication of *The Common Reader* in 1926, she noted her response to being invited by her cousin, H.A.L. Fisher, to contribute to his series for autodidact readers:

> Haven't I just written to Herbert Fisher refusing to do a book for the Home University Series on Post Victorian? – knowing that I can write a book, a better book, a book off my own bat, for the Press if I wish! (D3, pp. 42–43)

The shared terms (used again later in *The Years* for the novel's other working-class autodidact, Chipperfield) suggest a sense of her kinship with Wright and their shared educational status outside the elite male public schools.

The 'respect' that Woolf's diary registers for Wright also reflects the nature of his relationships with women; Snaith, drawing on Elizabeth Wright's biography of her husband, comments on his 'feminism'.[37] *The Pargiters* notes that Mr Brook (an early manifestation of Sam Robson) 'respected women [...] respected them, honoured them, just as if they were men!' (p. 153). This feminism is directly

---

[34] Anna Snaith and Christine Kenyon-Jones, 'Tilting at Universities: Virginia Woolf at King's College London', *Woolf Studies Annual*, Vol. 16 (2010), 1–44.

[35] The issue of Woolf and autodidacticism is a productive one that demands further consideration. The present chapter's focus on Woolf's relationship to the institutional structures of education precludes an extended discussion here.

[36] D.J. Palmer, 'English', in *The History of the University of Oxford VII*, ed. by Brock and Curthoys, pp. 397–411 (p. 407); Janet Howarth, 'The Self-Governing University, 1882–1914', in *The History of the University of Oxford VII*, ed. by Brock and Curthoys, pp. 599–643 (p. 629).

[37] *Public and Private*, p. 109.

associated with his lack of formal education: 'The force at the back of such opinions was not merely that Joseph Wright himself had received no schooling: he was not the product of Eton or Harrow, and King's and Christ Church' (p. 155). Instead, 'he was much more profoundly influenced by his mother' (pp. 155–56) who facilitated his education. The specific and unusual conditions of his autodidact educational 'training' led him to have 'highly original' (p. 158) opinions on marriage, as education informs gender relations.

Mitchell A. Leaska notes that Woolf presents Wright as her 'ideal model of manhood' (p. xii) in *The Pargiters*. *The Years*, however, renders Robson through Kitty's viewpoint:

> Sam [...] stepped forward and indicated with his stubby forefinger the picture of an old woman looking rather over life size in the photographer's chair.
>
>   'My mother,' he said [...]
>
> The unwieldy old lady, posed in all the stiffness of her best clothes, was plain in the extreme. And yet Kitty felt that admiration was expected.
>
>   'You're very like her, Mr Robson,' [...]
>
> Indeed they had something of the same sturdy look; the same piercing eyes; and they were both very plain. (pp. 52–53)

Kitty registers the 'stubby', 'unwieldy', 'plain', and 'over life size' Robsons, all terms which suggest a disdain towards their seeming inelegance. Her observation echoes Woolf's 1931 'Introductory Letter to Margaret Llewelyn Davies', a preface to a collection of testimonials by members of the Women's Cooperative Guild, entitled *Life as We Have Known It*, which references the 'sculpturesque' bodies of cooperative women.[38] Despite Kitty's ambivalence, Woolf's approval of Sam Robson's feminism avoids the polemical tone of *The Pargiters* by manifesting itself on a symbolical level through the contrasting, but corresponding, depiction of maternal images in the Pargiter and Robson families. Lara Feigel notes the recurrence of objects throughout *The Years*, which function 'as metonyms for [...] the passing of time'; these objects also recur within the same section as Woolf invests them with political significance within each period.[39] This is evident in the photograph of Sam Robson's mother, the description of which draws heavily upon the photographic representation of Joseph Wright's mother, Sarah Ann Wright, in *The Life of Joseph Wright*. Earlier in the chapter, the Pargiter girls are

---

[38] Virginia Woolf, 'Introductory Letter to Margaret Llewelyn Davies', in *Life as We Have Known It: The Voices of Working Class Women*, ed. by Margaret Llewelyn Davies (London: Virago, 2012), pp. ix–xxxvi (p. xxi). Further references to this edition will be included in brackets after the citation.

[39] Feigel, p. 172.

presided over by a portrait of their dying mother: 'Over the fireplace the portrait of a red-haired young woman in white muslin holding a basket of flowers on her lap smiled down on them' (p. 8). This portrait is referenced throughout the text and, as Feigel notes, its fading represents the passing of time.[40] The image is also politically weighted; the flowers, the virginal white muslin, and benign smile all connote an idealized portrait of the middle-class lady, akin to the 'angel in the house', the Coventry Patmore ideal that Woolf had so rebelled against in 'Professions for Women' (1931).[41] It departs so much from reality, that, as adults, the Pargiter children have no recollection of this figure bearing any semblance to their mother: 'Was it like her?', Peggy asks, 'Not as I remember her', Eleanor replies (p. 238). Woolf provides a critical commentary on a middle-class tendency to idealize women out of existence, leaving the reality unrecognizable in the image. Mrs Robson is erected as a formidable matriarchal power, while Rose Pargiter dies at the beginning of the novel, her image left to decay, as patriarchal society is enacted within the middle-class Pargiter family. An integral aspect of Sam Robson's heroism comes from his enlightened attitude to women – born of his autodidact education – which refuses the idealizing spirit that dominates middle-class conceptions of femininity.

After visiting the Robson family, Kitty is overwhelmed with affection for Sam: 'You are the nicest man I have ever met, she thought' (p. 53), and wonders of the family: 'Did they know how much she admired them?' (p. 53). The visit to the Robson home is presented as a defining formative experience for Kitty, echoing through the years: in '1910' Kitty remembers the 'very light room' at the Robsons'; 'that's the sort of life I like' (p. 135), she thinks.

'Present Day' and the children's song

In '1880', advances in working-class education are represented as a nascent force and a potential stimulant of social change. 'Present Day', however, presents a similarly class-divided society: at Delia's party, North questions 'where are the Sweeps and the Sewer-men [...] there were only Dons and Duchesses' (p. 296). The children's song towards the end of 'Present Day' provides a stark confrontation with social otherness for the party's guests, and represents a deeply ambiguous moment. Enigmatic and indeterminate, it has invited an

[40] Ibid.
[41] Virginia Woolf, 'Speech of January 21 1931' ['Professions for Women'], in *The Pargiters*, ed. by Leaska, pp. xxv–xliv.

array of critical interpretations. Anna Snaith has noted that, in the manuscript of *The Years*, one character suggests that the working-class voices 'might have been hottentot' rendering the song's 'otherness [...] as much about class as race'.[42] David Bradshaw and Ian Blyth have noted Woolf's knowledge of 'Greek, Latin, French and Italian', suggesting 'she appears to be drawing on all of these languages in this incomprehensible song', while Avrom Fleishman has suggested that it 'may be discovered to be a transformation of a classic text, mingling as it does a number of Greek and Latin syllables and words'.[43] The cultural politics of widening educational opportunity provide a further productive context against which to read the song, and suggest the influence of Joseph Wright in the characterization of Sam Robson. Alice Wood has noted Wright's occurrence in *The Pargiters*, *The Years*, and *Three Guineas*, suggesting that this reveals how 'Woolf [...] strove to ground her cultural analysis in fact'; I explore the influence of Joseph Wright on the novel as a culturally influential figure, and a transgressor of class and cultural boundaries.[44]

The children's song is given a climactic role in the novel, usurping Nicholas's fragmented speech, which was intended to provide the party with 'a fillip, a finish' (p. 308). The voice of the idolatrous individual is replaced with the voice of the working-class collective who comprise 'the younger generation' (p. 314). The children have notably learnt their song 'at school' and their education is repeatedly alluded to in this short scene: 'No school tomorrow?', 'Weren't you taught something at school?', 'What they teach 'em at school, you know' (p. 314; p. 315). The song is dissociated from the paradigm of middle-class facilitation of working-class education presented elsewhere in 'Present Day', in the depiction of 'Runcorn's Boy' and 'Chipperfield', who call on Edward Pargiter to 'direct [...] [their] reading' (p. 302); instead, it alienates the middle-class audience:

Etho passo tanno hai,
Fai donk to tu do,
Mai to, kai to, lai to see
Toh dom to tuh do –
[...]
Fanno to par, etto to mar,
Timin tudo, tido,

[42] *The Years*, ed. by Anna Snaith, p. 806; p. xlv.

[43] Virginia Woolf, *The Years*, ed. by David Bradshaw and Ian Blyth (Chichester: Wiley-Blackwell, 2012), p. 351; Avrom Fleishman, *Virginia Woolf: A Critical Reading* (London: Johns Hopkins University Press, 1977), p. 200.

[44] *Late Cultural Criticism*, p. 55.

Foll to gar in, mitno to par,
Eido, teido, meido –
(p. 314)

Woolf criticized the didactic learning method of the lecture in her 1934 essay
'Why?': 'Why, since life holds only so many hours, waste one of them on being
lectured?'.[45] The methods of elementary school education are implicitly figured
as similarly deficient; the chanting recalls rote methods of learning that are
positioned as effacing individuality, the children act 'with one impulse' (p. 314).
The extent to which the children themselves understand the song they have
performed is unclear, and the narrator, as if to affirm the song's inscrutability
to the reader, impartially notes 'that was what it sounded like. Not a word was
recognizable' (p. 314), it is a 'shriek', 'discordant [...] meaningless' (p. 314; p.
315).

Jane Marcus argues that Eleanor 'instinctively understands speech
unintelligible to others, [this] reflects a mystical communion between women
and children'.[46] The interrogatory intonation in Eleanor's assessment of the
song as 'beautiful?' (p. 315) suggests, however, the uncertainty of middle-class
response when confronted with this other cultural force. Eleanor is not allied
with the children in social or political intent, first assessing them with deep
ambivalence. The narrator neutrally observes that the children look 'awkward
and clumsy' (p. 313). But when rendered through Eleanor's viewpoint, they are
transposed into a Nordau-ian discourse of degeneration. With the gaze of an
anthropologist, she notes 'their hands [...] the shape of their ears' (p. 313). From
this, she deduces that they are 'the children of the caretaker, I should think' (p.
313). These children appear feral to Eleanor as they take large slices of cake with
'a curious fixed stare as if they were fierce' (p. 313).

Kitty's experiences in '1880' are evoked immediately prior to the song; she
attempts to recall the name of the man 'I used to like so much at Oxford' (p. 309),
eventually happening upon: 'Robson'. Such an allusion back to the early stages
of the text is productive for a reading of the children's song. Joseph Wright was
a transgressor of class barriers through his role as interpreter of working-class
cultures: he produced the first *English Dialect Dictionary* for Oxford University
Press. After the children sing their song, Patrick notes the children's 'Cockney

[45] Virginia Woolf, 'Why?', in *The Essays of Virginia Woolf Volume 6 1933–1941*, ed. by Clarke, pp. 30–36 (p. 32).
[46] *Languages of Patriarchy*, p. 38.

accent' (p. 315) and, indeed, there is evidence to suggest that Woolf was evoking the actual sounds of English dialects and accents in the song itself.

Woolf was familiar with the lexical contents of the *English Dialect Dictionary*. Proof pages from the *Dictionary* were included in *The Life of Joseph Wright*, the biography Woolf enthusiastically consumed.[47] Further, in addition to its status as a long-established surname dating back to the sixteenth century, Jane Marcus has noted Wright's *Dialect Dictionary* as a source for the 'Pargiter' family name.[48] Mitchell A. Leaska notes that 'pargiter' appears neither in Wright's dictionary, nor in the *OED*, but comments that 'parget' does appear in the *English Dialect Dictionary*, meaning 'plaster with cement or mortar', with 'pargeter' also appearing by extension, and defined as 'a plasterer'.[49] While both 'parget' and 'pargeter' also appear in the *OED*, Snaith has followed Marcus in suggesting that Wright's *Dictionary* is 'the most likely source' of the name.[50]

While the structure of the dictionary (from dialect word into English) makes it unlikely that Woolf was attempting to encode a particular message in the children's song, the words of the song are either directly evident in the dictionary or their sounds are evocative of English dialect sounds. 'Donk' is included as an adjective meaning 'damp, moist, wet'.[51] Various dialectal variants of 'To' are given over approximately two pages of the dialect dictionary, and 'Do' is similarly revealed to be a common dialect word in various grammatical forms: it occupies over four pages of Wright's dictionary.[52] 'Fai' is a variant of 'Fain', an adjective meaning 'glad, happy, well-pleased'.[53] 'Tanno' is found to be a variant of 'Tino', which is an adverb, '[a] negative expletive', in Somerset, Devon, and Cornwall.[54] Wright's dictionary included 'the complete vocabulary of all English dialect words which are still in use or are known to have been in use at any time during the last two hundred years in England, Ireland, Scotland, and Wales'.[55]

---

[47] Plate XVI, Plate XVII, Plate XVIII, in Elizabeth Wright, *The Life of Joseph Wright: Volume II*.

[48] *The Years*, ed. by Anna Snaith, p. 400; Marcus, *Languages of Patriarchy*, p. 39. See also Mitchell A. Leaska who acknowledges Marcus's lead in a footnote. Mitchell A. Leaska, 'Virginia Woolf, the Pargeter: A Reading of *The Years*', *The Bulletin of the New York Public Library: Virginia Woolf Issue*, Vol. 80 No. 2 (Winter 1977), 172–210 (p. 173).

[49] As cited in 'Virginia Woolf, the Pargeter', p. 173.

[50] *OED*, <www.oed.com> [accessed 3 March 2014]; *The Years*, ed. by Anna Snaith, p. 400.

[51] *The English Dialect Dictionary Volume II*, ed. by Joseph Wright, 6 vols (Oxford: Oxford University Press, 1898–1905), p. 120.

[52] For 'To' see *English Dialect Dictionary Volume VI*, pp. 170–72; for 'Do' see *English Dialect Dictionary Volume II*, pp. 95–100.

[53] *English Dialect Dictionary Volume II*, p. 278; p. 280.

[54] *English Dialect Dictionary Volume VI*, p. 28; p. 158.

[55] *English Dialect Dictionary Volume I*, p. v.

The lexicography in the dictionary is opposed to 'the literary language'; for inclusion, words must differ from the literary language in both meaning and pronunciation.[56] There is some indication here of the relevance of Wright for Woolf's search for a 'democratic' art (E5, p. 533) in 'The Niece of an Earl'. The narrator in the 'Introductory Letter' met the cooperative women's writing with a sense of ambivalence; 'whether that is literature or not literature I do not presume to say' (p. xxxv), but speculated that 'images and saws and proverbial sayings must still be current with them [working-class women] that have never reached the surface of print' (p. xxiii). Wright's dictionary gives access to such a lexicon. In the children's song, Woolf brings dialect words into relation with words of more directly classical and romance language origins, as identified by Blyth, Bradshaw, and Fleishman. On occasions, such words overlap: 'donk' – occurs, as noted, in Wright's dictionary and is also the French term for 'donkey'. This represents a suggestive lexical experiment that recalls the 'Introductory Letter's' hope that 'society will pool its possessions instead of segregating them' (p. xxiv); *The Years* presents an equivocal – and uneasy – vision of the implications of such 'democratic' art.

Jane Marcus argues that the children's song represents an 'ecstatic speaking in tongues', suggesting that it evokes the 'anguish of being excluded from language and culture [...] [Woolf] explained [...] in "On Not Knowing Greek"' (1925).[57] These comments are provocative given Edward Pargiter's refusal to translate his citation from Classical Greek: '"Translate it" he [North] said. Edward shook his head. "It's the language", he said' (p. 303). The phrase is from *Antigone*, and translates as: "'Tis not my nature to join in hating, but in loving.'[58] The translated citation occurs in *Three Guineas*, where Woolf notes that 'lame as the English rendering is, Antigone's five words are worth all the sermons of all the archbishops' (pp. 206–07). In 'Present Day', however, the missing translation renders both the meaning and effect of the original Ancient Greek inaccessible to North. Joan N. Burstyn notes that familiarity with Latin and Greek 'was the hallmark of a gentleman'.[59] Public-school-educated Edward is positioned as holding a monopoly on elite cultural forms; 'locked up in that fine head', this classical knowledge is inaccessible to outsiders: 'Why not prise it open? Why not share it?', North wonders (p. 299). Woolf's 'On Not Knowing Greek' (1925)

---

[56] Ibid.
[57] *Languages of Patriarchy*, p. 66; p. 65.
[58] *The Years*, ed. by Anna Snaith, p. 533.
[59] Burstyn, p. 17.

identified Greek as 'the language that has us most in bondage; the desire for that which perpetually lures us back'.[60] The acquisition of Greek is a perpetual charm, luring the individual out of the entrapment of philistinism. The sorcerous language of the essay is echoed as Edward's refusal to 'share' his knowledge elevates him to 'a priest, a mystery monger' (p. 299).

'Present Day' suggests education's role in cultivating both a social, and a cultural, class divide: the incomprehensible children's song represents the inadequacies of working-class education while the elite classical culture of the public school and university is rendered inaccessible. Carey suggests that modernists such as Woolf developed a literary style that worked to exclude the masses and counteracted the effects of democratic educational reform.[61] However, 'Present Day' is concerned with the very limits of such democratic reform, as the institutional structures of education manifest separate cultural forms, rather than a democratic culture in common.

Woolf made her final revisions to *The Years* in 1936: in the same year, the Haldane Education Act was passed, promising to raise the school-leaving age to fifteen (although the advent of the Second World War and underfunding meant such reforms were never instituted). Woolf's response to reviews of *The Years* suggests her frustration with attempts to assess the novel within received political categories: '*The TLS* spoke as if it were merely the death song of the middle classes' (D5, p. 68); 'As it is I'm discussed (as usual) & no one has yet seen the point – *my* point' (D5, p. 70, emphasis in original). Instead, Woolf sought to 'rethink politics very slowly into my own tongue' (D5, p. 114). In *The Years* this manifests itself in the ambivalent 'speaking in tongues' of the children's song.

Three Guineas: Exploring the marginalized in the marginalia

In 1938, an unemployed mill worker, Agnes Smith, wrote a fan letter to Virginia Woolf after reading *Three Guineas*: 'I suppose [...] that you dealt so exclusively with the "educated man's daughter" [...] for the very good reason that it is one of which you have firsthand knowledge.'[62] The letter is striking for its demonstration that although, as Naomi Black identifies, the text's 'primary audience' was

---

[60] Virginia Woolf, 'On Not Knowing Greek', in *The Essays of Virginia Woolf Volume IV 1925–1928*, ed. by Andrew McNeillie (London: Hogarth Press, 1994), pp. 38–52 (p. 48).

[61] See Carey, p. 21.

[62] Anna Snaith, 'Wide Circles: The *Three Guineas* Letters', *Woolf Studies Annual*, Vol. 6 (2000), 1–168 (p. 105).

middle-class women, it also attained a wide working-class readership, as Snaith has assessed.[63] *Three Guineas* has received considerable attention for its gender-based anti-fascist arguments, while the class politics of the text have been variously interpreted.[64] Although Jane Marcus has held that 'Woolf does not privilege gender over class', more typically, Woolf has attracted censure for the text's (perceived) myopic focus on the concerns of the 'daughters of educated men'.[65] Snaith notably argues that Woolf's refusal to advocate for the working class was a 'deliberate political stance' that demonstrates a 'consciousness of the limitations of her own class position', leading her to speak only to and about 'that class of women of which she has had experience'.[66] I argue that the textual marginalia of *Three Guineas* (in the form of its endnotes) demonstrate Woolf's examination of the particular conditions of working-class education and suggest that these endnotes expose the workings of the text's polemical focus on the 'daughters of educated men'.

In the process of compiling the text, Woolf amassed a 'mass' of research notes: three scrapbooks of newspaper cuttings and information gleaned through petitioning her friends – she wrote to Lady Shena Simon and Ethel Smyth, for instance, for details surrounding women's exclusion from Cambridge and their role in orchestras.[67] Unable to use all her research notes, she later had to explain to Smyth why she did not include the details surrounding the 'exclusion of women instrumentalists from the Bournemouth Municipal Orchestra' that

[63] Naomi Black, *Virginia Woolf as Feminist* (London: Cornell University Press, 2004), p. 4. See Snaith's discussion in 'The Reading Public: Respondents to *Three Guineas*', in *Public and Private*, pp. 113–29.

[64] Merry M. Pawlowski, 'Introduction: Virginia Woolf at the Crossroads of Feminism, Fascism and Art', in *Virginia Woolf and Fascism: Resisting the Dictators' Seduction*, ed. by Merry M. Pawlowski (Basingstoke: Palgrave, 2001), pp. 1–10 (p. 2). The essays in the collection similarly situate Woolf's anti-fascist politics in terms of a gender critique. See especially, Marie Louise Gättens, '*Three Guineas*, Fascism and the Construction of Gender', in *Virginia Woolf and Fascism*, ed. by Pawlowski, pp. 21–38; Lisa Low, '"Thou canst not touch the freedom of my mind": Fascism and Disruptive Female Consciousness in *Mrs Dalloway*', in *Virginia Woolf and Fascism*, ed. by Pawlowski, pp. 92–104.

[65] Marcus, *Languages of Patriarchy*, p. 13. Q.D. Leavis's 1938 review of the text damned Woolf for being 'quite insulated by class'. This condemnation is echoed by 'Theodore Dalrymple', who has argued that *Three Guineas* is 'a locus classicus of self-pity and victimhood', and Alex Zwerdling has noted: 'It is clear that Woolf wanted to think of herself not as privileged but as deprived.' Q.D. Leavis, 'Review', *Scrutiny*, September 1938, in *Virginia Woolf: The Critical Heritage*, ed. by Robin Majumdar and Allen McLaurin (London: Routledge Kegan & Paul, 1975), pp. 409–19 (p. 409); 'Theodore Dalrymple', 'Blame It on Bloomsbury', *The Guardian*, 17 August 2002, <http://www.theguardian.com/books/2002/aug/17/classics.highereducation> [accessed 2 May 2013]; Alex Zwerdling, *Virginia Woolf and the Real World* (London: University of California Press, 1986), p. 233.

[66] *Public and Private*, p. 114. The letter from Agnes Smith is alluded to at pp. 116–17.

[67] Virginia Woolf, *The Letters of Virginia Woolf Volume VI 1936–1941*, ed. by Nigel Nicolson (London: Hogarth Press, 1980), p. 235. See pp. 132–33 and p. 217 for Woolf's requests for information. Further references to this edition will be included in brackets after the citation, as L6 and then the page number.

Smyth had supplied her with: she wanted, she wrote, to retain 'some slimness, and not repeat inordinately' (L6, p. 234). The heterogeneous and heterodox character of the text's notes invites a flexible reading approach. Often, the notes simply provide publication details for a citation: '*A Memoir of Anne Jemima Clough*, by B. A. Clough, p. 32' (p. 296). On other occasions, as for the note defining the 'daughters of educated men', the information seems crucial to an understanding of the text itself. Other notes are digressive and amusing – *The TLS* observed that they contained 'the quintessence of the author's wit'.[68] One example is the note detailing the maid's role in English upper-middle-class life in protecting women's chastity:

> The maid played so important a part in English upper-class life from the earliest times until the year 1914 [...] that some recognition of her services seems to be called for. [...] It is much to be regretted that no lives of maids, from which a more fully documented account could be constructed, are to be found in the *Dictionary of National Biography*. (pp. 297–98)

Woolf's irreverent tone is pointedly aimed at her own family: Sir Leslie Stephen, Woolf's father, edited the *Dictionary of National Biography*, with its series of biographical portraits of great men.

Although the text first appeared in America as 'Women Must Weep' without its endnotes in the *Atlantic Monthly,* this omission is, as Black notes, a concession to the 'actual or anticipated dimensions of the magazine's nationality and audience' and the limitations imposed by the magazine publication context, rather than evidence of their insignificance.[69] Woolf's correspondence indicates that she perceived them to be intellectually central to the text:

> Notes. Yes that was a question; bottom of the page or end. I decided for end, thinking people might read them, the most meaty part of the book, separately. Gibbon wished to do this, but gave way to friends. Pippa Strachey writes that she's glad they are at the end. (L6, p. 235)

The decision to position the notes at the end allows Woolf's arguments to gain momentum and render it possible for her to make her polemical points more concisely. The positioning of the notes also illuminates Vita Sackville-West's response to the text's arguments as 'misleading' – a comment that was angrily received by Woolf:

---

[68] Unsigned review, 'Review in *The Times Literary Supplement*', 4 June 1938, in *Virginia Woolf: The Critical Heritage*, ed. by Majumdar and McLaurin, pp. 400–01 (p. 401).

[69] Black, p. 132.

If I said, I dont [sic] agree with your conception of Joan of Arc's character, thats [sic] one thing. But if I said, your arguments about her are 'misleading' shouldn't I mean, Vita has cooked the facts in a dishonest way in order to produce an effect which she knows to be untrue? If *thats* [sic] what you mean by 'misleading' then we shall have to have the matter out, whether with swords or fisticuffs. (L6, p. 243, emphasis in original)

Despite Woolf's ire, on occasion the notes do not fully support the argument put forward in the text. For instance, in a discussion of the special duties of the daughters of educated men, the main body of the text notes that 'the minds of educated men are more highly trained and their words subtler than those of working men' (p. 235). The note to this comment suggests the evidence for this:

16. By way of proof, an attempt may be made to elucidate the reasons given by various Cabinet Ministers in various Parliaments from about 1870 to 1918 for opposing the Suffrage Bill. An able effort has been made by Mrs Oliver Strachey (see chapter 'The Deceitfulness of Politics' in her '*The Cause*'). (pp. 311–12)

Such evidence may support the idea that educated men have 'highly trained' minds, but it does not necessarily support the comparative claim that the text puts forward: that their words are 'subtler' than those of working men. This manipulation of evidence offers a manifestation of Woolf's decision to focus on the daughters of educated men in *Three Guineas* as a special case.

The political cause of the working class is not, however, neglected in the text. It is in the text's 'meaty' marginalia that the conditions of the working class are more fully explored. In the main body of the third chapter, the 'Outsiders' Society' (p. 232) is represented as an organization for the 'daughters of educated men', as Woolf urges them to focus on their own social advancement: 'It would consist of educated men's daughters working in their own class – how indeed can they work in any other? – and by their own methods for liberty, equality and peace' (p. 232). In the note, Woolf advocates class separatism in the creation of social change, and offers readers an invitation for further research, referring them to narratives of working-class self-improvement through education:

For a more detailed account of working-class life, see *Life as We Have Known It*, by Co-operative working women, edited by Margaret Llewelyn Davies. The *Life of Joseph Wright* also gives a remarkable account of working class life at first hand. (pp. 310–11)

In Part One, the main body of *Three Guineas* is concerned with the educational inequities evident within Woolf's own social group. Woolf's narrator finds that although the men and women of the middle class have similar accents, manners, and positions in the social hierarchy in relation to the working class, they are in fact marked by a divide: 'But ... those three dots mark a precipice, a gulf so deeply cut between us ... ' (p. 118). This gulf is 'paid-for education' (p. 118), which has created 'two classes' (p. 132) divided by gender and educational experience. A note defining 'the daughters of educated men' outlines the grounds on which this distinction is made:

> It has been necessary to coin this clumsy term – educated man's daughter – to describe the class whose fathers have been educated at public schools and universities. Obviously, if the term 'bourgeois' fits her brother, it is grossly incorrect to use it of one who differs so profoundly in the two prime characteristics of the bourgeoisie – capital and environment. (p. 274)

The term itself, 'daughters of educated men', suggests an entirely relational position to the privileges of the middle class. Woolf's feminist struggle with Marxist terminology prompts her to grant these women an appositional relationship to the traditional privileges of the 'bourgeois': 'capital' and 'environment', specifically, here the public school and university. The notes to Part Three, however, establish an opposition between both the men and women of the middle class, and the working class, in a discussion of the educational methods appropriate for different social groups. The main body of *Three Guineas* suggests that the daughters of educated men should 'refuse to bolster up the vain and vicious system of lecturing by refusing to lecture' (p. 158), as she repeats her criticism of 'the lecture habit' established in her earlier essay 'Why?' (1934), written for *Lysistrata*, the Somerville Student College Magazine, and similarly targeted at an audience who were largely the 'daughters of educated men'. In *Three Guineas*, Woolf's note considers the 'mental docility' which lecturing creates in 'the young' (p. 286). She holds, however, one important exception:

> The words 'vain and vicious' require qualification. [...] The words in the text refer only to the sons and daughters of educated men who lecture their brothers and sisters upon English literature [...] [n]one of this applies of course to those whose homes are deficient in books. If the working class find it easier to assimilate English literature by word of mouth they have a perfect right to ask the educated class to help them thus. (pp. 285–86)

Woolf does not directly advocate for the working classes but she does recognize their 'right' to advance their own conditions and 'ask' for proper access to education, in her acknowledgement that the autodidact pedagogical strategies advocated for the middle class may not be suitable for the impoverished working class. 'A Daughter's Memories' (1932), published in *The Times* on the centenary of Leslie Stephen's birth, reveals the richly resourced nature of Woolf's own autodidact education: she had 'the free run of a large and quite unexpurgated library'.[70] The qualification to the footnote in *Three Guineas* represents Woolf's explicit recognition that the milieu and means of working-class readers necessitate a different pedagogical strategy that will facilitate their access to literature in comparison to the 'daughters of educated men' who are 'from the very class which should have learnt to read at home' (p. 286).

The notes render *Three Guineas* a text that reveals the mechanics of its polemic. The manoeuvres of logic that Woolf makes to construct her argument are physically marginalized at the end of the text, yet nonetheless rendered visible. Woolf's recognition of the notes as 'the most meaty' part of the text also cautions against readings which criticize the text's perceived myopia without acknowledging its status as a rhetorical performance that displaces consideration of working-class conditions into the notes in order to reinforce the text's polemic, rather than, necessarily, to undermine the working-class cause. The distinction drawn between the role of lectures in working-, as opposed to middle-class education in *Three Guineas* suggestively illuminates Woolf's decision to lecture to the WEA in 'The Leaning Tower' (1940), a text which engages with educational discourse in order to conceptualize egalitarian political structures and democratic cultural forms.

'The Leaning Tower', the WEA, and multilateral education

'The Leaning Tower', Woolf's 1940 lecture to the WEA, emerges from a distinctly wartime perspective that privileged the work of the adult education movement in the cultivation of social and cultural democracy. G.D.H. Cole, vice president of the WEA until 1938, found that 'such bodies as the Workers' Educational Association' were fundamental in shaping an educated post-war democracy: 'The weapons which we Socialists possess for fighting [...] are those of reason and education [...] [w]hile men's minds are keyed up by suspense, the chance is ours to organise and re-direct the democratic forces'.[71] 'The Leaning Tower' reflects Cole's concern to use the WEA to 'find new anchorage for their [working people's] minds' in the 'fight[ing] for cultural values' in the post-war world.[72]

---

[70] Virginia Woolf, 'A Daughter's Memories', in *The Platform of Time: Memoirs of Family & Friends*, ed. by S.P. Rosenbaum (London: Hesperus Press, 2007), pp. 58–64 (p. 63).

[71] G.D.H. Cole, *The War on the Home Front* (London: Fabian Society, 1939), p. 11; pp. 12–16.

[72] *The War on the Home Front*, p. 11.

Woolf was writing *Between the Acts* as she was producing 'The Leaning Tower', and where Marina Mackay suggests that the former text reveals Woolf to be 'on extraordinarily (and literally) conservative territory', Janet Montefiore reads 'The Leaning Tower' as a declaration of '"one nation" leftish patriotism'.[73]

The lecture represents a studied rhetorical performance, designed to appeal to its WEA audience. Erika Yoshida's analysis of the adaptations Woolf made between drafts of the speech held in the Berg Collection, and the version published in *Folios of New Writing* suggests that she wrote her lecture specifically for her working-class audience.[74] Maroula Joannou has used WEA records to explore the gender composition of Woolf's audience, commenting:

> While we do not know [...] it may well have included a sizeable number of women [...] the absence of men of military age made the W.E.A. nationally increasingly reliant on female students and Tutor Organizers. Thus Woolf's use of the pronoun 'we' includes the women listening with whom she would have identified more easily than with an audience of working men.[75]

As Joannou notes, Woolf aligns herself with her working-class audience as she opposes their collective educational fortunes with the educational privilege of the public-school-educated Auden Group: 'She [England] has left the other class, the immense class to which almost all of us must belong, to pick up what we can in village schools; in factories; in workshops; behind counters; and at home' (E6, p. 276). This list recalls pedagogic venues Woolf explored throughout the 1930s: 'the village school' of *The Waves Holograph I,* and the 'workshop' (p. xxxii) of the 'Introductory Letter' to *Life as We Have Known It.*[76] Woolf also rewrites the narrative positioning established in the 'Introductory Letter'. The narrator there emphasized working women's place 'behind a counter' (p. xiii), noting the impossibility of meeting the working classes 'not as masters or mistresses or customers with a counter between us' (pp. xxi–xxiii).

Such self-conscious narrative repositioning suggests the degree to which Woolf's voice in both texts is artfully constructed. Alice Wood recognizes

---

[73] Marina MacKay, *Modernism and World War II* (Cambridge: Cambridge University Press, 2007), p. 37; Montefiore, p. 13.

[74] Erika Yoshida, '"The Leaning Tower": Woolf's Pedagogical Goal of the Lecture to the WEA under the Threat of War', in *Virginia Woolf: Art, Education and Internationalism: Selected Papers from the Seventeenth Annual Conference on Virginia Woolf*, ed. by Diana Royer and Madelyn Detloff (Clemson: Clemson University Digital Press, 2008), pp. 33–39.

[75] Maroula Joannou, *Women's Writing, Englishness and National and Cultural Identity: The Mobile Woman and the Migrant Voice 1938–1962* (Basingstoke: Palgrave Macmillan, 2012), p. 18.

[76] Virginia Woolf, *The Waves: The Two Holograph Drafts*, ed. by J.W. Graham (London: Hogarth Press, 1976), p. 68.

Woolf's 'fictionalising' of her narrator-persona in the 'Introductory Letter' as a 'narrative strategy' designed to 'engage a middle-class reader'.[77] Woolf's direct recollection in 'The Leaning Tower' of the terms around which class division was figured in the 'Introductory Letter' further suggests the elements of performance in the former text, as her political positioning shifts as her sense of her audience shifts – Woolf, notably, wanted *Life as We Have Known It* to find a 'general public', and it was reviewed in *The Bookman* and *The Observer*, with a focus on Woolf's introduction.[78] The organ of the Women's Cooperative Guild, *Woman's Outlook,* notably, however, focused on the guildswomen's testimonies, only briefly noting the 1913 Congress 'about which Mrs. Virginia Woolf writes so vividly in an Introductory Letter to Miss Llewelyn Davies'.[79] Woolf's dialogic experimentation with rhetorical positioning implies that she tested different political positions as she explored her allegiance to different communal groups. Woolf's letters suggest the posed nature of the cross-class unity established in the lecture: she characterized her audience as '200 betwixt and betweens' (L6, p. 394) in a letter to Vita Sackville-West, noting 'thats [*sic*] what comes of yielding to the damnable importunity of a wretched little man who lives on tinned tomatoes on top of a hill. My swan song – positively my last public misery' (L6, p. 393).

Woolf's letter indicates that there were men in the audience, in addition to the women that Joannou suggests dominated. The WEA emerged from discourses surrounding adult education that sought to establish a new type of masculine ideal, taken from a different, unilaterally empowered, social class. Nick Kneale suggests that Ruskin College (founded in 1899 at Oxford) sought to establish a unique class and gender identity for its students as distinct from the bourgeois scholar. Walter Watkins Vrooman, who co-founded the college with Charles Austin, held 'unorthodox views on class and gender politics'.[80] Early editions of the college magazine suggest the negotiation of an alternative masculine identity as part of the college's agenda: 'Remember the workman has a culture

---

[77] Alice Wood, 'Facing *Life as We Have Known It*: Virginia Woolf and the Women's Cooperative Guild', *Literature & History*, Vol. 23 No. 2 (Autumn 2014), 18–34 (p. 31).

[78] Virginia Woolf to Margaret Llewelyn Davies, 14 September 1930, in Virginia Woolf, *The Letters of Virginia Woolf Volume IV 1929–1931*, ed. by Nigel Nicolson (London: Hogarth Press, 1978), p. 213; Unsigned review, 'Review of *Life as We Have Known It*', *The Bookman*, Spring 1931, p. 92; J.C. Stobart, 'Working Women's Lives: Review of *Life as We Have Known It*', *The Observer*, 7 June 1931, p. 4.

[79] Unsigned article, 'Better Than Fiction Is – *Life as We Have Known It*', *Woman's Outlook*, 4 April 1931, pp. 368–70 (pp. 368–69).

[80] Nick Kneale, 'The Science and Art of "Man-Making": The Class and Gender Foundations of Ruskin Hall, Oxford 1899', in *Ruskin College: Contesting Knowledge, Dissenting Politics*, ed. by Geoff Andrews, Hilda Kean, and Jane Thompson (London: Lawrence & Wishart, 1999), pp. 5–34 (p. 19).

of his own that the scholar possesses not.'[81] In Ruskin's foundational speech, Vrooman argued that the key to educational success was to establish 'clearly the ideal of manhood or special attitude to be striven for.'[82] This ideal was widely disseminated via in-college residency, correspondence courses, reading circles, extension lectures, and classes, which combined to have a 'significant impact' on workers' education.[83]

Although the WEA emerged from the University Extension movement, Anne Ockwell and Harold Pollins note the 'fear and distrust of Oxford in the working-class movement.'[84]A 1908 WEA pamphlet, *Oxford and Working Class Education* explored the WEA's institutional involvement with Oxford. Ramsay MacDonald expressed his concern over the issue in a letter to the WEA leader, Albert Mansbridge, rendering the competing models of WEA and Oxford masculinity clear: 'Oxford will assimilate [sic] them, not they Oxford. [...] [T]hey are the only good, and everything that takes them away from their internal sources of power and culture is bad.'[85] In 1913 Cole wrote that the new adult education movement was forming 'a type of man [...] capable of understanding the working class, and remaining of it, even if his standards rose higher than those of his fellows'.[86] Cole is circumspect, avoiding the suggestion that working-class education will create new leaders that would dominate the rest of their class. Instead, the focus is on improving the social group as a whole. Woolf had met Cole during his tenure as vice president of the WEA, and responded to him in terms that connote an awareness of this alternative masculine ideal: 'A positive domineering young man he seemed [...] I write from the outsiders [sic] unsympathetic point of view.'[87]

Woolf therefore explores the failure of a particular brand of public-school masculinity before an audience informed by alternative ontological and leadership ideals. The lecture notes the waning political and cultural dominance

[81] 'The University Don: A Letter from a Ruskin Hall Student Who Is Earning His Way through College Entirely by His Own Industry', *Young Oxford*, Vol. 1 No. 3 (December 1899), p. 8. Cited in Kneale, p. 6.

[82] Cited in Kneale, p. 19.

[83] Anne Ockwell and Harold Pollins, '"Extension" in All Its Forms', in *The History of the University of Oxford VII*, ed. by Brock and Curthoys, pp. 661–88 (p. 678).

[84] Ockwell and Pollins, p. 685.

[85] Ramsay MacDonald to Albert Mansbridge, 4 December 1908, as cited in Goldman, *Dons and Workers*, p. 163.

[86] G.D.H. Cole, *The World of Labour: A Discussion of the Present and Future of Trade Unionism* (London: Bell, 1913), p. 384.

[87] Virginia Woolf, *The Diary of Virginia Woolf Volume I 1915–1919*, ed. by Anne Olivier Bell (London: Hogarth Press, 1977), p. 268.

of 'Day-Lewis, Auden, Spender, Isherwood, Louis MacNeice', suggesting that they are 'tower dwellers like their predecessors' who went to 'public schools and universities' (E6, p. 267). However, during their literary ascension, from '1925' to '1939', there was 'everywhere change; everywhere revolution' (E6, p. 267). The shared 'tendency' of their writing thus expressed 'the tower of middle-class birth and expensive education – to lean' (E6, p. 267). 'The Leaning Tower' argues that the tower dwellers' 'self-consciousness […] class-consciousness […] consciousness of things changing' (E6, p. 273) have damaged their creative work, a claim that is in dialogue with her previous position in 'The Niece of an Earl', which granted the middle classes exemption from a 'self-conscious, or class-conscious' state, while the working classes were necessarily removed 'from their own class' by the 'education […] the act of writing implies' (E5, p. 532). 'The Leaning Tower' uses the terms of Wordsworth's 'Preface to the Lyrical Ballads' to establish a critique of the Auden Group's verse, suggesting 'there was no tranquillity in which they could recollect' (E6, p. 273), as a result, their work was 'full of confusion and of compromise' (E6, p. 269).[88] In contrast to this world of elites and towers, Woolf establishes a vision of a socially levelled post-war world as 'a world without classes and towers […] if they [the politicians] mean what they say' (E6, pp. 274–75).

Woolf's lecture inhabits the same conceptual space as T.C. Worsley's *Barbarians and Philistines: Democracy and the Public Schools* (1940), a text Woolf had read: her diary refers to 'little soft round Worsley's discourse on the young [?] – which should bring in my lecture' (D5, pp. 282–83). *Barbarians and Philistines* found that the public school's continued presence in the post-war world 'will effectively sabotage the establishment of democracy'.[89] Instead, Worsley advocated the establishment of 'common elementary schools for *all* children' to create a 'common cultural heritage' and 'social cohesion'.[90] Worsley's reference to the 'common elementary school' reflects contemporary debates on multilateral education, an early term for comprehensive schooling – a system widely established in 1965. In the late 1930s, the 'comprehensive' school was a conceptual category that was in the process of being realized. The term itself was variable: 'multilateral', 'multibias', 'common', and 'comprehensive' were all names

[88] William Wordsworth, 'Preface' to *The Lyrical Ballads* (1802), <http://web.mnstate.edu/gracyk/courses/web%20publishing/wordsworthpreface.htm> [accessed 19 April 2013].
[89] Worsley, *Barbarians and Philistines*, p. 280.
[90] *Barbarians and Philistines*, p. 281, emphasis in original.

used to denote this system.[91] Following the 1926 Hadow Report's advocacy of a selective secondary system, the call for multilateral education gained momentum during the 1930s. The *Times Educational Supplement (TES)* had argued for multilateralism throughout the decade, and, in 1930, the National Association of Labour Teachers pledged their support for the ideal. In 1939 the Labour Party's educational advisory committee urged multilateralism as 'an immediate practical policy'. The government's 1938 Spens Report deemed, however, that multilateralism was 'too subversive' to implement.[92] Woolf, notably, was aware of the report – it is mentioned by Worsley in *Barbarians and Philistines* – and it is also alluded to in W.H. Auden and T.C. Worsley's *Education Today and Tomorrow* (1939), published by the Hogarth Press.[93]

Informed by such debates, 'The Leaning Tower' suggests that wartime necessity, the 'income tax' (introduced by Sir John Simon in April 1940) is creating 'equal opportunities' by swallowing middle-class incomes: 'The income tax is saying to middle-class parents: You cannot afford to send your sons to public schools any longer; you must send them to the elementary schools' (E6, p. 275).[94] The lecture claims that economic pressure will fundamentally alter the social structure: 'Classes will disappear [...] [a]ll classes will be merged in one class' (E6, p. 275). Woolf cites a letter from the *New Statesman and Nation* written by a parent whose 'boy, who was to have gone to Winchester, had been [...] sent to the village school' (E6, p. 275). The letter explores the conditions of public-school and state education: the public school has 'the sense of the past [...] the gentle influences that belong to the best spirits of all ages', while the village elementary school has a 'young, highly qualified and enthusiastic' teacher, 'more effective' teaching, and 'the question of class does not arise'.[95] It concludes by calling for a 'fresh wind' to blow through the 'proud' public schools.[96] Woolf uses the letter as a stimulus for the lecture's exploration of new institutional forms:

---

[91] McKibbin notes that before the late 1940s, the 'common' school was usually called a 'multilateral' or 'multibias' school and was thereafter a 'comprehensive' school. The multilateral school was not synonymous with the comprehensive school, however, with the former containing internal streaming and encompassing the 'grammar' and 'modern' sides in one institution, while comprehensive schools increasingly referred to local non-selective secondary schools with weak or no streaming. *Classes and Cultures*, p. 231.

[92] Board of Education [The Spens Report], p. 291.

[93] Worsley, *Barbarians and Philistines*, p. 213; Auden and Worsley, *Education Today and Tomorrow*, in *W.H. Auden Volume I 1926–1938*, ed. by Mendelson, pp. 389–424 (p. 408).

[94] HMRC Tax Office, <http://www.hmrc.gov.uk/history/taxhis6.htm> [accessed 2 April 2013].

[95] Molly Fordham, 'Correspondence: The Public School Problem', *New Statesman and Nation*, 13 April 1940, p. 496.

[96] Ibid.

But it is in the future; and there is a deep gulf to be bridged between the dying world, and the world that is struggling to be born. For there are still two worlds, two separate worlds. 'I want [...] the best of both worlds for my son.' She wanted, that is, the village school, where he learnt to mix with the living; and the other school – Winchester it was – where he mixed with the dead. [...] She wanted the new world and the old world to unite, the world of the present and the world of the past. (E6, p. 276)

Steve Ellis notes that the lecture maintains that the 'post-war classless society' is to be achieved 'largely through the developing public library system'.[97] Here, however, the focus is on institutional education, as the mother's problem is rendered symptomatic of wider debates in education. The lecture previously suggested that the 1930s poet was 'a dweller in two worlds, one dying, the other struggling to be born' (E6, pp. 272–73) in an allusion to Matthew Arnold's 'Stanzas from the Grand Chartreuse': 'Wandering between two worlds, one dead, | The other powerless to be born'.[98] Now, similar terms are used to categorize the indeterminate state of the educational system, suspended between two social ideals. Stephen Spender's *The New Realism* (1939) had used these terms to describe the manner in which class conflict was informing his generation's aesthetics: 'The situation, as I have outlined it, leaves the artist [...] in a split position, between two worlds, "one dead the other waiting to be born".'[99] While Arnold's verse animates a sense of division as he explores a shift away from faith to modern rationalism and technological progress, in Woolf's and Spender's appropriation, passivity is transformed into action as educational systems and aesthetic forms are deemed complicit in the struggle away from middle-class liberalism and into working-class socialism. The image is later used by Richard Hoggart in *The Uses of Literacy* (1957), and applied to the working-class autodidact, rather than the middle-class artist, as he expresses the condition of the 'uprooted and the [a]nxious' who 'take up many kinds of self-improvement' and 'ask questions of themselves about their society, who are because of this, even though they may never have been to grammar-schools, "between two worlds, one dead, the other powerless to be born".'[100]

[97] Steve Ellis, *British Writers and the Approach of World War II* (Cambridge: Cambridge University Press, 2015), p. 188.

[98] Matthew Arnold, 'Stanzas from the Grand Chartreuse', <http://www.poetryfoundation.org/poem/172861> [accessed 4 October 2014].

[99] *The New Realism*, p. 17.

[100] Richard Hoggart, *The Uses of Literacy* (London: Chatto & Windus, 1957), p. 245.

Three Guineas used the term 'gulf' to represent the difference of 'paid-for education' (p. 118), which created 'two classes' of educated brothers and their uneducated sisters within the middle class. Here, 'gulf' connotes a difference between the upper and working classes with the discrepancy between the paid-for public school which is 'so very, very private[?]' in its exclusivity and 'the system of free national education' (E6, p. 276). Multilateralism is the 'bridge' between these two worlds. Woolf is alluding to this 'future' ideal as she identifies the struggle between the new world of the 'living' village school, and the old world of the 'dead' public school, echoing the mother's distinction between the vital nature of state education, as opposed to the traditional ethos of the public school. The two worlds, divided by social class, would 'unite' in the multilateral institution, which could both accommodate, and create the possibility, for social unity. The broad, allusive terms reflect the fact that multilateralism was an ideal in process, a concept in flux. Nonetheless, Woolf clearly alludes to its key feature of bringing together 'children differing in background', as identified by Spens.[101]

Multilateralism's resolution of different social classes in one institution could foster a unified cultural form:

> How will that change affect the writer who sits at his desk looking at human life? [...] The novel of a classless and towerless world should be a better novel than the old novel. The novelist will have more interesting people to describe [...] real people, not people cramped and squashed into featureless masses by hedges. The poet's gain is less obvious [...] [b]ut he should gain words; when we have pooled all the different dialects, the clipped and cabined vocabulary which is all that he uses now should be enriched. (E6, p. 275)

The novel of a world without elite leaders and social class holds direct implications for literature. In contrast to the culturally divided society presented in 'Present Day', Woolf suggests (in line with Worsley's thesis) that multilateralism cultivates a 'common culture'. The biblical implications of the Leaning Tower as the Tower of Babel are also in play here; Genesis 11. 1–9 functions as an aetiology of cultural differences, as God creates a polyglot nation following man's building of a tower in a previously monoglot city. H.A.L. Fisher's October 1931 article for *The Highway* (the WEA journal), 'The Tower of Babel', alluded to this biblical story as he advocated the benefits of language learning to members of the WEA.[102] 'The Leaning Tower' re-versions this biblical allusion; the 'leaning' tower is presented as ripe for dismantling through institutional overhaul.

---

[101] Board of Education [The Spens Report], p. 291.
[102] H.A.L. Fisher, 'The Tower of Babel', *The Highway*, October 1931, p. 3.

I consider elsewhere the significance of Woolf's engagement with autodidact networks, in particular the Women's Cooperative Guild, in her exploration of the status of working-class writing, arguing that in the 'Introductory Letter' Woolf's anticipation of a democratic literary discourse in the future refuses to marginalize the ambivalence surrounding her assessment of working-class writing in the present.[103] Woolf's position in 'The Leaning Tower' is not only reflective of her wider thesis on working-class writing, it is also in dialogue with articles published in *The Highway*, which consider the cultivation of working-class literature, asking: 'When Will the Industrial Worker Produce His Own Literature?'[104] The writer of this article is 'amazed [...] that the industrial workers of this country [...] have failed to produce a literature of their own', finding that 'if you wish to be a creative artist of working-class life you must remain loyal to your own class and traditions'.[105] The article calls for industrial workers to produce

> a new drama, or a new fiction or a new tradition of poetry. For it cannot be disputed that the great, raw material for literature to-day lies, not in Bloomsbury or Chelsea, but in the stress and circumstance of our contemporary industrial life.[106]

The socialist vision established in the 'Introductory Letter' is echoed in 'The Leaning Tower'; there, society 'will pool its possessions' and here this material sharing is figured on a lexical level: 'We have pooled all the different dialects.' This is opposed to the current division of 'human life' 'by hedges' that hold mastery ('dominion') over the poet. These 'hedges' of class division are held to curtail human potentiality. In *The Waves Holograph I*, Woolf suggested that it was the 'field labourers, factory workers, miners' who were part of this mass: 'features they had none' (p. 64). Now all social classes will become 'real people, not people cramped and squashed into featureless masses by hedges' through a common education system.

In the present, without a multilateral system ('that change'), the public library can offer the working classes access to literature. Woolf returns to the terms of her 1925 essay 'The Common Reader' as she holds her library book aloft and

---

[103] Natasha Periyan, 'Democratic Art or Working-Class Literature?: Virginia Woolf, the Women's Cooperative Guild and Literary Value in the "Introductory Letter"', in *Working-Class Writing: Theory and Practice*, ed. by Nick Hubble and Ben Clarke (London: Palgrave Macmillan, 2018).

[104] Professor Ifor Evans, 'When Will the Industrial Worker Produce His Own Literature?', *The Highway*, October 1932, pp. 8–10.

[105] Evans, p. 8; p. 10.

[106] Evans, p. 8.

proclaims that 'England lent it to a common reader, saying "It is time that even you, whom I have shut out from all my universities for centuries, should learn to read your mother tongue"' (E6, p. 276). The active ideal of the autodidact reader who 'create[s] for himself' from 'The Common Reader' is recalled as Woolf argues that readers should 'make yourselves critics' (E6, p. 276).[107] Melba Cuddy-Keane has read 'The Leaning Tower' as a straightforward advocacy of autodidactic methods, while Steve Ellis, commenting on the lecture's closure, has noted the 'powerful counter-strategy of private reading running through [...] [Woolf's] work in the late 1930s and early 1940s [...] which [...] offers a [...] convincing resolution of the problems of the relation between the community and the individual'.[108] Woolf's final peroration is also, however, haunted by the political potential of the institution. Traces remain of the multilateral institution's claims to cross-class communality:

> Let us trespass at once. Literature is no one's *private* ground; literature is *common* ground. It is not cut up into nations; there are no wars there. Let us trespass freely and fearlessly and find our own way for ourselves. It is thus that English literature will survive this war and *cross the gulf* – if commoners and outsiders like ourselves make that country our own country, if we teach ourselves how to read and how to write, how to preserve and how to create. (E6, p. 278, emphases added)

As Ellis acknowledges, the final phrase of 'The Leaning Tower' is a striking advocacy of autodidacticism, and here the common ground recalls the place of the Common Reader.[109] However, Woolf does not completely abandon the political significance of multilateral education; also written into these lines is a tacit awareness of the political role of the institution. Woolf's words recall the actions of her other great trespasser: the narrator of *A Room of One's Own* who 'audaciously' 'trespassed on the turf' (p. 6) of the Oxbridge college, an act of political rebellion against women's exclusion from education. The terms of Woolf's enclosure metaphor also mirror the names for different schools: the 'common' ground of the 'common', 'multilateral' or 'multibias' school is opposed to the 'private ground' of the public school, described previously in the lecture as 'so very very private'. 'Cross the gulf' echoes the phrase's previous usage to suggest how the multilateral institution would help overcome the divide of social class.

---

[107] Virginia Woolf, 'The Common Reader', in *The Essays of Virginia Woolf Volume IV 1925–1928*, ed. by McNeillie, p. 19.

[108] Cuddy-Keane, *Virginia Woolf*, pp. 108–10; Ellis, *British Writers*, p. 199.

[109] Ellis, *British Writers*, pp. 198–99.

Archival material in the Berg Collection reveals that Woolf went back and changed her citation of the mother's letter from the *New Statesman and Nation* to include the mother's opposition between the inclusive, free national education system and the exclusive public school at the same time as she typed up the lecture's final part.[110] The amended section and the closure are in the same blue typing ribbon, as opposed to the black typing ribbon used to type out the lecture's earlier sections. The amendment also appears on a loose leaf of paper at the end of her typed transcript, out of sync with its order in the text. Unlike the rest of the lecture, this sheet of paper has no staple marks, instead bearing holes made from a hole punch, further suggesting its status as a later revision. This detail about Woolf's writing processes supports an interpretation that privileges her concern with contemporary debates surrounding the benefits of multilateralism, revealing that she deliberately generated textual resonances between the lecture's closure and the mother's earlier words on contemporary schooling. Such allusive references make 'The Leaning Tower' a more complex advocacy of autodidactic methods than it may – at first – appear.

In 1940 Woolf drafted a letter to Ben Nicolson, which implored: 'What is the kind of education people ought to have?' (L6, p. 420); a question that reflects upon her exploration of both institutional and anti-institutional methods of education. Mary Childers comments that the 'multivocality' of Woolf's style of writing 'may be said to suppress any political reading of it as always too simple and too polemical'.[111] The critical trend that has focused on Woolf's democratizing, class and gender-crossing concept of the Common Reader as the measure of her engagement with working-class education has evaded the narrative of her direct confrontation with issues of social class and institutional education. Such a focus demonstrates Woolf's analysis of the educational institution's role in shaping social and cultural class division, and her speculative anticipation of its potential to cultivate a politically and culturally democratic future in the post-war world that is 'struggling to be born' (E6, p. 276).

[110] Berg Collection, 66B0309, Typescript, signed with the author's ms. Corrections 39p. The Henry W. and Albert A. Berg Collection of English and American Literature, The New York Public Library.
[111] Mary M. Childers, 'Virginia Woolf on the Outside Looking Down', *Modern Fiction Studies*, Vol. 38 No. 1 (1992), 61–79 (p. 70).

5

'Making Him Our Master': The Eton Writers George Orwell, Cyril Connolly, and Henry Green

In March 1922 *The Eton Candle* was published. The showy vividness of the cover, a flash of magenta pink with gold lettering, was matched by the literary ambitions of its editors, Brian Howard and Harold Acton, who were in their final year at Eton. Howard contributed essays, short stories, and poems; Acton contributed poems, translations, and the first chapter of a planned novel; while a few other students, such as Anthony Powell, contributed illustrations. Also included in the volume was an Old Etonian Supplement, which included the work of Aldous Huxley (who taught at Eton between 1917 and 1919) and Osbert and Sacheverell Sitwell, who had supported the production of the volume.[1] Published in the year of *Ulysses* and *The Waste Land*, *The Eton Candle* aligned itself with modernist aesthetics. Brian Howard launched a passionate invective against the 'appallingly stupid opposition to *vers libre*' in his essay on the subject, and celebrated the work of the imagist poets and Aldous Huxley, who was 'a brilliant young genius'.[2] The volume represented a confident aesthetic statement on the part of its precociously erudite schoolboy editors and was reviewed remarkably widely for a school magazine. Indeed, while a reviewer in *The Times* was dismissive ('it would be unfair to treat it seriously'), Edith Sitwell (a supporter of Howard's work) reviewed the volume as 'a very promising and interesting book, [...] [it] augurs well for the next generation of English writers'.[3]

---

[1]   See Nicholas Murray, *Aldous Huxley: An English Intellectual* (London: Little, Brown, 2002), pp. 96–109 for details surrounding Huxley at Eton.

[2]   Brian Howard, cited in *Brian Howard: Portrait of a Failure*, ed. by Marie-Jacqueline Lancaster (London: Blond, 1968), pp. 63, 71.

[3]   Unsigned review, 'Essays in Verse – Keats and Modern Writers', *The Times*, 11 April 1922, p. 19; Percival Garratt, Edith Sitwell, F.C. Field-Hyde, and G.A. Pfister, 'New Publications', *The Sackbut*, June 1922, p. 35.

Martin Green has – rather over-emphatically – suggested that the volume reveals how 'the modern movement was perceptibly, at Eton, launched'.[4] The three Eton contemporaries this chapter considers – Henry Green, Cyril Connolly, and George Orwell – were not included in the volume, yet their work was informed by this climate of literary experimentation. Connolly later noted, 'I wrote a parody of Acton myself but do not remember being asked to contribute. I think I would have been too shy; for the *Eton Candle* represented the only element in the school which was *avant-garde*.'[5] Connolly's statement is not quite accurate – other attempts were made by the Eton boys to engage with modernist culture. Henry Green was secretary to the Eton Arts Society, founded in 1922, alongside fellow members Acton and Howard.[6] This experience is mentioned in *Pack My Bag* (1940), and fictionalized in Green's first novel *Blindness* (1926), in which John Haye, the protagonist, proudly announces that he is 'Secretary to the Noat Art Society' at the opening of his diary, which also occupies the opening portion of the novel.[7] Noat, as Jeremy Treglown comments, was originally called 'Note' in the draft manuscripts of the novel, an anagram of Eton, and at one point in the text, Haye comments that his school 'might be Eton' (p. 345).[8] In 1942 Orwell wrote, 'I don't feel that Eton has been much of a formative influence in my life.'[9] Orwell's biographer, Bernard Crick, agrees with this summation but cites one of Orwell's schoolfriends, who noted the influence of being taught by Huxley on the young Eric Blair: 'Eric Blair ... would in particular make us note Aldous's phraseology [...]. The taste for words and their accurate and significant use remained.'[10] This chapter considers these three writers: Orwell, the resister of Eton's exclusivity; Connolly, Eton's eulogizer; and Green, whose satirical depiction of Eton in *Blindness* is

---

[4] Martin Green, *Children of the Sun: A Narrative of 'Decadence' in England after 1918* (London: Constable, 1977), p. 159.

[5] Cyril Connolly, cited in *Brian Howard: Portrait of a Failure*, ed. by Lancaster, p. 56.

[6] Various critics have noted how Green reworks the Eton Arts Society in *Blindness*. Keith C. Odom, *Henry Green* (Boston: Twayne, 1978), p. 31; Michael North, *Henry Green and the Writing of His Generation* (London: University Press of Virginia, 1984), p. 17; Marius Hentëa, 'The Fiction of Blindness and Real Life: The Diary Portion of Henry Green's *Blindness* (1926)', *Notes and Queries*, Vol. 59 (July 2012), 421–24 (p. 423); Cyril Connolly, *Enemies of Promise* (London: Penguin, 1979), p. 266. Further references to this edition will be included in brackets after the citation; Martin Green, *Children of the Sun*, p. 173.

[7] Henry Green, *Nothing/Doting/Blindness* (London: Vintage, 2008), p. 343. Further references to this edition will be included in brackets after the citation.

[8] Jeremy Treglown, *Romancing: The Life and Work of Henry Green* (London: Faber & Faber, 2000), p. 62.

[9] Bernard Crick, *George Orwell: A Life* (London: Secker & Warburg, 1980), p. 47.

[10] Crick, p. 59.

rendered far more enigmatic in his late-1930s portrayal. I focus particularly on these writers' autobiographical works, to suggest how their literary style and class and cultural critique are formulated in both response and resistance to the privilege of their exclusive Etonian education.

George Orwell and *The Road to Wigan Pier*: Anti-heroic rhetoric, anti-heroic politics

In 1931 Eric Blair reviewed a biography of Thomas Carlyle, critiquing Carlyle's fetishization of the heroic to suggest that it is matched by a concomitant egotism and an inflated rhetorical style that veils an impoverishment of thought:[11] Blair suggests that Carlyle is 'that fairly subtilised form of egoist, an orator', commenting that his key text, *Heroes and Hero-worship*, is

> nothing better than oratory. There are [...] fine adjectives – adjectives which, living a strange life of their own, give an air of profundity – but no real depth of thought. It is only a splendid vestment of words, draped about a few worn, rather mean ideas.[12]

The association posited here, between inflated political ideals and inflated literary forms, contains the seeds of *Nineteen Eighty-Four*'s Newspeak, with its aim to 'narrow the range of thought' as rhetoric was linked to the heroics of totalitarian politics and the 'leader-worship' of Big Brother.[13]

Max Saunders finds a parallel between Orwell's own self-depiction and his relationship to literary form, noting that he 'wants to make himself transparent (as he wanted to make language transparent) so we can see society, and social injustice'.[14] Eric Blair's adoption of a pseudonym signals that any 'transparency' of self and language is, however, a literary pose – an artful political tool. I consider *The Road to Wigan Pier* (1937) alongside Orwell's other novels and essays to

---

[11] John Holloway's study of Victorian rhetoric focuses on Carlyle's distinctive oratorical style, whereby 'no part of Carlyle's prose seems quite unrelated to his overriding purpose'. John Holloway, *The Victorian Sage: Studies in Argument* (London: Macmillan, 1953), p. 57.

[12] George Orwell, 'Review of *the Two Carlyles* by Osbert Burdett', *The Adelphi*, March 1931, in *The Complete Works of George Orwell Volume 10 A Kind of Compulsion 1903–1936*, ed. by Peter Davison (London: Secker & Warburg, 1998), pp. 195–97 (p. 196). Further references to this essay will be included in brackets after the citation as CW10 and then the page number.

[13] George Orwell, *Nineteen Eighty-Four* (London: Penguin, 1966), p. 45; p. 109. Further references to this edition will be included in brackets after the citation.

[14] Saunders, p. 510. Nick Hubble considers Saunders's critique in relation to *Homage to Catalonia* in 'Orwell and the English Working Class: Lessons in Autobiografiction for the Twenty-First Century', in *Orwell Today*, ed. by Richard Lance Keeble (Bury St Edmunds: Abramis, 2012), pp. 30–45 (p. 36).

suggest how his earlier critique of the vacuous nature of literary and political heroisms informed the development of Orwell's 1930s rhetoric and politics. In this, I am in dialogue with Ben Clarke's analysis of 'Orwell's political ideas by analyzing both the content and strategies of his texts'.[15] Where Clarke positions Orwell against the Auden Group to suggest how his 'style [...] developed in opposition to the specialist discourses he associated with cultural and political elites', analysis of the ways in which Orwell inflected education with rhetorical and political values suggests how he politicized aesthetics, rendering his literary style integral to the political intent of his texts.[16] Orwell's educational ideals in the 1930s are bound up with his engagement with the 'myth of the proletariat' which has been positioned as a cornerstone of Orwell's class politics by critics. Stephen Ingle and Ben Clarke suggest that Orwell was conscious that this myth may have had 'shortcomings', but maintain its validity for his socialist vision: Clarke argues that Orwell 'both critiques and uses popular myths, attempting to reconstruct their meaning rather than reveal them as illusions'.[17] Orwell's mercurial, ventriloquial, and rhetorical style renders his ironic engagement with the 'myth of the proletariat' opaque. This is a rhetorical style that, in its occupation of multiple subject positions, can be conceived of in opposition to the 'egoism' Orwell finds in Carlyle, as a rejection of hierarchical politics is paralleled by a rejection of hierarchical rhetoric. Education provides the site of this engagement, as Orwell explores its role as a determinant of cultural and political ideals.

The straightforward school autobiography was the 1930s project Orwell never quite managed to write: 'I'm always meaning one of those days to write a book about St. Cyprian's' (CW11, p. 254). Orwell described his later essay on his schooldays, 'Such, Such Were the Joys', as 'a sort of pendant to Cyril Connolly's *Enemies of Promise*'.[18] Like Connolly's work, it considers life at St Cyprian's, but the tone is much darker – the essay relays a vicious beating by Orwell's headmaster, an experience which provoked

---

[15] Ben Clarke, 'George Orwell: Politics, Rhetoric, and the Public Intellectual', *Studies in the Humanities*, Vol. 35 No. 2 (2008), 231–49 (p. 232).

[16] Ibid.

[17] Stephen Ingle, *The Social and Political Thought of George Orwell: A Reassessment* (London: Routledge, 2006), p. 65; Ben Clarke, *Orwell in Context: Communities, Myths, Values* (Basingstoke: Palgrave Macmillan, 2007), p. 3.

[18] The essay is attributed by Bernard Crick to 1940, but is commonly dated to 1947, and was published in 1952. For a detailed discussion of the dating of the essay see Appendix B, Crick, pp. 410–12; as cited in Crick, p. 410.

a sense of desolate loneliness and helplessness, of being locked up not only in a hostile world but in a world of good and evil where the rules were such that it was actually not possible for me to keep them.[19]

Elements of autobiography shape *The Road to Wigan Pier* and early critics saw the autobiographical second part of the text as compromising the integrity of the documentary vision of northern industrial life, represented in Part I. Victor Gollancz found that 'Mr Orwell is still a victim of that early atmosphere, in his home and public school', while Storm Jameson argued that the second, autobiographical section revealed Orwell's 'flounderings' within 'the gulf, mental and moral, between the public school boy [*sic*] turned Socialist and the socialist worker'.[20] *The Road to Wigan Pier* was influential in setting the terms within which Jameson formulated her 'Documents' essay:

> A task of the greatest value, urgent and not easy, is waiting to be done. George Orwell has begun on it in the first half of *The Road to Wigan Pier*. The instinct which drives a writer to go and see for himself may be sound [...] he must be able to give an objective report [...] [w]ithout feeling heroic, or even adventurous, or curious about their own spiritual reactions.[21]

Part II presents itself as both a digression and an explanation of the positions established in the first part of the text: 'I shall have to digress and explain how my own attitude towards the class question was developed' (p. 106). A dialogic relationship is established between the two sections, where the observations of Part I are recontextualized through exposure of the prejudices behind the documentary lens in Part II. Such an analysis elucidates the text's depiction of the 'myth of the proletariat'. Part I evokes the heroic manual workers of socialist realism: on seeing the miners work, Orwell's narrator celebrates 'what splendid men they are [...] nearly all of them have the most noble bodies' (p. 21). Their physicality is lingered over in awe: 'wide shoulders tapering to slender supple waists, and small pronounced buttocks and sinewy thighs' (p. 21). They are monumentalized like 'hammered iron statues' (p. 21). Orwell's research notes for his trip record the results of the 1931 census which reveal the strong presence of working women in the regions he visited:

[19] George Orwell, 'Such, Such Were the Joys', in *The Complete Works of George Orwell Volume 19 It Is What I Think 1947–1948*, ed. by Peter Davison (London: Secker & Warburg, 1998), pp. 356–87 (p. 359). Further references to this essay will be included in brackets after the citation as CW19 and then the page number.

[20] Victor Gollancz, 'Foreword to *The Road to Wigan Pier* [1937]', in *George Orwell: The Critical Heritage*, ed. by Jeffrey Meyers (London: Routledge & Kegan Paul, 1975), pp. 91–99 (p. 95); Storm Jameson, 'Socialists Born and Made', *Fact*, May 1937, pp. 87–90 (p. 87).

[21] Jameson, 'Writing in Revolt 1. Theory – Documents', pp. 12–13.

Mining 7,708 (118 females.) Textiles (not dress) and cellulose, 5,386, mainly women. Manufacture of machinery 2,139. Manufacture of clothing (not knitted) 2,438, mainly women. Transport and communication, 1,966. In business 5,133, about a quarter women.[22]

Despite this, *The Road to Wigan Pier* discusses only all-male mining work, deliberately excluding discussion of women's labour. Such a move is a sign of Orwell's deliberate participation in an image of the proletariat as aligned with the male, manual worker. The final chapter of *The Road to Wigan Pier* critiques this image, however, as a piece of '"proletarian" cant' (p. 199):

> In order to symbolize the class war, there has been set up the more or less mythical figure of a 'proletarian', a muscular but downtrodden man in greasy overalls, in contradistinction to a 'capitalist', a fat, wicked man in a top hat and fur coat. It is tacitly assumed that there is no one in between [...]. If you are going to harp on the 'dictatorship of the proletariat', it is an elementary precaution to start by explaining who the proletariat *are*. But because of the Socialist tendency to idealize the manual worker as such, this has never been made sufficiently clear. How many of the wretched shivering army of clerks and shopwalkers, who in some ways are actually worse off than a miner or a dock-hand, think of themselves as proletarians? A proletarian – so they have been taught to think – means a man without a collar. So that when you try to move them by talking about 'class war', you only succeed in scaring them; they forget their incomes and remember their accents, and fly to the defence of the class that is exploiting them. (p. 199, emphasis in original)

The inverted commas signal Orwell's sense of the misconceptions surrounding these terms – 'proletarian', 'capitalist', 'dictatorship of the proletariat', 'class war' – as he argues that the 'mythical figure' of the 'proletarian' as a manual worker serves as a prop to the class divide. Orwell's use of the passive ('has been set up') contributes to an effacement of his participation in the creation of the myth of the proletariat in Part I of *The Road to Wigan Pier*; in these terms, his previous description of the working miners seems to spill over into a parodic appropriation of the iconography of socialist realism. This masculinized, proletarian ideal is later positioned as defunct in 'The Lion and the Unicorn' (1940): 'The old-style "proletarian" – collarless, unshaven and with muscles warped by heavy labour – still exists, but he is constantly decreasing in

---

[22] George Orwell, 'Appendix 2: Orwell's Notes for *The Road to Wigan Pier*', in *Complete Works Volume 10*, ed. by Davison, pp. 538–84 (p. 542). Further references to this appendix will be included in brackets after the citation as CW10 and then the page number.

numbers'; while *Nineteen Eighty-Four* exposes the falsity of 'the physical type set up by the Party as an ideal' (p. 52).[23]

Orwell acknowledges a cultural class difference (in the form of 'accents') between the lower middle class and the working class, while advocating an economic identification. The relationship between cultural and economic determinants of the class divide was critiqued in his review of Alec Brown's *The Fate of the Middle Classes,* written while in the north:

> A man with £3 a week who can pronounce his aitches regards himself – and is regarded by other people, to some extent – as the superior of a man with £10 a week who can't. [...] [I]t is because of this that the aitch-pronouncing section of the population tend to side with their natural enemies and against the working class, even when they grasp the economic side of the question fairly clearly.[24]

Orwell's contention is that there is a vast cultural difference between those who are economically in the same bracket. The issue of 'aitch-pronouncing' becomes metonymic for the cultural class divide in *The Road to Wigan Pier,* where the final chapter is an exposition of these concerns and the difficulty of 'escap[e][ing], culturally, from the class into which you have been born' (p. 198). With the threat of 'Fascism [...] coming' (p. 203), Orwell argues that the cultural class divide must be temporarily tolerated in favour of economic identification:

> We must drop that misleading habit of pretending that the only proletarians are manual labourers. [...] They [the middle class] must not be allowed to think that the battle is between those who pronounce their aitches and those who don't; for if they think that, they will join in on the side of the aitches.
>
> I am implying that different classes must be persuaded to act together without, for the moment, being asked to drop their class-differences. And that sounds dangerous. (p. 200)

Dropping 'class-differences' and dropping 'habit[s]' are idiomatically reminiscent of 'dropping your aitches'. Clarke has noted that Orwell's sense of the significance of cultural differences 'shape[s]' the text, while Lynette Hunter gives a summary of the text's argument: 'Cultural and class differences are central and very difficult to solve, but should be separate from financial issues over which the

[23] George Orwell, 'The Lion and the Unicorn: Socialism and the English Genius', in *Complete Works Volume 12,* ed. by Davison, pp. 391–434 (p. 408). Further references to this essay will be included in brackets after the citation as CW12 and then the page number.

[24] George Orwell, 'Review of *The Fate of the Middle Classes,* by Alec Brown', in *Complete Works Volume 10,* ed. by Davison, p. 478.

classes could cooperate.'[25] Orwell's thinking on financial and cultural differences in this text finds itself in a double bind. Paradoxically, although Orwell critiques socialist behaviour and action for its economic emphasis and trivialization of cultural differences, he also suggests that the cultural should not stand in the way of class identification: 'Different classes must be persuaded to act together without, for the moment, being asked to drop their class-differences' (p. 200).

The Road to Wigan Pier is aware of the challenge its political message denotes. The focus on accent and dialect as the locus of the 'terribly difficult issue of class-distinctions' (p. 203) is deliberately reductive, reflecting the nexus of a series of highly contentious culturally based class prejudices. The text's closure, 'we have nothing to lose but our aitches' (p. 204), is disingenuous: after such a long focus on the significance of the cultural divide, the true psychological value of the 'aitches' has been fully realized. It is worth pausing over the rhetoric of the final section of *The Road to Wigan Pier*, as the final pages are replete with features designed to persuade the reader to disavow the cultural allegiances the text has explored, in favour of a cross-class identification that would benefit the socialist cause. Parallelism is used: 'Economically, I am in the same boat with the miner, the navvy, and the farmhand [...] [b]ut culturally I am different from the miner, the navvy, and the farm-hand' (p. 202). Colloquialisms are deployed: 'The only possible policy for the moment is to go easy' (p. 203). Rhetorical questions are used: 'Which class do I belong to?' (p. 198), 'Why?' (p. 199). A summative peroration is given: 'to sum up' (p. 202). Metaphor is used: 'The sinking middle class [...] are clinging to their gentility under the impression that it keeps them afloat. It is not good policy to *start* by telling them to throw away the life-belt' (p. 202). Finally, the unifying force of the collective pronoun operates a rallying cry to the down-at-heel, if not quite down-and-out, middle classes: 'we of the sinking middle class – the private schoolmaster, the half-starved free-lance journalist [...] the jobless Cambridge graduate' (p. 204). The persuasive stylistics of the text attempt to compensate for the politically contentious content, persuading his middle-class readership to forsake their cultural class prejudices in favour of allegiance with the working class. Orwell's flexible rhetorical style, his subtle shifts of tone and ventriloquist nature, can be conceived of in opposition to the heroic and egotistical quality he identified in Carlylean discourse and goes on to find in totalitarian politics. It is the very subtlety of Orwell's rhetoric that has

---

[25] Clarke, *Orwell in Context*, p. 50; Lynette Hunter, *George Orwell: The Search for a Voice* (Milton Keynes: Open University Press, 1984), pp. 67–68.

led critics to detect in *The Road to Wigan Pier* an advocacy of the myth of the proletariat that the text works to debunk.

Working-class education – or rather, a lack of working-class education – is an integral aspect of the cultivation of this myth. The Wigan Pier diary registers a keen sense of the incipient political threat of an uneducated working class, as Orwell records his 'dismay' at the reaction of the working-class crowd to a public meeting held by Oswald Mosley and the British Union of Fascists: 'how easy it is to bamboozle an uneducated audience if you have prepared beforehand a set of repartees with which to evade awkward questions' (CW10, p. 457). A few days later, Orwell wrote to Jack Common of the meeting in similar terms: 'It sickens one to see how easily a man of that type can win over and bamboozle a working class audience' (CW10, p. 458). The uneducated working class are figured as ripe for fascist indoctrination and represent a keen political threat. Despite this, *The Road to Wigan Pier* seemingly celebrates the working-class 'manual worker' as opposed to the 'educated man' at the end of Part I:

> I should say that a manual worker, if he is in steady work and drawing good wages – an 'if' which gets bigger and bigger – has a better chance of being happy than an 'educated' man [...]. I have often been struck by the peculiar easy completeness, the perfect symmetry as it were, of a working-class interior at its best. Especially on winter evenings after tea, when the fire glows in the open range and dances mirrored in the steel fender, when Father, in shirt-sleeves, sits in the rocking chair at one side of the fire reading the racing finals, and Mother sits on the other with her sewing, and the children are happy with a pennorth of mint humbugs, and the dog lolls roasting himself on the rag mat – it is a good place to be in, provided that you can be not only in it but sufficiently *of* it to be taken for granted [...] In that age when there is no manual labour and everyone is 'educated', it is hardly likely that Father will still be a rough man with enlarged hands who likes to sit in shirt sleeves and says 'Ah wur coomin' oop street'. (pp. 104–05, emphasis in original)

This romanticized image relies upon an uneducated, in-work working class for its survival; education has no place in this idyllic image of working-class culture. Conversely, in the projected, socialist 'Utopian future [...] the scene is totally different' (p. 105) as education connotes a disruption to working-class culture and discourse. This is an image that Orwell can objectify, precisely because he is excluded from it. The different relationship Orwell claims to have had with the working-class mining community, and the supposedly classless tramping community, where people 'completely failed to notice' (p. 135) his 'educated' accent is figured by his parallel statements: the idealized working-class home 'is

a good place to be in, provided that you can be not only in it but sufficiently *of* it
to be taken for granted' (p. 104, emphasis in original), while the tramping world
accepted him: 'Once you are in that world and seemingly *of* it, it hardly matters
what you have been in the past' (p. 136, emphasis in original).

Orwell deliberately enacts the operation of class prejudice to support the ends
of his thesis. In Part II, he comments that 'snobbishness is bound up with a species
of idealism' (p. 115), and here the universalized image of the working-class
family with 'Father', 'Mother', and 'children' presents a deliberately conservative
and propagandistic image. Hynes has found that its 'political implications are
essentially conservative [...] [i]t is a very odd paragraph indeed for a socialist
to write'.[26] The tableau is, however, of indeterminate factual provenance. The
narrator claims it to be a 'memory of working-class interiors' and presents it as a
'scene' and 'picture' that has been 'called up' by his imagination (p. 105). In either
case, for its successful realization, it is positioned in the subjunctive mood of
full-time employment ('if'). Indeed, the fulfilment of these conditions is under
threat: 'This scene is still reduplicated in a majority of English homes, though
not in so many as before the war' (p. 105).

Further ironies are present at the end of Part I when Orwell's narrator exposes
the hypocrisies of class prejudice in an exploration of the relationship between
masculine ideals and education. Orwell takes umbrage when his own public-
school education is associated with emasculation: 'Lawrence tells me that because
I have been to a public school I am a eunuch. [...] [I]f you tell me I am a eunuch
you are tempting me to hit back in any way that seems feasible' (p. 147). Orwell
spoils for a fight in the face of Lawrence's perceived slight to his masculinity,
based on an extrapolation of Lawrence's attitude to Lord Chatterley in *Lady
Chatterley's Lover*. However, his narrator earlier makes the same association
between emasculation and education when dismissing working-class education:

> Take the working-class attitude towards 'education'. How different it is from
> ours, and how immensely sounder! [...] I used to lament over quite imaginary
> pictures of lads of fourteen dragged protesting from their lessons and set to work
> at dismal jobs. It seemed to me dreadful that the doom of a 'job' should descend
> upon anyone at fourteen. [...] I know now that there is not one working-class
> boy in a thousand who does not pine for the day when he will leave school. He
> wants to be doing real work, not wasting his time on ridiculous rubbish like
> history and geography. To the working class, the notion of staying at school till
> you are nearly grown-up seems merely contemptible and unmanly. The idea of

---

[26] *Auden Generation*, p. 276.

a great big boy of eighteen, who ought to be bringing a pound a week home to his parents, going to school in a ridiculous uniform and even being caned for not doing his lessons! Just fancy a working-class boy of eighteen allowing himself to be caned! He is a man when the other is still a baby [...]. There is much in middle-class life that looks sickly and debilitating when you see it from a working-class angle. (pp. 103–04)

Education for the working classes is (seemingly) emasculating and infantilizing. This passage is open to accusations of a reactionary politics and, indeed, it has attracted much criticism as such. Frank Gloversmith has condemned Orwell as 'reactionary [...] hypocritical. [...] This is a deadlock, insofar as Orwell writes at a time when the map of class divisions and the charting of educational opportunity would have the closest possible correlation.'[27] The *Left Review* found the passage 'simply absurd': 'It is a healthy instinct which prompts many working people to seek education in the face of every difficulty, and Englishmen like Ruskin and William Morris had better vision than Mr. Orwell in this matter', while Philip Toynbee called Orwell's thinking 'a piece of idiocy': 'because the beloved adopts this attitude then Orwell himself will jolly well adopt it too.'[28] This passage is more ambiguous than it initially appears, however. The inverted commas around '"education"' signal that Orwell is not presenting an objection to education in itself; the punctuation is suggestive of both the misconceptions of working-class ideas surrounding education and the false education of the middle class. The ventriloquism of Orwell's narrator is revealed in the use of free indirect speech; the exclamatory forms and colloquial asides ('[j]ust fancy', '[t]he time was'), alongside the simplistic antithesis 'man'/'baby' indicate his switch into ventriloquism as he identifies the 'working-class attitude' on '"education"' before switching back into a more sophisticated register: 'There is much in middle-class life that looks sickly and debilitating.'

Walter Greenwood was 'infuriated [...] by some of the things he [Orwell] says' in *The Road to Wigan Pier*.[29] In this instance, however, the 'working-class angle' is not necessarily Orwell's own. He participates in the cultivation of the myth of the proletariat that is debunked in Part II, in his objection to the stereotyped vision of the working class by 'quantities of middle-class people' that

---

[27] Frank Gloversmith, 'Changing Things: Orwell and Auden', in *Class, Culture and Social Change*, ed. by Gloversmith, pp. 101–41 (p. 121).

[28] Derek Kahn, 'Review of *The Road to Wigan Pier*', *Left Review*, April 1937, p. 187; Philip Toynbee, *Encounter*, August 1959, pp. 81–82, in *George Orwell: Critical Heritage*, ed. by Meyers, pp. 115–18 (p. 117).

[29] Walter Greenwood, *Tribune*, 12 March 1937, p. 12, in *George Orwell: Critical Heritage*, ed. by Meyers, pp. 99–100 (p. 100).

leads to a 'notion that the working class have been absurdly pampered, hopelessly demoralized by doles, old age pensions, free education, etc.' (p. 116). *The Road to Wigan Pier*'s narrator ventriloquizes the attitudes of class prejudice, rather than necessarily acting as a mouthpiece for Orwell's own values. Such manipulation is designed to point up the relationship between social stereotyping and class prejudice whereby 'snobbishness is bound up with a species of idealism' (p. 115). The myth of the proletariat is rejected as a sign and prop of the class divide: a 'mythical' (p. 199) symbol of the 'class war' (p. 199).

Education, social class, leadership: Wigan and beyond

Arthur Calder-Marshall's review of *The Road to Wigan Pier* suggested that Orwell 'sees the cultural and political hope of the present and future' as lying with the working class, while Hynes and Clarke similarly position the working class as leaders of Orwell's socialist future.[30] Bernard Crick, however, argues that *The Road to Wigan Pier* is formative in Orwell's advancement of the role of the lower middle classes in socialism:

> From his visit to the North and reaching its peak in the novel *Coming Up for Air* and [...] *The Lion and the Unicorn*, he developed a theory that the future of socialism depended precisely on the leadership of the lower middle classes and on persuading them that they had an identity of interest with the industrial working class.[31]

Crick's analysis of the group targeted in Orwell's political message corresponds with Stephen Ingle's identification of Orwell's readers as 'middle-class, predominantly Southern'.[32]

Such a perception of the class background and political engagement of his readership elucidates Orwell's omission of details surrounding the organized and politically committed nature of working-class socialism – an omission that

---

[30] Arthur Calder-Marshall, *Time and Tide*, 20 March 1937, p. 382, in *George Orwell: Critical Heritage*, ed. by Meyers, pp. 101–03 (p. 102). Hynes argues that Orwell's socialism sees the 'working-class socialists' as 'heroes', noting that this 'would be a movement of the sentimental, good-hearted English working class and of such others as could achieve that state', while Clarke finds that the 'image of the English working-class man emerges from the texts, conceived as [...] instrument of social transformation'. Hynes, *Auden Generation*, p. 277; Clarke, *Orwell in Context*, p. 170.

[31] Crick, p. 189.

[32] Stephen Ingle, *George Orwell: A Political Life* (Manchester: Manchester University Press, 1993), p. 49.

provoked criticism from the *Left Review*.[33] The Wigan Pier diary repeatedly suggests the active presence of the localized and associative organizations of Labour Party politics in the north: on 11 February 1936 Orwell records that '*[l]ast night to Co-Op hall with various people from the N.U.W.M. [...] [w]as surprised by the amount of Communist feeling here*' (CW10, p. 424, emphasis in original); on 15 February he '*[w]ent with N.U.W.M. collectors on their rounds*' (CW10, p. 426, emphasis in original); on 19 February he went to an NUWM social event, with '*[a]bout 200 people, preponderantly women*' (CW10, p. 431, emphasis in original); and on 29 February Orwell acknowledged in a letter to Richard Rees 'The lads at the N.U.W.M. have been of great service to me' (CW10, p. 442). These political structures are acknowledged in *The Road to Wigan Pier* to ambivalent effect:

> I have seen a good deal of the N.U.W.M., and I greatly admire the men, ragged and underfed like the others, who keep the organization going. [...] [T]he English working class do not show much capacity for leadership, but they have a wonderful talent for organization. (p. 75)

The working classes are to provide reinforcement but not leadership, as Orwell's evasion of the extent and influence of working-class political networks in *The Road to Wigan Pier* is designed to empower a middle-class audience in order to cultivate the socialist cause. 'The Lion and the Unicorn' later criticized the Left for 'alienating the middle classes from Socialism' (CW12, p. 419); the essay called for a form of socialism that would 'win over the middle classes instead of antagonizing them' (CW12, p. 421). This need to 'win over' the middle class elucidates Orwell's analysis of the educated as natural leaders:

> In Lissagaray's *History of the Commune* there is an interesting passage describing the shootings that took place after the Commune had been suppressed. The authorities were shooting the ringleaders, and as they did not know who the ringleaders were, they were picking them out on the principle that those of better class would be the ringleaders. An officer walked down a line of prisoners, picking out likely-looking types. One man was shot because he was wearing a watch, another because he 'had an intelligent face' [...]. I do agree that in almost any revolt the leaders would tend to be people who could pronounce their aitches. (p. 44)

---

[33] Kahn, p. 187.

Lissagaray's text was foundational in Marxist thought. Eleanor Marx wrote the introduction to the first English translation, which appeared in 1886, suggesting that the text detailed 'the first attempt of the proletariat to govern itself'.[34] Orwell's description of the incident reveals how he diverges from Marxist orthodoxy in advancing his social theory. The original notes merely:

> 'You seem intelligent,' said he to some one; 'step out of the ranks.' 'You have a watch,' said he to another; 'you must have been a functionary of the Commune,' and he placed him apart [...] he chose eighty-three men and three women, made them draw up along the talus of the fortifications and had them shot.[35]

There is no mention in the original of 'those of better class', a detail that collapses intelligence with social standing. Orwell's commentary on the episode, 'leaders [...] tend to be people who could pronounce their aitches', is also absent. *History of the Paris Commune of 1871* repeatedly dichotomizes the causes of the proletariat and the bourgeoisie, in a way that would subvert the ends of Orwell's thesis: 'so much for the judges and the justice which the bourgeoisie gave those proletarians they had not shot down'; 'the people alone had been great [...] [t]he bourgeoisie, on the contrary, had displayed all its total cowardice'.[36] Orwell's appeal to his 'intelligent', 'better class' of reader is designed to empower a middle-class readership to effect social change.

In *Coming Up for Air* (1939), Orwell carefully codes George Bowling in social and educational terms. Critics have variously associated Bowling with the mundane: Frank Gloversmith suggests that, in Orwell's work, 'the hero – a Comstock or a George Bowling – may be small'; Crick calls Bowling a 'non-intellectual antihero'; Cunningham calls him a 'version of Orwell's ordinary bloke on the bus', while Alison Light suggests that he is part of a wider shift towards the depiction of the 'gelded', emasculated male in interwar fiction.[37] 'Boys' Weeklies' (1940) argued that the corner shop, stocked full of 'boys' penny weeklies', offered 'the best available indication of what the mass of the English people really feels and thinks'; Bowling's reading matter positions him as part of the mass. Influenced by mainstream culture, he starts off reading

[34] Prosper Olivier Lissagaray, *History of the Paris Commune of 1871*, trans. by Eleanor Marx (London: Verso, 2012), p. 3.

[35] Lissagaray, pp. 314–15.

[36] Lissagaray, p. 338; p. 332.

[37] Gloversmith, 'Changing Things: Orwell and Auden', p. 140. Crick, p. 254; Cunningham, *British Writers*, p. 207; Light, *Forever England*, p. 7.

'the boys' penny weeklies [...] a bit later it was books'.[38] His time spent on the West Coast Defence Force in the First World War guarding twelve tins of bully beef, during which he spent a year reading – among others – 'Wells, Conrad, Kipling, Galsworthy' (p. 121), represents 'the only real education, in the sense of book-learning, that I've ever had' (p. 122). At the end of the war, Bowling sought work as a salesman and 'wasn't a highbrow any longer' (p. 128). His formal education is a means of establishing his 'lower middle class' status. 'Boys' Weeklies' found that 'in England education is mainly a matter of status' (CW, p. 62) and, indeed, this is reflected in Bowling's education as a boy: 'we went to the dame-school [...] [m]ost of the shopkeepers' children went there, to save them from the shame and come-down of going to the board school, though [...] Mother Howlett was [...] worse than useless as a teacher' (p. 55). While H.E. Bates in *The Old School* noted his grammar school's 'unnecessary attempts at conformation with public school standards, the constant talk of tradition and the honour and good name of the school' (p. 29), Bowling's time at grammar school is rendered distinct from a public-school-education: 'You'd no sentiment of loyalty, no goofy feeling about the old grey stones [...] there was no Old Boy's tie and not even a school song' (p. 67). 'The Lion and the Unicorn' rejected public-school values as inadequate to the challenge of war ('The difference between going down fighting, and surrendering without a fight, is by no means a question of "honour" and schoolboy heroics' (CW12, pp. 431–32)), and, similarly, the suburban, unintellectual Bowling is privy to a level of insight to which Old Porteus, his former schoolmaster, a 'public-school chap[s]' (p. 159), is blind:

> I'm not a fool, but I'm not a highbrow either [...] [a]nd yet I've enough sense to see that the old life we're used to is being sawn off at the roots. [...] And I'm not even exceptional in this. There are millions of others like me. Ordinary chaps that I meet everywhere, chaps I run across in pubs, bus drivers and travelling salesmen [...] have got a feeling that the world's gone wrong. [...] And yet here's this learned chap, who's lived all his life with books and soaked himself in history [...] [d]oesn't think Hitler matters. Refuses to believe there's another war coming. (pp. 157–58)

[38] George Orwell, 'Boys' Weeklies', in *Complete Works Volume 12*, ed. by Davison, pp. 57–79 (p. 58). Further references to this essay will be included in brackets after the citation as CW12 and then the page number; George Orwell, *Coming Up for Air* (London: Penguin, 1962), p. 88. Further references to this edition will be included in brackets after the citation.

Bowling's mundane rather than 'exceptional' status ('[t]here are millions of others like me') is reflected in the text's linguistic register: Alex Zwerdling argues that

> Orwell is [...] a poor ventriloquist [...]. [His] experiment [...] is constantly being pulled in two directions – the need to articulate a political warning clearly and forcefully, and the need to be true to the colloquial, impoverished vocabulary of the narrator and the audience he is designed to represent and reach.[39]

'Politics and the English Language' (1946) rejects the 'inflated' rhetoric of political language, finding that political systems tarnish and degrade language: 'I should expect to find [...] that the German, Russian and Italian languages have all deteriorated [...] as a result of dictatorship'; Blair/Orwell's 1931 review suggests that Carlylean rhetoric held similar qualities – his 'oratory' is empty, a 'splendid vestment of words' (CW10, p. 196), and the 'egoism' (CW10, p. 196) of his rhetoric parallels the egoism of his heroic politics.[40] Instead, in Bowling's discourse, colloquial forms – 'chap' (p. 157), 'shoved down my throat' (p. 88) – establish the fallible ('name I forget' (p. 88)) protagonist. George Bowling, who is 'not [...] exceptional', occupies a register that is deflated in comparison with Carlyle's style – in this deflation there is an accompanying sincerity which renders the text's register a vehicle for its politics, and seems to anticipate the finding of 'Politics and the English Language' that '[t]he great enemy of clear language is insincerity' (CW17, p. 428).

While Crick suggests that *Coming Up for Air* is the 'peak' of Orwell's suggestion that the success of socialism 'depended [...] on the leadership of the lower middle classes', Bowling seems to eschew conventional leadership ideals.[41] 'The Lion and the Unicorn's' egalitarian vision of 'a world-state of free and equal human beings' (CW12, p. 411) echoes this departure from conventional models of leadership, presenting a vision of a technocratic, socialist government, inclusive of the Labour Party, trade unions and the middle class. This government 'will not set up any explicit class dictatorship [...] it will never lose touch with the tradition of compromise and the belief in a law that is above the State' (CW12, p. 427). The rhetoric of George Bowling, which occupies a studied political register, reflects a shift away from the high oratory Orwell critiqued in his 1931 review, a form

[39] Alex Zwerdling, *Orwell and the Left* (London: Yale University Press, 1974), p. 126.

[40] George Orwell, 'Politics and the English Language', in *The Complete Works of George Orwell Volume 17 I Belong to the Left 1945*, ed. by Peter Davison (London: Secker & Warburg, 1998), pp. 421–32 (p. 428). Further references to this edition will be included in brackets after the citation as CW17 and then the page number.

[41] Crick, p. 189.

of which is figured in the 'didactic[ally]' (p. 230) rhetoric of O'Brien in *Nineteen Eighty-Four*, as he functions as the mouthpiece for Big Brother's totalitarian oppression. The novel adapts ideas present in D.H. Lawrence's *Fantasia of the Unconscious* (1922) to develop a polarized education system into a condition of totalitarianism: the Proles, who make up 85 per cent of the population, leave school for heavy labour at twelve: '*[u]ntil they become conscious they will never rebel*' (p. 60, emphasis in original). Carey sees in *Nineteen Eighty-Four* a depoliticization of the masses, as the uneducated Proles are 'transposed to an innocent, pre-industrial existence', but 'The Lion and the Unicorn' renders clear that such a predicament is a condition of totalitarianism, rather than a wish fulfilment on Orwell's part.[42] The essay argues for the 'abolition of all hereditary privilege, especially in education' (CW12, p. 410); 'reform of the educational system along democratic lines' (CW12, p. 422) is proposed, in order to create a 'classless educational system' (CW12, p. 427).

Throughout the 1930s, education figures as a testing ground of Orwell's rejection of hierarchical politics on both a linguistic and a political level. This has implications for Eric Blair's own self-fashioning as George Orwell: in a 1948 letter to Julian Symons, Orwell wrote of George Bowling: 'Of course you are perfectly right about my own character constantly intruding on that of the narrator'; the shared first name signalling this slippage in personal identification.[43] For Cyril Connolly, Orwell's schoolfriend and keen critic, the association between inflated literary forms and vacuous content was problematic: seemingly in dialogue with his friend, Connolly found that 'mastery of form has lately been held [...] to conceal a poverty of content but this is not inevitably so' (p. 94). As I shall suggest, Connolly does, however, share Orwell's concern with the ways in which education informed the social and cultural codes of literary discourse.

Cyril Connolly and *Enemies of Promise*: The self-reflexive 'text-book'

In his 1948 'Introduction' to *Enemies of Promise* (1938), Cyril Connolly objected to reviews which had found that the book's autobiographical Part III had 'nothing to do with' (p. 9) the rest of the work: two sections of literary criticism.

---

[42] Carey, p. 44.

[43] As cited in Jeffrey Meyers, 'Orwell's Apocalypse: *Coming Up For Air*', in *Modern Critical Views: George Orwell*, ed. by Harold Bloom (New York: Chelsea House, 1987), pp. 85–96 (p. 94).

Evelyn Waugh was one such critic. He found that the book was 'structurally jerry-built' and felt that Connolly's 'attempt to pass' the three books off as 'the expansion of a single theme' was 'very near to dishonesty'.[44] The book is, indeed, curiously hybrid: Alex Woloch has described it as a 'striking mixture of formal and sociological concerns'.[45] As Auden's review identified, referencing also MacNeice's *Modern Poetry* and Isherwood's *Lions and Shadows*, this 'combination of criticism with autobiography is a feature of our time [...] [t]here is a close relation between the ideas which men hold and the way in which they live'.[46] Another parallel to this exists, of course, in the work of George Orwell. This analysis considers how Part III of the text deconstructs the cultural values advanced in Parts I and II. Latent within Connolly's examination is a concern over what – and whose – cultural values will survive, a concern that, I suggest, can be elucidated with reference to contemporaneous debates surrounding the role of the classics in education.

Connolly conceives of Parts I and II in language that is suggestive of the pedagogic; the book's 1948 introduction describes it as a 'didactic inquiry' (p. 9), a 'text-book' (p. 9) – the presence of an index as a tool to the readers' ability to locate the information they seek in the study formally reinforces this pedagogic intent. Throughout the book, scientific language is used to describe Connolly's method, suggesting the emulation of an objective rationale: the book's (in)famous '*The Theory of Permanent Adolescence*' (p. 271, emphasis in original) – that boys' public-school years 'are so intense as to dominate their lives and to arrest their development' (p. 271) – is one such example, as well as Connolly's 'experiment' (p. 82) where he merges the voices of Hemingway, Orwell, and Isherwood, to note the homogenous literary discourse of the New Vernacular. Connolly's taxonomic imagination tends towards listing, categorizing, and classifying. He includes a 'production chart' (p. 73) of Mandarins and New Vernacular writers, with writers' works listed by year and sub-classified by type: '1931. V. Woolf, *The Waves* (M); Roy Campbell, *The Georgiad* (V); A. Powell, *Afternoon Men* (V)' (pp. 74–75). Also evident is an idiosyncratic table assessing the 'Characteristics of the Clever Young Men and their Dirty Deals' (p. 55), which offers a comparative analysis of the qualities of the male protagonists of works by writers including Huxley, Joyce, and Eliot. Part II is constructed via an idiosyncratic methodology,

[44] Evelyn Waugh, 'Present Discontents', *Tablet*, 3 December 1938, in *The Essays, Articles and Reviews of Evelyn Waugh*, ed. by Donat Gallagher (London: Methuen, 1983), pp. 238–41 (p. 238).

[45] Alex Woloch, 'Foreword', in Cyril Connolly, *Enemies of Promise* (Chicago: University of Chicago Press, 2008), pp. vii–xviii (p. xiii).

[46] Auden, 'How Not to Be a Genius', p. 19.

whereby Connolly cites a ten-line extract from George Crabbe's 'The Village', and uses the poem's description of the realities of village life as a lens through which to consider 'the conditions which govern the high rate of mortality among contemporary writers' (p. 97), with each chapter in Part II addressing different factors, taken from the poem.

Woloch suggests that this merging of genres, the scientific with literary criticism, has the effect of 'suggesting that literary criticism, properly pursued, is always threatening (or aspiring) to turn into a different mode of writing altogether'.[47] However, the quixotic nature of the methodology of Part II of the text, where there is a satirical leap of logic between Crabbe's poem and the failure of contemporary writers, seems to undermine notions of literary criticism's aspiration to a more objective mode of analysis. There is an attempt in Part III to expose the fallacy of the seeming objectivity behind the critic's lens and to deconstruct the cultural assumptions that become naturalized by the critic's authoritative stance: 'A critic is an instrument which registers certain observations; before the reader can judge of their value he must know sufficient of the accuracy of the instrument to allow for the margin of error' (p. 155). Through this analogy of the critic-as-lab-instrument, Part III becomes an act of scientific self-calibration. By exposing the critic's 'margin of error' the reader can 'judge' the validity of the conclusions the text reaches.

The 'Introduction' notes that, in Part III, 'Romanticism is measured against a romantic education' which 'further[s] the growth of those literary speculations on which the first part is based' (p. 9). The education explored in Part III crucially elucidates the text's most abiding classification, between two types of literary style, the Mandarin and the New Vernacular, which is self-reflexively informed by Connolly's analysis of his own educational background. In Part III, Connolly notes that 'Homer and Virgil were the pillars of an Eton education' (p. 232). After winning the Rosebery History Prize, Connolly was co-opted into Division One (the top stream within Block A at Eton, a block designated for Oxford and Cambridge preparation), which was usually reserved for winners of the Newcastle Prize, open only to Classicists.[48] Connolly records being 'initiated' into the 'inner culture' of the 'eighteenth-century Etonian tradition of classical humanism' (p. 231) in 1921, when he studied the classics via John William

---

[47] Woloch, p. xvi.
[48] Jeremy Lewis, *Cyril Connolly: A Life* (London: Cape, 1997), p. 76; see *Enemies of Promise*, p. 243.

Mackail's *Greek Anthology* and Butcher and Lang's translations of Homer, both translations tainted by a romantic vein:[49]

> A sensitive Etonian with a knowledge of Homer and Virgil through these translations and a good ear, would be unable to detect in poems like *Tithonus*, *Ulysses,* or the *Lotus Eaters* any note foreign to the ear of Homer and Virgil. [...] The two classics had been 'romanticized' for him. (p. 233)

English Literature did not form part of the formal curriculum at Eton until the 1960s; until then it was assumed that students would read texts in English in their spare time, and while Connolly records reading English literature as part of his knowledge of the literature of the 'five civilizations' (p. 239), such a curriculum informed his perception of literary value and his creative composition: 'I didn't see how one could write well in English, and my Greek and Latin were still not good enough. [...] [T]o compose in a dead language was the creative activity toward which my education was inexorably tending' (pp. 264–65).[50] The demotic use of contractions here stylistically exemplifies Connolly's point. This 'eighteenth-century Etonian tradition of classical humanism' (p. 231) shapes Connolly's analysis of the Mandarins' 'romantic' (p. 61) and 'elaborate' style (p. 61). It is defined as the style of the elites – those who have a classical education and emulate this discourse in an anglicized form:

> It is characterized by long sentences with many dependent clauses, by the use of the subjunctive and conditional, by exclamations and interjections, quotations, allusions, metaphors, long images, Latin terminology, subtlety, and conceits. Its cardinal assumption is that neither the writer nor the reader is in a hurry, that both are in possession of a classical education and a private income. It is Ciceronian English. (pp. 29–30)

Mandarin style is conceived as a Latinate form of English; a translation of classical rhetoric into the mother tongue, rather than an evolution of a modern tradition for prose. Where the Mandarin style is Latinate, the New Vernacular is demotic. This is associated with the 'left-wing' (p. 82) writers Christopher Isherwood and George Orwell, who are 'superlatively readable' (p. 82). The writing style is 'colloquial' (p. 75) and informed by 'the talkies' (p. 75). Orwell's later analysis of the

---

[49] Jean-Christophe Murat comments that Connolly's 'strictures of romanticism remain narrowly class-bound' in *Enemies of Promise* – a deficiency of which Connolly is, I suggest, aware. Jean-Christophe Murat, 'The Cost of Myth: Cyril Connolly and "Romanticism"', *The Space Between*, Vol. IV No. 1 (2008), 101–22 (p. 111). A contemporary reviewer of Mackail's anthology comments that his translations 'please by their style' and are 'attractive'. Walter Headlam, 'Mackail's Greek Anthology', *Classical Review*, Vol. 6 No. 6 (June 1892), 269–71 (p. 270).

[50] See Murray, p. 97.

defamation of the English language in 'Politics and the English Language' suggests the extent to which his own style is conceived in opposition to the inflated terms of a Latinate style, a fiscal image used repeatedly by Connolly to characterize Mandarin style: 'inflation [...] of language' (p. 67), 'inflationism of Bloomsbury' (p. 85). As noted, Orwell later uses this term in 'Politics and the English Language' as he objects to 'pretentious, Latinized style' (CW12, p. 426) and suggests that a classical lexicon obscures meaning: 'A mass of Latin words falls upon the facts like soft snow, blurring the outlines and covering up all the details' (CW12, p. 428). Connolly perceives that the danger of the New Vernacular is its susceptibility to succumbing to the very journalistic styles of which it is a symptom. He notes

> the penalty of writing for the masses. As the writer goes out to meet them half-way he is joined by other writers going out to meet them half-way and they merge into the same creature – the talkie journalist, the advertising, lecturing, popular novelist. (p. 83)

Informed by mass culture, the New Vernacular is a style that is perceived to be accessible for a mass audience. Connolly's 'Introduction' suggests that his 'recommendation towards a certain solution in Parts I and II is meant to be illustrated by the style which emerges in Part III' (p. 10). This style 'combines the rapidity of the colloquial with an elasticity permitting incursions into the Mandarin of prose poetry' (p. 10). Connolly's exhortative introduction 'hope[s] that my readers of today will be more perceptive' in noticing such rhetorical manoeuvrings and the text's 'evolving' style (p. 10). To some extent it is possible to see this dynamic in evidence, although it is not so entirely self-evident as to warrant Connolly's censorious tone. Descriptions of his early childhood contain a high frequency of simple, direct sentences: 'I became a snob. [...] In 1910 I was sent home from Africa for good. [...] By now I was an aesthete. [...] Sunsets were my preoccupation.' (p. 161). Later sections of the narrative give way to a more complex rhetorical style, particularly in Part III, which expresses an anxiety that the classical cultural values Connolly imbibed in his Eton education render him redundant:

> We exercised our dreams of literary composition through the medium of another language. [...] No one who did his verses well could write poetry afterwards. There would be one slim Eton-blue volume with a few translations, a *Vale*, and a couple of epigrams, then silence. For the culture of the lilies, rooted in the past, divorced from reality, and dependent on a dead foreign tongue, was by nature sterile. (p. 235)

Connolly's anxiety is expressed in the very Mandarin style that the New Vernacular is supposedly rendering obsolete with his use of 'long sentences with many dependent clauses' (p. 29), 'long images', and 'conceits' (p. 30).

The image of the 'lilies' is an abiding conceit of this chapter and symbolizes the aestheticism of Eton. Elsewhere, this floral imagery is evident in the metaphorical descriptions of the 'very soil of the Eton lilies' (p. 233): classical culture. Immersed in archaic cultural forms, 'the civilization of the lilies' demonstrates the 'limitations of good taste […]. I had such knowledge of the masterpieces of the past yet remained timidly at sea among the creations of the present' (p. 242).

The text starts from the self-confident position of the cultural elite, addressing 'my educated fellow bourgeois, whose interests and whose doubts I share' (p. 17), and takes an uncompromising position on class division and its consequences for literary style: 'The way I write and the things I like to write about make no appeal to the working class nor can I make any bridge to them till they are ready for it.' (p. 17). However, it goes on to register a profound unease surrounding the viability of bourgeois literary discourse and cultural values in the face of social change. Connolly cites a defence of the vernacular style that is 'often heard':

> 'If culture is to survive it must survive through the masses; if it cannot be made acceptable to them there is no one else who will be prepared to guarantee it, since the liberal capitalist society who protected it will not be in a position to do so after another slump and a war. Much that is subtle in literature and life will have to be sacrificed if they are to survive at all; consequently it is necessary for literature to approach its future custodians in a language they will understand.'
> The old world is a sinking ship, to get a place in the boats that are pushing off from it not money nor leisure, the essayist's elegance nor the pedant's erudition will avail […] Nothing will admit us but realism and sincerity, an honest appeal in downright English […] as the time for making him [the poor man] our master grows nearer, so his education becomes more necessary since on it depend the cultural values which he will choose to preserve. (p. 81)

The 'educated bourgeois' are positioned as complicit in the very transference of power that will endanger their own cultural and political transcendence. Assurance of the quality of working-class education becomes the only way in which bourgeois values can survive. Concern over the forms of education available to the working class was evident in government reports which considered the status of the classics in schools. The 1921 Crewe Report observed a similar link between transitions of power and cultural values. It notes that the representatives of the Labour Party were 'seriously concerned' about the 'lack of opportunity for children of the working classes to get a classical education'.[51] The classics are rendered both culturally and politically relevant:

> They realise that, if Labour is to become a governing power in the country, the average worker must attain a wider outlook on the problems with which the country will be faced, and that this will best be given by the study of the Classics.[52]

The report found that learning the classics was 'of great and almost irreplaceable value as a means of promoting the proper use of the English language both in speech and writing by all classes of the community'.[53] It recommended securing a 'substantial position' for the classics for all pupils: 'That which contributes to the development of the finest minds should not be denied to any of our people'.[54] Connolly's analysis that 'downright English' is the way to reach out to the working man suggests a cynicism surrounding the feasibility of democratizing the classical values that he previously suggests underpins the Mandarin style, while nonetheless hoping for an 'education' that will render intact existing 'cultural values'. Connolly's attempt in *Enemies of Promise* to arrive at a literary style that assimilates elements of the Latinate Mandarin with elements of the popularist New Vernacular in his autobiographical testimony can be read as a self-conscious attempt to render himself relevant, to find a solution to 'the problem that is obsessing me', the problem of how 'to write a book that will hold good for ten years afterwards' (p. 16). The solution he finds is haunted by a sense of vulnerability and personal anachronism as he attempts to find his place in a new world order.

Henry Green and *Pack My Bag*: Self-camouflage and class-inflected discourse

In a 1958 *Paris Review* interview, Henry Green observed that 'if you are trying to write something which has a life of its own […] the author must keep completely out of the picture'.[55] The same interview observed that when his works are 'about

---

[51] Crewe Report, *The Position of the Classics in the Educational System of the United Kingdom* (London: H.M. Stationery Office, 1921), p. 21.

[52] Ibid.

[53] Crewe Report, pp. 11–12.

[54] Crewe Report, p. 269; p. 268.

[55] Terry Southern, interview with Henry Green, 'The Art of Fiction', *The Paris Review*, 1958, in *Surviving: The Uncollected Writings of Henry Green*, ed. by Matthew Yorke (London: Chatto & Windus, 1992), pp. 234–50 (p. 244).

myself, they are not necessarily accurate as a portrait; they aren't photographs. After all, no one knows what he is like, he just tries to give some sort of general picture of his time.'[56] This desire to remain anonymous was reflected in the publicity and marketing strategies Green adopted: he resisted his publishers' attempts to distribute biographical information about him, and, as one *Life* magazine journalist noted, Green 'dislikes having his face photographed' – the article was accompanied by a sidelong image of Green at a bar.[57] His hand, holding a cigarette, is raised to hide his head, his knee defensively drawn up and propped on a bar stool, as he tries to keep 'out of the picture' of the photograph. This elusive mode of self-representation is paradoxically represented in his public-school autobiography, *Pack My Bag* (1940).

One of the text's early readers, Evelyn Waugh, wrote to Green noting that *Pack My Bag* was '*a book no-one else could have written and it makes me feel I know [you] far less well than I did before which, in a way, I take to be its purpose*'.[58] This analysis of the elusive self-representation of the text as integral to its 'purpose' renders it a stark contrast to the 'disrobing' (p. 155) of the self in Cyril Connolly's *Enemies of Promise*. Rod Mengham argues that, in *Pack My Bag*, 'the absence of an authorizing self is replaced by the presence of the text as a rival self' while desire can 'recapture the self for identity'.[59] Mengham's analysis hints at the significance of the very materiality of the text, while suggesting an opposition between text and selfhood that does not account for the ways in which Green both manipulates and critiques discourse as a means to represent a form of selfhood constituted by literary style. Green commented in a 1941 essay that

> a man's style is like the clothes he wears, an expression of his personality. But what a man is, also makes the way he writes, as the choice of a shirt goes to make up his appearance which is, essentially, a side of his character.[60]

[56] 'Art of Fiction', p. 238.

[57] Nigel Dennis, 'The Double Life of Henry Green', *Life* magazine, 4 August 1952, p. 83.

[58] As cited in Sebastian Yorke, 'Introduction', in Henry Green, *Pack My Bag: A Self-Portrait* (London: Hogarth Press, 1992), pp. v–xiii (p. ix), italics in original. See also observations by Greene's Eton contemporary, Antony Powell, who described *Pack My Bag* as 'at once reticent and revealing'; and Jeremy Treglown who suggests that in Green's work there is a 'deep argument [...] between self-revelation and secrecy'. Powell as cited in Marius Hentëa, *Henry Green at the Limits of Modernism* (Eastbourne: Sussex Academic Press, 2014), p. 81; Treglown, p. 6.

[59] Rod Mengham, *The Idiom of the Time: The Writings of Henry Green* (Cambridge: Cambridge University Press, 1982), p. 55.

[60] Henry Green, 'Apologia: Published in No. 4 *Folios of New Writing*, 1941', in *Surviving*, ed. by Matthew Yorke, pp. 90–97 (p. 92).

This association renders literary style, like clothes, a function of outward self-expression. In such terms, *Pack My Bag*'s observation that on Green's arrival at Oxford, he was 'sorry I was what I am' elucidates the stylistic basis of the text as a manifestation of ontological unease and self-loathing.[61] Marius Hentëa notes that *Pack My Bag* has traditionally posed difficulties to Green scholars because of 'the widespread view that his writing is anti-mimetic and indifferent to social reality, an autobiographical work surfacing out of the anxieties of late 1930s Britain is uneasily accommodated within the corpus of Green criticism'.[62] My reading points to the ways in which formalist and historicist understandings complement one another in an understanding of *Pack My Bag* that acknowledges its rendering of discourse and identity as both socially and historically coded and resolutely textual. I offer a historicized reading of the text as a resistance to First World War commemoration rites, before considering how Green aligns the style of *Pack My Bag* with the ontological and social effects of a public-school-education. The final stage of this analysis will contextualize *Pack My Bag* and Green's novels against debates surrounding technical education to argue that his rejection of the working-class reader and desire to preserve an authentic working-class discourse is part of his retreat from the values of his own social group.

Autobiography, naming, and commemoration

Published in October 1940, *Pack My Bag* explicitly grounds itself in a state of suspended uncertainty symptomatic of the post-Munich Agreement mood: Green notes the terror of 'this absolute bewilderment of July 1939' (p. 153), and the novel's final signature is 'London 1938–39' (p. 159).[63] Hentëa has suggested that *Pack My Bag* is 'a memorial' for the dead First World War heroes; the text also acts

---

[61] Henry Green, *Pack My Bag: A Self-Portrait* (London: Vintage, 2000), p. 129. Further references to this edition will be included in brackets after the citation.

[62] Marius Hentëa, 'A Guilty Self-Portrait: Henry Green's *Pack My Bag*', *Cambridge Quarterly*, Vol. 40 No. 1 (2011), 36–52 (p. 37).

[63] Critical studies of *Pack My Bag* often ground it in a Second World War context, for instance MacKay, *Modernism and World War II* and Mark Rawlinson, *British Writing of the Second World War* (Oxford: Clarendon Press, 2000). For a critical perspective that argues that Green is part of the 1930s generation, despite the fact that he published only one novel in the 1930s (*Party Going*) see North, pp. 1–13. *Pack My Bag* was published in October 1940. Green had applied pressure to the Hogarth Press, who had wanted to publish in Spring 1941, or by Christmas 1940 if possible, in order to secure this earlier release. See J. Howard Woolmer, *A Checklist of the Hogarth Press 1917–1946* (Revere: Woolmer Brotherson, 1986), p. 161. Further details surrounding the conditions of the publication of *Pack My Bag* can be found in J.H. Willis Jr., *Leonard and Virginia Woolf as Publishers: The Hogarth Press, 1917–1941* (London: University Press of Virginia, 1992), pp. 346–47.

as a resistance to the memorialization of Green's own generation.[64] While Walter Allen saw the elusive self-presentation in *Pack My Bag* as a Freudian 'expression of a death-wish', the autobiographical subject of *Pack My Bag* repeatedly rails against the harbinger of mortality that the Second World War augurs: 'Surely it would be asking much to pretend one had a chance to live' (p. 1).[65] Theorists of life-writing have considered how the elegiac, memorialization mode is encrypted within autobiography itself: Laura Marcus notes the thanatographical function of life-writing, while for Paul De Man this function is embedded in the condition of the proper name.[66] De Man argues that 'prosopopeia is the trope of autobiography, by which one's name [...] is made as intelligible and memorable as a face'.[67] This has an inherently elegiac function: 'Death is a displaced name for a linguistic predicament, and the restoration of mortality by autobiography (the prosopopeia of the voice and the name) deprives and disfigures to the precise extent that it restores.'[68]

This theoretical perspective elucidates an understanding of the commemorative weight behind the proper name. Naming had formed a significant part of Connolly's autobiography, which reads as a 'Who's who' of the 1930s generation: he names Henry Green, George Orwell, and Cecil Beaton, among others. The threat of war after the Munich Agreement renders the elegiac value of the proper name clear. Green finds that the writer of autobiography has to 'decide whether he will mention the living', or, alternatively 'another way is to mention only those who have died but my trouble here is that not enough have died yet' (p. 55). The final 'yet' is hung significantly at the end of the sentence, as Green anticipates the death of his generation in another war. The elegiac function of the proper name was reflected in First World War memorial rites: Bob Bushaway notes that, after 1918, 'the obsession with lists and rolls' was symptomatic of 'the concern of the bereaved to see proper recognition accorded to the individuality of their loss'.[69] The place of the roll call in public-school life (in registers and school speech days) combined with the heavy and disproportionate fatality rate of the public-school

---

[64] Hentëa, 'A Guilty Self-Portrait', p. 45; *Limits of Modernism*, p. 84.

[65] Walter Allen, 'An Artist of the Thirties', *Folios of New Writing* (Spring 1941), pp. 149–58 (p. 157). Allen alludes to Spender's *The Backward Son* in his analysis of *Pack My Bag*.

[66] Laura Marcus, *Auto/biographical Discourses: Theory, Criticism, Practice* (Manchester: Manchester University Press, 1994), p. 210.

[67] Paul De Man, 'Autobiography as De-facement', *MLN*, Vol. 94 No. 5 (December 1979), 919–30 (p. 926).

[68] De Man, p. 930.

[69] Bob Bushaway, 'Name upon Name: The Great War and Remembrance', in *Myths of the English*, ed. by Roy Porter (Cambridge: Polity Press, 1992), pp. 136–67 (p. 139).

officer class meant that the commemorative value of the proper name found particular resonance with writers depicting public-school life.[70] Literature of the period repeatedly reflected this association between public-school life and the elegiac, commemorative function of the name. Non-modernists, such as James Hilton in *Goodbye Mr Chips* (1934), preserve the solemnity of the assembly roll call of the dead, while for Vera Brittain in *Testament of Youth*, the memory of Roland's name repeated among the prize-winners in the Uppingham Speech Day programme recalls a happier time before 'the Flood' (p. 72). For 1930s writers, the inscribed name on the memorial provided an opportunity for irony. Auden satirizes the neuroses of the schoolboys with 'names to live up to' in *The Orators* (1931), and Isherwood's *The Memorial* (1932) sees the memorial ceremony of Richard the 'hero' at his public school, who is killed in the First World War, aligned with the 'callover she [Lily] had heard on a Speech Day at Eric's school'.[71]

Patricia Rae has argued that 1930s texts reveal a sense of '[p]roleptic [e]legy'.[72] However, Green is in dialogue with this trend. Drawing on De Man's association of naming and death, and the 1930s generation's relationship to the dead war heroes of the First World War, Green's refusal to name is part of a historical predicament as he refuses to inscribe elegy into his autobiography. He defies the heroic tradition by writing himself out of its forms, one of which is the commemorative function of the proper name. The fact that one of the few proper names Green uses in *Pack My Bag* is that of his 'heroic' brother, Philip, whom he 'hero-worshipped' (p. 49) and later died, reflects this elegiac function. Thus, instead of being privy to Green's real surname (Yorke), the reader is only told of aborted pseudonyms; 'Henry Michaelis' (p. 105), as the memorializing, thanatographical function of the proper name is averted.[73]

---

[70] Adrian Gregory notes that 'the top echelons of British society suffered *proportionately* more' in both the First and the Second World War. In the First World War, 20 per cent of Etonians who had served were killed, a figure 80 per cent greater than the average number of fatalities. Mark Bostridge notes that Uppingham School 'lost about one in five of every old boy that served'. Adrian Gregory, *The Silence of Memory* (Oxford: Berg, 1994), p. 213; Mark Bostridge, 'Introduction', in *Testament of Youth* (London: Virago, 2009), pp. ix–xxii (p. xvii).

[71] Christopher Isherwood, *The Memorial* (Minneapolis: University of Minnesota Press, 1999), p. 133; p. 97.

[72] Patricia Rae, 'Double Sorrow: Proleptic Elegy and the End of Arcadianism in 1930s Britain', in *Modernism and Mourning*, ed. by Patricia Rae (London: Associated University Presses, 2007), pp. 213–38.

[73] Shepley notes that although all editions of *Pack My Bag* attribute Green's surname as Henry Michaelis, *College Days*, the Eton ephemeral in which he published, publishes his name as 'Henry Michaels'. Shepley notes that 'it seems bizarre' that a typographical error would be repeated over so many reprints and speculates that it could be 'a consciously oblique reinvention of another version of the author'. See Nick Shepley, *Henry Green Class, Style and the Everyday* (Oxford: Oxford University Press, 2016), pp. 27–28, n. 23.

School and the stylistics of estrangement

Henry Green's use of a pseudonym represents a rupture in the 'autobiographical contract' between author and reader.[74] Peter Hitchcock reads the surname 'Green' as, like another he toyed with – 'Browne' – 'a gesture to the "commoner".[75] Nick Shepley's analysis of Green's assumption of a pseudonym encourages a reading of Green's authorial identity that works not within a dichotomized model (Henry Yorke versus Henry Green) but one that encompasses a multiplicity of selves, something signalled by the properties of his assumed name.[76] The surname 'Green' was a common proper name and was present in literary circles: (Henry) Graham Greene published his poetry collection, *Babbling April* in 1923.[77] The assumption of 'Green' as a pseudonym thus allows a slippage into other forms of literary identity. Shepley notes the 'wealth of connotations' of the term 'Green', but it is also a word that hints at its own textuality, existing as a noun (as in the synecdoche of the village 'green'), an adjective, and a verb.[78] This pseudonym thus also aligns the written self with the amorphousness of a word that itself gestures to its own lexical multiplicity through its occupation of different parts of speech, and different grammatical functions.

Pack My Bag's focus on the textual is recognized by Marius Hentëa: 'Rather than a life, it is writing that must be explained.'[79] The text recognizes this duality of purpose; noting initially that it demonstrated 'how one changed from boy to man' (p. 1), and later suggesting, in between extracts and analyses of his own literary style, that 'my task is to show how [...] the style [...] emerged into 1928 [...] how this self-expression grew and how it altered' (p. 107). Green's focus on his school years, his time at Oxford, and in his father's factory, suggests how these social experiences were formative in influencing the development of his literary style. There is a seeming transparency in the inclusion of extracts from Green's juvenile fiction to represent the evolution of literary style, yet the inclusion of such extracts also reinforces style as a construct and the text, rather than the self, as the true object of analysis in *Pack My Bag*, as the layers of opacity between the biographer and his reader accumulate. Green's post-war broadcast, 'A Novelist

---

[74] Laura Marcus, *Auto/biographical Discourses*, p. 191.
[75] Peter Hitchcock, 'Passing: Henry Green and Working-Class Identity', *Modern Fiction Studies*, Vol. 40 No. 1 (Spring 1994), 1–31 (p. 8).
[76] See Shepley, pp. 32–33.
[77] See Shepley, p. 30.
[78] Ibid. See OED entry for 'green', <www.oed.com> [accessed 14 August 2017].
[79] 'A Guilty Self-Portrait', p. 49.

to His Readers: I', found that 'reading is a kind of unspoken communication with print, a silent communion with the symbols which are printed to make up words.'[80] Shepley's commentary on this broadcast notes that 'the text is constantly depersonalized [...] any sense of an authorial voice is rendered resoundingly ambivalent'.[81] There is an emphasis also on the materiality of the text, its very constructedness, in the focus on the physicality of text's component parts, the 'print' and the 'symbols' that make up 'words'. The intimacy of the act of reading is reflected in an earlier iteration of this idea in *Pack My Bag*:

> Names distract, nicknames are too easy and if leaving both out as it often does makes a book look blind then that to my mind is no disadvantage. Prose is not to be read aloud but to oneself alone at night, and it is not quick as poetry but rather a gathering web of insinuations which go further than names however shared can ever go. Prose should be a long intimacy between strangers with no direct appeal to what both may have known. It should slowly appeal to feelings unexpressed [...] and feelings are not bounded by the associations common to place names or to persons with whom the reader is unexpectedly familiar. (pp. 55–56)

This contemplation of the effect of an anonymous text comes before his introduction of Eton in non-specific terms as 'The public school I went to ... ' (p. 56) to limit the social and cultural associations of the school. An occasion on which Green uses names in the book's opening is a time 'of which I remember [...] hardly anything' (p. 7): 'Most things boil down to people, or at least most houses to those who live in them, so Forthampton boils down to Poole' (p. 1). The emphatic repetition of 'boils down' punningly continues Green's concern that he should be 'taking stock' (p. 1) but also suggests that Green sees the naming process as reductive. The absence of names is a means of estranging the text from the reader. Green's analogy between the relationship between the reader and the prose text, and the uncertain status of human friendships plays with the known and unknown, the revealed and repressed in narrative.

There is a correspondence between the estranged discourse of the text and the experience of self-estrangement that is associated with upper-class schooling: 'Going to boarding school is the biggest change one could have, nothing can ever so estrange a nursery boy from himself' (p. 11). Marina MacKay notes Green's 'defiantly aristocratic' usage of 'one' in the opening of *Pack My Bag* ('before one

---

[80] Henry Green, 'A Novelist to His Readers: I', BBC Broadcast published in *The Listener*, November 1950, in *Surviving*, ed. by Matthew Yorke, pp. 136–42 (p. 140).

[81] Shepley, p. 7.

is killed').[82] The depersonalized, third-person form also reflects on a lexical level the sense of self-alienation occasioned by starting school. A sense of self-division is augmented in the second clause which fractures further into the 'nursery boy' and 'himself'. *Pack My Bag's* distinctive literary style forms a stark contrast to the opening diary portion of *Blindness* which renders the naive voice of public schoolboy John Haye. In *Blindness*, Green inverts the structure of *A Portrait of the Artist as a Young Man* (1916), where Joyce allows Stephen to take over the narrative at the end of the novel; Green instead takes his aspiring writer's voice away at the point of debility at the beginning of the novel, with a switch from the intimacy of the first-person voice that captures public-school discourse ('Am I considered the school idiot?' (p. 352)) into Green's distinctive alienated, and alienating, literary discourse.

Pack My Bag's preoccupation with the status of friends and friendships is inscribed in the social relations at Green's school, as well as the literary style of the text:

> More and more often my *friends* played with *strangers* in friendly games. [...] A fives court is twelve foot across. Walking between you could go from one foursome to the next, so fast from one quick game to another in which *friends* might be engaged with couples *strange* to you but not to them. Now he who takes service, crouching behind the pepperbox to make his return, is out of sight so that in each court you could see only three players at a glance [...] we had to watch for the fourth player to come out in the rallies as our *friends* were now on such terms that one had been known to play with three *strangers*.
>
> It would have been *friendly* to stand by a game to praise the play thus getting to know the players *strange* to us. (pp. 85–86, emphases added)

In his letter to Green, Evelyn Waugh commented on the use of class-inflected language in the text:

> Only one thing disconcerted me – more in this book than any of the novels. The proletarian grammar – the 'likes' for 'ases', the 'bikes' for 'bicycles', 'hims' for 'hes', etc. and then the sudden resumption of gentleman's language whenever you write of sport.[83]

Green's language here is technical and specialized, and by implication of its social context, 'gentlemanly'. The 'pepperbox' is an object particular to Eton Fives: *The Eton Glossary* notes 'one of the great differences between Eton fives and

---

[82] 'Doing Business', p. 735.
[83] As cited in Sebastian Yorke, 'Introduction', p. ix.

Rugby fives is the pepper-box, the irregular buttress sticking into the court.'[84] There is a voyeuristic opportunism as a subtext of the game, independent of the winning or losing. In a BBC broadcast Green commented on the significance of the arrangement of words in prose: 'It is the *context* in which they lie that *alone* gives them life.'[85] The terms 'friend', 'friendly', 'strangers' are repeated in different contexts, allowing them to accumulate irony as relations in Green's social group seem consumed with politics. The animus within the social relationships at the school is set into relief by an encounter with a destitute man when Green abandoned his schoolfriends during left-wing protests at a Conservative meeting:

> A small ragged working man we had not noticed said: 'Would they be friends of yours in there?' With a strong sense of guilt we admitted it. 'Well then' he said 'my lads you go back to your pals what is in trouble,' and we went back, ashamed. (p. 143)

The 'proletarian grammar' Evelyn Waugh noted appears in the speech Green reports directly – it is not incorporated into his own speech patterns. Green employed the colloquial term 'pals' (used here by the 'ragged working man') in an effusive interview he gave to *The Star* in 1929, on the publication of *Living* (1929), inspired by his experiences while he was working at his father's factory in Birmingham between 1927 and 1929: 'the men, I loved them. They are fine fellows, generous, open hearted, and splendid pals.'[86] There is an easy affiliation with the working class here that the observational reticence of *Living* resists. In *Pack My Bag*, the term punctures the ironies previously accumulated around the term 'friend', as the working man helps Green and his friends see their own weaknesses by exposing the failure of public-school loyalty.

Technical education and working-class readers in *Living* and *Pack My Bag*

Waugh's reading of *Pack My Bag* is tainted by his own class feeling, but is also responsive to the text's analysis of the class-inflected nature of discourse. Green's own class politics, as discernible in his novels, is notoriously indirect, a point

---

[84] C.R. Stone, *The Eton Glossary* (Eton: Spottiswoode, 1902), p. 25. As cited in *OED*, <http://www.oed.com> [accessed 7 January 2014].

[85] 'A Novelist to His Readers: I', p. 141, emphases in original.

[86] As cited in Treglown, p. 99.

reinforced by Nick Shepley.[87] John Lehmann, who knew Green personally, suggested Green was 'not really interested in politics at all' and that his novels were apolitical: 'he's never got a political or social axe to grind, he sees it in a completely detached but in an extraordinarily precise way'; Marius Hentëa notes that Green's 'politics were never clear', while Valentine Cunningham suggests that he was 'at best a Tory radical'.[88]

Other readings suggest that Green's affection for working-class culture is rooted in an idealizing spirit that maintains social difference. Peter Hitchcock finds that 'an identification with the Other does not erase difference but produces it in the realm of the symbolic'.[89] Marina MacKay notes Green's aspiration to a brand of 'evasive neutrality that he associated with high artistic disinterestedness', but, writing of *Living*, she aligns the process observed by Hitchcock with a social conservatism:

> A sympathetic fascination with the working classes is not [...] exclusively the preserve of left politics in the 1930s; rather, a liking for the cultural specificities of class difference becomes almost tautologically compatible with an interest in their perpetuation [...] sympathetic representation can be a conservative [...] response to social change as well as a radical one, and not least when what's being represented is in the process of radical transformation.[90]

Shepley finds this reading persuasive, but objects to the 'politicized' tendency of MacKay's readings of Green, which he finds 'reductive'.[91] To some degree, the multiplicity and indirection of a Green text resists alignment to any singular political position, a resistance which itself is a carefully crafted result of the prose. This is recognized by MacKay as she notes *Pack My Bag*'s 'intransigence to an identifiable politics'.[92] A recognition of the ways in which Green's text is responsive to historical contexts surrounding technical education offers a means of understanding the complexity of his class feeling. The text's closure demonstrates an affection for working-class culture that is representative of an escapist retreat from literary and educated discourse into a preservationist desire to maintain the purity of working-class culture as a release from the values of his

---

[87] Shepley, p. 80.
[88] Keith C. Odom and John Lehmann, 'An Interview with John Lehmann about Henry Green', *Twentieth Century Literature*, Vol. 29 No. 4 (Winter 1983), 395–402 (p. 399; p. 397); Hentëa, 'A Guilty Self-Portrait', p. 37; Cunningham, *British Writers*, p. 234.
[89] Hitchcock, p. 23.
[90] *Modernism and World War II*, p. 116; pp. 97–98.
[91] Shepley, p. 80.
[92] 'Doing Business', p. 735.

own social group. *Living* provides a corollary to *Pack My Bag*, which alludes to his work in his father's factory, H. Pontifex & Sons after he left Oxford. Green writes a version of himself into his novel in the guise of Dick Dupret, the public-school-educated, factory owner's son, who tries to ingratiate himself with the workers in conversation: 'Dupret used what he thought was Mr Tarver's language' (p. 299). Both texts allude to factory workers attending technical classes at 'technical school in evenings' (*Living*, p. 310) or 'night school' (*Pack My Bag*, p. 154).

Junior technical schools were first introduced in 1905 with schools recruiting at thirteen that were not linked to further education.[93] Typically underfunded, the rarity of the technical school meant that the 1938 Spens Report found that there is 'much ignorance [...] of the aims, scope and work of the Technical Schools'.[94] Spens found that it was '*of great importance to establish a new type of higher school of technical character, wholly distinct from the traditional academic grammar (secondary) school*' yet with 'equality of status with [g]rammar [s]chools'.[95] The report affirms the presence of traditional, academic content in technical education: the technical school 'differs', 'in the methods of approach and treatment' (rather than content), from the 'science side' of the grammar school, and the Spens Committee was 'satisfied that it is the aim and purpose of Junior Technical Schools to liberalize every subject in their curriculum'.[96] While Spens equivocated over the relative academic claims of technical education, other commentators were more direct: C.T. Millis found that technical education as a whole is a 'contrast' to 'the literary type of education afforded by the Public and older Secondary schools'.[97] The deficiencies in technical education, indicated by the Spens Report, meant that much technical education was conducted at evening classes in Mechanics' Institutes.

The ambitious Bert Jones in *Living* wants to 'get on' (p. 214) and attends technical school to improve his work prospects. Lily, his girlfriend, supports him in his ambitions, as Green wryly notes: 'Mr Jones began going to technical school where she sent him' (p. 301). Millis, writing in 1925, finds that the period in which Green wrote *Living* saw a particular burgeoning of interest in technical education after the unemployment of the First World War.[98] Birmingham, the site of both *Living* and Green's father's factory, was at the forefront of the technical

---

[93] Simon, p. 21.
[94] Board of Education [The Spens Report], p. 281.
[95] Board of Education [The Spens Report], p. 274; p. 281, emphases in original.
[96] Board of Education [The Spens Report], p. 275; p. 276; p. 270.
[97] C.T. Millis, *Technical Education: Its Development and Aims* (London: Arnold, 1925), p. 1.
[98] Millis, p. 11.

education movement. Millis outlines Birmingham's 'claim to have had the first Mechanics' Institute in Great Britain' and notes that these institutions 'have developed into Technical Institutes and Colleges'.[99] Elsewhere in Birmingham, local industrial magnates redressed deficiencies in technical education by opening schools attached to their factories, with George Cadbury opening a school at his factory in 1913. Cadbury noted that 'some firms have found it necessary to plan quite extensive programmes of evening classes for their adult employees, thus supplementing in a very marked degree the provision made by Local Education Authorities'.[100] At the conference, Cadbury favoured 'at least part-time education' beyond the official school-leaving age.[101] He suggests that technical education could (arguably) support a conservative end:

> The strike is a barbarous weapon, and is an appeal to force, soon destined, I hope, to give way to arbitration and consultation appealing to reason which must triumph in the long run. A fuller education is the best approach to this.[102]

Skills-based technical education did not necessarily connote, therefore, a method of social transformation, but rather promised to produce a workforce more imbued with the ideals that could lead to efficient production. *Pack My Bag* suggests that technical education reinforced working-class identity, rather than prompted social transformation: 'Almost everyone of the age I had reached who was not a labourer went to night school to learn more of whatever trade he was in' (p. 154). The cultivation of a technically proficient working-class leader was an aspiration of technical education: referring to a report on 'Education for Foremanship' by Mr N.J. MacLean, later published by the Birmingham-based Association for Industry and Commerce in 1928, Cadbury noted that 'it is very noticeable in our business how the men who have taken up adult education are those who become leaders and who can intelligently discuss their problems with the management and their fellows'.[103]

In *Living*, Lily has precisely such promotional aims for Bert; she 'saw him as being foreman one day soon' (p. 276). Despite Bert's desire to secure a job that would give him 'advancement and satisfaction', he quickly becomes disillusioned: 'What was the good in trying to better yourself when you couldn't hold a better

---

[99] Millis, p. 12; p. 20.

[100] George Cadbury, *Why We Want Education in Industry: Presidential Address Delivered by Alderman George Cadbury at the Annual Conference of the Association for Education in Industry and Commerce June 10th 1926* (Birmingham: Association for Education in Industry and Commerce, 1926), p. 11.

[101] Cadbury, p. 5.

[102] Cadbury, p. 11.

[103] Cadbury, p. 10; p. 11.

job' (p. 360), and stops attending evening classes: 'he told Lily Gates he went to technical school in evenings when he never went after first three times' (p. 310). In *Living*, education is a matter of cultural habit. In the view of others, Bert does not have the strength of character to deviate from the norms of working-class life: 'He would never go. He hadn't the stuff in him' (p. 310). Mr Craigan's hostility to Lily's relationship with Bert, prompted by his own affection for Lily and his fear of losing his home, finds expression in his resistance to working-class education:

> If I 'ad a son I wouldn't educate 'im above the station 'e was born in. It's hard enough to be a moulder and 'ave the worry of the job forty-seven hours in the week but to be on the staff, or foreman even, with the man above you doggin' at you and them under you never satisfied, like the young chaps never am nowadays, it aint like living at all. (p. 306)

The gerund 'living' is striking because it preserves the final 'g', which is dropped elsewhere in Craigan's speech ('doggin'') as Green evokes a form of dialect which, Hitchcock suggests, is closer to that of the streets around his father's offices than his Birmingham factory.[104] When contextualized here, the novel's title is expressive of a working-class condition that is 'satisfied' with stasis: Craigan here implicitly opposes striving to improve one's self, 'like the young chaps' who are 'never satisfied', with something that 'aint like living at all'. 'Living' is here associated with contentment, not aspiration.

Phrases in Mr Craigan's speech are recontextualized in scenes of him reading 'the works of Dickens', a writer, Lily thinks in frustration, that he returns to 'over and over again' (p. 242), as he reflects and revisits the predicament of Lily's relationship with Bert ('this trouble' (p. 312)). The narrator notes that 'Mr Craigan was reading Dickens' (p. 311), and the specific Dickens text he is reading is *Little Dorrit*, a social critique of poverty and debtors' prisons in Victorian London. However, the narrative does not invoke a sense of protest in Mr Craigan. Instead it repeatedly (and ironically) prompts reflections of personal matters, rather than engrossment in the plot and story:

> *Little Dorrit* laid on his knee, he thought it was selfishness that was all of Miss Gates [...] He began talking aloud to himself. [...] 'An' she aint been out so often with Bert Jones,' he said. [...] Suddenly he broke out into loud voice: 'I wouldn't educate my son above the station 'e was born in [...] what is there in it.' (pp. 311–12)

Later, when Craigan is 'picking out *Little Dorrit* from the bookshelf', rather than reading the text, he is 'so satisfied at how he found the house after his time in

---

[104] Hitchcock, p. 20.

bed, and above all so satisfied with his legs that they had not given way as he
went downstairs […] that he fell into doze over open book' (p. 341). Reading
most emphatically prompts satisfaction, inertia, and escape.

Where Walter Greenwood politicizes working-class depoliticization through
Larry Meath and narrative structure, as discussed in Chapter 3, there is an
observational detachment in Green's representation that is missing in *Pack My
Bag*'s rejection of the working-class reader, which is cloaked in a resistance to the
class values associated with education itself:

> It would be equally absurd to say that, if these men had had the time to take
> up books, they would have been better able to stand reading than those whose
> excess of leisure or whose boredom had driven them to it. On the contrary they
> will make bad readers when, if we are not to have a war and hours are to get
> shorter, they will be pitchforked into it if their gardens are not made very much
> larger. One and all are violently opinionated, it is not lack of education, I do not
> know what it is, and reading does surely require an open mind. (p. 156)

Reading is a sign of rentier indulgence – 'excess of leisure […] boredom' – a last
resort ('driven them to it') for the, quite literally, unproductive. There appears to
be a response in these lines to a perception of social changes that will occur if war
does not arrive: shorter working hours, increased leisure. If the working class
do not get 'larger' gardens through the tending of which they will expend their
leisure time, they will be 'pitchforked' into reading. Shepley's analysis of Green's
sympathy for the working class is absent here; rather, there is an exasperation ('I
do not know what it is').[105] The suggestion that the 'opinionated' working class
are unsuited to reading is reinforced in *Caught* (1943) as working-class fireman
Pye presents education as merely a prop for self-determinism: 'Take education,
what is education? I say it is a man's capability to see rightly for 'isself'.[106] Pye's
proclamations which undermine education are in ungrammatical speech
('rightly'); however, rather than undercutting his assertion, his speech patterns
reflect his rebellion against the value of education itself.

Party Going has an acute sense of the modalities of linguistic difference as it
depicts a mysterious man who switches easily between different regional and
class-inflected speech, which is variously identified as speaking 'ordinarily', and
with 'Brummagem' and 'educated accents'.[107] His chameleon-like speech patterns

---

[105] Shepley, p. 80.
[106] Henry Green, *Caught* (London: Harvill Press, 2001), pp. 35–36.
[107] Henry Green, *Loving/Living/Party Going* (London: Penguin, 1993), p. 477. Further references to this
edition will be included in brackets after the citation.

destabilize his identity, and prompt other characters to identify him as the 'hotel detective' (p. 479). This transgression of speech boundaries is something of a stumbling block for Green's father in *Pack My Bag*. An 'amateur' of his servants' working-class dialect, he was 'always consulting his Dialect Dictionary' (p. 4). The patterns of working-class speech resist codification and systematization: in practising his new vocabulary with the servants, Green's father would use an 'Elizabethan word' but 'was at once corrected with a Saxon monosyllable he had never heard' (p. 5). Although *Pack My Bag* acknowledges that 'there are not two or three social classes but hundreds well defined throughout Britain' (p. 125), the text is concerned with a polarized sense of linguistic difference, presenting the speech of a 'labourer' (p. 156) before relaying 'a story from Oxford' (p. 157). The labourer's earthy story of 'great hilarity' (p. 156) is relayed in simple sentences, while the Oxford anecdote is far more sedate, its punchline cloaked in sophistry and allusion: 'so he drops off for a bit but when he woke up the cow was gone' versus 'his modern Arabic is good but his ancient Arabic is like attar of roses' (p. 157). The accent of Birmingham working-class speech is evoked on the page: 'A hyphen in the middle of the word beautiful so as to pronounce it be-eautiful' (p. 156) and, indeed, working-class culture is based on orality:

> In putting my point this way I am of course confusing conversation with stories written here but meant to be told aloud which, when so told, escape the deadening effect print has so that anything in manuscript is more lively than the selfsame words whatever they may be after having been set in type at the printers. (p. 157)

Green's emphatic analysis of working-class culture as oral is rendered through the assonance of 'told aloud' and his repetition of 'told'. This is polarized with the 'deadening effect' of 'print' as he revisits his earlier analysis of how prose should be read, 'to oneself alone at night' (p. 55). This suggests a deep ambivalence towards literary production and the business of being a writer, given Green's situation of the self as a textual product. Literate and literary culture is associated with morbidity and mortality in *Pack My Bag* while working-class speech 'unadulterated by literature' (p. 156) offers incentive for heroism: 'they would be worth dying for by those heroic comparisons in simple words so well chosen and arranged, so direct a communication they made one silly with laughing' (p. 158). This elevation of 'direct [...] communication' offers a self-reflexive commentary on Green's own indirectness and obliqueness. It is this rejection of his own class values that prompts a hyperbolic embrace of working-class discourse. Green's uneasiness at the loss of variegated culture and discourse in an era of social levelling is further figured in *Concluding* (1948), which depicts a state-run training academy with a mass of girls, all with names beginning with 'M': Merode, Mary, Marion, Moira; as state education signals a homogenization of identity and literary discourse.

Pack My Bag's complex relationship to class, education, and discourse raises wider questions about the class implications of Green's own literary style, with its absence of definite and indefinite articles ('he fell into doze over open book'). Waugh had marvelled at Green's style, commenting on his ability to 'take language one step further than its grammatical limits allow'.[108] Contemporary commentators read Green's literary style in class-inflected terms. One suggested that it was a symptom of his education, damningly commenting that

> had the author been at an elementary school he would have been caned into a better syntax, and thereby might have gained a more normal and competent means of self-expression, the better to equip himself to mix with the workmen whom he later chose to make his fellows.[109]

Walter Allen commented of *Living*: 'No working-class writer, I think, could have written the book' while this novel, was, for Isherwood, 'the "best proletarian novel ever written"'.[110] Harold Heslop mistook Green, a blue-blooded Eton- and Oxford-educated writer, and son of an industrial magnate of aristocratic origin, as a humble working man at the 1930 Second International Conference of Revolutionary and Proletarian Writers: 'A new school of writers has branched off from the old [...][s]ome of these writers, especially James Hanley and Henry Green, are of proletarian stock.'[111] However erroneously, Green thus was deemed to engender the patterns of working-class speech he found to be 'heroic' as part of his retreat from the idea of liberal education for the working class in *Pack My Bag*, which itself can be positioned in a broader literary continuum that recognizes the conflicted ways in which public-school writers engaged with debates surrounding expansions in educational provision to develop a class-based critique of literary discourse.

[108] Evelyn Waugh, 'The Books You Read: A Neglected Masterpiece', *Graphic*, 14 June 1930, p. 588.
[109] Richard Church, 'A Fight for Identity', *The Spectator*, 22 November 1940, pp. 548–50 (p. 548).
[110] Allen, p. 152; Christopher Isherwood, as cited in Green and Southern, 'Art of Fiction', p. 247.
[111] Harold Heslop, as cited in Hentëa, *Limits of Modernism*, p. 37.

Coda

'Arthur, listen to me! Can we go on like this?'

'Why, what is it now?' he cried irritably. 'What on earth d'you mean?'

'Oh I know I'm being vile,' Diana wailed. 'But can all your terrific work be worth the candle?'

'You don't suppose I like slavery for its own sake, surely to goodness! [....] And what about Peter? He has to be paid for, and educated; you know it as well as I do!'

'Occasionally I ask myself if the darling wouldn't be better off in a council school.'

'Diana! Stop! He'd never in after life forgive us if I didn't give him the start I got from my father.'

'And where did that land you?'

'No really, Diana,' her husband protested, but with some signs, at last, of unease 'what are you trying to insinuate? That we've been failures?' (p. 258)

Henry Green, *Doting*, 1952

Henry Green described his 1952 novel *Doting* as a 'hard and sharp' social comedy of the 'upper classes'.[1] The novel's action takes place in Peter Middleton's holidays from St Olaf's, a version of Eton. Like Arthur, Green sent his son to his old school and, like Arthur, Green submitted to the regime of office life: *Life* magazine profiled Green's 'double life' on the publication of *Doting*, presenting Green's novel-writing as his '"secret" vice', after office hours.[2] In this episode, education in the novel is deliberately depoliticized: the wailing mother, the hyperbolic terms and overblown sentiment are all reminiscent of melodrama as education is rendered the subject of familial dispute. Peter Middleton is reduced to a comedic stereotype, nothing more than a plot device: he reminds Annabel, his father's fling, of the hearty Tom Brown: 'You're talking now just like the boy out of a school story book' (p. 194); clichéd and strangely out of step with his age.

---

[1]   Green and Southern, 'Art of Fiction', in *Surviving*, ed. by Matthew Yorke, p. 247.

[2]   Dennis, 'The Double Life of Henry Green', p. 83. North notes the novel's autobiographical implications, p. 195.

With the Butler Education Act (1944), Peter could gain secondary education outside the public-school system via a 'council school', as Diana suggests. Marina MacKay argues that the post-war Labour government left Green 'unambiguously grumpy'.[3] Clement Attlee was elected Prime Minister on 26 July 1945 with a landmark victory: he secured 47.7 per cent of the vote, and 393 seats in the House of Commons. This government represented the triumph of a vision for a new kind of Britain: egalitarian and socialist. It was a government composed of scholarship boys and autodidacts. Fourteen members of the Labour government, including the chancellor of the exchequer, had some involvement in the Workers' Educational Association (WEA) in an official or pedagogic capacity, while fifty-six active WEA 'adherents' sat on the backbenches.[4] The adult education movement as a whole had an even greater influence on this Labour government: over one hundred Labour MPs had been tutors or students in adult education.[5]

Ross McKibbin concludes that between 1918 and 1951 'the old "ideological apparatus of the state" [was] largely intact'.[6] He notes that 'social change and institutional rigidity' worked against each other, resulting in 'a society with powerful democratic impulses but political structures and habits of mind which could not adequately contain them'.[7] Although the public schools remained untouched by the Butler Education Act, there was a feeling that their products were emerging into a less amenable world, and that they were somehow not responsive to the values of post-Second World War Britain. This is registered in Green's novel: Arthur's creeping suspicion that 'we' are 'failures', and his wife's suggestion that the council school would do as good a job in educating her son as a public school, encapsulates a sense of upper-class vulnerability in the climate of post-war reforms: with their inviolable hegemony compromised, Green's characters register an uneasy sense that they are becoming redundant.

By 1940 the shift towards a state-maintained secondary system remained, of course, incontrovertibly in the subjunctive tense of the post-war world that is 'struggling to be born' (E6, p. 273). Through their novels, autobiographies, poems, and plays, as well as in classrooms, lecture halls, and textbooks, writers of the 1930s helped bring it into being.

[3] *Modernism and World War II*, p. 117.
[4] See Goldman, *Dons and Workers*, p. 239.
[5] See Margaret Cole, *Growing Up into Revolution* (London: Longmans, Green, 1949), pp. 118–19.
[6] *Classes and Cultures*, p. 536.
[7] Ross McKibbin, *Parties and People: England 1914–1951* (Oxford: Oxford University Press, 2010), pp. 201–02.

Bibliography

A., E. and B.H.S., eds., *Impressions of L. H. M. S.* (London: Miss Austin, 1927)

Abel, Elizabeth, *Virginia Woolf and the Fictions of Psychoanalysis* (London: University of Chicago Press, 1989)

Abel Travis, Molly, 'Eternal Fascism and Its "Home Haunts" in the Leavises' Attacks on Bloomsbury and Woolf', in *Virginia Woolf and Fascism: Resisting the Dictators' Seduction*, ed. by Merry M. Pawlowski (Basingstoke: Palgrave, 2001), pp. 165–77

Alaya, Flavia M., 'Two Worlds Revisited: Arnold, Renan, The Monastic Life, and the Stanzas from the Grande Chartreuse', *Victorian Poetry*, Vol. 5 (1967), 237–54

Alberti, Johanna, 'The Turn of the Tide: Sexuality and Politics, 1928–31', *Women's History Review*, Vol. 3 No. 2 (1994), 169–90

Allen, Judith, *Virginia Woolf and the Politics of Language* (Edinburgh: Edinburgh University Press, 2010)

Allen, Walter, 'An Artist of the Thirties', *Folios of New Writing* (Spring 1941), pp. 149–58

Anderson, Robert D., *Universities and Elites in Britain since 1800* (Cambridge: Cambridge University Press, 1995)

Andrews, Geoff, Hilda Kean and Jane L. Thompson, eds., *Ruskin College: Contesting Knowledge, Dissenting Politics* (London: Lawrence & Wishart, 1999)

Arnold, Matthew, 'Stanzas from the Grand Chartreuse', <http://www.poetryfoundation.org/poem/172861> [accessed 4 October 2014]

Auden, W.H., *Collected Poems*, ed. by Edward Mendelson (London: Faber & Faber, 1991)

Auden, W.H., *The Complete Works of W.H. Auden Prose and Travel Books in Prose and Verse Volume I 1926–1938*, ed. by Edward Mendelson (London: Faber & Faber, 1996)

Auden, W.H., *The Complete Works of W.H. Auden Prose, Volume II 1939–1948*, ed. by Edward Mendelson (London: Faber & Faber, 2002)

Auden, W.H., *The Dance of Death* (London: Faber & Faber, 1933)

Auden, W.H., 'Democracy's Reply to the Challenge of Dictators', in *The Complete Works of W.H. Auden Prose and Travel Books in Prose and Verse Volume I 1926–1938*, ed. by Edward Mendelson (London: Faber & Faber, 1996), pp. 463–66

Auden, W.H. and Christopher Isherwood, *The Dog beneath the Skin or Where Is Francis?* (London: Faber & Faber, 1935)

Auden, W.H. and T.C. Worsley, *Education Today and Tomorrow*, in *The Complete Works of W.H. Auden Prose and Travel Books in Prose and Verse Volume I 1926–1938*, ed. by Edward Mendelson (London: Faber & Faber, 1996), pp. 389–424

Auden, W.H. and T.C. Worsley, *Education Today and Tomorrow* (London: Hogarth Press, 1939)

Auden, W.H., *The English Auden: Poems, Plays and Dramatic Writings 1927–1939*, ed. by Edward Mendelson (London: Faber & Faber, 1986)

Auden, W.H., 'Gentleman versus Player', in *The Complete Works of W.H. Auden Prose and Travel Books in Prose and Verse Volume I 1926–1938*, ed. by Edward Mendelson (London: Faber & Faber, 1996), pp. 31–33

Auden, W.H., 'How Not to Be a Genius', in *The Complete Works of W.H. Auden Prose Volume II 1939–1948*, ed. by Edward Mendelson (London: Faber & Faber, 2002), pp. 18–21

Auden, W.H., 'Introduction to *The Oxford Book of Light Verse*', in *The Complete Works of W.H. Auden Prose and Travel Books in Prose and Verse Volume I 1926–1938*, ed. by Edward Mendelson (London: Faber & Faber, 1996), pp. 430–37

Auden, W.H. and John Garrett, 'Introduction to *The Poet's Tongue*', in *The Complete Works of W.H. Auden Prose and Travel Books in Prose and Verse Volume I 1926–1938*, ed. by Edward Mendelson (London: Faber & Faber, 1996), pp. 105–09

Auden, W.H., 'Letter to Lord Byron', in *The English Auden: Poems, Essays and Dramatic Writings 1927–1939*, ed. by Edward Mendelson (London: Faber & Faber, 1977), pp. 169–99

Auden, W.H., 'The Liberal Fascist [Honour]', in *The Complete Works of W.H. Auden Prose and Travel Books in Prose and Verse Volume I 1926–1938*, ed. by Edward Mendelson (London: Faber & Faber, 1996), pp. 55–61

Auden, W.H., 'Life's Old Boy', in *The Complete Works of W.H. Auden Prose and Travel Books in Prose and Verse Volume I 1926–1938*, ed. by Edward Mendelson (London: Faber & Faber, 1996), pp. 62–66

Auden, W.H., Letter to E.R. Dodds, 13 November 1938, 'Textual Notes: Education', in *The Complete Works of W.H. Auden Prose and Travel Books in Prose and Verse Volume I 1926–1938*, ed. by Edward Mendelson (London: Faber & Faber, 1996), pp. 805–10

Auden, W.H., 'Matthew Arnold', in *The English Auden: Poems, Essays and Dramatic Writings, 1927–1939*, ed. by Edward Mendelson (London: Faber, 1986), p. 241

Auden, W.H., 'Morality in an Age of Change', in *The Complete Works of W.H. Auden Prose and Travel Books in Prose and Verse Volume I 1926–1938*, ed. by Edward Mendelson (London: Faber & Faber, 1996), pp. 477–86

Auden, W.H., 'XIX', in *The English Auden: Poems, Essays and Dramatic Writings, 1927–1939*, ed. by Edward Mendelson (London: Faber, 1986), p. 33

Auden, W.H. and Christopher Isherwood, *On the Frontier* (London: Faber & Faber, 1938)

Auden, W.H., *The Orators: An English Study* (London: Faber & Faber, 1932)

Auden, W.H., *The Orators: An English Study*, 3rd edn (London: Faber & Faber, 1966)

Auden, W.H., 'Out on the Lawn', in *The English Auden: Poems, Essays and Dramatic Writings 1927–1939*, ed. by Edward Mendelson (London: Faber & Faber, 1977), pp. 136–38

Auden, W.H., 'Poetry, Poets, and Taste', in *The Complete Works of W.H. Auden Prose and Travel Books in Prose and Verse Volume I 1926–1938*, ed. by Edward Mendelson (London: Faber & Faber, 1996), pp. 162–65

Auden, W.H., 'Poetry, Poets and Taste', *The Highway*, December 1936, pp. 43–44

Auden, W.H., *The Poet's Tongue* (London: George Bell & Sons, 1935)

Auden, W.H., 'Private Pleasure', in *The Complete Works of W.H. Auden Prose and Travel Books in Prose and Verse Volume I 1926–1938*, ed. by Edward Mendelson (London: Faber & Faber, 1996), pp. 25–27

Auden, W.H., 'Problems of Education', in *The Complete Works of W.H. Auden Prose and Travel Books in Prose and Verse Volume I 1926–1938*, ed. by Edward Mendelson (London: Faber & Faber, 1996), pp. 27–28

Auden, W.H., 'The Prolific and the Devourer', in *The English Auden: Poems, Essays and Dramatic Writings, 1927–1939*, ed. by Edward Mendelson (London: Faber, 1986), pp. 394–406

Auden, W.H., 'Psychology and Art Today', in *The Complete Works of W.H. Auden Prose and Travel Books in Prose and Verse Volume I 1926–1938*, ed. by Edward Mendelson (London: Faber & Faber, 1996), pp. 93–105

Auden, W.H., 'A Review of *Culture and Environment*, by F.R. Leavis and Denys Thompson, and Other Books', in *The Complete Works of W.H. Auden Prose and Travel Books in Prose and Verse Volume I 1926–1938*, ed. by Edward Mendelson (London: Faber & Faber, 1996), pp. 37–39

Auden, W.H., 'A Review of *English Poetry for Children* by R.L. Mégroz', in *The Complete Works of W.H. Auden Prose and Travel Books in Prose and Verse Volume I 1926–1938*, ed. by Edward Mendelson (London: Faber & Faber, 1996), pp. 70–71

Auden, W.H., 'A Review of *The Evolution of Sex*, Dr Gregorio Marañón and *The Biological Tragedy of Women*, by Anton Nemilov', in *The Complete Works of W.H. Auden Prose and Travel Books in Prose and Verse Volume I 1926–1938*, ed. by Edward Mendelson (London: Faber & Faber, 1996), pp. 29–31

Auden, W.H., 'Schoolchildren', in *Collected Poems*, ed. by Edward Mendelson (London: Faber & Faber, 1991), pp. 126–27

Auden, W.H., 'Schoolchildren', in *The English Auden: Poems, Essays and Dramatic Writings 1927–1939*, ed. by Edward Mendelson (London: Faber & Faber, 1986), pp. 216–17

Auden, W.H., 'September 1, 1939', in *The English Auden: Poems, Essays and Dramatic Writings 1927–1939*, ed. by Edward Mendelson (London: Faber & Faber, 1986), pp. 245–47

Auden, W.H., 'T.E. Lawrence', in *The Complete Works of W.H. Auden Prose and Travel Books in Prose and Verse Volume I 1926–1938*, ed. by Edward Mendelson (London: Faber & Faber, 1996), pp. 61–62

Auden, W.H., 'XXXI', in *The English Auden: Poems, Essays and Dramatic Writings 1927–1939*, ed. by Edward Mendelson (London: Faber & Faber, 1986), pp. 48–49

Auden, W.H., 'To Unravel Happiness', in *The Complete Works of W.H. Auden Prose and Travel Books in Prose and Verse Volume I 1926–1938*, ed. by Edward Mendelson (London: Faber & Faber, 1996), pp. 77–79

Auden, W.H., 'Writing', in *The Complete Works of W.H. Auden Prose and Travel Books in Prose and Verse Volume I 1926–1938*, ed. by Edward Mendelson (London: Faber & Faber, 1996), pp. 12–24

Auerbach, Nina, *Communities of Women: An Idea in Fiction* (Cambridge: Harvard University Press, 1978)

Baldick, Chris, *Literature of the 1920s: Writers among the Ruins: The Edinburgh History of Twentieth-Century Literature in Britain: Volume 3* (Edinburgh: Edinburgh University Press, 2012)

Baldick, Chris, *The Oxford English Literary History Volume 10: 1910–1940 The Modern Movement* (Oxford: Oxford University Press, 2004)

Ball, Stephen J., *Class Strategies and the Education Market: The Middle Classes and Social Advantage* (London: Routledge Falmer, 2003)

Banks, Olive, *Parity and Prestige in English Secondary Education: A Study in Educational Sociology* (London: Routledge and Paul, 1955)

Beer, Gillian, *Virginia Woolf: The Common Ground* (Edinburgh: Edinburgh University Press, 1996)

Beetham, Margaret and others, *Women's Worlds: Ideology, Femininity and the Woman's Magazine* (Basingstoke: Palgrave, 1991)

Bell, Kathleen, 'A Change of Heart: Six Letters from Auden to Professor and Mrs E.R. Dodds Written at the Beginning of World War II', in *W.H. Auden: 'The Map of All My Youth' Auden Studies 1*, ed. by Katherine Bucknell and Nicholas Jenkins (Oxford: Clarendon Press, 1990), pp. 95–115

Bell, Quentin, '*A Room of One's Own* and *Three Guineas*', in *Virginia Woolf and Fascism: Resisting the Dictators' Seduction*, ed. by Merry M. Pawlowski (Basingstoke: Palgrave, 2001), pp. 13–20

Bell, Quentin, *Virginia Woolf: A Biography Volume I and II* (London: Hogarth Press, 1972)

Berg, James J. and Chris Freeman, eds., *The Isherwood Century: Essays on the Life and Work of Christopher Isherwood* (London: University of Wisconsin Press, 2000)

Bergonzi, Bernard, *Reading the Thirties: Texts and Contexts* (London: Macmillan, 1978)

Berman, Jessica, 'Of Oceans and Opposition: *The Waves*, Oswald Mosley and the New Party', in *Virginia Woolf and Fascism: Resisting the Dictators' Seduction*, ed. by Merry M. Pawlowski (Basingstoke: Palgrave, 2001), pp. 105–21

Berman, Ronald, *Modernity and Progress: Fitzgerald, Hemingway, Orwell* (Tuscaloosa: University of Alabama Press, 2005)

Berry, Paul and Mark Bostridge, *Vera Brittain: A Life* (London: Chatto & Windus, 1995)

Bertram, Anthony, 'Books for the W.E.A. Student', *The Highway*, March 1937, p. 168

Birch, Dinah, *Our Victorian Education* (Oxford: Blackwell, 2008)

Birch, Dinah, '"What Teachers Do You Give Your Girls?": Ruskin and Women's Education', in *Ruskin and Gender*, ed. by Dinah Birch and Francis O'Gorman (Basingstoke: Palgrave Macmillan, 2002), pp. 121–36

Black, Naomi, *Virginia Woolf as Feminist* (London: Cornell University Press, 2004)

Blair, John G., *The Poetic Art of W.H. Auden* (London: Princeton University Press, 1965)

Blake, Nicholas, *A Question of Proof* (London: Penguin, 1935)

Blaszak, Barbara J., *Matriarchs of England's Cooperative Movement: A Study in Gender Politics and Female Leadership 1883–1921* (London: Greenwood Publishing Group, 2000)

Blewitt, Trevor, ed., *The Modern Schools Handbook* (London: Gollancz, 1934)

Bloom, Harold, ed., *Modern Critical Views: George Orwell* (New York: Chelsea House Publishers, 2009)

Bloom, Harold, ed., *Modern Critical Views: W.H. Auden* (New York: Chelsea House Publishers, 1986)

Bluemel, Kristin, *George Orwell and the Radical Eccentrics: Intermodernism in Literary London* (Basingstoke: Palgrave, 2004)

Board of Education, *The Education of Backward Children with Special Reference to Children Who Are Backward Because They Are Dull* (London: His Majesty's Stationery Office, 1937)

Board of Education, *The Public Schools and the General Educational System* [The Fleming Report] (London: His Majesty's Stationery Office, 1944)

Board of Education, *Report of the Consultative Committee on Secondary Education with Special Reference to Grammar Schools and Technical High Schools: Chairman* [The Spens Report] (London: His Majesty's Stationery Office, 1938)

Boly, John R., *Reading Auden: The Returns of Caliban* (London: Cornell University Press, 1991)

Bonham, John, *The Middle Class Vote* (London: Faber & Faber, 1954)

Boobbyer, Philip, *The Spiritual Vision of Frank Buchman* (Philadelphia: Pennsylvania State University Press, 2013)

Bostridge, Mark, 'Introduction', in *Testament of Youth* (London: Virago, 2009), pp. ix–xxii

Bourke, Joanna, *Dismembering the Male: Men's Bodies, Britain and the Great War* (London: Reaktion Books, 1996)

Bourke, Joanna, *Working-Class Cultures in Britain 1890–1960: Gender, Class and Ethnicity* (London: Routledge, 1994)

Bowen, Elizabeth, 'Introduction', in Antonia White, *Frost in May* (London: Virago, 1981), pp. v–x

Bowlby, Rachel, *Feminist Destinations and Further Essays on Virginia Woolf* (Edinburgh: Edinburgh University Press, 1997)

Bozorth, Richard R., *Auden's Games of Knowledge: Poetry and the Meanings of Homosexuality* (Chichester: Columbia University Press, 2001)

Bradley, S.A.J., trans. and ed., *Anglo-Saxon Poetry* (London: Dent, 1982)

Bradshaw, David, 'British Writers and Anti-Fascism in the 1930s, Part I: The Bray and Drone of Tortured Voices', *Woolf Studies Annual*, Vol. 3 (1997), 3–27

Bradshaw, David, 'British Writers and Anti-Fascism in the 1930s, Part II: Under the Hawk's Wings', *Woolf Studies Annual*, Vol. 4 (1998), 41–66

Bradshaw, David, ed., *The Cambridge Companion to E.M. Forster* (Cambridge: Cambridge University Press, 2007)

Bradshaw, David, 'Hyam's Place: *The Years*, the Jews and the British Union of Fascists', in *Women Writers of the 1930s: Gender, Politics and History*, ed. by Maroula Joannou (Edinburgh: Edinburgh University Press, 1999), pp. 179–91

Branson, Noreen, *History of the Communist Party of Great Britain 1927–1941* (London: Lawrence & Wishart, 1985)

Bricheno, Patricia and Mary Thornton, 'Role Model, Hero or Champion? Children's Views Concerning Role Models', *Educational Research*, Vol. 49 No. 4 (2007), 383–96

Briggs, Julia, 'Between the Texts: Virginia Woolf's Acts of Revision', *Text*, Vol. 12 (1999), 143–65

Briggs, Julia, *Virginia Woolf: An Inner Life* (London: Allen Lane, 2005)

Brittain, Vera, *Chronicle of Friendship: Vera Brittain's Diary of the Thirties*, ed. by Alan Bishop (London: Gollancz, 1986)

Brittain, Vera, *Honourable Estate* (London: Virago, 2000)

Brittain, Vera and Geoffrey Handley-Taylor, eds., *The Selected Letters of Winifred Holtby and Vera Brittain (1920–1935)* (London: Brown, 1960)

Brittain, Vera, *Testament of Friendship: The Story of Winifred Holtby* (London: Virago, 2012)

Brittain, Vera and Winifred Holtby, *Testament of a Generation: The Journalism of Vera Brittain and Winifred Holtby*, ed. by Paul Berry and Mark Bostridge (London: Virago Press, 1985)

Brittain, Vera, *Testament of Youth* (London: Virago Press, 2009)

Brockliss, Laurence and Nicola Sheldon, *Mass Education and the Limits of State Building, 1870–1930* (Basingstoke: Palgrave Macmillan, 2012)

Brooker, Peter and Andrew Thacker, eds., *The Oxford Critical and Cultural History of Modernist Magazines Volume I: Britain and Ireland 1880–1955* (Oxford: Oxford University Press, 2009)

Brown, Ivor, 'Looking Backward. Public Schools and Others', *The Observer*, 12 August 1934, p. 5

Bryant, Marsha, *Auden and Documentary in the 1930s* (London: University Press of Virginia, 1997)

Bucknell, Katherine and Nicholas Jenkins, *W.H. Auden: 'The Language of Learning and the Language of Love' Auden Studies 2* (Oxford: Clarendon Press, 1994)

Buell, Frederick, *W.H. Auden as a Social Poet* (London: Cornell University Press, 1973)

Burgess, Anthony, 'Class of '34', *The Observer*, 19 August 1984, p. 19

Burstyn, Joan N., *Victorian Education and the Ideal of Womanhood* (London: Croom Helm, 1980)

Burt, Cyril, *The Backward Child* (London: University of London Press, 1937)

Burt, Stephen, *The Forms of Youth: Twentieth-Century Poetry and Adolescence* (Chichester: Columbia University Press, 2007)

Bushaway, Bob, 'Name upon Name: The Great War and Remembrance', in *Myths of the English*, ed. by Roy Porter (Cambridge, Polity Press, 1992), pp. 136–67

Butler Education Bill Reading, 19 January 1944, <http://hansard.millbanksystems.com/commons/1944/jan/19/education-bill> [accessed 13 November 2017]

Cadbury, George, *Why We Want Education in Industry: Presidential Address Delivered by Alderman George Cadbury at the Annual Conference of the Association for Education in Industry and Commerce June 10th 1926* (Birmingham: Association for Education in Industry and Commerce, 1926)

Caesar, Adrian, *Dividing Lines: Poetry, Class and Ideology in the 1930s* (Manchester: Manchester University Press, 1991)

Caine, Barbara, 'Stefan Collini, Virginia Woolf, and the Question of Intellectuals in Britain', *Journal of the History of Ideas*, Vol. 68 (2007), 369–73

Calder, Angus, *Disasters and Heroes: On War, Memory and Representation* (Cardiff: University of Wales Press, 2004)

Calder, Angus, *The People's War: Britain 1939–1945* (London: Cape, 1969)

Calder-Marshall, Arthur, *Challenge to Schools: A Pamphlet on Public-School-Education* (London: Hogarth Press, 1935)

Calder-Marshall, Arthur, *Dead Centre* (London: Cape, 1935)

Calder-Marshall, Arthur, 'Fiction', *Fact*, July 1937, pp. 38–44

Calder-Marshall, Arthur, *The Magic of My Youth* (London: Hart-Davis, 1951)

Calder-Marshall, Arthur, *Time and Tide*, 20 March 1937, p. 382, in *George Orwell: The Critical Heritage*, ed. by Jeffrey Meyers (London: Routledge & Kegan Paul, 1975), pp. 101–03

Callan, Edward, *Auden: A Carnival of Intellect* (Oxford: Oxford University Press, 1983)

Carey, John, *The Intellectuals and the Masses: Pride and Prejudice among the Literary Intelligentsia 1880–1939* (London: Faber & Faber, 1992)

Carlyle, Thomas, 'Biography', in *English and Other Critical Essays* (London: Everymans Library, 1975), pp. 65–79

Carlyle, Thomas, *The French Revolution* (London: Continuum, 2010)

Carlyle, Thomas, *On Heroes and Hero-Worship* (London: Ward Lock, 1910)

Carpenter, Humphrey, *W.H. Auden: A Biography* (London: Allen & Unwin, 1981)

Carroll, Berenice A., '"To Crush Him in Our Own Country": The Political Thought of Virginia Woolf', *Feminist Studies*, Vol. 4 (1978), 99–132

Caudwell, Christopher, *Illusion and Reality: A Study of the Sources of Poetry* (London: Macmillan, 1937)

Caughie, Pamela, ed., *Virginia Woolf in the Age of Mechanical Reproduction* (London: Garland Publishing, 2000)

Chapman, Wayne K. and Janet M. Manson, eds., *Women in the Milieu of Leonard and Virginia Woolf: Peace, Politics, and Education* (New York: Pace University Press, 1998)

Charteris, Charlotte, 'Playing Up: Edward Upward in Cambridge and Beyond', in *Edward Upward and Left-Wing Literary Culture in Britain*, ed. by Benjamin Kohlmann (Farnham: Ashgate, 2013), pp. 19–33

Childers, Mary M., 'Virginia Woolf on the Outside Looking Down', *Modern Fiction Studies*, Vol. 38 No. 1 (1992), 61–79

Christ, Carol T., 'Woolf and Education', in *Woolf in The Real World: Selected Papers from the Thirteenth International Conference on Virginia Woolf, Smith College, Northampton, Massachusetts 5–8 June 2003*, ed. by Karen V. Kukil (Clemson: Clemson University Digital Press, 2005), pp. 2–9

Church, Richard, 'A Fight for Identity', *The Spectator*, 22 November 1940, pp. 548–50

Clark, Jon and others, eds., *Culture and Crisis in Britain in the Thirties* (London: Lawrence and Wishart, 1979)

Clark, Thekla, *Wystan and Chester: A Personal Memoir* (London: Faber & Faber, 1995)

Clarke, Ben, 'George Orwell: Politics, Rhetoric, and the Public Intellectual', *Studies in the Humanities*, Vol. 35 No. 2 (2008), 231–49

Clarke, Ben, *Orwell in Context: Communities, Myths, Values* (Basingstoke: Palgrave Macmillan, 2007)

Clay, Catherine, *British Women Writers 1914–1945: Professional Work and Friendship* (Aldershot: Ashgate, 2006)

Clewell, Tammy, 'Consolation Refused: Virginia Woolf, the Great War and Modernist Mourning', *MFS*, Vol. 50 No. 1 (Spring 2004), 197–223

Cole, G.D.H., *Socialism and Fascism, 1931–1939* (Basingstoke: Palgrave Macmillan, 2002)

Cole, G.D.H., *The War on the Home Front* (London: Fabian Society, 1939)

Cole, G.D.H., *The World of Labour: A Discussion of the Present and Future of Trade Unionism* (London: Bell, 1913)

Cole, Margaret, *Growing Up into Revolution* (London: Longmans, Green, 1949)

Collini, Stefan, *Absent Minds: Intellectuals in Britain* (Oxford: Oxford University Press, 2006)

Collini, Stefan, 'Author's Response', *Journal of the History of Ideas*, Vol. 68 (2007), 395–405

Collini, Stefan, *Public Moralists: Political Thought and Intellectual Life in Britain 1850–1930* (Oxford: Clarendon Press, 1991)

Colt, Rosemary M. and Janice Rossen, eds., *Writers of the Old School: British Novelists of the 1930s* (Basingstoke: Macmillan, 1992)

Comstock, Margaret, 'The Loudspeaker and the Human Voice: Politics and the Form of *The Years*', *The Bulletin of the New York Public Library: Virginia Woolf Issue*, Vol. 80 No. 2 (Winter 1977), 252–75

Connolly, Cyril, *The Condemned Playground Essays 1927–1944* (London: Routledge, 1945)

Connolly, Cyril, *Enemies of Promise* (London: Penguin, 1979)

Connolly, Cyril, *Enemies of Promise* (Chicago: University of Chicago Press, 2008)

Connolly, Cyril, *The Evening Colonnade* (London: David Bruce & Watson, 1973)

Connolly, Cyril, 'Review', *New Statesman and Nation*, February 1936, in *W.H. Auden: The Critical Heritage*, ed. by John Haffenden (London: Routledge & Kegan Paul, 1983), pp. 185–88

Connolly, Cyril, *The Selected Works of Cyril Connolly*, ed. by Matthew Connolly (London: Picador, 2002)

Constantine, Stephen, 'Love on the Dole and Its Reception', *Literature and History*, Vol. 8 No. 2 (1982), 232–47

Coombes, B.L., 'The Leaning Tower Replies: Below the Tower', *Folios of New Writing* (Spring 1941), pp. 30–36

Coombes, B.L., 'Sabbath Night', *Folios of New Writing* (Autumn 1940), pp. 42–53

Coombes, John, 'British Intellectuals and the Popular Front', in *Class, Culture and Social Change: A New View of the 1930s*, ed. by Frank Gloversmith (Brighton: Harvester Press, 1980), pp. 70–100

Coombes, John, *Writing from the Left: Socialism, Liberalism and the Popular Front* (London: Harvester Wheatsheaf, 1989)

Corr, Helen, 'Sexual Politics in the National Union of Teachers 1870–1920', *Women, Education and the Professions: History of Education Society Occasional Publication*, Vol. 8 (1987), 53–65

Corrigan, Gordon, *Mud, Blood and Poppycock: Britain and the First World War* (London: Cassell Military, 2004)

Coupland, Philip, 'H. G. Wells's "Liberal Fascism"', *Journal of Contemporary History*, Vol. 35 No. 4 (2000), 541–58

Couto, Maria, *Graham Greene: On the Frontier: Politics and Religion in the Novels* (Basingstoke: Macmillan, 1988)

Crewe Report, *The Position of the Classics in the Educational System of the United Kingdom* (London: H.M. Stationery Office, 1921)

Crick, Bernard, *George Orwell: A Life* (London: Secker & Warburg, 1980)

Croft, Andy, *Red Letter Days: British Fiction in the 1930s* (London: Lawrence & Wishart, 1990)

Cuddy-Keane, Melba, '"Are Too Many Books Written and Published?" by Leonard and Virginia Woolf', *PMLA*, Vol. 121 (2006), 235–44

Cuddy-Keane, Melba, 'The Politics of Comic Modes in Virginia Woolf's *Between the Acts*', *PMLA*, Vol. 105 No. 2 (March 1990), 273–85

Cuddy-Keane, Melba, *Virginia Woolf, the Intellectual and the Public Sphere* (Cambridge: Cambridge University Press, 2003)

Cunningham, Valentine, *British Writers of the Thirties* (Oxford: Oxford University Press, 1988)

Cunningham, Valentine, 'Neutral?: 1930s Writers and Taking Sides', in *Class, Culture and Social Change: A New View of the 1930s*, ed. by Frank Gloversmith (Brighton: Harvester Press, 1980), pp. 45–69

Cunningham, Valentine, ed., *The Penguin Book of Spanish Civil War Verse* (London: Penguin, 1980)

Curthoys, M.C. and Janet Howarth, 'Origins and Destinations: The Social Mobility of Oxford Men and Women', in *The History of the University of Oxford VII: Nineteenth Century Oxford, Part Two*, ed. by M.G. Brock and M.C. Curthoys (Oxford: Clarendon Press, 2000), pp. 571–95

Curtis, Vanessa, 'Thoby Stephen at Clifton College', *Virginia Woolf Bulletin*, No. 28 (May 2008), 62–66

Dale, Iain, ed., *Labour Party General Election Manifestos, 1900–1997* (London: Routledge, 1999)

Dalgarno, Emily, *Virginia Woolf and the Migrations of Language* (Cambridge: Cambridge University Press, 2012)

Dalgarno, Emily, *Virginia Woolf and the Visible World* (Cambridge: Cambridge University Press, 2001)

'Dalrymple, Theodore', 'Blame It on Bloomsbury', <http://www.guardian.co.uk/books/2002/aug/17/classics.highereducation> [accessed 3 October 2012]

Danson Brown, Richard, *Louis MacNeice and the Poetry of the 1930s* (Tavistock: Northcote House, 2009)

Dataller, Roger, *Oxford into Coal-Field* (London: Dent, 1934)

Dataller, Roger, *A Pitman Looks at Oxford* (London: Dent, 1933)

Daugherty, Beth Rigel, 'Learning Virginia Woolf: Of Leslie, Libraries and Letters', in *Virginia Woolf and Communities*, ed. by Jeanette McVicker and Laura Davis (New York: Pace University Press, 1999), pp. 10–17

Daugherty, Beth Rigel, 'Virginia Woolf Teaching/Virginia Woolf Learning: Morley College and the Common Reader', in *New Essays on Virginia Woolf*, ed. by Helen Wussow (Dallas: Contemporary Research Press, 1995), pp. 61–77

Davenport-Hines, Richard, *Auden* (London: Heinemann, 1995)

Davenport-Hines, Richard, 'School Writings', in *W.H. Auden: 'The Language of Learning and the Language of Love'*, Auden Studies 2, ed. by Katherine Bucknell and Nicholas Jenkins (Oxford: Clarendon Press, 1994), pp. 1–47

Davidson, Mary R., 'An Aesthete in the Foundry: Henry Green's Living', in *Writers of the Old School: British Novelists of the 1930s*, ed. by Rosemary M. Colt and Janice Rossen (Basingstoke: Macmillan, 1992), pp. 39–54

Davies, Margaret Llewelyn, ed., *Life as We Have Known It: The Voices of Working-Class Women*, (London: Virago, 2012)

Davison, John, *Graham Greene and the Berkhamsted Connection: A Lecture* (Berkhamsted: Graham Greene Birthplace Trust, 1998)

Day-Lewis, Cecil, *Starting Point* (London: Cape, 1937)

Deane, Patrick, 'Auden's England', in *The Cambridge Companion to W.H. Auden*, ed. by Stan Smith (Cambridge: Cambridge University Press, 2004), pp. 25–38

De Gay, Jane, *Virginia Woolf's Novels and the Literary Past* (Edinburgh: Edinburgh University Press, 2006)

De Lyon, Hilary and Frances Widdowson Migniuolo, *Women Teachers Issues & Experiences* (Milton Keynes: Open University Press, 1989)

De Man, Paul, 'Autobiography as De-facement', *MLN*, Vol. 94 No. 5 (December 1979), 919–30

Delamont, Sara, 'The Domestic Ideology and Women's Education', in *The Nineteenth Century Woman: Her Cultural and Physical World*, ed. by Sara Delamont and Lorna Duffin (London: Croom Helm, 1978), pp. 164–87

Dennis, Nigel, 'The Double Life of Henry Green', *Life Magazine*, 4 August 1952, pp. 83–94

Dent, H.C., *1870–1970: Century of Growth in English Education* (London: Longman, 1970)

Dickinson, Renée, *Female Embodiment and Subjectivity in the Modernist Novel: The Corporeum of Virginia Woolf and Olive Moore* (London: Routledge, 2009)

Diemert, Brian, *Graham Greene's Thrillers and the 1930s* (London: McGill-Queen's University Press, 1996)

Duchêne, François, *The Case of the Helmeted Airman: A Study of W.H. Auden's Poetry* (London: Chatto and Windus, 1972)

Dutt, R.P., *Fascism and Social Revolution: A Study of the Economics and Politics of the Last Stages of Capitalism in Decay* (London: Martin Lawrence, 1935)

Dyhouse, Carol, *Girls Growing Up in Late Victorian and Edwardian England* (London: Routledge and Kegan Paul, 1981)

Dyhouse, Carol, *No Distinction of Sex?: Women in British Universities, 1870 –1939* (London: University College London Press, 1995)

Ellis, Steve, *British Writers and the Approach of World War II* (Cambridge: Cambridge University Press, 2015)

Ellis, Steve, *Virginia Woolf and the Victorians* (Cambridge: Cambridge University Press, 2007)

Ensor, Beatrice, 'The Outlook Tower', *The New Era*, January 1920, p. 3

Esty, Joshua, *A Shrinking Island: Modernism and National Culture in England* (Oxford: Princeton University Press, 2003)

Evans, Professor Ifor, 'When Will the Industrial Worker Produce His Own Literature?', *The Highway*, October 1932, pp. 8–10

Ewins, Kristin, '"Revolutionizing a Mode of Life": Leftist Middlebrow Fiction by Women in the 1930s', *ELH*, Vol. 82 No.1 (Spring 2015), 251–79

Eyles, Leonora, '*Love on the Dole*', *The Times Literary Supplement*, 29 June 1933, p. 444

Farrar, Frederic W., *Eric; or, Little by Little* (Edinburgh: Black, 1890)

Feigel, Lara, *Literature, Cinema and Politics, 1930–1945: Reading between the Frames* (Edinburgh: Edinburgh University Press, 2010)

Fenwick, Gillian, *George Orwell A Bibliography* (Winchester: Oak Knoll Press, 1998)

Ferguson, R.W., *Education in the Factory: An Account of the Educational Schemes & Facilities at Cadbury Brothers Ltd. Bournville Works* (Bournville: Publications Department Bournville Works, c.1923)

Ferrer, Daniel, *Virginia Woolf and the Madness of Language*, trans. by Geoffrey Bennington and Rachel Bowlby (London: Routledge, 1990)

Firchow, Peter E., 'Private Faces in Public Places: Auden's *The Orators*', *PMLA*, Vol. 92 (1977), 253–72

Firchow, Peter E., *W.H. Auden: Contexts for Poetry* (London: Associated University Presses, 2002)

Fisher, H.A.L., *Educational Reform: Speeches Delivered by the Right Hon H.A.L. Fisher, MP President of the Board of Education* (Oxford: Clarendon Press, 1918)

Fisher, H.A.L., 'The Home University Library', *The Highway*, November 1935, p. 28

Fisher, H.A.L., 'The Tower of Babel', *The Highway*, October 1931, pp. 3–4

Fisher, H.A.L., *An Unfinished Autobiography* (London: Oxford University Press, 1940)

Fitch, Sir Joshua, 'Preface', in *Stanley's Life Thomas Arnold* (London: John Murray, 1901)

Fleishman, Avrom, *Virginia Woolf: A Critical Reading* (London: Johns Hopkins University Press, 1977)

Flint, Kate, 'Virginia Woolf and the General Strike', *Essays in Criticism*, Vol. 36 No. 4 (October 1986), 319–34

Fordham, Finn, *I Do I Undo I Redo: The Textual Genesis of Modernist Selves* (Oxford: Oxford University Press, 2010)

Fordham, Molly, 'Correspondence: The Public-School Problem', *New Statesman and Nation*, 13 April 1940, p. 496

Forster, E.M., *The Longest Journey* (London: Penguin, 2006)

Forster, E.M., 'Review of *The Old School*', *The Spectator*, 27 July 1934, p. 136

Foucault, Michel, *The History of Sexuality Volume 1: The Will to Knowledge*, trans. by Robert Hurley (London: Penguin, 1998)

Fox, Pamela, *Class Fictions: Shame and Resistance in the British Working-Class Novel, 1890–1945* (London: Duke University Press, 1994)

Fox, Ralph, 'Lawrence the 20th Century Hero', *Left Review*, July 1935, pp. 391–96

Fraser, Robert, *A Social Philosophy for Fabians* (London: The Fabian Society, 1930)

Freud, Sigmund, *Group Psychology and the Analysis of the Ego*, trans. and ed. by James Strachey (London: Hogarth Press, 1959)

Freud, Sigmund, 'Introduction to Psychoanalysis and the War Neuroses', trans. by Ernest Jones, in *The Complete Psychological Works of Sigmund Freud Vol XVII (1917–1919)*, trans. by James Strachey (London: Hogarth Press, 1995), pp. 205–15

Froula, Christine, *Virginia Woolf and the Bloomsbury Avant-Garde: War, Civilization, Modernity* (Chichester: Columbia University Press, 2005)

Fuller, John, *W.H. Auden: A Commentary* (London: Faber & Faber, 1998)

Gagnier, Regenia, *Subjectivities: A History of Self-Representation in Britain, 1832–1920* (Oxford: Oxford University Press, 1991)

Gardiner, Juliet, *The Thirties: An Intimate History* (London: Harper Collins, 2010)

Garnett, David, 'Current Literature: Books in General', *New Statesman and Nation*, 25 August 1934, p. 239

Garratt, Percival, Edith Sitwell, F.C. Field-Hyde, and G.A. Pfister, 'New Publications', *The Sackbut*, June 1922, pp. 34–36

Gättens, Marie Louise, 'Three Guineas, Fascism and the Construction of Gender', in *Virginia Woolf and Fascism: Resisting the Dictators' Seduction*, ed. by Merry M. Pawlowski (Basingstoke: Palgrave, 2001), pp. 21–38

Gaughan, Matthew, 'Palatable Socialism or "The Real Thing"?: Walter Greenwood's *Love on the Dole*', *Literature & History*, Vol. 17 No. 2 (2008), 47–61

Gibson, Wilfred, 'Five New Novels', *The Manchester Guardian*, 3 May 1940, p. 7

Giles, Judy, *Women, Identity and Private Life in Britain 1900–1950* (Basingstoke: Macmillan, 1995)

Glendinning, Victoria, *Leonard Woolf* (London: Simon & Schuster, 2006)

Gloversmith, Frank, 'Changing Things: Orwell and Auden', in *Class, Culture and Social Change: A New View of the 1930s*, ed. by Frank Gloversmith (Brighton: Harvester Press, 1980), pp. 101–41

Gloversmith, Frank, 'Defining Culture: J.C. Powys, Clive Bell, R.H. Tawney and T.S. Eliot', in *Class, Culture and Social Change: A New View of the 1930s*, ed. by Frank Gloversmith (Brighton: Harvester Press, 1980), pp. 15–44

Glynn, Sean and John Oxborrow, *Interwar Britain: A Social and Economic History* (London: Allen and Unwin, 1976)

Goldman, Jane, *The Feminist Aesthetics of Virginia Woolf: Modernism, Post-Impressionism and the Politics of the Visual* (Cambridge: Cambridge University Press, 1998)

Goldman, Lawrence, *Dons and Workers: Oxford and Adult Education since 1850* (Oxford: Clarendon Press, 1995)

Gollancz, Victor, 'Foreword to *The Road to Wigan Pier* [1937]', in *George Orwell: The Critical Heritage*, ed. by Jeffrey Meyers (London: Routledge & Kegan Paul, 1975), pp. 91–99

Golubov, Nattie, 'English Ethical Socialism: Women Writers, Political Ideas and the Public Sphere between the Wars', *Women's History Review*, Vol. 14 No. 1 (2005), 33–60

Gordon, Peter, Richard Aldrich, and Dennis Dean, *Education and Policy in England in the Twentieth Century* (London: Woburn, 1991)

Graham, J.W., 'Manuscript Revision and the Heroic Theme of *The Waves*', *Twentieth Century Literature*, Vol. 29 No. 3 (1983), 312–32

Graves, John, *Policy and Progress in Secondary Education 1902–1942* (London: Thomas Nelson & Sons, 1943)

Graves, Robert, *Goodbye to All That* (London: Penguin, 2000)

Green, Henry, 'Apologia: Published in No. 4 *Folios of New Writing*, 1941', in *Surviving: The Uncollected Writings of Henry Green*, ed. by Matthew Yorke (London: Chatto & Windus, 1992), pp. 90–97

Green, Henry and Terry Southern, '"The Art of Fiction" published in the *Paris Review*, 1958', in *Surviving: The Uncollected Writings of Henry Green*, ed. by Matthew Yorke (London: Chatto & Windus, 1992), pp. 234–50

Green, Henry, *Caught* (London: Harvill Press, 2001)

Green, Henry, *Concluding* (London: Harvill Press, 1997)

Green, Henry, *Loving/Living/Party Going* (London: Penguin, 1993)

Green, Henry, *Nothing/Doting/Blindness* (London: Vintage, 2008)

Green, Henry, 'A Novelist to His Readers: I', BBC Broadcast published in *The Listener*, November 1950, in *Surviving: The Uncollected Writings of Henry Green*, ed. by Matthew Yorke (London: Chatto & Windus, 1992), pp. 136–42

Green, Henry, *Pack My Bag: A Self-Portrait* (London: Hogarth Press, 1992)

Green, Henry, *Pack My Bag: A Self-Portrait* (London: Vintage, 2000)

Green, Henry, *Surviving: The Uncollected Writings of Henry Green*, ed. by Matthew Yorke (London: Chatto & Windus, 1992)

Green, Martin, *Children of the Sun: A Narrative of 'Decadence' in England after 1918* (London: Constable, 1977)

Greene, Graham, *Brighton Rock* (London: Vintage, 2006)

Greene, Graham, 'The Cinema', *The Spectator*, 25 November 1938, p. 901

Greene, Graham and Henry J. Donaghy, *Conversations with Graham Greene* (London: University Press of Mississippi, 1992)

Greene, Graham, *England Made Me* (London: Vintage, 2004)

Greene, Graham, 'Fiction', *The Spectator*, 30 June 1933, p. 956

Greene, Graham, 'The Films', *Night & Day*, 14 October 1937, p. 39

Greene, Graham, 'The Films', *Night & Day*, 28 October 1937, p. 31

Greene, Graham, *Fragments of Autobiography: A Sort of Life and Ways of Escape* (London: Penguin, 1991)

Greene, Graham, *Graham Greene: A Life in Letters*, ed. by Richard Greene (London: Little, Brown, 2007)

Greene, Graham, *It's a Battlefield* (London: Penguin, 1940)

Greene, Graham, *The Lawless Roads* (London: Penguin, 1992)

Greene, Graham, ed., *The Old School* (Oxford: Oxford University Press, 1985)

Greene, Graham, ed., *The Old School: Essays by Divers Hands* (London: Cape, 1934)

Greene, Graham, 'Three Poets', *Oxford Magazine*, 10 November 1932, in *W.H. Auden: The Critical Heritage*, ed. by John Haffenden (London: Routledge & Kegan Paul, 1983), pp. 115–16

Greenwood, Walter, *Love on the Dole* (London: Vintage, 2004)

Greenwood, Walter and Ronald Gow, *Love on the Dole [A Play]* (London: Jonathan Cape, 1935)

Greenwood, Walter, 'On the Dole', *The Spectator*, 17 July 1936, pp. 93–94

Greenwood, Walter, 'Poverty and Freedom', *The Spectator*, 22 November 1935, pp. 860–61

Greenwood, Walter, *Tribune*, 12 March 1937, p. 12, in *George Orwell: The Critical Heritage*, ed. by Jeffrey Meyers (London: Routledge & Kegan Paul, 1975), pp. 99–100

Gregory, Adrian, *The Silence of Memory* (Oxford: Berg, 1994)

Grimble, Simon, '"Only Degradation and Slavery?": The Figure of the Teacher in the Writing of Edward Upward', in *Edward Upward and Left-Wing Literary Culture in Britain*, ed. by Benjamin Kohlmann (Farnham: Ashgate, 2013), pp. 69–82

Gualtieri, Elena, "'The Essay as Form: Virginia Woolf and Literary Tradition'", *Textual Practice*, Vol. 12 No. 1 (1998), 46–67

Gualtieri, Elena, *Virginia Woolf's Essays: Sketching the Past* (Basingstoke: Macmillan, 2000)

Gullace, Nicoletta, *The Blood of Our Sons: Men, Women, and the Renegotiation of British Citizenship during the Great War* (Basingstoke: Palgrave Macmillan, 2002)

Haffenden, John, ed., *W.H. Auden: The Critical Heritage* (London: Routledge & Kegan Paul, 1983)

Hamley, H.R., 'Introductory Survey', in *The Education of Backward Children and Juvenile Delinquency in England and Wales*, ed. by Sir Percy Nunn (London: Evans Brothers, 1937), pp. 5–19

Harker, Ben, 'Adapting to the Conjuncture: Walter Greenwood, History and *Love on the Dole*', *Keywords*, Issue 7 (2009), 55–72

Harker, Ben, "'On Different Levels Ourselves Went Forward": Pageantry, Class Politics and Narrative Form in Virginia Woolf's Late Writing', *ELH*, Vol. 78 (2011), 433–56

Harris, Alexandra, 'Common Readers in Wartime', *Virginia Woolf Bulletin*, Vol. 31 No. 21 (May 2009), 10–15

Headlam, Walter, 'Mackail's Greek Anthology', *Classical Review*, Vol. 6 No. 6 (June 1892), 269–71

Hegel, G.W.F., *Elements of the Philosophy of Right*, ed. by Allen W. Wood, trans. by H.B. Nisbet (Cambridge: Cambridge University Press, 1991)

Hentëa, Marius, 'The Fiction of Blindness and Real Life: The Diary Portion of Henry Green's *Blindness* (1926)', *Notes and Queries*, Vol. 59 (July 2012), 421–24

Hentëa, Marius, 'A Guilty Self-Portrait: Henry Green's *Pack My Bag*', *Cambridge Quarterly*, Vol. 40 No. 1 (2011), 36–52

Hentëa, Marius, *Henry Green at the Limits of Modernism* (Eastbourne: Sussex Academic Press, 2014)

Hill, M.E., *The Education of Backward Children* (London: Harrap, 1939)

Hilliard, Christopher, 'Modernism and the Common Writer', *The Historical Journal*, Vol. 18 No. 3 (September 2005), 769–87

Hilliard, Christopher, *To Exercise Our Talents: The Democratization of Writing in Britain* (London: Harvard University Press, 2006)

Hilton, James, *Goodbye Mr Chips* (London: Hodder & Stoughton, 2001)

Hirst, Esther, 'As Ithers See Us', *The Cooperative News*, 21 June 1913, p. 800

Hitchcock, Peter, 'Passing: Henry Green and Working-Class Identity', *Modern Fiction Studies*, Vol. 40 No. 1 (1994), 1–31

HMRC Tax Office, <http://www.hmrc.gov.uk/history/taxhis6.htm> [accessed 2 April 2013]

Hodgkin, T.L., 'The Individual and the Group', *Left Review*, November 1937, pp. 627–29

Hoggart, Richard, *The Uses of Literacy* (London: Chatto & Windus, 1957)

Holder, R.W., *The Dictionary Men: Their Lives and Times* (Bath: Bath University Press, 2004)

Hollander, Rachel, 'Novel Ethics: Alterity and Form in *Jacob's Room*', *Twentieth Century Literature*, Vol. 53 No. 1 (Spring 2007), 40–66

Holloway, John, *The Victorian Sage: Studies in Argument* (London: Macmillan, 1953)

Holroyd, Michael, *Lytton Strachey: A Critical Biography Volume 1, The Unknown Years* (London: Heinemann, 1967)

Holt, Jenny, *Public School Literature, Civic Education and the Politics of Male Adolescence* (Farnham: Ashgate, 2008)

Holtby, Winifred, *Anderby Wold* (London: Virago, 2011)

Holtby, Winifred, *The Astonishing Island* (London: Lovat Dickson, 1933)

Holtby, Winifred, 'The Best of Life', in *Testament of a Generation: The Journalism of Vera Brittain and Winifred Holtby*, ed. by Paul Berry and Mark Bostridge (London: Virago Press, 1985), pp. 87–89

Holtby, Winifred, 'Fear and the Woman Who Earns', in *Testament of a Generation: The Journalism of Vera Brittain and Winifred Holtby*, ed. by Paul Berry and Mark Bostridge (London: Virago Press, 1985), pp. 81–83

Holtby, Winifred, 'King George V Jubilee Celebrations', in *Testament of a Generation: The Journalism of Vera Brittain and Winifred Holtby*, ed. by Paul Berry and Mark Bostridge (London: Virago Press, 1985), pp. 89–93

Holtby, Winifred, *The Land of Green Ginger* (London: Virago, 2011)

Holtby, Winifred, *Letters to a Friend*, ed. by Alice Holtby and Jean McWilliam (London: Collins, 1937)

Holtby, Winifred, 'Nijinsky', *The Schoolmistress*, 16 November 1933, p. 189 and p. 196

Holtby, Winifred, 'The Old School', *The Schoolmistress*, 9 August 1934, p. 493 and p. 500

Holtby, Winifred, *South Riding* (London: Collins, 1949)

Holtby, Winifred, *Virginia Woolf: A Critical Memoir* (London: Wishart, 1932)

Holtby, Winifred, 'The Voice of Youth', *The Schoolmistress*, 16 May 1935, p. 185

Holtby, Winifred, 'The Wearer and the Shoe', in Vera Brittain and Winifred Holtby, *Testament of a Generation: The Journalism of Vera Brittain and Winifred Holtby*, ed. by Paul Berry and Mark Bostridge (London: Virago Press, 1985), pp. 64–67

Holtby, Winifred, *Women* (London: John Lane The Bodley Head, 1941)

Hopkins, Chris, *English Fiction in the 1930s: Language, Genre, History* (London: Continuum, 2006)

Hopkins, Eric, *A Social History of the English Working Classes 1815–1945* (London: Edward Arnold, 1979)

Howarth, Janet, '"In Oxford but ... not of Oxford": The Women's Colleges', in *The History of the University of Oxford Volume VII Nineteenth Century Oxford, Part Two*, ed. by M.G. Brock and M.C. Curthoys (Oxford: Clarendon Press, 2000), pp. 237–307

Howarth, Janet and Mark Curthoys, 'The Political Economy of Women's Higher Education in Late Nineteenth and Early Twentieth-Century Britain', *Historical Research*, Vol. 60 No. 142 (June 1987), 208–31

Howarth, Janet, 'The Self-Governing University, 1882–1914', in *The History of the University of Oxford VII: Nineteenth Century Oxford, Part Two*, ed. by M.G. Brock and M.C. Curthoys (Oxford: Clarendon Press, 2000), pp. 599–643

Howarth, Janet, 'Women', in *The History of the University of Oxford Volume VIII The Twentieth Century*, ed. by Brian Harrison (Oxford: Clarendon Press, 1994), pp. 345–75

Howarth, Peter, *Play Up and Play the Game: The Heroes of Popular Fiction* (London: Eyre Methuen, 1973)

Howatson, Alastair, *Mechaniks in the Universitie: A History of Engineering Science at Oxford* (Oxford: University of Oxford Department of Engineering Science, 2008)

Howkins, Alun, 'Class against Class: The Political Culture of the Communist Party of Great Britain: 1930–1935', in *Class, Culture and Social Change: A New View of the 1930s*, ed. by Frank Gloversmith (Brighton: Harvester Press, 1980), pp. 240–57

Hubble, Nick, 'George Orwell and Mass Observation: Mapping the Politics of Everyday Life in England 1936–1941' (unpublished doctoral thesis, University of Sussex, 2002)

Hubble, Nick, *Mass Observation and Everyday Life: Culture, History, Theory* (Basingstoke: Palgrave Macmillan, 2006)

Hubble, Nick, 'Orwell and the English Working Class: Lessons in Autobiografiction for the Twenty-First Century', in *Orwell Today*, ed. by Richard Lance Keeble (Bury St Edmunds: Abramis, 2012), pp. 30–45

Hughes, Thomas, 'The Public Schools of England Part II', *The North American Review*, Vol. 129 (July 1879), 37–52

Hughes, Thomas, *Tom Brown's Schooldays*, adapted for use in schools by Fred W. Bewsher (London: George Bell & Sons, 1913)

Hughes, Thomas, *Tom Brown's Schooldays* (Cambridge: Macmillan, 1857)

Hulcoop, John F., 'Percival and the Porpoise: Woolf's Heroic Theme in *The Waves*', *Twentieth Century Literature*, Vol. 34 No. 4 (1988), 468–88

Hunter, Lynette, *George Orwell: The Search for a Voice* (Milton Keynes: Open University Press, 1984)

Hurst, Isobel, *Victorian Women Writers and the Classics: The Feminine of Homer* (Oxford: Oxford University Press, 2006)

Hussey, Mark, *The Singing of the Real World: The Philosophy of Virginia Woolf's Fiction* (Columbus: Ohio State University Press, 1986)

Hussey, Mark, ed., *Virginia Woolf and War: Fiction, Reality, and Myth* (Syracuse: Syracuse University Press, 1991)

Hussey, Mark and Vara Neverow, eds., *Virginia Woolf: Emerging Perspectives Third Annual Conference on Virginia Woolf* (New York: Pace University Press, 1994)

Hynes, Samuel, *The Auden Generation: Literature and Politics in England in the 1930s* (London: Bodley Head, 1976)

Hynes, Samuel, 'What Is a Decade?: Notes on the Thirties', *Sewanee Review*, Vol. 88 (1980), 506–11

Ingle, Stephen, *Decency versus Ideology: The Politics of George Orwell* (Hull: University of Hull, Department of Politics, 1984)

Ingle, Stephen, *George Orwell: A Political Life* (Manchester: Manchester University Press, 1993)

Ingle, Stephen, *The Social and Political Thought of George Orwell: A Reassessment* (London: Routledge, 2006)

Ironside, Philip, *The Social and Political Thought of Bertrand Russell: The Development of an Aristocratic Liberalism* (Cambridge: Cambridge University Press, 1996)

Isherwood, Christopher, *Lions and Shadows: An Education in the Twenties* (London: Minerva, 1996)

Isherwood, Christopher, *The Memorial* (Minneapolis: University of Minnesota Press, 1999)

Isherwood, Christopher, 'Some Notes on Auden's Early Poetry', *New Verse No. 26–27*, November 1937, pp. 4–9

Isherwood, Christopher, 'The Youth Movement in the New Germany', *Action*, 10 December 1931, p. 18

Jackson, Anna, *Diary Poetics: Form and Style in Writers' Diaries, 1915–1962* (London: Routledge, 2010)

Jameson, Storm, 'Socialists Born and Made', *Fact*, May 1937, pp. 87–90

Jameson, Storm, 'Writing in Revolt 1. Theory – Documents', *Fact*, July 1937, pp. 9–18

Jeffares, A. Norman, *W.B. Yeats: A New Biography* (London: Continuum, 2001 [1988])

Jenkins, Nicholas, 'Eleven Letters from Auden to Spender', in *W.H. Auden 'The Map of All My Youth' Auden Studies 1*, ed. by Katherine Bucknell and Nicholas Jenkins (Oxford: Clarendon Press, 1990), pp. 55–93

Joannou, Maroula, ed., *Women Writers of the 1930s: Gender, Politics and History* (Edinburgh: Edinburgh University Press, 1999)

Joannou, Maroula, *Women's Writing, Englishness and National and Cultural Identity: The Mobile Woman and the Migrant Voice 1938–1962* (Basingstoke: Palgrave Macmillan, 2012)

Jones, Chris, *Strange Likeness: The Use of Old English in Twentieth-Century Poetry* (Oxford: Oxford University Press, 2006)

Jones, Clara, *Virginia Woolf Ambivalent Activist* (Edinburgh: Edinburgh University Press, 2016)

Joyce, James, *A Portrait of the Artist as a Young Man* (Oxford: Oxford University Press, 2008)

Joyce, Simon, 'On or About 1901: The Bloomsbury Group Looks Back at the Victorians', *Victorian Studies*, Vol. 46 No. 4 (Summer 2004), 631–54

Julien, Heather, 'School Novels, Women's Work and Maternal Vocationalism', *NWSA Journal*, Vol. 19 No. 2 (Summer 2007), 118–37

Jury, Louise, 'Auden's Schoolboy Inspiration Tells the Truth about Their Love', *Independent*, 18 March 2000, <http://www.independent.co.uk/news/media/audens-schoolboy-inspiration-tells-the-truth-about-their-love-284829.html> [accessed 26 July 2017]

Kahn, Derek, 'Review of *The Road to Wigan Pier*', *Left Review*, April 1937, pp. 186–87

Kavanagh, Matthew, '"Against Fascism, War and Economies": The Communist Party of Great Britain's Schoolteachers during the Popular Front, 1935–1939', *History of Education*, Vol. 43 No. 2 (2014), 208–31

Kavanagh, Matthew, 'British Communism, Periodicals and Comprehensive Education: 1920–56', *Twentieth Century Communism*, Vol. 12 (April 2017), 88–120

Kennard, Jean, *Vera Brittain & Winifred Holtby: A Working Partnership* (London: University Press of New England, 1989)

Kettle, Arnold, 'W.H. Auden: Poetry and Politics in the Thirties', in *Culture and Crisis in Britain in the Thirties*, ed. by Jon Clark and others (London: Lawrence & Wishart, 1979), pp. 83–101

King-Hall, Stephen, 'Public Schools and Public Boys', *Time and Tide Second Spring Book Supplement*, p. 467

Kinkead-Weekes, Mark, *D.H. Lawrence: Triumph to Exile 1912–1922* (Cambridge: Cambridge University Press, 1996)

Kinsella, Elaine L., Timothy D. Ritchie, and Eric R. King Igou, 'Zeroing in on Heroes: A Prototype Analysis of Hero Features', *Journal of Personality and Social Psychology*, Vol. 108 (2015), 114–27

Klugman, James, 'Introduction: The Crisis of the Thirties: A View from the Left', in *Culture and Crisis in Britain in the Thirties*, ed. by Jon Clark and others (London: Lawrence & Wishart, 1979), pp. 13–36

Kneale, Nick, 'The Science and Art of "Man-Making": The Class and Gender Foundations of Ruskin Hall, Oxford 1899', in *Ruskin College: Contesting Knowledge, Dissenting Politics*, ed. by Geoff Andrews, Hilda Kean, and Jane Thompson (London: Lawrence & Wishart, 1999), pp. 5–34

Knorin, V.G, *Fascism, Social-Democracy and the Communists, Thirteenth Plenum of the E.C.C.I. Reports and Speeches* (London: Modern Books, 1934)

Kohlmann, Benjamin, *Committed Styles: Modernism, Politics, and Left-Wing Literature in the 1930s* (Oxford: Oxford University Press, 2014)

Kohlmann, Benjamin, ed., *Edward Upward and Left-Wing Literary Culture in Britain* (Farnham: Ashgate, 2013)

Kohlmann, Benjamin, 'Writing of the Struggle: An Introduction to Edward Upward's Life & Works', in *Edward Upward and Left-Wing Literary Culture in Britain*, ed. by Benjamin Kohlmann (Farnham: Ashgate, 2013), pp. 1–17

Kolocotroni, Vassiliki, Jane Goldman, and Olga Taxidou, eds., *Modernism: An Anthology of Sources and Documents* (Edinburgh: Edinburgh University Press, 1998)

Koutsantoni, Katerina, *Virginia Woolf's Common Reader* (Farnham: Ashgate, 2009)

Kynaston, David, *Austerity Britain 1945–1951* (London: Bloomsbury, 2007)

Laing, Stuart, 'Presenting "Things as They Are": John Sommerfield's *May Day* and Mass Observation', in *Class, Culture and Social Change: A New View of the 1930s*, ed. by Frank Gloversmith (Brighton: Harvester Press, 1980), pp. 142–60

Lamb, J.B., 'Carlyle's "Chartism," the Rhetoric of Revolution, and the Dream of Empire', *Victorians Institute Journal*, Vol. 23 (1995), 129–50

Lancaster, Marie-Jacqueline ed., *Brian Howard: Portrait of a Failure* (London: Blond, 1968)

Lane, Homer, *Talks to Parents and Teachers* (London: Allen & Unwin, 1928)

Latham, Sean, *'Am I a Snob?': Modernism and the Novel* (London: Cornell University Press, 2003)

Lawrence, D.H., *Fantasia of the Unconscious and Psychoanalysis and the Unconscious* (London: Penguin, 1975)

Lawson, John and Harold Silver, *A Social History of Education in England* (London: Metheun, 1978)

Lawton, Denis, *Education and Labour Party Ideologies, 1900–2001 and Beyond* (London: Routledge, 2005)

Layard, J.W., 'Malekula: Flying Tricksters, Ghosts, Gods, and Epileptics', *The Journal of the Royal Anthropological Institute of Great Britain and Ireland*, Vol. 60 (1930), 501–24

Leaska, Mitchell A., 'Introduction', in Virginia Woolf, *The Pargiters: The Novel-Essay Portion of The Years*, ed. by Mitchell A. Leaska (London: Hogarth Press, 1978), pp. vii–xxiv

Leaska, Mitchell A., 'Virginia Woolf, the Pargeter: A Reading of *The Years*', *The Bulletin of the New York Public Library: Virginia Woolf Issue*, Vol. 80 No. 2 (Winter 1977), 172–210

Leavis, F.R., Unsigned review, *Listener*, 22 June 1932, in *W.H. Auden: The Critical Heritage*, ed. by John Haffenden (London: Routledge & Kegan Paul, 1983), pp. 100–01

Leavis, Q.D., 'Review', *Scrutiny*, September 1938, in *Virginia Woolf: The Critical Heritage*, ed. by Robin Majumdar and Allen McLaurin (London: Routledge Kegan & Paul, 1975), pp. 409–19

Lee, Hermione, 'Introduction', in Antonia White, *Strangers* (London: Virago, 1981), pp. i–vii

Lee, Hermione, *The Novels of Virginia Woolf* (London: Methuen, 1977)

Lee, Hermione, *Virginia Woolf* (London: Chatto & Windus, 1996)

Leighton, Joseph Alexander, *Social Philosophies in Conflict: Fascism and Nazism, Communism, Liberal Democracy* (London: Appleton, 1937)

Leonardi, Susan J., *Dangerous by Degrees: Women at Oxford and the Somerville College Novelists* (London: Rutgers University Press, 1989)

Lesnik-Oberstein, Karin, ed., *Children in Culture, Revisited: Further Approaches to Childhood* (Basingstoke: Palgrave Macmillan, 2011)

Levenback, Karen L., *Virginia Woolf and the Great War* (Syracuse: Syracuse University Press, 1998)

Levy, Heather, *The Servants of Desire in Virginia Woolf's Shorter Fiction* (New York: Peter Lang, 2010)

Lewis, Jeremy, *Cyril Connolly: A Life* (London: Cape, 1997)

Light, Alison, *Forever England: Femininity, Literature and Conservatism between the Wars* (London: Routledge, 1991)

Light, Alison, *Mrs Woolf and the Servants* (London: Penguin, 2007)

Lipking, Joanna, 'Looking at the Monuments: Woolf's Satiric Eye', *The Bulletin of the New York Public Library: Virginia Woolf Issue*, Vol. 80 No. 2 (Winter 1977), 141–45

Lissagaray, Prosper Olivier, *History of the Paris Commune of 1871*, trans. by Eleanor Marx (London: Verso, 2012)

Livesey, Ruth, 'Socialism in Bloomsbury: Virginia Woolf and the Political Aesthetics of the 1880s', *The Yearbook of English Studies*, Vol. 37 No. 1 (2007), 126–44

Lodge, David, *The Practice of Writing* (London: Secker & Warburg, 1996)

Low, Lisa, '"Thou Canst Not Touch the Freedom of My Mind": Fascism and the Disruptive Female Consciousness in *Mrs Dalloway*', in *Virginia Woolf and Fascism: Resisting the Dictators' Seduction*, ed. by Merry M. Pawlowski (Basingstoke: Palgrave Macmillan, 2001), pp. 92–104

Lucas, John, 'Auden's Politics: Power, Authority and the Individual', in *The Cambridge Companion to W.H. Auden*, ed. by Stan Smith (Cambridge: Cambridge University Press, 2004), pp. 152–64

Luebbert, Gregory M., *Liberalism, Fascism, or Social Democracy: Social Classes and the Political Origins of Regimes in Interwar Europe* (Oxford: Oxford University Press, 1991)

Lynch, A.J., *The Rise and Progress of the Dalton Plan* (London: Philip, 1926)

MacDonald, James Ramsay, *Labour's Appeal to the Nation* (London: St. Clements Press, 1929)

Mack, Edward Clarence, *Public Schools and British Opinion: 1780 to 1860* (London: Methuen, 1938)

Mack, Edward Clarence, *Public Schools and British Opinion since 1860* (New York: Columbia University Press, 1941)

MacKay, Marina, '"Doing Business with Totalitaria": British Late Modernism and Politics of Reputation', *ELH*, Vol. 73 No. 3 (Fall 2006), 729–53

MacKay, Marina, *Modernism and World War II* (Cambridge: Cambridge University Press, 2007)

MacNeice, Louis, *Autumn Journal* (London: Faber & Faber, 2012)

MacNeice, Louis, 'The Leaning Tower Replies: The Tower That Once', *Folios of New Writing* (Spring 1941), pp. 37–41

MacNeice, Louis, *Modern Poetry: A Personal Essay* (Oxford: Oxford University Press, 1938)

MacNeice, Louis, *The Strings Are False* (London: Faber & Faber, 1996)

Mangan, J.A., *Athleticism in the Victorian and Edwardian Public School: The Emergence and Consolidation of an Educational Ideology* (Cambridge: Cambridge University Press, 1981)

Mangan, J.A., 'Bullies, Beatings, Battles, and Bruises: "Great Days and Jolly Days"', in *Disreputable Pleasures: Less Virtuous Victorians at Play*, ed. by Mike Huggins and J.A. Mangan (London: Frank Cass, 2004), pp. 3–34

Mangan, J.A. and James Walvin, eds., *Manliness and Morality: Middle-Class Masculinity in Britain and America, 1800–1940* (Manchester: Manchester University Press, 1987)

Mangan, J.A., ed., *Tribal Identities: Nationalism, Europe, Sport* (London: Frank Cass, 1996)

Mao, Douglas and Rebecca L. Walkowitz, 'The New Modernist Studies', *PMLA*, Vol. 123 No. 3 (May 2008), 737–48

Marcus, Jane, 'Britannia Rules *The Waves*', in *Decolonizing Tradition: New Views of Twentieth Century 'British' Literary Canons*, ed. by. Karen R. Lawrence (Chicago: University of Illinois Press, 1992), pp. 136–62

Marcus, Jane, ed., *The Bulletin of the New York Public Library: Virginia Woolf Special Issue*, Vol. 80 No. 2 (Winter 1977)

Marcus, Jane, ed., *Virginia Woolf and Bloomsbury: A Centenary Celebration* (Basingstoke: Macmillan, 1987)

Marcus, Jane, *Virginia Woolf and the Languages of Patriarchy* (Bloomington: Indiana University Press, 1987)

Marcus, Laura, *Auto/biographical Discourse: Criticism, Theory, Practice* (Manchester: Manchester University Press, 1994)

Marks, Peter, 'Art and Politics in the 1930s: *The European Quarterly* (1934–1935), *Left Review* (1934–1938) and *Poetry and the People* (1938–1940)', in *The Oxford Critical and Cultural History of Modernist Magazines Volume 1 Britain and Ireland 1880–1955*, ed. by Andrew Thacker and Peter Brooker (Oxford: Oxford University Press, 2009), pp. 623–46

McClellan, Ann K., 'Adeline's (bankrupt) Education Fund: Woolf, Women and Education in the Short Fiction', *Journal of the Short Story in English*, Vol. 50 (Spring 2008), 2–12

McClellan, Ann K., *How British Women Writers Transformed the Campus Novel: Virginia Woolf, Dorothy L. Sayers, Margaret Drabble, Anita Brookner, Jeanette Winterson* (Lampeter: Edwin Mellen Press, 2012)

McClellan, Ann K., '"I Was My War; My War Was I": Vera Brittain, Autobiography and University Fiction during the Great War', *Paedagogica Historica*, Vol. 52 (2016), 121–36

McCulloch, Gary, *Cyril Norwood and the Ideal of Secondary Education* (Basingstoke: Palgrave Macmillan, 2007)

McCulloch, Gary, *Failing the Ordinary Child?: The Theory and Practice of Working-Class Secondary Education* (Buckingham: Open University Press, 1998)

McGee, Patrick, 'The Politics of Modernist Form; or Who Rules the Waves?', *MFS*, Vol. 38 No. 3 (Fall 1992), 631–50

McGowan, John, *Democracy's Children: Intellectuals and the Rise of Cultural Politics* (London: Cornell University Press, 2002)

McIntire, Gabrielle, *Modernism, Memory, and Desire: T.S. Eliot and Virginia Woolf* (Cambridge: Cambridge University Press, 2008)

McKibbin, Ross, *Classes and Cultures: England 1918–1951* (Oxford: Oxford University Press, 1998)

McKibbin, Ross, *The Ideologies of Class: Social Relations in Britain 1880–1950* (Oxford: Clarendon Press, 1990)

McKibbin, Ross, *Parties and People: England 1914–1951* (Oxford: Oxford University Press, 2010)

McLaurin, Allen, *Virginia Woolf: The Echoes Enslaved* (Cambridge: Cambridge University Press, 1973)

McManus, Patricia, 'Virginia Woolf: From a Moral to a Political Reading', *Woolf Studies Annual*, Vol. 14 (2008), 91–138

Mehta, Digish, *Stephen Spender: A Bibliography 1928 to 1955* (Ahmedabad: Gujarat University, 1983)

Mellor, Leo, 'George Barker in the 1930s: Narcissus and the Autodidact', *Modernist Cultures*, Vol. 10 (2015), 250–68

Mendelson, Edward, *Early Auden* (London: Faber & Faber, 1981)

Mendelson, Edward, 'The Auden-Isherwood Collaboration', *Twentieth Century Literature*, Vol. 22 (1976), 276–85

Mengham, Rod, 'Auden, Psychology and Society', in *The Cambridge Companion to W.H. Auden*, ed. by Stan Smith (Cambridge: Cambridge University Press, 2004), pp. 165–74

Mengham, Rod and N.H. Reeve, eds., *The Fiction of the 1940s: Stories of Survival* (Basingstoke: Palgrave, 2001)

Mengham, Rod, *The Idiom of the Time: The Writings of Henry Green* (Cambridge: Cambridge University Press, 1982)

Mengham, Rod, 'The Thirties: Politics, Authority, Perspective', in *The Cambridge History of Twentieth-Century English Literature*, ed. by Laura Marcus and Peter Nicholls (Cambridge: Cambridge University Press, 2004), pp. 359–78

Mepham, John, *Virginia Woolf* (Basingstoke: Macmillan, 1991)

Meyers, Jeffrey, ed., *George Orwell: The Critical Heritage* (London: Routledge & Kegan Paul, 1975)

Meyers, Jeffrey, 'Orwell's Apocalypse: *Coming Up for Air*', in *Modern Critical Views: George Orwell*, ed. by Harold Bloom (New York: Chelsea House, 1987), pp. 85–96

Miller, Monica J., 'Odds, Ends and Others: Objects and the Narration of Woolf's Servant Characters', *Woolf Studies Annual*, Vol. 16 (2010), 111–31

Miller, Tyrus, *Late Modernism: Politics, Fiction and the Arts between the World Wars* (London: University of California Press, 1999)

Millis, C.T., *Technical Education: Its Development and Aims* (London: Arnold, 1925)

Minow-Pinkney, Makiko, *Virginia Woolf and the Problem of the Subject: Feminine Writing in the Major Novels* (Brighton: Harvester, 1987)

Mitchell, Julian, *Another Country* (Oxford: Amber Lane Press, 2014)

Mitchison, Naomi, ed., *An Outline for Boys & Girls and Their Parents* (London: Victor Gollancz, 1932)

Mitchison, Naomi, 'Review', *Weekend Review*, October 1930, in *W.H. Auden: The Critical Heritage*, ed. by John Haffenden (London: Routledge 1983), pp. 81–83

Montefiore, Janet, *Men and Women Writers of the 1930s: The Dangerous Flood of History* (London: Routledge, 1996)

Moorehead, Caroline, *Bertrand Russell: A Life* (London: Sinclair-Stevenson, 1992)

Morris, Max, *The People's Schools: The New People's Library Volume XX* (London: Left Book Club; Gollancz, 1939)

Murat, Jean-Christophe, 'The Cost of Myth: Cyril Connolly and "Romanticism"', *The Space Between*, Vol. IV No. 1 (2008), 101–22

Murray, Nicholas, *Aldous Huxley: An English Intellectual* (London: Little, Brown, 2002)

Neill, A. S., *All the Best, Neill: Letters from Summerhill*, ed. by Jonathan Croall (London: Deutsch, 1983)

Neill, A.S., *A Dominie in Doubt* (London: Jenkins, 1920)

Neill, A.S., *That Dreadful School* (London: Jenkins, 1937)

Neill, A.S., *The Problem Teacher* (London: Jenkins, 1939)

Neill, A.S., *Summerhill* (Harmondsworth: Penguin, 1980)

Neverow, Vara S., 'Freudian Seduction and the Fallacies of Dictatorship', in *Virginia Woolf and Fascism: Resisting the Dictators' Seduction*, ed. by Merry M. Pawlowski (Basingstoke: Palgrave Macmillan, 2001), pp. 56–72

Nicolson, Harold, *The Development of English Biography* (London: Hogarth Press, 1933)

North, Michael, *Henry Green and the Writing of His Generation* (London: University Press of Virginia, 1984)

Nunn, Sir Percy, ed., *The Education of Backward Children and Juvenile Delinquency in England and Wales* (London: Evans Brothers, 1937)

Oakeley, E.M. and Rev. J.M. Wilson, *Clifton College Register 1862 to 1887* (London: Rivingtons, 1887)

Ockwell, Anne and Harold Pollins, '"Extension" in All Its Forms', in *The History of the University of Oxford VII: Nineteenth Century Oxford, Part Two*, ed. by M.G. Brock and M.C. Curthoys (Oxford: Clarendon Press, 2000), pp. 661–88

Odom, Keith C., *Henry Green* (Boston: Twayne, 1978)

Odom, Keith C. and John Lehmann, 'An Interview with John Lehmann about Henry Green', *Twentieth Century Literature*, Vol. 29 No. 4 (Winter 1983), 395–402

O'Neill, Michael, *The All-Sustaining Air: Romantic Legacies and Renewals in British, American, and Irish Poetry since 1900* (Oxford: Oxford University Press, 2007)

Oram, Alison, *Women Teachers and Feminist Politics 1900–1939* (Manchester: Manchester University Press, 1996)

Orton, William, 'The Social Philosophy of Mr Bertrand Russell', *The American Economic Review*, Vol. 14 (1924), 209–26

Orwell, George, 'Appendix 2: Orwell's Notes for *The Road to Wigan Pier*', in *The Complete Works of George Orwell Volume 10 A Kind of Compulsion 1903–1936*, ed. by Peter Davison (London: Secker & Warburg, 1998), pp. 538–84

Orwell, George, 'Boys' Weeklies', in *The Complete Works of George Orwell Volume 12 A Patriot After All 1940–1941*, ed. by Peter Davison (London: Secker & Warburg, 1998), pp. 57–79

Orwell, George, *A Clergyman's Daughter* (London: Penguin, 1975)

Orwell, George, *Coming Up for Air* (London: Penguin, 1962)

Orwell, George, *The Complete Works of George Orwell Volume 10 A Kind of Compulsion 1903–1936*, ed. by Peter Davison (London: Secker & Warburg, 1998)

Orwell, George, *The Complete Works of George Orwell Volume 11 Facing Unpleasant Facts 1937–1939*, ed. by Peter Davison (London: Secker & Warburg, 1998)

Orwell, George, *The Complete Works of George Orwell Volume 12 A Patriot After All 1940–1941*, ed. by Peter Davison (London: Secker & Warburg, 1998)

Orwell, George, *Down and Out in Paris and London* (London: Penguin, 2001)

Orwell, George, 'Foreword to *The End of the Old School Tie*', May 1941, in *The Complete Works of George Orwell Volume 12 A Patriot After All 1940–1941*, ed. by Peter Davison (London: Secker & Warburg, 1998), pp. 486–87

Orwell, George, *Homage to Catalonia* (London: Penguin, 2000)

Orwell, George, 'Inside the Whale', in *The Complete Works of George Orwell Volume 12 A Patriot After All 1940–1941*, ed. by Peter Davison (London: Secker & Warburg, 1998), pp. 86–115

Orwell, George, 'The Lion and the Unicorn: Socialism and the English Genius', in *The Complete Works of George Orwell Volume 12 A Patriot After All 1940–1941*, ed. by Peter Davison (London: Secker & Warburg, 1998), pp. 391–434

Orwell, George, *Nineteen Eighty-Four* (London: Penguin, 1966)

Orwell, George, 'Politics and the English Language', in *The Complete Works of George Orwell Volume 17 I Belong to the Left 1945*, ed. by Peter Davison (London: Secker & Warburg, 1998), pp. 421–32

Orwell, George, 'Review', in *The Complete Works of George Orwell Volume 12 A Patriot After All 1940–1941*, ed. by Peter Davison (London: Secker & Warburg, 1998), pp. 163–65

Orwell, George, 'Review of *Barbarians and Philistines: Democracy and the Public Schools* by T.C. Worsley', *Time and Tide*, 14 September 1940, in *The Complete Works of George Orwell Volume 12 A Patriot After All 1940–1941*, ed. by Peter Davison (London: Secker & Warburg, 1998), pp. 261–62

Orwell, George, 'Review of *The Fate of the Middle Classes*, by Alec Brown', in *The Complete Works of George Orwell Volume 10 A Kind of Compulsion 1903–1936*, ed. by Peter Davison (London: Secker & Warburg, 1998), p. 478

Orwell, George, 'Review of *The Two Carlyles* by Osbert Burdett', *The Adelphi*, March 1931, in *The Complete Works of George Orwell Volume 10 A Kind of Compulsion 1903–1936*, ed. by Peter Davison (London: Secker & Warburg, 1998), pp. 195–97

Orwell, George, *The Road to Wigan Pier* (London: Penguin, 1984)

Orwell, George, 'Such, Such Were the Joys', in *The Complete Works of George Orwell Volume 19 It Is What I Think 1947–1948*, ed. by Peter Davison (London: Secker & Warburg, 1998), pp. 356–87

Ostrem, William, 'The Dog beneath the Schoolboy's Skin: Isherwood, Auden and Fascism', *The Isherwood Century: Essays on the Life and Work of Christopher Isherwood*, ed. by James J. Berg and Chris Freeman (London: University of Wisconsin Press, 2000), pp. 162–71

Overy, Richard, *The Morbid Age: Britain between the Wars* (London: Penguin, 2009)

Owen, Patricia, '"Who Would Be Free, Herself Must Strike the Blow" The National Union of Women Teachers, Equal Pay, and Women within the Teaching Profession', *Journal of the History of Education Society*, Vol. 17 No. 1 (1988), 83–99

Palmer, D.J., 'English', in *The History of the University of Oxford VII: Nineteenth Century Oxford, Part Two*, ed. by M.G. Brock and M.C. Curthoys (Oxford: Clarendon Press, 2000), pp. 397–411

Pandey, Surya Nath, *Stephen Spender: A Study in Poetic Growth* (Salzburg: Institut für Anglistik und Amerikanistik, Universität Salzburg, 1982)

Parker, Peter, *The Old Lie: The Great War and the Public School Ethos* (London: Constable, 1987)

Parliamentary Paper, Cmd 6397 Royal Commission on Equal Pay, Minutes of Evidence. London, HMSO, 1945, 23 March 1945, statement submitted by Association of Assistant Mistresses

Patterson, Ian, *Guernica and Total War* (London: Profile Books, 2007)

Patterson, Ian, 'The Translation of Soviet Literature: John Rodker and PresLit', in *Russia in Britain 1880–1940: From Melodrama to Modernism*, ed. by Rebecca Beasley and Philip Bullock (Oxford: Oxford University Press, 2013), pp. 188–208

Patterson, Ian, 'Wild Geese over the Mountains: Melodrama and the Sublime in the English Imaginary 1933–1939', <http://www.tate.org.uk/research/publications/tate-papers/wild-geese-over-mountains-melodrama-and-sublime-english-imaginary> [accessed 4 August 2014]

Pawlowski, Merry M., 'Introduction: Virginia Woolf at the Crossroads of Feminism, Fascism and Art', in *Virginia Woolf and Fascism: Resisting the Dictators' Seduction*, ed. by Merry M. Pawlowski (Basingstoke: Palgrave, 2001), pp. 1–10

Pawlowski, Merry M., 'Toward a Feminist Theory of the State: Virginia Woolf and Wyndham Lewis on Art, Gender and Politics', in *Virginia Woolf and Fascism: Resisting the Dictators' Seduction*, ed. by Merry M. Pawlowski (Basingstoke: Palgrave, 2001), pp. 39–55

Peach, Linden, 'No Longer a View: Virginia Woolf in the 1930s and the 1930s in Virginia Woolf', in *Women Writers of the 1930s: Gender, Politics and History*, ed. by Maroula Joannou (Edinburgh: Edinburgh University Press, 1999), pp. 192–204

Peach, Linden, *Virginia Woolf* (Basingstoke: Macmillan, 2000)

Pekin, L.B., *Coeducation in Its Historical and Theoretical Setting* (London: Hogarth Press, 1939)

Pekin, L.B., *Progressive Schools: Their Principles and Practice* (London: Hogarth Press, 1934)

Pekin, L.B., *Public Schools: Their Failure and Their Reform* (London: Hogarth Press, 1932)

Pelling, Henry, *A Short History of the Labour Party* (London: Macmillan, 1972)

Periyan, Natasha, 'Democratic Art or Working-Class Literature?: Virginia Woolf, the Women's Cooperative Guild and Literary Value in the "Introductory Letter"', in *Working-class Writing: Theory and Practice*, ed. by Nick Hubble and Ben Clarke (London: Palgrave Macmillan, 2018)

Phillips, Kathy J., *Virginia Woolf against Empire* (Knoxville: University of Tennessee Press, 1994)

Phipps, Emily, *History of the National Union of Women Teachers* (London: National Union of Women Teachers, 1928)

Piette, Adam, *Imagination at War: British Fiction and Poetry, 1939–1945* (London: Papermac, 1995)

Podnieks, Elizabeth, *Daily Modernism: The Literary Diaries of Virginia Woolf, Antonia White, Elizabeth Smart, and Anaïs Nin* (London: McGill-Queen's University Press, 2000)

Pridmore-Brown, Michelle, '1939–1940: Of Virginia Woolf, Gramophones and Fascism', *PMLA*, Vol. 113 No. 3 (May 1998), 408–21

Quigly, Isabel, *The Heirs of Tom Brown: The English School Story* (London: Chatto & Windus, 1982)

Rae, Patricia, 'Double Sorrow: Proleptic Elegy and the End of Arcadianism in 1930s Britain', in *Modernism and Mourning*, ed. by Patricia Rae (London: Associated University Presses, 2007), pp. 213–38

Rae, Patricia, 'Orwell's Heart of Darkness: *The Road to Wigan Pier* as Modernist Anthropology', *Prose Studies*, Vol. 22 No. 1 (April 1999), 71–102

Rawlinson, Mark, *British Writing of the Second World War* (Oxford: Clarendon Press, 2000)

Raynes Park High School website, 'The Beginnings', <http://www.rphs.org.uk/76/the-beginnings> [accessed: 17 July 2017]

Raynes Park High School website, 'School History 1935 and Onwards', <http://www.rphs.org.uk/75/1935-and-onwards> [accessed 17 July 2017]

Raynes Park High School website, 'The School Song', <http://www.rphs.org.uk/77/the-school-song> [accessed 17 July 2017]

Reed, John R., *Old School Ties: The Public Schools in British Literature* (New York: Syracuse University Press, 1964)

Regan, Lisa, *Winifred Holtby's Social Vision: 'Members One of Another'* (London: Pickering and Chatto, 2012)

Reilly, Patrick, *George Orwell: The Age's Adversary* (Basingstoke: Macmillan, 1986)

Replogle, Justin, 'Auden's Marxism', *PMLA*, Vol. 80 No. 5 (1965), 584–95

Rhondda, Lady Margaret, 'Some Letters from Winifred Holtby', *Time and Tide*, 11 April 1936, pp. 518–20

Richmond, Kenneth, *The Curriculum* (London: Constable, 1919)

Richmond, Kenneth, *Education for Liberty* (London: Collins, 1918)

Richmond, Kenneth, *The Permanent Values in Education* (London: Constable, 1917)

Riggs, Erica, 'W.H. Auden as Seriocomic Critic', *Twentieth Century Literature*, Vol. 37 No. 2 (1991), 207–24

Roberts, Michael, *New Signatures* (London: Hogarth Press, 1932)

Roberts, Michael, 'Preface', in *New Country*, ed. by Michael Roberts (London: Hogarth Press, 1933), pp. 9–21

Roberts, Michael, Untitled Review, *Adelphi*, August 1932, in *W.H. Auden: The Critical Heritage*, ed. by John Haffenden (London: Routledge 1983), pp. 107–10

Robinson, Peter, *In the Circumstances: About Poems and Poets* (Oxford: Clarendon Press, 1992)

Rodden, John, ed., *The Cambridge Companion to George Orwell* (Cambridge: Cambridge University Press, 2007)

Romilly, Giles and Esmond Romilly, *Out of Bounds* (London: Hamish Hamilton, 1935)

Rose, Jonathan, *The Intellectual Life of the British Working Classes* (London: Yale University Press, 2001)

Rosenberg, Beth Carole, *Virginia Woolf and Samuel Johnson: Common Readers* (New York: St. Martin's Press, 1995)

Rosenfeld, Natania, *Outsiders Together: Virginia and Leonard Woolf* (Oxford: Princeton University Press, 2000)

Ross, Stephen, 'Authenticity Betrayed: The "Idiotic Folk" of *Love on the Dole*', *Cultural Critique*, No. 56 (Winter 2004), 189–209

Ruskin, John, *The Works of John Ruskin Volume 1 Sesame and Lilies* (Orpington: Allen, 1887 [1864])

Russell, Bertrand, *Education and the Social Order* (London: Allen & Unwin, 1932)

Russell, Bertrand, *On Education: Especially in Early Childhood* (London: George Allen & Unwin, 1926)

Russell, Bertrand, *Principles of Social Reconstruction* (London: Allen & Unwin, 1916)

Sanderson, Michael, 'Educational and Economic History: The Good Neighbours', in *Social Change in the History of British Education*, ed. by Joyce Goodman, Gary McCulloch, and William Richardson (London: Routledge, 2008), pp. 27–44

Sarker, Sonita, 'Locating a Native Englishness in Virginia Woolf's *The London Scene*', *NWSA Journal*, Vol. 13 No. 2 (2001), 1–30

Saunders, Max, *Self-Impression: Life-Writing, Autobiografiction, and the Forms of Modern Literature* (Oxford: Oxford University Press, 2010)

Saville, Victor, dir., *South Riding* (London Film Studios, Victor Saville Productions, 1938) [on DVD]

Schiedeck, Jürgen and Martin Stahlmann, 'Totalizing of Experience: Educational Camps', in *Education and Fascism: Political Identity and Social Education in Nazi Germany*, ed. by Heinz Sünker and Hans-Uwe Otto (London: Falmer Press, 1997), pp. 54–80

Schweizer, Bernard, *Radicals on the Road: the Politics of English Travel Writing in the 1930s* (London: University Press of Virginia, 2001)

Seigel, Jules Paul, ed., *Thomas Carlyle: The Critical Heritage* (London: Routledge and Kegan Paul, 1971)

Sellers, W.H., 'New Light on Auden's *The Orators*', *PMLA*, Vol. 82 No. 5 (1967), 455–64

Sharpe, Tony, *W.H. Auden* (London: Routledge, 2007)

Shaw, Marion, *The Clear Stream: A Life of Winifred Holtby* (London: Virago, 1999)

Shelden, Michael, *Friends of Promise: Cyril Connolly and the World of Horizon* (London: Hamilton, 1989)

Shepley, Nick, *Henry Green Class, Style and the Everyday* (Oxford: Oxford University Press, 2016)

Sherry, Norman, *The Life of Graham Greene Volume I 1904–1939* (London: Cape, 1989)

Silver, Brenda, 'Textual Criticism as Feminist Practice: Or, Who's Afraid of Virginia Woolf Part II', in *Representing Modernist Texts: Editing as Interpretation*, ed. by George Bornstein (Ann Arbor: University of Michigan Press, 1991), pp. 193–222

Silver, Brenda, *Virginia Woolf's Reading Notebooks* (Guildford: Princeton University Press, 1983)

Simmons, J.S.G., 'All Souls', in *The History of the University of Oxford VII: Nineteenth Century Oxford, Part Two*, ed. by M.G. Brock and M.C. Curthoys (Oxford: Clarendon Press, 2000), pp. 209–20

Simon, Brian, *The Politics of Educational Reform 1920–1940* (London: Lawrence & Wishart, 1974)

Simon, Brian, ed., *The Search for Enlightenment: The Working Class and Adult Education in the Twentieth Century* (London: Lawrence & Wishart, 1990)

Skelton, Robin, ed., *Poetry of the Thirties* (London: Penguin Books, 1964)

Skidelsky, Robert, *English Progressive Schools* (Harmondsworth: Penguin Books, 1969)

Smith, Stan, ed., *The Cambridge Companion to W.H. Auden* (Cambridge: Cambridge University Press, 2004)

Smith, Stan, 'The Dating of Auden's "Who Will Endure" and the Politics of 1931', *The Review of English Studies*, New Series, Vol. 41 (1990), 351–62

Smith, Stan, *Inviolable Voice: History and Twentieth-Century Poetry* (Dublin: Gill and Macmillan, 1982)

Smith, Stan, 'Loyalty and Interest: Auden, Modernism and the Politics of Pedagogy', *Textual Practice*, Vol. 4 No. 1 (1990), 54–72

Smith, Stan, 'Remembering Bryden's Bill: Modernism from Eliot to Auden', in *Rewriting the Thirties: Modernism and After*, ed. by Keith Williams and Steven Matthews (London: Longman, 1997), pp. 53–70

Smith, Stan, *W.H. Auden* (Oxford: Basil Blackwell, 1985)

Snaith, Anna, 'Introduction', in Virginia Woolf, *The Years*, ed. by Anna Snaith (Cambridge: Cambridge University Press, 2012), pp. xxxix–xcix

Snaith, Anna and Michael H. Whitworth, eds., *Locating Woolf: The Politics of Space and Place* (Basingstoke: Palgrave Macmillan, 2007)

Snaith, Anna, ed., *Palgrave Advances in Virginia Woolf Studies* (Basingstoke: Palgrave Macmillan, 2007)

Snaith, Anna and Christine Kenyon-Jones, 'Tilting at Universities: Virginia Woolf at King's College London', *Woolf Studies Annual*, Vol. 16 (2010), 1–44

Snaith, Anna, *Virginia Woolf: Public and Private Negotiations* (Basingstoke: Macmillan, 2000)

Snaith, Anna, 'Wide Circles: The *Three Guineas Letters*', *Woolf Studies Annual*, Vol. 6 (2000), 1–168

Snee, Carole, 'Working-Class Literature or Proletarian Writing?', in *Culture and Crisis in Britain in the Thirties*, ed. by Jon Clark and others (London: Lawrence and Wishart, 1979), pp. 165–91

Soulsby, L.H.M., *Stray Thoughts for Girls* (London: Longmans, Green, 1910 [1893])

Southworth, Helen, *Leonard and Virginia Woolf, the Hogarth Press and the Networks of Modernism* (Edinburgh: Edinburgh University Press, 2010)

Soviet Writers' Congress 1934: The Debate on Socialist Realism and Modernism in the Soviet Union (London: Lawrence & Wishart, 1977)

Spears, M.K., *The Poetry of W.H. Auden: The Disenchanted Island* (Oxford: Oxford University Press, 1963)

Spender, Stephen, *The Backward Son* (London: Hogarth Press, 1940)

Spender, Stephen, *Collected Poems 1928–1953* (London: Faber & Faber, 1955)

Spender, Spender, *Cyril Connolly: A Memoir* (Edinburgh: Tragara Press, 1978)

Spender, Stephen, 'An Elementary School Classroom', *The London Mercury*, Vol. 32 No. 187 (May 1935), 8

Spender, Stephen, *Forward from Liberalism* (London: Left Book Club, 1937)

Spender, Stephen, *Journals 1939–1983*, ed. by John Goldsmith (London: Faber, 1985)

Spender, Stephen, 'Letters to the Editor: Adult Education', *The Times*, 25 February 1942, p. 5

Spender, Stephen, *New Collected Poems* (London: Faber & Faber, 2004)

Spender, Stephen, 'New Poetry', *Left Review*, July 1937, pp. 358–61

Spender, Stephen, *The New Realism: A Discussion* (London: Hogarth Press, 1939)

Spender, Stephen, *New Selected Journals: 1939–1955*, ed. by Lara Feigel, John Sutherland with Natasha Spender (London: Faber & Faber, 2012)

Spender, Stephen, 'Oxford to Communism', *New Verse*, Nos. 26–27, November 1937, pp. 9–10

Spender, Stephen, *The Still Centre* (London: Faber & Faber, 1939)

Spender, Stephen, *The Thirties and After: Poetry, Politics and People 1933–1975* (London: Macmillan, 1978)

Spender, Stephen, *W.H. Auden: A Memorial Address Delivered at Christ Church Cathedral, Oxford on 27 October, 1973* (London: Faber & Faber, 1973)

Spender, Stephen, '"Where No One Was Well": Review of British Writers of the Thirties by Valentine Cunningham', *The Observer*, 7 February 1988, p. 24

Spender, Stephen, *World within World* (London: Hamish Hamilton, 1951)

Spender, Stephen, 'Writing in Revolt – Poetry', *Fact*, July 1937, pp. 18–30

Sponenberg, Ashlie, 'The Long Arm of Discipline: *South Riding*, Documentary Writing, and the Cinematic Gaze', *The Space Between*, Vol. III No. 1 (2007), 65–78

Stanford Friedman, Susan, '"Virginia Woolf"'s Pedagogical Scenes of Reading: *The Voyage Out, The Common Reader* and Her "Common Readers"', *Modern Fiction Studies*, Vol. 38 (1992), 101–25

Stannard, Martin, *Evelyn Waugh: The Early Years 1903–1939* (London: Dent, 1986)

Stannard, Martin, 'In Search of Himselves: The Autobiographical Writings of Graham Greene', *Prose Studies*, Vol. 8 No. 2 (1985), 139–55

Steedman, Carolyn, *Strange Dislocations: Childhood and the Idea of Human Interiority 1780–1930* (London: Virago Press, 1995)

Stephen, Leslie, *Samuel Johnson* (London: Macmillan, 1887)

Stephen, Leslie, 'Thomas Carlyle', *Cornhill Magazine*, March 1881, pp. 349–58

Stephen, Leslie, 'Thoughts of an Outsider: Public Schools', *Cornhill Magazine*, March 1873, pp. 281–92

Stephen, Leslie, 'Thoughts of an Outsider: The Public Schools again', *Cornhill Magazine*, November 1873, pp. 605–15

Stephens, W.B., *Education in Britain, 1750–1914* (Basingstoke: Macmillan, 1998)

Sternlicht, Sanford, *Stephen Spender* (New York: Twayne; Toronto: Maxwell Macmillan Canada, 1992)

Stobart, J.C., 'Working Women's Lives: Review of *Life as We Have Known It*', *The Observer*, 7 June 1931, p. 4

Stray, Christopher, *Classics Transformed: Schools, Universities and Society in England, 1830–1960* (Oxford: Clarendon Press, 1998)

Suh, Judy, 'Woolf and the Gendering of Fascism', in *Virginia Woolf and Communities: Selected Papers from the Eighth Annual Conference*, ed. by Jeannette McVicker and Laura Davis (New York: Pace University Press, 1999), pp. 141–46

Summerfield, Penny, 'Women and the Professional Labour Market 1900–1950: The Case of the Secondary Schoolmistress', *Women, Education and the Professions: History of Education Society Occasional Publication*, Vol. 8 (1987), 37–52

Sünker, Heinz and Hans-Uwe Otto, eds., *Education and Fascism: Political Identity and Social Education in Nazi Germany* (London: Falmer Press, 1997)

Sutherland, John, *Stephen Spender: The Authorized Biography* (London: Penguin, 2004)

S.W., 'The Truth about School', *The Manchester Guardian*, 17 September 1935, p. 5

Swingler, Randall, 'Spender's Approach to Communism', *Left Review*, March 1937, pp. 110–13

Symons, Julian, *The Thirties: A Dream Revolved* (London: Cresset Press, 1960)

Tambling, Jeremy, 'Repression in Mrs Dalloway's London', *Essays in Criticism*, Vol. XXXIX No. 2 (1989), 137–55

Tawney, R.H., *Education: The Socialist Policy* (London: Independent Labour Party, 1924)

Tawney, R.H., *Equality* (London: George Allen & Unwin, 1931)

Tawney, R.H., *Secondary Education for All: A Policy for Labour* (London: Labour Party Education Advisory Committee and George Allen Unwin, 1922)

Taylor, Elinor, 'Popular Front Politics and the British Novel, 1934–1940' (unpublished doctoral thesis, University of Salford [2014])

Temple, William, *Lecture on the Place of the W.E.A. in English Education* (Manchester: Workers' Educational Association, North-Western District, 1932)

Thacker, Andrew, *Moving through Modernity: Space and Geography in Modernism* (Manchester: Manchester University Press, 2003)

Toynbee, Philip, *Encounter*, August 1959, pp. 81–82, in *George Orwell: The Critical Heritage*, ed. by Jeffrey Meyers (London: Routledge & Kegan Paul, 1975), pp. 115–18

Tratner, Michael, *Modernism and Mass Politics: Joyce, Woolf, Eliot, Yeats* (Stanford: Stanford University Press, 1995)

Treglown, Jeremy, *Romancing: The Life and Work of Henry Green* (London: Faber & Faber, 2000)

Trudgill, Peter, *Sociolinguistics: An Introduction to Language and Society* (Harmondsworth: Penguin, 1983)

Tsuzuki, Chushichi, 'Anglo-Marxism and Working-Class Education', in *The Working Class in Modern British History: Essays in Honour of Henry Pelling*, ed. by Jay Winter (Cambridge: Cambridge University Press, 1983), pp. 187–99

Ulich, Robert, *The Education of Nations* (Cambridge: Harvard University Press, 1961)

Unsigned article, 'Better Than Fiction Is – *Life as We Have Known It*', *Woman's Outlook*, 4 April 1931, pp. 368–70

Unsigned article, 'The Discovery of the Working Woman', *The Cooperative News*, 21 June 1913

Unsigned article, 'The Right Book Club Success', *The Observer*, 25 April 1937, p. 12

Unsigned article, 'Some Books Recommended by Our Contributors', *The New Era in Home and School*, January 1939, p. 26

Unsigned article, 'Towards a Classless Education', *New Statesman and Nation*, 4 August 1934, pp. 145–46

Unsigned article, 'Wednesday at Congress', *The Cooperative News*, 21 June 1913, p. 794

Unsigned article, 'When Democracy Is a "Sham"', *Birmingham Post*, 24 October 1938, p. 13

Unsigned editorial, *The Times*, 16 April 1880, p. 9

Unsigned review, 'Essays in Verse – Keats and Modern Writers', *The Times*, 11 April 1922, p. 19

Unsigned review, '*The Old School* Review', *The Times*, 24 July 1934, p. 8

Unsigned review, 'Review in *The Times Literary Supplement*', 4 June 1938, in *Virginia Woolf: The Critical Heritage*, ed. by Robin Majumdar and Allen McLaurin (London: Routledge Kegan & Paul, 1975), pp. 400–01

Unsigned review, 'Review of *Life as We Have Known It*', *The Bookman*, Spring 1931, p. 92

Unsigned review, 'Some Thoughts on *The Old School*', *The Manchester Guardian*, 31 July 1934, p. 5

Upward, Edward, *Journey to the Border* (London: Enitharmon Press, 1994)

Upward, Edward, 'The Leaning Tower Replies: The Falling Tower', *Folios of New Writing* (Spring 1941), pp. 24–29

Vaninskaya, Anna, '"It Was a Silly System": Writers and Schools, 1870–1939', *The Modern Language Review*, Vol. 105 (2010), 952–75

Verschoyle, Derek, 'Review', *Spectator*, February 1936, in *W.H. Auden: The Critical Heritage*, ed. by John Haffenden (London: Routledge & Kegan Paul, 1983), pp. 183–85

Vicinus, Martha, *Independent Women: Work and Community for Single Women 1850–1920* (London: Virago, 1985)

Walker, Barbara M., 'No More Heroes Any More: The "Older Brother as Role Model"', *Cambridge Journal of Education*, Vol. 37 No. 4 (December 2007), 503–18

Wallace, Diana, *Sisters and Rivals in British Women's Fiction 1914–1939* (Basingstoke: Macmillan, 2000)

Waugh, Evelyn, 'The Books You Read: A Neglected Masterpiece', *Graphic*, 14 June 1930, p. 588

Waugh, Evelyn, *Decline and Fall* (London: Penguin, 2001)

Waugh, Evelyn, *Letters of Evelyn Waugh* (London: Weidenfeld and Nicolson, 1980)

Waugh, Evelyn, 'Present Discontents', *Tablet*, 3 December 1938, in *The Essays, Articles and Reviews of Evelyn Waugh*, ed. by Donat Gallagher (London: Methuen, 1983), pp. 238–41

Weatherhead, A. Kingsley, *Stephen Spender and the Thirties* (London: Associated University Presses, 1975)

Webster, Anthony, ed., *The Hidden Alternative: Cooperative Values, Past, Present and Future* (Manchester: Manchester University Press, 2011)

Webster, Roger, '*Love on the Dole* and the Aesthetic of Contradiction', in *The British Working-Class Novel in the Twentieth Century*, ed. by Jeremy Hawthorn (London: Arnold, 1984), pp. 49–61

Wetzsteon, Rachel, *Influential Ghosts: A Study of Auden's Sources* (London: Routledge, 2007)

White, Antonia, *As Once in May: The Early Autobiography of Antonia White and Other Writings*, ed. by Susan Chitty (London: Virago, 1983)

White, Antonia, 'David Garnett', *The Schoolmistress*, 23 November 1933, p. 217 and p. 234

White, Antonia, *Diaries 1926–1957 Volume I*, ed. by Susan Chitty (London: Constable, 1991)

White, Antonia, 'Dr. Jordan Lloyd', *The Schoolmistress*, 26 October 1933, p. 93 and p. 96

White, Antonia, 'Flora Robson', *The Schoolmistress*, 12 October 1933, p. 33 and p. 36

White, Antonia, *Frost in May* (London: Virago Press, 1981)

White, Antonia, 'Mr Gordon Selfridge', *The Schoolmistress*, 14 September 1933, p. 601 and p. 604

White, Antonia, 'The Position of Women in the World To-day', *The Schoolmistress*, 28 December 1933, p. 345

White, Antonia, 'Sir Alfred Hopkinson', *The Schoolmistress*, 9 November 1933, p. 157 and p. 160

White, Antonia, 'Sir William Crawford', *The Schoolmistress*, 28 September 1933, p. 658 and p. 674

White, Antonia, *Strangers* (London: Virago, 1981)

White, Antonia, *Strangers* (London: Harvill Press, 1954)

White, Evelyne, *Winifred Holtby as I Knew Her* (London: Collins, 1938)

White, Steven H., 'What Is a Hero? An Exploratory Study of Students' Conception of Heroes', *Journal of Moral Education*, Vol. 28 No. 1 (1999), 81–95

White, Susanna, dir., 'Tell Me the Truth about Love', BBC4, 17 May 2009 [first broadcast in 2000]

Whittier-Ferguson, John, 'Repetition, Remembering, Repetition: Virginia Woolf's Late Fiction and the Return of War', *MFS*, Vol. 57 No. 2 (Summer 2011), 230–53

Whitworth, Michael H., *Virginia Woolf* (Oxford: Oxford University Press, 2005)

Williams, Keith, and Steven Matthews, eds., *Rewriting the Thirties: Modernism and After* (London: Longman, 1997)

Williams, Raymond, *Culture and Materialism: Selected Essays* (London: Verso, 2010)

Williams, Raymond, 'The Future of Cultural Studies', in *Politics of Modernism* (London: Verso, 1989), pp. 151–62

Williams, Raymond, 'The Idea of a Common Culture (1967)', in *Raymond Williams On Culture & Society: Essential Writings*, ed. by Jim McGuigan (London: Sage, 2014), pp. 93–100

Williams, Raymond, *The Long Revolution* (London: Chatto & Windus, 1961)

Willis Jr., J.H., *Leonard and Virginia Woolf as Publishers: The Hogarth Press, 1917–1941* (London: University Press of Virginia, 1992)

Wilson, Nicola, *Home in British Working-Class Fiction* (London: Ashgate, 2017)

Wilson, Duncan, *Leonard Woolf: A Political Biography* (London: Hogarth Press, 1978)

Windle, Jack, '"What Life Means to Those at the Bottom": *Love on the Dole* and Its Reception since the 1930s', *Literature & History*, Vol. 20 No. 2, 35–50

Winter, Jay, *Sites of Memory, Sites of Mourning: The Great War in European Cultural History* (Cambridge: Cambridge University Press, 1995)

Wipf-Miller, Carol A., 'Fictions of "Going Over": Henry Green and the New Realism', *Twentieth Century Literature*, Vol. 44 No. 2 (summer 1998), 135–54

Woloch, Alex, 'Foreword' in Cyril Connolly, *Enemies of Promise* (Chicago: University of Chicago Press, 2008), pp. vii–xviii

Wood, Alice, 'Facing *Life as We Have Known It*: Virginia Woolf and the Women's Cooperative Guild', *Literature & History*, Vol. 23 No. 2 (Autumn 2014), 18–34

Wood, Alice, *Virginia Woolf's Late Cultural Criticism* (London: Bloomsbury, 2013)

Wood, Neal, *Communism and British Intellectuals* (London: Victor Gollancz, 1959)

Woolf, Leonard, *Beginning again: An Autobiography of the Years 1911–1918* (London: Hogarth Press, 1964)

Woolf, Leonard, *Downhill All the Way: An Autobiography of the Years 1919–1939* (London: Hogarth Press, 1967)

Woolf, Leonard, *Women's Cooperative Guild Papers for Guides January 1914: Education and the Cooperative Movement* (London: Women's Cooperative Guild, 1914)

Woolf, Virginia, 'The Art of Biography', in *The Essays of Virginia Woolf Volume VI 1933–1941*, ed. by Stuart N. Clarke (London: Hogarth Press, 2011), pp. 181–89

Woolf, Virginia, 'The Artist and Politics', in *Collected Essays Volume II*, ed. by Leonard Woolf (London: Hogarth Press, 1966), pp. 230–32

Woolf, Virginia, *Between the Acts* (Oxford: Oxford University Press, 2000)

Woolf, Virginia, *The Common Reader I* (London: Vintage, 2003)

Woolf, Virginia, 'The Common Reader', in *The Essays of Virginia Woolf Volume IV 1925–1928*, ed. by Andrew McNeillie (London: Hogarth Press, 1994), p. 19

Woolf, Virginia, 'The Cook', in *The Platform of Time Memoirs of Family and Friends*, ed. by S.P. Rosenbaum (London: Hesperus Press, 2007), pp. 179–83

Woolf, Virginia, 'A Daughter's Memories', in *The Platform of Time: Memoirs of Family & Friends*, ed. by S.P. Rosenbaum (London: Hesperus Press, 2007), pp. 58–64

Woolf, Virginia, *The Diary of Virginia Woolf Volume I 1915–1919*, ed. by Anne Olivier Bell (London: Hogarth Press, 1977)

Woolf, Virginia, *The Diary of Virginia Woolf Volume II 1920–1924*, ed. by Anne Olivier Bell (London: Hogarth Press, 1978)

Woolf, Virginia, *The Diary of Virginia Woolf Volume III 1925–1930*, ed. by Anne Olivier Bell (London: Hogarth Press, 1980)

Woolf, Virginia, *The Diary of Virginia Woolf Volume IV 1931–1935*, ed. by Anne Olivier Bell (London: Hogarth Press, 1982)

Woolf, Virginia, *The Diary of Virginia Woolf Volume V 1936–1941*, ed. by Anne Olivier Bell (London: Hogarth Press, 1984)

Woolf, Virginia, *Flush* (Oxford: Oxford University Press, 1998)

Woolf, Virginia, *A Haunted House: The Complete Shorter Fiction* (London: Vintage, 2003)

Woolf, Virginia, 'How Should One Read a Book?', in *The Essays of Virginia Woolf Volume IV 1925–1928*, ed. by Andrew McNeillie (London: Hogarth Press, 1994), pp. 388–400

Woolf, Virginia, 'Introductory Letter to Margaret Llewelyn Davies', in *Life as We Have Known It: The Voices of Working Class Women*, ed. by Margaret Llewelyn Davies (London: Virago, 2012), pp. ix–xxxvi

Woolf, Virginia, *Jacob's Room* (Oxford: Oxford University Press, 2008)

Woolf, Virginia, 'The Leaning Tower', in *The Essays of Virginia Woolf Volume VI 1933–1941*, ed. by Stuart N. Clarke (London: Hogarth Press, 2011), pp. 259–83

Woolf, Virginia, *The Letters of Virginia Woolf Volume II 1912–1922*, ed. by Nigel Nicolson (London: Hogarth Press, 1976)

Woolf, Virginia, *The Letters of Virginia Woolf Volume IV 1929–1931*, ed. by Nigel Nicolson (London: Hogarth Press, 1978)

Woolf, Virginia, *The Letters of Virginia Woolf Volume VI 1936–1941*, ed. by Nigel Nicolson (London: Hogarth Press, 1980)

Woolf, Virginia, 'Memoir of Julian Bell', in *The Platform of Time: Memoirs of Family and Friends*, ed. by S.P. Rosenbaum (London: Hesperus Press, 2008), pp. 19–32

Woolf, Virginia, *Mrs Dalloway* (London: Penguin, 1996)

Woolf, Virginia, 'The Niece of an Earl', in *The Essays of Virginia Woolf Volume 5 1929–1932*, ed. by Stuart N. Clarke (London: Hogarth Press, 2009), pp. 529–34

Woolf, Virginia, *Night and Day* (St. Albans: Granada Publishing, 1978)

Woolf, Virginia, 'The Novels of Thomas Hardy', in *The Essays of Virginia Woolf Volume 5 1929–1932*, ed. by Stuart N. Clarke (London: Hogarth Press, 2009), pp. 561–72

Woolf, Virginia, 'On Not Knowing Greek', in *The Essays of Virginia Woolf Volume IV 1925–1928*, ed. by Andrew McNeillie (London: Hogarth Press, 1994), pp. 38–52

Woolf, Virginia, *Orlando* (London: Penguin, 1993)

Woolf, Virginia, *The Pargiters: The Novel-Essay Portion of The Years*, ed. by Mitchell A. Leaska (London: Hogarth Press, 1978)

Woolf, Virginia, *The Platform of Time Memoirs of Family and Friends*, ed. by S.P. Rosenbaum (London: Hesperus Press, 2007)

Woolf, Virginia, 'Poetry, Fiction and the Future', in *The Essays of Virginia Woolf Volume IV 1925–1928*, ed. by Andrew McNeillie (London: Hogarth Press, 1994), pp. 428–41

Woolf, Virginia, *Roger Fry: A Biography* (London: Hogarth Press, 1940)

Woolf, Virginia, *A Room of One's Own and Three Guineas* (London: Penguin, 2000)

Woolf, Virginia, *Selected Diaries* (London: Vintage, 2008)

Woolf, Virginia, 'Sketch of the Past', in *Moments of Being: Autobiographical Writings*, ed. by Jeanne Schulkind (London: Pimlico, 2002), pp. 78–160

Woolf, Virginia, 'Speech of January 21, 1931'['Professions for Women'], in Virgina Woolf, *The Pargiters: The Novel Essay Portion of The Years*, ed. by Mitchell A. Leaska (London: Hogarth Press, 1978), pp. xxv–xliv.

Woolf, Virginia, *To the Lighthouse* (Oxford: Oxford University Press, 2000)

Woolf, Virginia, *The Years*, ed. by David Bradshaw and Ian Blyth (Chichester: Wiley-Blackwell, 2012)

Woolf, Virginia, *The Years*, ed. by Jeri Johnson (London: Penguin, 2002)

Woolf, Virginia, *The Years*, ed. by Anna Snaith (Cambridge: Cambridge University Press, 2012)

Woolf, Virginia, *The Waves* (Hertfordshire: Wordsworth Classics, 2000)

Woolf, Virginia, *The Waves*, ed. by Gillian Beer (Oxford: Oxford University Press, 2008)

Woolf, Virginia, *The Waves*, ed. by Kate Flint (London: Penguin, 1992)

Woolf, Virginia, *The Waves*, ed. by Michael Herbert and Susan Sellers (Cambridge: Cambridge University Press, 2011)

Woolf, Virginia, *The Waves: The Two Holograph Drafts*, ed. by J.W. Graham (London: Hogarth Press, 1976)

Woolf, Virginia, Henry Baerlein, Arnold Bennett, J.D. Beresford, Hamilton Fyfe, John Galsworthy, Compton Mackenzie, Alfred Ollivant, John Oxenham, and Eden Phillpotts, Hugh Walpole, 'What Is a Good Novel? A Symposium', *The Highway*, Summer 1924, pp. 100–10

Woolf, Virginia, 'Why?', in *The Essays of Virginia Woolf Volume 6 1933–1941*, ed. by Stuart N. Clarke (London: Hogarth Press, 2011), pp. 30–36

Woolf, Virginia, 'Why Art To-day Follows Politics', in *The Essays of Virginia Woolf Volume 6 1933–1941*, ed. by Stuart N. Clarke (London: Hogarth Press, 2011), pp. 75–79

Woolmer, J. Howard, *A Checklist of the Hogarth Press 1917–1946* (Revere: Woolmer Brotherson, 1986)

Wordsworth, William, 'Preface' to *The Lyrical Ballads* (1802), <http://web.mnstate.edu/gracyk/courses/web%20publishing/wordsworthpreface.htm> [accessed 19 April 2013]

Worsley, Thomas Cuthbert, *Barbarians and Philistines: Democracy and the Public Schools* (London: Hale, 1940)

Worsley, Thomas Cuthbert, 'Father to the Man: *The Backward Son* by Stephen Spender', *New Statesman and Nation*, 4 May 1940, p. 594

Worsley, Thomas Cuthbert, 'The Past Tense, *Selected Poems*: Henry Newbolt', *New Statesman and Nation*, 16 November 1940, p. 500

Wright, Basil, dir., commentary by H. Wilson, produced by John Grierson, *Children at School* (Realist Film Unit, 1937)

Wright, Elizabeth Mary, *The Life of Joseph Wright*, 2 vols (Oxford: Oxford University Press; Humphrey Milford, 1932)

Wright, Joseph, ed., *The English Dialect Dictionary*, 6 vols (Oxford: Oxford University Press, 1898–1905)

Wright, Joseph, *English Dialect Grammar* (Oxford: Oxford University Press, 1905)

Yorke, Sebastian, 'Introduction', in Henry Green, *Pack My Bag: A Self-Portrait* (London: Hogarth Press, 1992), pp. v–xiii

Yoshida, Erika, '"The Leaning Tower": Woolf's Pedagogical Goal of the Lecture to the WEA under the Threat of War', in *Virginia Woolf: Art, Education and Internationalism: Selected Papers from the Seventeenth Annual Conference on Virginia Woolf*, ed. by Diana Royer and Madelyn Detloff (Clemson: Clemson University Digital Press, 2008), pp. 33–39

Young, John Wesley, *Totalitarian Language: Orwell's Newspeak and Its Nazi and Communist Antecedents* (London: University Press of Virginia, 1991)

Zwerdling, Alex, *Orwell and the Left* (London: Yale University Press, 1974)

Zwerdling, Alex, *Virginia Woolf and the Real World* (London: University of California Press, 1986)

Contemporaneous Journals, Newspapers, and Little Magazines Referenced

Action, 1931
Daily Worker, 1931
Folios of New Writing, 1940–1941
The Guardian
The Highway, 1920–1940
Left Review
The London Mercury, May 1935
The New Era in Home and School
New Statesman and Nation
New Verse, Nos. 26–27, November 1937
Night & Day
The Observer
The Spectator

Archives

Winifred Holtby Collection at the Hull Archive and History Centre Archives

Collection of 9 items on Somerville College 1921–1923, LWH/5/5.12/01a-0li

Holtby, Winifred, 'After the Election', *The Schoolmistress*, 29 October 1931, front page, WH/2/2.21/01/05c

Holtby, Winifred, 'Arnold Bennett's Library', *The Schoolmistress*, 19 November 1931, front page WH/2/2.21/01/06a

Holtby, Winifred, 'My Weekly Journal', *The Schoolmistress*, 18 June 1931, p. 329, WH/2/2.21/01/01a

Holtby, Winifred, 'My Weekly Journal', *The Schoolmistress*, 25 June 1931, front page, WH/2/2.21/01/01b

Holtby, Winifred, 'My Weekly Journal: What a Revue Should Be', *The Schoolmistress*, 27 June 1935, front page, Centre WH/2/2.21/04/06b

Holtby, Winifred, 'On the NUT Conference', *The Schoolmistress*, 27 April 1933, front page, WH/2/2.21/02/04c

Holtby, Winifred, 'The Scarborough Conference', *The Schoolmistress*, 2 May 1935, p. 122, WH/2/2.21/04/05a

Holtby, Winifred, 'Speech Day at St. Cyprian's, 2028', *Time and Tide*, 6 July 1928, pp. 655–56. LWH/1/1.12/01g

Labour and Education (London: The Labour Party, 1934), WH/8/8.2/03a
'Minutes of the Proceedings of the Education Committee', WH/8/8.3/01b
South Riding materials, L WH/8/8.22
Wilkinson, Ellen, 'Winifred Holtby's Last Novel', *Time and Tide,* 7 March 1936, p. 324, in *South Riding* materials, L WH/8/8.22

Winifred Holtby Collection at the Bridlington Local Studies Centre

'Annotated Typescript of Vera Brittain's "Testament of Friendship"'
Series of sixteen manuscript notebooks

British Library Archives

British Library Sound Archive, Stephen Spender, *The Backward Son,* dir. by Richard Wortley, adapted by Pauline Spender. *Saturday Playhouse,* BBC Radio 4 (20 March 1993)
British Library Western Manuscripts Collection, L.C.P. 1935/33, 22.10.1936, Auden/Isherwood, *Dog Beneath the Skin.* Lic: 14254
British Library Western Manuscripts Collection, RP 7965, W.H. Auden, Case histories
British Library Western Manuscripts Collection, RP 6712/1, W.H. Auden, Transcript of draft manuscript of 'T.E. Lawrence'

Archives from the Berg Collection at New York Public Library

Virginia Woolf Collection of Papers, 1882–1894 [bulk 1912–1940] Berg Coll MSS Woolf, The Henry W. and Albert A. Berg Collection of English and American Literature, The New York Public Library [Berg Collection, 66B0309, Typescript, signed with the author's ms. Corrections 39p]
W.H. Auden Collection of Papers, 1909–1979 [bulk 1927–1973], Berg Coll MSS Auden, The Henry W. and Albert A. Berg Collection of English and American Literature, The New York Public Library [Public-school letters. Holograph Transcripts of 13 letters]

National Union of Women Teachers Archive at the UCL Institute of Education

'Condolences and Obituaries', UWT/D/43/6
'Educational Week-end Conference and Equal Pay Luncheon', UWT/B/5/35
'Equal Pay Meeting 18 October 1929', UWT/D/1/42

'Equal Pay Olympia 1938', UWT/D/1/72

'Equal Rights Committee (Evidence for the Royal Commission on the Civil Service)',
    UWT/D/32/5

'Important Letters', UWT/D/48/5

'Married Women Teachers', UWT/D/11/5

'NUWT Manchester Unit – Minute Book', UWT/F/74/5

'Obituaries and Notes on Speakers', UWT/D/14/3

'Six Point Group – Deputation to LCC on Married Women Teachers', UWT/D/11/28

'Victory Luncheon', UWT/B/10/1

'War and Peace', UWT/D/20/9

'War and Peace', UWT/D/20/7

'Women's Peace Movement', UWT/D/20/5

The Walter Greenwood Collection at the University of Salford

Author's Proof Copy of *Love on the Dole* WGC/1/2/2

Manuscript of *Love on the Dole* WGC/1/2/1

Index